ENEMIES OF ALL HUMANKIND

RE-MAPPING THE TRANSNATIONAL

A Dartmouth Series in American Studies

SERIES EDITOR
Donald E. Pease
Avalon Foundation Chair of Humanities
Founding Director of the Futures of American Studies Institute
Dartmouth College

The emergence of Transnational American Studies in the wake of the Cold War marks the most significant reconfiguration of American Studies since its inception. The shock waves generated by a newly globalized world order demanded an understanding of America's embeddedness within global and local processes rather than scholarly reaffirmations of its splendid isolation. The series Re-Mapping the Transnational seeks to foster the cross-national dialogues needed to sustain the vitality of this emergent field. To advance a truly comparativist understanding of this scholarly endeavor, Dartmouth College Press welcomes monographs from scholars both inside and outside the United States.

For a complete list of books available in this series, see www.upne.com.

Sonja Schillings, *Enemies of All Humankind: Fictions of Legitimate Violence*
Günter H. Lenz, edited by Reinhard Isensee, Klaus J. Milich, Donald E. Pease, John Carlos Rowe, *A Critical History of the New American Studies, 1970–1990*
Helmbrecht Breinig, *Hemispheric Imaginations: North American Fictions of Latin America*
Jimmy Fazzino, *World Beats: Beat Generation Writing and the Worlding of U.S. Literature*
Zachary McCleod Hutchins, editor, *Community without Consent: New Perspectives on the Stamp Act*
Kate A. Baldwin, *The Racial Imaginary of the Cold War Kitchen: From Sokol'niki Park to Chicago's South Side*
Yuan Shu and Donald E. Pease, *American Studies as Transnational Practice: Turning toward the Transpacific*
Melissa M. Adams-Campbell, *New World Courtships: Transatlantic Alternatives to Companionate Marriage*
David LaRocca and Ricardo Miguel-Alfonso, editors, *A Power to Translate the World: New Essays on Emerson and International Culture*
Elèna Mortara, *Writing for Justice: Victor Séjour, the Mortara Case, and the Age of Transatlantic Emancipations*
Rob Kroes, *Prison Area, Independence Valley: American Paradoxes in Political Life and Popular Culture*

SONJA SCHILLINGS

ENEMIES OF ALL HUMANKIND

Fictions of Legitimate Violence

DARTMOUTH COLLEGE PRESS
HANOVER, NEW HAMPSHIRE

Dartmouth College Press
An imprint of University Press of New England
www.upne.com

Manufactured in the United States of America
Typeset in Sabon and Scala Sans Pro by Integrated Publishing Solutions

Library of Congress Cataloging-in-Publication Data

Names: Schillings, Sonja, author.
Title: Enemies of all humankind: fictions of legitimate violence / Sonja Schillings.
Other titles: Violence in Anglo-American modernity
Description: Hanover, N.H.: Dartmouth College Press, 2016. | Series: Re-mapping the transnational: a Dartmouth series in American studies | Includes bibliographical references and index.
Identifiers: LCCN 2016019825 (print) | LCCN 2016038426 (ebook) | ISBN 9781512600155 (cloth: alk. paper) | ISBN 9781512600162 (pbk.: alk. paper) | ISBN 9781512600179 (epub, mobi & pdf)
Subjects: LCSH: American fiction—History and criticism. | Violence in literature. | English literature—History and criticism. | Pirates in literature. | Violence—Philosophy. | Civilization—Philosophy—History.
Classification: LCC PS374.V58 S34 2016 (print) | LCC PS374.V58 (ebook) | DDC 813.009/355—dc23
LC record available at https://lccn.loc.gov/2016019825

5 4 3 2 1

This study is dedicated to Günter F. Müller, my father

CONTENTS

ACKNOWLEDGMENTS

This book began as a dissertation at the Graduate School of North American Studies (GSNAS) at the John F. Kennedy Institute for North American Studies at the Freie Universität Berlin. I would like to thank the faculty of the John F. Kennedy Institute for North American Studies, as well as the staff of the GSNAS, for four wonderful and formative years.

Without the faith and support of my dissertation supervisor, Winfried Fluck, this book would not exist and I would not be a scholar. Ursula Lehmkuhl and Sabine Schülting provided invaluable insights and advice throughout the writing process. Donald E. Pease, Ingo Berensmeyer, Dieter Dörr, and Ulla Haselstein were invaluable conversation partners at crucial points of my argument's formation.

James Arvanitakis, Joel Baer, Gina Caison, Martin Fredriksson, Sophia Frese, Garnet Kindervater, Daniel Lange, Wojciech Malecki, Klaus J. Milich, Ethan Zane Miller, Katharina Motyl, Janna Obadas, Greta Olson, Julia Püschel, Christoph Raetzsch, Wibke Schniedermann, Boris Vormann, Birte Wege, and the members of Carmen Birkle's colloquium at the Philipps-Universität Marburg also deserve special mention for their helpful comments and suggestions at various stages of this book. The International Graduate Centre for the Study of Culture at the Justus-Liebig-Universität Giessen provided a great and supportive environment during the revision process.

My thanks go to Richard Pult, Amanda Dupuis, and Susan A. Abel of University Press of New England, to Jeanne Ferris for copyediting, to Madeleine LaRue for proofreading, to Connie Binder for indexing, and to Cathérine Ludwig-Ockenfels for her help with citations.

My husband, Matthias Schillings, has had my back during the entire writing process and provided me with coffee, love, and a home.

This work was generously funded by the Excellence Initiative of the German federal and state governments.

ENEMIES OF ALL HUMANKIND

INTRODUCTION

WHAT IS VIOLENCE?

Violence is physically immediate and unpredictably intimate, and thus difficult to grasp from within the language of scholarly argument. Because scholarly reasoning cannot easily recreate the logic of a violent situation, arguments on violence tend to focus on some of the more negotiable basic elements of violence. The most well-established of these elements is the notion that an act of violence is fundamentally uncontrollable by those subjected to it. The question of legitimate violence derives from this basic observation and raises the following questions: Is violence, understood as the physical enforcement of one person's will over another's, always and necessarily a bad thing? Are there any circumstances in which violence could be good, or even virtuous? If so, what are those circumstances?

The Calas affair of 1764–65 was a well-known and controversial case in France that points to the complex bundle of problems that informs any such discussion of legitimate violence in Western modernity specifically. Jean Calas was suspected of having murdered his son even though an overwhelming body of evidence pointed toward death by suicide. Calas was tortured to obtain a confession of murder, and sentenced to death on the breaking wheel. Because the Calases were Protestant and Jean's accusers were Catholic, the case attracted the attention of the Enlightenment thinker Voltaire, who took the lead in charging that the court had been biased against Calas. In his defense of Calas, Voltaire argued that the monarch and the clergy had abused their power to destroy Calas for reasons unrelated to the charge. In response to the ensuing scandal, King Louis XV eventually annulled the sentence, and Calas was posthumously rehabilitated.

In the Western modern tradition, legitimate violence is conventionally conceptualized as acts of defense against aggression, and the Calas affair illustrates what a broad range of concepts can be evoked as defensible in principle. The notion of threatened and reinstated statehood, the negotiation of institutional procedure, and the influence of cultural generalizations all play important roles in the construction of legitimate violence in the course of the Calas affair. Regarding the role of legitimate violence in text, it is particularly illustrative to consider that the ground for Voltaire's charge of illegitimate violence changed over time, as he moved from a critique of the motives for the use of violence to a critique of the type of violence used. His argument evolved from an accusation of religious bigotry to a claim that torture was inherently at odds with universal human sensibility. This shift in perspective is interesting because, as Lynn Hunt points out, Voltaire was not initially moved by these allegedly spontaneous and universal human sensibilities when he first reviewed the case. Rather, he established them as a normative premise for his criticism later on, when the assumption of such sensibilities began to constitute a necessary premise for an evolved argument about the basic conditions of legitimate violence (L. Hunt, *Inventing Human Rights*, 73–76).

In this study, legitimate violence is very broadly understood as defensive. Whoever claims legitimate violence marks something as worthy of protection —say, a community—and simultaneously formulates the expectation that even those who are (potentially) the target of violence accept this community's basic worthiness of protection. In this sense, an act of legitimate violence does not begin but ends conflict; it simply reacts to a violent attack that transgresses a boundary, puts a stop to the attack, and thus protects both the boundary and everything "behind" it. The invocation of legitimate violence therefore tends to refer to overarching values rather than to concrete interests. Legitimate violence, in all the discourses and examples discussed here, is also understood to occur only between human beings. Classic notions of legitimate violence against nonhumans, such as the case of the hunter who kills an animal to still his hunger, are not considered.

As the king's eventual rehabilitation of Calas and the development of Voltaire's premises indicate, it is not easy to determine what the boundary worthy of protection is, where it lies, who resides "behind" it, or even what counts as an attack on it. Neither the reference to state authority nor that to "natural" human sensibilities provides an uncontested basis of what exactly can make an act of violence legitimate. In a sense, legitimate violence is like a perfect circle: able to be formulated as a concept, but never found in the real world. Acts of legitimate violence are most unambiguously encountered in texts, such as narratives that focus on the notion of "poetic justice"—a phrase that, in its original meaning in Thomas Rymer's 1678 "The Tragedies of the Last Age Consider'd," simply referred to a distinction between good and evil characters, and meant that the good will be rewarded while the evil will be punished. However, the grounds for the recognition of "good" and "evil" characters as legitimately rewarded or punished are subject to change, just as the verdict in a murder case can be.

This study is not intended to develop a comprehensive definition of legitimate violence. Instead, it asks how legitimate violence is formulated—how, in other words, claims to legitimate violence can be made and maintained in spite of, and usually in conscious anticipation of, disagreement. It also asks how claims to legitimate violence can evolve that may be based on wholly new parameters, as in the case of Voltaire's universal human sensibilities, and how such values are introduced as worthy of protection.

More specifically, the study focuses on the discussion of a concept that has been extraordinarily effective in enabling the successful narrative construction of legitimate violence in texts and across the text forms used in modern Western (and, especially, Anglo-American) discourse. This concept, called *hostis humani generis* (the enemy of all humankind), was first established in the language of international law, and the general claim of this study is that properly understood, the concept can serve as a kind of formula to expose structural continuities in text-based claims to legitimate violence across the centuries.

In its explicitly legal context, the status of hostis humani generis is somewhat vague. It has been described variously as a concept and as a term of art. I understand it as a special kind of legal fiction. Legal fictions are considered "the growing pains of the language of the law" (Fuller, *Legal Fictions*, 22). They serve as transitional metaphors, in the sense that the "metaphor assimilates the known to the unknown" (Curl, "Metaphors," 233), or, in this case, that the law adapts to contexts it had not previously considered when unprecedented conflicts arise. The law has to adapt to these unanticipated circumstances and must be able to function in this new context as well as in the old. To bridge the gap between the familiar and the unfamiliar, the law often uses the basic notion of "as if" to apply existing categories to an unknown problem and roughly delineate the basic relations that characterize the new conflict. For example, one makes corporations liable for wrongdoing by treating them "as if" they were natural persons until (ideally) a corporate law is established that makes the legal fiction's analogy unnecessary.

Legal fictions thus serve a pragmatic function: they allow a comparatively swift legal reaction to a historically specific crisis, and thus they reduce pressure on the law to improvise lasting solutions all too quickly. The breathing room secured by a legal fiction allows the law to remain coherent as law, since it enables a more careful institutional adaptation to change. The usefulness of the conventional legal fiction generally ends when a more sophisticated, and thus more appropriate, body of law has been established, even though the first basic relationship established by the legal fiction often remains decisive (Moglen, "Legal Fictions"). Legal fictions' transitional status, though often left implicit, is a well-established legal convention. The notorious example of the corporation as a person arouses such heated debate at least in part because in this case, the crude and transitional vehicle of the legal fiction has remained a permanent legal arrangement (see, for example, Esposito, "Person"; Teubner, "Enterprise Corporatism").

Among legal fictions, hostis humani generis assumes a special position because it was never intended to be transitional. It was never meant to be made moot by the development of a more appropriate legal framework. Its function in the law is to describe conflict with a perpetrator whose actions against certain people or groups are thought to betray a fundamental hostility toward humankind and the laws that govern humanity. These perpetrators cannot be assimilated into the law because hostis humani generis defines them as entities that act "as if" they absolutely resist any such assimilation. They are defined as enemies of the rule of law itself—"as if" they personally epitomized anarchic chaos, nightmarish oppression, or any other radical and violent refusal of the law. Because they are constructed as perpetrators of violence, and because their violence is defined as inherently illegitimate, violence against such perpetrators is, in turn, inherently legitimate. Each and every violent act that defines enemies of all humankind can be considered a violation of a constitutive boundary worthy of protection, so violence against them protects this boundary almost by default. In legal history, figures such as the pirate; the slave trader; the committer of crimes against humanity (especially the torturer); and, most recently, the international terrorist have been identified as such enemies in Anglo-American legal discourse.

As this heterogeneous list of criminal figures indicates, the grounds for evoking hostis humani generis in law have changed considerably over time. Nevertheless, the basic interpretive pattern provided by hostis humani generis imposes certain regularities on its use. Certain conditions must be met so that a claim to legitimate violence against any enemy of all humankind can be persuasive. These regularities have never been discussed extensively, and it is the object of this study to carve them out.

From the mid-nineteenth century to the late twentieth, hostis humani generis did not attract much academic interest. In legal studies and disciplines such as political science, it tended to be mentioned only in substantiating notes to the main text; its discussion was a mere formal appendix to some more interesting topic, such as the question of a legal right to territorial expansion, the division of branches of government, the implementation of human rights law, just war theory and universal jurisdiction, and the historical properties of maritime piracy. It was not seen as a category that merited attention in its own right.

This perception has changed in recent years. In fields from legal studies to the humanities, and especially in American studies, hostis humani generis has begun to attract much attention. The sudden interest in this particular legal fiction has to do with two intertwined political developments: first, the War on Terror's construction of international terrorists as "unlawful combatants" in direct reference to hostis humani generis in the years following the 9/11 attacks, and second, the "pirate-terrorist nexus" that was identified in the context of Somali piracy. A brief digression is necessary to explain the importance of these developments for the debate that this study engages in.

The term "pirate-terrorist nexus" was coined by Charles Dragonette in an outraged letter to the editor of a journal on maritime security in 2005 ("Lost at Sea"). Dragonette was responding to an article that represented, in his view, a number of other articles that alleged there was a direct link between Somali maritime pirates and terrorists associated with Al-Qaeda. Dragonette condemned this nexus as a nonsensical, purely strategic fabrication, completely disconnected from established facts. But in the United States especially, the idea of a pirate-terrorist nexus continued to influence international security policies for reasons that went far beyond the phenomenon of maritime piracy (Mahnkopf, "Piratenhatz"; Lehr, *Violence at Sea*). The pirate analogy was indeed pushed by the administration of President George W. Bush to substantiate a new definition of international terrorism, a political decision that was supported by popular and scholarly arguments from terrorism studies and maritime security studies in particular (see, for example, Burgess, *World for Ransom*; Burnett, *Dangerous Waters*; Sekulich, *Terror on the Seas*; Shay, *Terror Triangle*; Skaridov, "Hostis Humani Generis"). Nevertheless, many political scientists saw the belief in the pirate-terrorist nexus as not based on the assessment of actual political phenomena, but instead as a means to concrete political ends, such as obtaining greater funding and resources (see, for example, Lehr and Lehmann, "Somalia"; Murphy, *Weak States*).

This dubious use of hostis humani generis in the War on Terror might not have become obvious to observers, had Somali pirates not provided a clear example of how eerily similar the legal constructions of pirates and terrorists were. Maritime violence around the Horn of Africa received a great deal of attention especially after the hijacking of the American ship *Maersk Alabama* in 2009 (see Phillips, *A Captain's Duty*), and this introduced the particular problems of the nexus to a much wider array of critics. The peculiar artificiality of the pirate-terrorist nexus began to attract the interest of scholars outside of legal studies and political science. Hostis humani generis emerged as the common denominator underlying such outwardly diverse phenomena as the legal construction of people imprisoned at Guantánamo Bay as unlawful combatants, the strategic association of violent non-Westerners with terrorism as in the case of Somali piracy, or the portrayal of the events of 9/11 as an attack on humanity as a whole.

In the first influential critical assessments of the nexus, the use of hostis humani generis itself was largely criticized as a sign of bad scholarship and/or political cynicism (Dragonette, "Lost at Sea"; Engels, "Floating Bombs"; Kaplan, "Guantánamo"; Murphy, *Weak States*). Indeed, the blatantly strategic use of hostis humani generis in the course of the War on Terror merited the alarmed reactions it provoked. After all, this legal fiction's core function is to help construct an antagonist against whom any kind of counterviolence—including indefinite detention, torture, and assassination in or beyond sovereign territory—may be legitimate, even though such counterviolence may contradict the essence of national traditions and international conventions regarding justifiable forms of violence.

My point is not that prevailing traditions and conventions are voided by such acts of counterviolence; but that there has always been a legal exception to those traditions and conventions, and this loophole was now systematically exploited. The direct implication of the legal use of hostis humani generis is the perpetrator's subjection to universal jurisdiction. The notion of universal jurisdiction has been conditioned by the application of hostis humani generis at least since 1705. It means that, because the enemy of all humankind constitutes a universal threat, any sovereign power may destroy him anywhere and by any means necessary. Usually, sovereigns' ability to conduct legitimate extraterritorial interventions in peacetime is severely restricted,[1] and charges of illegitimate aggression may ensue if sovereigns violate these restrictions. In singular deviation from this principle, the identification of an enemy of all humankind allows sovereigns to intervene violently, as well as legitimately, even if they use violence in contexts that are far outside their customary boundaries. Universal jurisdiction is the reason why hostis humani generis has never been completely forgotten or abandoned by policy makers, and why it has been periodically rediscovered even after decades of nonuse.

If the use of this loophole is based on relations as artificial as the pirate-terrorist nexus, the literary and cultural critic is called on to investigate not only the logic of this artificial link but also why it is persuasive even when it is clearly not based on fact. The most obvious starting point for a critical analysis of hostis humani generis seems to be the question of against whom can one claim universal jurisdiction. The history of the legal fiction's application in law seems to suggest, in Adeno Addis's words, "that it [is] not the nature of the act but the nature of the actor that matter[s]" ("International Community," 139).

This assessment has indeed informed all prevailing understandings of hostis humani generis. Since hostis humani generis as a legal fiction has been intimately bound up with the crime of piracy for the vast majority of its uses (which go back between six hundred and more than two thousand years, depending on the interpretive breaks one allows for), and since it is associated with piracy again today, scholars tend to assume that to make sense of hostis humani generis, they must first understand the pirate. As a result, the enemy of all humankind is often described as a somewhat abstracted pirate figure that is coherent enough to merit comparable responses across the centuries.

I disagree with the assumption that the pirate, or any other single figure, can be used to explain the meaning of hostis humani generis. In terms of the choices and methods of my argument, therefore, it makes sense to start out with this difference in approach.

The idea that the pirate figure determines the meaning of hostis humani generis runs counter to the way in which hostis humani generis is used in law. It is incorrect to assume that there has ever been a coherent figure that served as a model for the application of the concept, even if we restrict ourselves to the pirate alone. The term "pirate" has always been far too flexible to invite any consistent analytical treatment. Historically, the term can refer to rogue privateers, mutineers, unruly villagers, predatory coastal clans, stable pirate ports, sovereign states (for example, imperial states such as Great Britain and revolutionary ones such as the United States), and many other entities. Even in the narrowest possible range of applications—namely, in the context of piracy law in modern European history—the entities encompassed by the term are far too diverse to permit any comprehensive definition of the pirate.[2]

The difficulty is increased by the fact that, after the early nineteenth century, hostis humani generis ceased to be inevitably linked to piracy. Since then, hostis humani generis has been used in a variety of cases that have absolutely nothing to do with piracy. Again, if we only restrict ourselves to the narrowest range of application, hostis humani generis is now equally applicable to figures like the international slave trader and the perpetrator of crimes against humanity (a group of crimes that, like piracy, is diverse and constantly expanding). The use of hostis humani generis to describe the international terrorist, then, is simply the most recent in a long history of variations; it is a historically telling, but certainly not a conceptually defining, application of the legal fiction. Especially since the twentieth century, the conceivable perpetrators have become such a heterogenous group that, as Eugene Kontorovic ("Piracy Analogy") has famously observed, the normative premises underlying the application of hostis humani generis in law seem to have become too inconsistent to be useful.

Despite this history of inconsistency in terms of perpetrators, however, it is a fact that hostis humani generis remains understandable and applicable. It remains so applicable, in fact, that unsuitable usages are immediately and almost instinctively recognized. Throughout the centuries, such inappropriate lapses have been met with the same kind of reaction: spontaneous condescending laughter meets the British attorney who claims that a pirate has to personally attack representatives of all nations to be called a enemy of all humankind (Tindal, *Law of Nations*, 25), and unbelieving and total congressional refusal meets President Franklin Pierce, who seeks to cover up a diplomatic disaster with the allegation of having encountered "a piratical resort of outlaws" (quoted in Moss, *Undeclared War*, 59; see also Wormuth and Firmage, *Dog of War*, 37–41).

If there is generally no obvious coherence in the application of hostis humani generis to perpetrators, how is it that the legal fiction still has a clearly recognizable lineage of correct interpretations?

In my view, this question can be addressed only by discussing hostis humani generis as referring not to a figure, but to a constellation. Like any legal fiction, hostis humani generis is not narrative in the strict sense but instead serves to enable a range of uses based on the basic relation it delineates. The object of this study is to trace the defining properties of these basic relations and render them visible as operative in texts across time and disciplines. I suggest that the legal fiction constitutes only the most basic version of a culturally overarching concept of legitimate violence. The hostis humani generis constellation, in short, allows the unambiguous assignment of legitimate and illegitimate positions in a wide variety of contexts.

Piracy scholars today are not blind to this dimension of the enemy of all humankind, but they usually do not theorize about it. When hostis humani generis is used in arguments about the pirate, it usually tends to serve as a marker of one understanding of piracy (piracy that is defined by maritime violence) to the exclusion of other understandings. There are, indeed, many conversations about the pirate that do not rely in the least on a discussion of hostis humani generis, and they are all excluded from discussion in this study. These are especially discussions of the fictional (or fictionalized) pirate as a cultural stock character (see, for example, Gerassi-Navarro, *Pirate Novels*; G. Moore, *Pirates and Mutineers*; Paul, Ganser, and Gerund, *Figures of Mobility*; Turley, *Rum, Sodomy and the Lash*); the debates about piracy in the wider context of the Internet and touching on themes such as copyright, sharing economies, and mash-up authorship (see, for example, Eckstein and Schwarz, *Postcolonial Piracy*; Fredriksson and Arvanitakis,

Leakages; Philip, "Technological Author"); and the increasing use of the term "piracy" as a methodological description of interdisciplinary research (see, for example, Puzar, "Piratical Cultural Studies"; de Sutter, "Piracy as Method").

Considering this diversity of conversations about piracy, hostis humani generis has been acknowledged to be a useful shorthand marker to specify the academic conversation on piracy at hand. The conversation about pirates as committers of maritime violence—and explicitly as enemies of all humankind—has resulted in publications such as Michael Kempe's study *Fluch der Weltmeere,* which provides a rich, in-depth understanding of the legal history of piracy and its contribution to the development of international law. Studies such as Amedeo Policante's study *The Pirate Myth* and Mikkel Thorup's *Intellectual History of Terror* use a discussion of maritime piracy as the foundation for a critique of the history of imperialism and modern capitalism. Monographs such as these have been accompanied by a number of noteworthy articles that, in their own ways, address both piracy (Jenisch, "Law of the Sea"; Risso, "Cross-Cultural Perceptions") and hostis humani generis (Greene, "Hostis Humani Generis") as terms that actively produce, rather than merely describe, a certain perspective on legitimate violence. However, all of these contributions remain invested in speaking about the perpetrators that are being produced, rather than hostis humani generis, which does the producing.

The study that my own argument mainly responds to is, somewhat predictably, the one with the premise and research interest most comparable to mine. Daniel Heller-Roazen's *The Enemy of All* (2009) constitutes the most comprehensive reading of hostis humani generis from the perspective of literary and cultural studies to date. It attempts to construct a pirate figure that is so abstract and general in its properties that it may be used to explain the international terrorist as well. Heller-Roazen's study focuses on identifying criteria for recognizing the piratical enemy of all that have endured over time. Heller-Roazen postulates that a pirate as a more universally understandable figure always requires a spatial realm in which exceptional conditions of rule apply; that the pirate as an agent must be considered universally hostile (presumably by a nation-state or empire); that this combination of space and agent brings about a normative collapse of political and criminal categories; and that, therefore, piracy is able to transform prevailing concepts of war (*Enemy of All*, 10–11). Although his study is impressively researched and often beautifully argued, its explanatory potential is limited by the idea of an internally coherent perpetrator figure. The enemy of all humankind is cast as one archetypical pirate figure; the international terrorist thus becomes recognizable as a quasi pirate. Especially in the last chapters of Heller-Roazen's study, it becomes evident that hostis humani generis is virtually the same thing to him that it is for scholars like Amy Kaplan in her scathing critique of American imperialism ("Guantánamo"): a legalist fig leaf that helps produce *homines sacri* (in the Agambian sense of carriers of bare life) through an arbitrary charge of piracy. In other words, he understands hostis humani generis as a vehicle that enables sovereigns to systematically use the notion of universal jurisdiction to produce human life that is radically excluded from the law, as well as violently objectified by sovereign force.

In my view, such a conclusion does injustice both to hostis humani generis and to Giorgio Agamben's theory of the *homo sacer.* Agamben does not characterize the homo sacer as a figure endowed with coherent properties; indeed, he refers to a range of extremely diverse figures that may be conceptualized as homines sacri (see, for example, Agamben, *Homo Sacer*, 50, 72, 76, 84, 90, 97, 104, and 185). Instead of abstracting the properties of specific figures, as Heller-Roazen does with the pirate, Agamben foregrounds an analytically interesting relationship established in law—an "ideal type" of relationship (Vasilache, "'Homines sacri,'" 62; my translation)—that may help identify and illuminate comparable relations in a much broader context than even the law itself. The relationship described in *Homo Sacer* is imagined to exist between the sovereign and the carrier of bare life, two figures that permanently arrest each other at the threshold of the law. This ideal and permanent type of relationship is what I understand as a constellation in this study, insofar as it describes a fixed relationship among several figures and, moreover, is mediated by the properties of the realm in which they relate. In the case of Agamben's homo sacer, this is the relationship between the homo sacer and the sovereign, mediated by the "threshold" of a law that is described in the spatial terms of a "zone" (*Homo Sacer*, 65).

If hostis humani generis is understood as a constellation in this way, it is precisely not "the nature of the actor" (Addis, "International Community," 139) that matters. What matters instead are the relations that such a constellation determines in the characterization of a conflict, and the realm that is characterized as a specific kind of realm because this fixed relationship among figures occurs in it. The "nature of the act" that Addis dismisses as insignificant thus becomes important again, because the violent relationship among these figures and the representation of their various allegiances cause some of these violent acts to emerge as inherently legitimate acts.

So, according to the argument presented here, what are the defining features of hostis humani generis as a constellation? Hostis humani generis describes a relationship among three figures, each of whom commits violence, and each of whom represents a realm that is constructed in spatial terms: a good realm, an evil realm, and the realm of the encounter itself. The figures confront each other in a space considered to be the unruly, transformative middle space between a realm of good and a realm of evil. Typically, the violence committed by the representative of civilization (the good realm) is cast as legitimate violence and that of the other two figures as illegitimate violence; but as the American tradition of use especially shows, some formal variation of the constellation is possible. Since the late nineteenth, but especially since the twentieth century, the elusive representative of the unruly in-between zone, the *pirata*, can likewise emerge as a potential committer of legitimate violence. Only the *praedo*, the representative of the evil realm, remains fixed as a committer of illegitimate violence (as explained below, here I am using Hugo Grotius's terms).

By inserting concrete figures into this constellation, it becomes possible to identify certain historically specific acts as acts of legitimate violence. Indeed, as the later chapters of this study will show in a number of close readings, the pirate is only one of many historically specific figures that can be inserted into the constellation to investigate the legitimacy of violence in a text—others are not only obvious figures such as the slave trader and the committer of crimes against humanity, but also ambiguously positive figures such as American frontiersman, the hard-boiled detective, the racialized underdog of the protest novel, and the twenty-first century's scholar-activist. The constellation of hostis humani generis provides an exceptionally wide range of possible applications in texts because other than the legal fiction, the constellation has been in consistent and active use in modernity.

This study will essentially provide an interpretive history of hostis humani generis as a constellation, discussing central interpretive breaks as well as important theoretical and historical influences and events. After all, the constellation is not timeless, though it is designed to approach a timeless question (What is legitimate violence?). It has developed within very specific discourses and draws its persuasiveness not least from its compatibility with core cultural assumptions of Anglo-American modernity.

The history of hostis humani generis significantly predates modernity, and two especially central cultural backdrops to any discussion of hostis humani generis should be mentioned here: Christian theology and the theory of just war. Christianity remains the all-important backdrop for the enduring racialized construction of Islam in the early hostis humani generis constellation, and Christian theology generally informs the constellation's structural properties. Certain constructions of the biblical cosmos can be read as rather apt descriptions of the spatial structure presupposed in the hostis humani generis constellation—for instance, the construction of the Christian worldview as having a "three-storied structure, consisting of a heaven above, a hell below and an earth in the middle. The earth is the scene of the supernatural activity of God and his angels on the one hand, and of Satan and his demons on the other" (Coupe, *Myth*, 10).

Likewise, modern categories of civilization often rely on Christian traditions of rendering difference meaningful. The differences between the religious and the secular, the state and the human being, the just and the legal, and the active representative agent and the passive innocent are all somewhat informed by the categories developed by Western European Christianity (see Goldenberg, *Changing*). The Enlightenment discourses on the state of nature that I use as central philosophical reference points also stand in direct continuity with specifically Christian traditions of constructing history (Greenblatt, *The Swerve*, 191–98).

In the modern history of hostis humani generis, references to Christianity in texts that rely on the constellation tend to be restricted to a dramatization of threatened and reinstated integrity of faith, especially in characterizations of the representative of civilization. In the discussion of literary texts especially, this study focuses solely on character transformations that are occasioned by discernible key events in an in-between zone that may confirm or permanently change the representative status of a figure, and thus its function in the constellation.

In the context of these more general notes on Christianity, the specific relationship of hostis humani generis to just war theory should be outlined at least briefly. Hostis humani generis is a legal fiction that postulates the existence of legitimate violence between civilization and its Other. While hostis humani generis has never officially been part of just war theory, theorists and commentators who use the hostis humani generis fiction typically also affirm the possibility of just war. For instance, Augustine of Hippo and Hugo Grotius, the theorists whose categories are used most extensively in this study to conceptualize hostis humani generis as a constellation, are both famous for their foundational contributions to just war theory (Holmes, "Just War Theory," 323; Solis, *Law of Armed Conflict*, 18). Just war theory is the best-known discourse that postulates the ability of violence to be legitimate. In just war theory, the accepted core property of legitimate violence is, again, its defensive nature, but hostis humani generis transcends the context of just war insofar as it helps negotiate the source of legitimacy for violence in any context that goes beyond the central case of just war. Enemies of all humankind are always enemies of all humankind, in both war and peace. This unique property of the legal fiction is, indeed, explicitly developed as the defining element of hostis humani generis in early modernity.

Only with the onset of early modernity does hostis humani generis as I understand it come into use, and while many European scholars contributed to its genesis, I will mainly focus on the English and Scottish[3] context to trace its early European history. The bulk of this study, however, is dedicated to the constellation's particularly nuanced and far-reaching interpretation in the United States from the nineteenth century until the present. It is only in this US context that hostis humani generis is truly separated from the crime of piracy and demonstrates its potential to negotiate the question of legitimate violence on a fundamental level. The conscious and sophisticated use of hostis humani generis as a constellation could, indeed, be called an American invention.

The origin of hostis humani generis in law is often identified as Cicero's construction of pirates as the enemies of all humankind. As I will show in part 1, Cicero imagined the hostis humani generis constellation as a simple binary of inherent good versus inherent evil. The Roman Empire, to him, was inherently legitimate because it was the empire; the pirate was inherently illegitimate because he violently attacked the empire and simultaneously rejected its exclusive claim to legitimate violence. In Cicero's view, because the pirate is by definition an illegitimate invader, conflict with a pirate is always an act of self-defense and is therefore always legitimate and just, regardless of the means of violence. This is the legal origin of the link between piracy and universal jurisdiction.

Augustine of Hippo made this legal fiction available as a constellation of broader cultural relevance. He provided a twist to the static Ciceronian relation between the representative of empire and the pirate, arguing that a violent act on behalf of the empire does not automatically translate into a normatively legitimate act. He complicated Cicero's assessment by removing the assumption of *inherent* legitimacy and illegitimacy in violent confrontation. After Augustine's important intervention, the maritime pirate as a figure is increasingly conventionalized as a figure that helps interrogate claims to legitimacy and to render new forms of claiming legitimacy to violence thinkable.

However, the establishment of the hostis humani generis constellation itself—a gradual process—did not begin until the sixteenth century. Imperial expansion, along with the taking of land from and war with native populations, constituted a new context for violent conflict that had to be actively legitimated because it stood in direct conflict with prevailing European notions of legitimate warfare and the appropriation of territory (see Fisch, *Europäische Expansion*). In this complex process of imperial legitimation, hostis humani generis helped reconceptualize the grounds for legitimate violence, combining the stable and inherent antagonism between legitimate and illegitimate entities, as proposed by Cicero, with the deeply ambiguous negotiation of legitimacy proposed by Augustine. Thus, two complementary enemies of all humankind emerged in early modernity, as noted above: the praedo and the pirata.

In the modern imperial context, which I discuss in part 2, hostis humani generis emerges as a constellation that assumes the existence of delimited realms of inherent civilization and inherent, invasive Otherness. These two realms stand in violent and existential conflict with each other. As explained above, there is a zone between them (in these earliest examples, a sea) that constitutes the main site of their violent engagement, and that neither realm can dominate. In this in-between zone, three figures appear (originally as maritime entities): a representative of civilization, a representative of the illegitimate Other realm, and a treacherous renegade who switches to the Other side without being able to shed his original association with civilization.

These three figures must all exist in the in-between zone, and all of them must commit violence there. Only under these circumstances can both the representative of the Other realm and the renegade be conceptualized as hostis humani generis. Hugo Grotius has defined these two complementary incarnations of the enemy of all humankind as *praedones* (inherent antagonists and representatives of the Other realm) and *piratae* (treacherous renegades), a distinction I have used as the basis of my own terminology, and discuss most thoroughly in part 2. Importantly, both antagonists must exist simultaneously. If they do not, the application of hostis humani generis fails in ways that are typically characterized as "off the mark" and "embarrassing" (see Cassese, *Politics*, 66–68; Wormuth and Firmage, *Dog of War*, 7–41).

These figures as representatives of a civilized realm, an Other realm, and a zone in between them are derived from a classic model of civilization that is used to legitimate much of European imperial expansion. In early modernity, two rival approaches to civilization inform European imperial expansion. I call these the essentialist model of civilization and the progressivist model. The basic assumption of both is that Christian Europe—and, later, industrial Europe (Schmitt, *Land und Meer*, 73)—is the epitome of civilization, and that this civilization is confronted with an Other that is either uncivilized (meaning that it lacks the properties of civilization), in the progressivist model, or outright barbaric (it is actively hostile to civilization), in the essentialist model. The two models of civilization thus differ in how they describe the same Other encountered outside of Europe.

Scholars in the tradition of Francisco de Vitoria and the Enlightenment thinker Christian Wolff argue that civilization, rather than the Other, is endowed with specific properties. Civilization, in their view, is characterized by certain features that can be adopted by all nations and peoples that do not already possess them. In this progressivist model, there is no inherent outsider to civilization, there are only actual and potential carriers of civilization. Noncivilized nations do not lose their claims to sovereignty over territory simply because they are noncivilized; instead, their expected development as sovereigns is conceptualized as a one-way street leading toward the adoption of civilization. This model does not acknowledge the existence of independently developed, culturally specific characteristics of the Other (however distortedly they may be presented in the rival essentialist model). Rather, the progressivist model tends to conceptualize non-Europeans as vessels yet to be filled, or children yet to reach maturity.

In contrast, scholars in the legal tradition of Juan Ginés de Sepúlveda (1490–1573) assume that there is an inherent and unbridgeable difference between civilization and barbarians. In this essentialist model, the barbarian by definition stands outside of, and in violent conflict with, civilization and what it represents (Foucault, *Society*, 195). This model primarily defines the properties of the Other and derives the characteristics of civilization from the opposite of these traits—for instance, through the rejection of the Other's "typical" customs such as cannibalism, sodomy, and the enslavement of "their women" (Pearce, *Savagism*, 84). Because the barbarian is so inherently and threateningly Other, a barbarous nation is not considered to have a legitimate claim to sovereignty and territory. For instance, the early modern positivist Alberico Gentili argued that the corsairs who had been commissioned by the Barbary States of North Africa were pirates, because the states themselves were barbarous and one could not accept their letters of marque as legitimate documents (Benton, "Legalities of the Sea," 279).

In summary, the essentialist model postulates that Other peoples or so-called races are irreducibly barbarous and must be removed or replaced for there to be peace. Civilization can advance only territorially—in space. In contrast, the progressivist approach accepts the Other's territorial claims as legitimate but argues that Others must advance culturally to the state of civilization. Only when they have reached the same state of civilization as civilization itself can they be regarded as equal. Civilization can advance only by making Others imitate it—in time. As Edward Said has pointed out, both of these generalizing characterizations of Otherness have fictional core elements that are crucial for the legitimation of violence. Concrete characterizations of the Other are constantly written and rewritten within the narrative logic of these models' construction of progress (either expansion or development), "always with various silences and elisions, always with shapes imposed and disfigurements tolerated, so that 'our' East, 'our' Orient [and 'our' Other in general] becomes 'ours' to possess and direct" (Said, *Orientalism*, xviii).

The hostis humani generis constellation is necessarily embedded in the essentialist model of civilization, as the fixed relationship between the representative of civilization and the praedo corresponds directly with the conflict lines of civilizer and barbarian drawn in that model. At the same time, hostis humani generis adds a helpful further dimension to the essentialist binary, because the third figure—the pirata—helps negotiate and adapt the normative boundaries of such a struggle. The pirata becomes a figure that conflates the inconflatable and thus absorbs the inevitable contradictions that arise from essentialist conflict. If the representative of civilization (obviously) represents the realm of civilization, and the praedo the barbarian realm, the pirata represents the elusive in-between zone, and his presence marks this zone as such.

In imperial discourse, the praedo, the inherent foe, is conventionally determined as Other on a racial basis. The modern understanding of "realms" and "inconflatable" aspects is informed by a specific definition of race that, I argue, directly informs any modern usage of hostis humani generis. I borrow from Hazel Rose Markus and Paula Moya in referring to a "conversation" about race that underlies the term's analytical definition in this study ("Doing Race," 15–16). Because hostis humani generis is necessarily based on the assumption of an inherent and unbridgeable difference between two spatialized realms, I will refer to a "conversation" that is "both one of the oldest and one of the most current. It is the conversation that says . . . 'It's in their culture; it can't be helped.' This version . . . draws on a narrow . . . understanding of culture as being so deeply rooted in a person, and so stable and predictable in its effects, that even important changes in a person's social environment are unlikely to make a difference in his or her values and behavior" (Markus and Moya, "Doing Race," 15).

As Ania Loomba demonstrates, this particular construction of an "unchangeable [cultural] essence" (*Shakespeare*, 56) can be directly linked back to constructions emerging in the early modern period. A "deep-seated hostility to Islam had been shaped by the long legacy of the Crusades" (ibid., 71) and was subsequently translated into the "complex rather than mechanical interrelation between ideologies of European/Christian/white superiority and colonial practices. . . . [I]deologies of skin colour complicated and hardened the concept of religious difference" that was originally established in relation to Islam and then reinforced in confrontation with Others in precolonial settings around the world (ibid., 42). As the notion of an Other culture already implies, race in this understanding always indicates a political collective whose structure is conceptualized as unified as well as illegitimate in its claims to power. At the same time, the Other's presupposed cultural and moral inferiority does not necessarily correspond to an actual political, infrastructural, or military inferiority. Instead, this racialized political collective is a violent antagonist who may destroy civilization if not held at bay; this is why the essentialist struggle is always existential. Both historical contexts that Loomba cites as foundational for the genesis of this understanding of race—the maritime conflict with the Barbary States as well as early colonialism, especially in the Americas—are also precisely the contexts of antagonism that brought the hostis humani generis constellation into existence.

While racialized essentialism was and remains the basis for understandings of the praedo, the figure of the pirata dramatizes the fundamental negotiations of legitimacy that Augustine introduced into the debate. Associated first with notions of religious conversion in the case of the Barbary corsairs, then with the adoption of nonwhite behavior in a colonial setting, the pirata is a figure originally situated inside civilization who recalls the features of the praedo, who stands outside it.

In contrast to the earliest versions of the constellation, which imagine the pirata as a renegade and traitor, in the more mature stages of colonialism something interesting happens to the pirata. This shift, too, is discussed in part 2 of the book. In British law of the eighteenth century, praedo and pirata are often conceptualized in reference to man in the state of nature in Hobbes's sense, but most significantly to the invader who occasions the transitional stage between the state of nature and the state of order in Locke's work. Because the pirata reduces himself to the cultural expressions of the praedo (who is arrested in a permanent state of nature) without being able to merge with the praedo, the pirata becomes something like a primitive man in colonial space, and thus a starting point of history in his own right.

It is in this way that the pirata becomes a figure that helps negotiate not only the legitimacy of expansive violence, but also the legitimacy of rule in general and of specific political orders that eventually rule this territory in his wake. In this context, the pirata is increasingly imagined as an unwitting pioneer that helps define precolonial space as empty. Some of the most sophisticated constructions of the constellation in this altered context can be found in literary writings of the United States. James Fenimore Cooper's novel *The Deerslayer, or The First Warpath* (1841) helps disentangle the problems, but also the potential, of a state of nature–based understanding of legitimate violence in the margins of empire.

In part 3, then, this study begins to focus completely on the significance of the hostis humani generis constellation in the United States. Since its founding, that nation had been burdened with the problem of its civilizational status. Because the two dominant civilizational discourses (essentialist and progressivist) presupposed Europe to be the only epitome of civilization, a former colony that defied European rule was, by definition, not civilized. At the same time, citizens of the United States tended to understand themselves as sharing the basic properties of European civilization, such as whiteness, Christianity, and other aspects of cultural or institutional ways of life that were considered defining markers of civilization. To resolve this contradiction, I argue, they used the hostis humani generis constellation to formulate a third model of civilization that both harmonized with and superseded the previous models. This third model was formulated in the late nineteenth century, at a time when racialized Other collectives, in their role as existentially threatening military antagonists, were deemed phenomena of the past. In the third model of civilization, which I call the frontier model, the hostis humani generis constellation is no longer used to legitimize imperial conquest of Other realms but to manage issues of unequal institutional representation within the nation-state itself.

The frontier thesis postulated by Frederick Jackson Turner in 1893 placed the pirata at its center as a foundational entity, as the frontier thesis uses the hostis humani generis constellation to render "the American" thinkable as a foundational pirata that is distinct from both Native Americans (as praedones) and Europeans (as representatives of civilization). Turner's bold interpretation of the constellation resulted in a model of civilization that imagined a perpetual process of civilizing disruption within national space and quickly began to address the legitimacy of institutional force as a main concern.

In the most astute twentieth-century narrative interpretations of the model, the praedo is reimagined as the representative of an illegitimate institutional structure of oppression that has to be countered by the renewed appearance of a foundational pirata, who reminds the corrupted nation of its own original values. This pirata figure is recognized as a foundational entity by the representative of civilization, who translates the pirata's violent intervention into a relegitimating institutional transformation. The pirata's most important feature becomes his transformative impact on the institutional structure of the nation by violently claiming an agency illegitimately denied to him.

World War II enlarged the scope of the frontier model's possible application to the whole word but also exposed the fact that this nationalist model always relied on the parallel existence of the essentialist model in the international sphere. The fourth and final part of this book addresses this problem. During the Cold War, the United States came face to face with the different implications of the essentialist and the frontier models, as these models use the same constellational premises of hostis humani generis to arrive at different conclusions about the nature of legitimate violence. This is especially the case as these models assign to different figures within the constellation the ability to use violence legitimately, which may even result in squarely opposing assessments of concrete violent scenarios.

In response to the ensuing conflicts and insecurities regarding the proper construction of legitimate violence, a legitimate American position was claimed via the combination of the notions of national exceptionalism (legitimated by the frontier model) and US claims to global political, military, and economic dominance (legitimated by the essentialist model). However, this solution did not resolve the core problem of the very different narrative emphases in these models' interpretation of the hostis humani generis constellation, and therefore it offered little more than temporary relief from a fundamental categorical disorientation regarding the nature of legitimate violence. In a reading of Kurt Vonnegut's 1962 novel *Mother Night*, I trace the problem of situating the notion of civilizing self-disruption in a new debate about the legitimacy of mass warfare. I also address the preliminary solution of the early Cold War years—namely, to cast the United States as the protector of human rights, which required worldwide defense against the mortal enemies of human rights (such as the Soviet Union) as well as to claim the United States was the proper agent to help ensure the global actualization of the human rights regime (anywhere, and preferably in the so-called Third World). This explicit inclusion of the global dimension after World War II leads to an important break in the legal interpretation of hostis humani generis, as the legal fiction is now incorporated into human rights law. In this new legal context, perpetrators were no longer identified as enemies of all humankind because of their random attacks, but because they attacked the human essence of their victims.

In the later Cold War years, however, the increasingly powerful representatives of a counterdiscourse on legitimate violence took issue with this break in legal interpretation. To delink the notion of legitimate violence from the defense of human rights and reintroduce classic essentialist understandings of hostis humani generis, the figure of the international terrorist was established in the 1980s. The neoconservative scholars who propagated this new understanding of terrorism significantly gained influence after the end of the Cold War, and especially after the events of 9/11 (see Yoo, "Memorandum"), but, as my initial discussion of the pirate-terrorist nexus has shown, it has not remained uncontested. This study's analysis of Mohsin Hamid's 2007 novel, *The Reluctant Fundamentalist*, indicates that a new formal reinterpretation of the hostis humani generis constellation may emerge from the discursive context of a global War on Terror.

As is already evident from this brief overview, hostis humani generis is a constellation with considerable analytical baggage. It is necessarily based on an understanding of Otherness as inherently hostile. In modernity specifically, it is typically used not to resist invasion, but rather to legitimate acts of violent invasion—whether the invasion be of territory, sovereignty, or privilege. Some of these invasive applications may seem more commendable to readers than others, but it should not be forgotten that they are all based on someone's dehumanization and subjection to violence. At the same time, hostis humani generis emerges as an effective resource for rethinking and critiquing dominant or rival understandings of legitimate violence, especially since Turner's all-important formal reinterpretation of the constellation.

To substantiate my claim of the constellation's central cultural role, especially in the United States, I will use a body of texts that can be roughly divided into two categories—namely, legal, political, and philosophical or theoretical texts; and literary texts. These two categories intimately interact with each other in my analysis.

I use legal, political, and philosophical or theoretical texts to track the historical developments in the use of hostis humani generis as a legal fiction—that is, as a category that is used in legal discourse to describe political antagonists. My definition of hostis humani generis in law draws especially on the writings of Hugo Grotius and William Blackstone, while the constellation's philosophical foundation in law is largely provided by Augustine of Hippo, John Locke, and Thomas Hobbes. Variations are explored using the works of, for example, Giorgio Agamben, Hannah Arendt, Robert Cover, Elaine Scarry, and Claire Sterling. This body of texts helps pinpoint interpretive patterns in the history of the constellation and indicates instructive breaks in these patterns.

The second body of texts, the literary ones, provides an insight into the complexities of the constellation's cultural interpretation in Anglo-American discourse. Apart from a discussion of anatomies of roguery such as Captain Charles Johnson's *A General History of the Pyrates* (1724 and 1728) and Charles Ellms's *The Pirates' Own Book* (1837) in the first part of this book, all the literary texts that are discussed more extensively are novels. These novels—James Fenimore Cooper's *The Deerslayer* (1841), Dashiell Hammett's *Red Harvest* (1929), Richard Wright's *Native Son* (1940), Kurt Vonnegut's *Mother Night* (1962), and Mohsin Hamid's *The Reluctant Fundamentalist* (2007)—each address a pressing cultural conflict of their time. Their use of the constellation is intended to develop a slightly different, slightly new, yet still persuasive perspective on—respectively—settlers' rights to the American continent, the city as a site of intense social conflict, the exclusionary conditions endured by African American citizens, the moral dilemma of the veteran who has experienced mass warfare, or the role of the Muslim immigrant during the War on Terror.

Historically, hostis humani generis, as a philosophical and legal concept and the novel form both originated in early modernity (Watt, *Rise*), which facilitates an analysis of the various ways in which the selected texts and contexts react to each other, overlap in what they say about the issue of legitimate violence, and reinforce each other in their shaping of culture. I have also chosen to work with novels because of their length: in contrast with, for example, the much more condensed form of the short story, the novel form has to grapple with a greater variety of problematic narrative implications of the constellation. Not only do the formal solutions found by writers illustrate the cultural negotiations that rage in the background of seemingly clear-cut applications of the constellation in text, but the openness and messiness of the novel require deliberate and sophisticated formal strategies to manage the constellation. It thereby becomes possible to appreciate the considerable formal effort that is required to apply hostis humani generis for the purpose of rethinking a problem of legitimate violence, which makes the novels themselves visible as important and influential interpretations of the constellation.

As the list of works discussed in this study indicates, it is a specific kind of novel—the kind that relies on text alone to produce meaning—that is incorporated into my analysis. This is not a general feature of the novel (see, for example, Plascencia, *The People of Paper*), but it is a basic restriction that I require to facilitate comparison with legal and political texts. To be able to compare texts across disciplines, I focus on their shared formal restriction to the written word to negotiate the question of legitimate violence. In addition, other factors have led me to choose these particular novels. It almost goes without saying that all of them focus thematically on the meaning of violence between humans; furthermore, the popularity and canonic status of these novels recommend them as particularly resonant negotiations of legitimate violence at different historical moments. Furthermore, the chosen novels offer a variety of territorial spaces within which the constellation can operate. These are all spaces that deviate from the sea as the original space associated with the constellation (and that still assumes center stage in the anatomies of roguery, for example). Like the anatomies of roguery, Cooper's novel is set in a space far from civilization and yet to be subjected to legitimate imperial expansion. Hammett's and Wright's novels, in contrast, take place in the heart of the American city, using this urban space to negotiate civilization and legitimate violence. Vonnegut's and Hamid's novels, finally, are set in a thoroughly globalized space.

The question of gender immediately arises in the context of the selection of novels to analyze. An attentive reader may have noticed that I have not only restricted myself to novels written by male authors (who, with the exception of Hamid, write for a decidedly male readership), but that I even tend to use a generic "he" when I speak, for instance, of the figures within the constellation. I have restricted myself to male authors and male perspectives not out of habit or preference, but for two analytical reasons. First, this focus on men underlines the fact that the discourses analyzed in this book are always also masculinity discourses. In the discursive traditions addressed here, the use of legitimate violence is conventionally the prerogative of men. Part 3 introduces a complication of naturalized masculinity in the usage of the constellation. However, in most of the narrative examples available to me that operate with hostis humani generis, men tend to remain the central agents, even after the fundamental discursive revision of legitimacy discourses in the twentieth century. There are, of course, various types of female characters that can be read with the hostis humani generis constellation—witches, ambitious wives, and pre-twentieth-century *femmes fatales* could make particularly interesting figures of analysis in this respect. However, that is not the project of the present study. In this book, the use of the generic "he" and the focus on male writers are not intended to universalize a particular perspective, but to indicate that the question of legitimate violence is directly bound up with a representative status traditionally (and often still) attributed exclusively to men. Masculinity is thus treated as one of the common denominators that conventionally unite the three figures in the in-between zone—the representative of civilization, the barbarian praedo, and the transgressive pirata—as representatives of a larger spatialized realm.

Second, the generic "he" indicates an unspoken but constitutive hierarchy that hostis humani generis is based on. The following question may arise: Why, if I use a generic "he," do I still insist on speaking of an enemy of humankind rather than mankind? While men are conventionally cast as representative agents of violence, the universalist legitimacy of an act of violence depends on the claim that all nonviolent figures cast as innocent—regardless of gender, origin, race, or religion—are in fact protected by it. The use of the term "humankind" indicates this important condition of a successful use of the hostis humani generis constellation.

In this sense, then, masculinity is treated like other notoriously elusive and changeable concepts that take center stage in this study, such as the notion of civilization. Entities such as "civilization" and "men" are never comprehensively defined across the ages. When discussed in this study, such concepts are exclusively understood in relation to the hostis humani generis constellation: the term "civilization" simply indicates an inherently legitimate realm that is presupposed in a text—a realm that can and must be defended, as it is faced with an existential barbarian threat. A specific threat certainly always accommodates more specific understandings of civilization; there is a difference, for example, between a civilization that faces a threat to its territorial dominance and one facing a threat to values that inform an institutional landscape. The reason such very different civilizations and men can be discussed together is that the hostis humani generis constellation generally helps invest such categories with concrete meaning in text, even though such categories in and of themselves defy comprehensive definition. The internal flexibility of terms such as "masculinity" and "civilization," as well as "race" and "space," allows them to operate as analytical continuities to help delineate an overarching discursive history of the negotiation of legitimate violence.

[I]

THE EMPEROR AND THE PIRATE: LEGITIMATE VIOLENCE AS A MODERN DILEMMA

AS I INDICATED AT VARIOUS POINTS in the introduction, the hostis humani generis constellation in its modern form does not emerge in a vacuum. Before the discussion of the constellation itself can begin, the common foundations of both the legal fiction as a specifically legal instrument and the constellation as a formula for the dramatization of a specific question (namely, that of the legitimacy of violence) must be addressed and set in their historical context. This part of the book focuses on how and why the question of the legitimacy of violence came to be associated with modern Anglo-American piracy law in the first place, but it also indicates where and how the pirate and hostis humani generis part ways.

Even though the pirate figure and hostis humani generis have been considered synonymous for centuries, the figure predates the legal fiction, which emerged only in early modernity. This section attempts to establish the constitutive common ground between the figure and the constellation that, I suggest, can be led back to the usage and modern reinterpretation of an antique anecdote relayed by Augustine of Hippo.

This part of the book thus traces the history of the pirate figure insofar as it negotiates legitimate violence. It thus provides the historical background for the construction of hostis humani generis as a constellation that is capable of dramatizing the question of legitimate violence. In addition, the part seeks to identify some specific aspects of the pirate figure that have been particularly influential for the formation of the hostis humani generis constellation. Lastly, and relatedly, the arguments in this part of the book help pinpoint the first interpretive differences between the imperialist European (primarily British) and nationalist US perspectives on the pirate. These interpretive differences inform many of the arguments of later chapters: in short, this part of the book helps establish some specific features of the US perspective on the constellation and introduces important discursive influences that inform the use of the constellation up to the present.

To address all of these issues, the discussion must begin by turning to ancient

Rome. Scholars of pirate law routinely cite the Roman statesman and philosopher Cicero as the first person to formulate the principle of hostis humani generis, even though he used a different terminology (*communis hostis omnium*). According to Cicero, pirates were such radically alien and threatening entities that they stood outside of the law of war and could even be deceived and destroyed without rendering the imperial agent who did so dishonorable, or his cause illegitimate (Heller-Roazen, *Enemy of All*, 17–22; see also Policante, *Pirate Myth*). Cicero postulated that the legitimacy question was resolved from the start: legitimacy was the inherent property of the empire, and illegitimacy was the inherent property of the pirate who preyed on imperial citizens and trade structures. Consequently, aggression against pirates was inherently just. As a case in point, the politician Cicero applauded the swift and massive retaliation against predatory coastal communities by his contemporary, Pompey the Great (Lätsch, *Insularität*, 162).

Cicero's sharp distinction between realms of absolute legitimacy and illegitimacy remains a property of the modern hostis humani generis constellation. However, he formulated these legal opinions on the pirate at a time when Roman hegemony in the maritime realm was uncontested, at least in Rome itself. The more fundamental legitimacy question that remained untheorized by Cicero was eventually addressed by Augustine of Hippo in late antiquity. Augustine's contribution to the development of Western piracy constructions is often overlooked by piracy scholars, but it is illuminating to consider that contribution for the purpose of this study's argument.

In Augustine's time, the Roman Empire was threatened by invasion and internal turmoil, and the rise of Christianity as a political ideology raised fundamental disagreements about the proper sources of legitimacy within the empire. In this context, legitimacy constituted a central issue not so much in any conflict with actual pirates, but quite generally in the conflict over who would rule Rome. Augustine first introduced a notion of piracy that reached significantly beyond the mere legal description of an anti-imperial offense (*City of God*, 413–26). His contribution mainly lies in a reinterpretation of an anecdote originally attributed to Cicero, whose original version is lost today (Kempe, *Fluch der Weltmeere*, 234). While Cicero insisted on a clear normative divide between the illegitimate pirate and the legitimate empire that stopped the pirate, Augustine introduced an ambiguity to this confrontation that allowed him to capture a more profound dilemma of legitimate violence. Augustine used the pirate as a metaphor of illegitimate rule rather than as the representative of a specific political community. This conceptualization of the pirate as a metaphor required that rulers who claimed to use legitimate violence had to address the question of how exactly their claim differed from that of the pirate.

The Augustinian anecdote that introduces this new metaphorical function of the pirate tends to be mentioned, quoted, or dramatized whenever the core problem of sovereign legitimacy arises in the West. This part of the book focuses on the narrative analysis of three passages that trace the genesis of the anecdote's modern reading. In the first chapter, I discuss the anecdote, analyze some of its narrative strategies, and clarify its philosophical context. Then I will analyze two influential modern rewritings of the anecdote. Both are taken from texts that belong to a popular variation of the essay genre, called anatomies of roguery. An anatomy of roguery usually describes the lifestyle, professional organization, and trials of criminals such as organized beggars, highwaymen, or—in these cases—pirates. One of the rewritings is Charles Johnson's *A General History of the Pyrates* (1724 and 1728), the most authoritative standard reference on early modern colonial piracy. This book was published in Great Britain at a time of fundamental political and economic paradigm shifts, as trade-based colonialism forcefully began to replace plunder-based colonialism. The justice of this regime change is critically interrogated in the *General History* and also addressed in the passage discussed here.

The second reinterpretation I analyze is found in Charles Ellms's *The Pirates' Own Book* (1837), a popular volume on piracy that has a decidedly US perspective and topic. Although Ellms's book directly reproduces some chapters of the *General History* and other British sources, its real contribution lies in its discussion of American pirates and antipirate measures of the time. Like the *General History*, *The Pirates' Own Book* is part of a larger debate on contemporary paradigm shifts. Ellms was an abolitionist, and his presentation of piracy is embedded in a general argument about the injustice of slavery and the slave trade. In this sense, the paradigm shift here lies in the expansion of the hostis humani generis fiction to encompass, for the first time, crimes other than piracy (namely, the international slave trade).

The central analytical concern of this entire part of the book is the arrangement of figures evoked by the anecdote: the pirate and the emperor, as well as the legitimate ruler who is an alternative to both, and the innocent who is a victim of both. It should be mentioned, too, that the examples of the Augustinian anecdote discussed in this part are not the only examples to be found in this study. For instance, I also mention Noam Chomsky's 1986 rereading of the anecdote (*Pirates and Emperors*) in the final part of this book.

[1]

AUGUSTINE OF HIPPO: *THE CITY OF GOD*

IN *THE CITY OF GOD*, Augustine outlines the conflict between two possible normative orientations of an individual, represented by the earthly City of Man and the divine City of God. The City of Man represents an orientation toward the world and its written and unwritten rules (a normative view of the dictate of necessity, or alternatively a view that considers tradition normative), whereas the City of God represents an orientation toward God's commands (an idealist point of view that considers the world from the perspective not of what the norm is among humans, but of what God's will is). *The City of God* is a defense of the superior justice of Christianity in both transcendental and worldly matters, and notions of legitimacy are a central concern of the book. Augustine determines the legitimacy of any activity, including violence and war, according to the normative orientation of the committer and/or ruler. The same act can be either just or unjust depending on the normative framework within which it is positioned.

Augustine locates both empire and pirate in the realm of the City of Man, and thus in the realm of imperfect justice. He argues that it is a structural property of worldly rule to include predatory (in other words, piratical) components (Mattox, *Just War*, 50). Because imperial rule specifically requires perpetual war as a stabilizing practice (rather than reserving war as a last resort), empires in particular are structurally predatory and therefore inherently unjust: "to make war on your neighbors, and thence to proceed to others, and through mere lust of dominion to crush and subdue people who do you no harm, what else is this to be called than great robbery?" (*City of God*, 103). War, Augustine notes, violates the humanity of everyone involved, notably including those who commit acts of violence. He rhetorically asks "what prudence there is in wishing to glory in the greatness and extent of the empire, when you cannot point out the happiness of men who are always rolling, with dark fear and cruel lust, in warlike slaughters and in blood, which, whether shed in civil or foreign war, is still human blood" (ibid., 100).

Because Augustine considers the empire itself a "great robbery," his view of the pirate as the antagonist of the empire is more ambiguous than Cicero's. According to Augustine, the structures of both empire and pirate depend on the violent exploitation of their neighbors. His famous polemical equation of the emperor and the pirate as equally illegitimate committers of violence is the most frequently cited maxim on piracy to date, and it has been enormously influential in imagining the nature of piracy throughout Western history. The passage reads as follows:

> Justice being taken away, then, what are kingdoms but great robberies? For what are robberies themselves, but little kingdoms? The band itself is made up of men; it is ruled by the authority of a prince, it is knit together by the pact of the confederacy; the booty is divided by the law agreed on. If, by the admittance of abandoned men, this evil increases to such a degree that it holds places, fixes abodes, takes possession of cities, and peoples, it assumes the more plainly the name of a kingdom, because the reality is now manifestly conferred on it, not by the removal of covetousness, but by the addition of impunity. *Indeed, that was an apt and true reply which was given to Alexander the Great by a pirate who had been seized. For when that king had asked the man what he meant by keeping hostile possession of the sea, he answered with bold pride, "What you mean by seizing the whole earth; but because I do it with a petty ship, I am called a robber, while you who do it with a great fleet are styled emperor."* (*City of God*, 101; emphasis added)

It is the highlighted anecdote that, in contemporary and modern readings, is usually cited without any reference to its argumentative context. The pirate's function in Augustine's own argument becomes clearer when other comparisons in the text are considered. In the same chapter, Augustine argues that "the bad man, even if he reigns, is a slave, and that not of one man, but, what is far more grievous, of as many masters as he has vices" (*City of God*, 101). In principle, the comparison to the pirate works the same way as the comparison to the slave. Both slave and pirate are evoked not as representatives of an actual political and social position (Augustine explicitly explains this in the case of the slave), but as the abstract representations of a certain deficient nature in the emperor. Whereas slavery is redefined as lacking the ability to control one's own vicious desires, piracy is redefined as having the insolence to claim that an injustice, if it is only committed brazenly and successfully enough, can in fact be called justice. In the anecdote, the pirate's equating of himself to Alexander is, in Augustine's words, "bold" because there is no comparison between them in status or military force.

Because the pirate's answer is nevertheless characterized as an "apt and true" observation, this characterization can only be directed at a parallel between the pirate's and the emperor's innermost nature—both are parasitical impostors at heart. In Augustine, the pirate functions hyperbolically to show the extent of Alexander's illegitimacy as a ruler, and Alexander serves as the personification of an imperial regime that is "always rolling, with dark fear and cruel lust."

Alexander is indeed not a randomly chosen figure; he provides additional information about the properties that both ruler and pirate represent for Augustine. In one sense, Alexander may represent traditional Roman imperial rule in the passage, since in Cicero's time he was considered a positive, heroic model of rule that was excessively cited in the visual representations of Roman emperors (Zanker, *Macht der Bilder*, 42). At the same time, the legitimacy of Alexander's conquests has never been completely uncontested. The righteousness of his motives for conquest was doubted even by his allies. Alexander has been characterized as rash, hot-blooded, and bordering on the barbaric even by writers who otherwise defend his actions as heroic in principle (Arrian, *Alexanderzug*, 607). Alexander's individual cultural legacy is largely a debate about the legitimacy of his motives for conquest (Wiemer, *Alexander der Große*, 190–211), as his sudden death prevented historians from knowing what kind of ruler he would have been had he eventually achieved "impunity" by establishing a stable empire. All that anyone can ever know of Alexander is that he was an emperor, "great" because of his unparalleled military success (Rubincam, "Two 'Magni'"). The explicit comparison to Alexander thus freezes the pirate in a state of eternal potentiality. Like Alexander, the pirate is always at the same time a potential sovereign and a potential convict because his desires are insatiable and pursued with a strong sense of entitlement, but it is impossible to determine conclusively the justice of their motivation.[1] The inherent ambiguity of bold pursuit without a specific or stable end would remain one of the defining features of the pirate figure. In early modernity, the pirate's "archetypical sin" came to be ambition (Baer, introduction, xiii): the indefinite desire to seize for seizure's sake.

The expansive rule embodied by pirate and emperor comes with a corresponding regime of justice that Augustine specifies in the passage surrounding the anecdote. Both figures represent a community: Alexander an army and a kingdom, the pirate a small regional community.[2] The violent abuse of some strata of humankind (namely, innocent neighbors as the victims of conquest) defines and structures these predatory communities. The members of the "band," as Augustine calls the community members, are protected by the law, whereas the innocent neighbors are violated by the very existence of a law that is based on their exploitation. It is such a flawed normative basis of the law that squarely locates all expansive political regimes in the City of Man.

The passage is more than a fatalist statement about the inevitable injustice of worldly rule, however. An element of potential true justice does exist within a legal structure that cannot rid itself of injustice. This element is the individual. Rulers in Augustine are understood as actual people who are individually measured according to ideals of good leadership. Alexander and the unnamed pirate are identified as the prototypical representatives of a bad rule, which is a rule defined by the love of conquest alone. Their rule affirms the aspect responsible for the injustice of worldly rule: a rule's general structural predisposition for exploitation is significantly exacerbated by a sovereign's unpardonable blood lust. With such a leader, the community produces, without necessity, innocent victims that could otherwise be peaceful neighbors (Augustine, *City of God*, 100).

Because of its aggravating effect, the exceptionally bad rule of a military emperor like Alexander is instructive about the true nature of worldly law, bringing into sharp relief the ways in which worldly rule's injustice operates on a structural level. As was indicated above, the rule associated with the emperor is split into a rule of law over the members of his band for whom laws are made, and a rule of violence over the people who come with the conquered territory. For the law to apply only to the band and not to its victims, the normative core of the law must lie in relational structures (such as necessity and tradition) rather than in absolute moral standards. The emperor's law is a primarily distributive law that presupposes the exploitation and ruin of those who provide, or even constitute, booty. Augustine assumes the existence of a confederacy, which is a regime firmly based on the regulation of the distribution of spoils. The injustice of this rule is caused by the fact that such a regime relies on producing a stream of victimized Others who bear no relationship to one another apart from their common humanity and their common experience of victimization by the emperor's band. This is the central reason why the pirate figuratively represents this kind of rule: the structural components of a piratical community based on plunder are the purest expression of a politically evil deed that corresponds with, and exacerbates, the inherent structural injustice of worldly rule in general.

In the anecdote of Alexander and the pirate, then, four figures are implied. First and second are the pirate and the emperor, who constitute each other because their normative orientation is the City of Man in its purest form, actualized by their fellow violent exploitation of the innocent. Third is God, the legitimate ruler. On earth, his reign is actualized by individual Christians who act in his spirit (a group of individuals that ideally includes rulers). Finally, the innocent are a faceless collective, objectified by the law, and will therefore not experience justice until the day of judgment, when the divine reign over all humans begins. As is apparent, the least active and least defined figure in this constellation—the innocent—is the figure that actualizes the legitimacy argument in Augustine, because the two possible normative orientations of rulers are made visible in respect to the innocent. The innocent cannot be included in the structure of worldly (distributive) law, as this kind of law is based on the exploitation of someone. Because they are themselves inactive, the innocents' fate directly reflects on the legitimacy of a ruler. Christian mercy granted to the innocent by the legitimate ruler despite unjust laws on the one hand, and the innocents' cruel victimization by the exacerbation of the law's unjust elements by the pirate-emperor on the other hand, become the defining poles in a legitimacy spectrum of violence. It is therefore in respect to the innocent that the legitimate Christian ruler and the pirate-emperor are defined. Each rule constitutes itself either by emphasizing the merciful inclusion or the violent depredation of the innocent neighbor who stands outside of the law.

The translation of these two core forms of rule into modern debates of sovereign statehood has been captured well in Wendy Brown's discussion of the gendered state (*States of Injury*). Brown portrays the pirate-emperor and the legitimate ruler as two complementary forms of masculinity that constitute Western prototypes of sovereignty, the protective father and the threatening brigadier. The innocent, in this altered and accentuated model, are the women-and-children[3] who, essentially, submit to the good man to be protected from the bad man. The brigadier thus becomes the all-important legitimating counterpart to the father, as he makes the father meaningful as a protector (ibid., 188–91). The gender perspective is useful at this point because it emphasizes the essentialized difference made between either ruler and the passive, helpless innocent, in Brown's case represented by the difference between men and women-and-children.

While Brown's model obviously has decisive differences from that of Augustine, her analysis draws attention to some aspects of Augustine's argument that will become central for his modern reception. First, as mentioned above, Brown makes explicit the essentialized difference made between those who rule and those who are subjected to sovereign law. She shows that the pirate-emperor and the legitimate ruler have more in common with each other than either one has with the innocent. The pirate-emperor, albeit firmly condemned as illegitimate, is still the only viable alternative if the legitimate ruler fails or is challenged fundamentally. Second, Brown foreshadows a decisive modern alternation. In her analysis of the gendered state, distinctions between the legitimate fatherly ruler and the illegitimate pirate-emperor tend to be located in the political, economic, and legal structures of statehood itself: they are problems internal to the band. The constitutive exploitative practices against the innocent, which underlies modern states' core notion of the law as fundamentally distributive, have significantly changed their position from the victimized neighbors of bad men to the victimized family members of good men.

It is not an accident that Augustine's treatment of violent rulers cast such a long shadow in later conversations on legitimate rule as well as violence. Due to Augustine's use of the pirate figure as the personification of two philosophical questions—namely, whether violence can ever be inherently legitimate, and by what right certain forms of violence are distinguished from each other along an abstract spectrum of justice—scholars regularly began to raise the topic of piracy when they discussed the legitimacy of violence in general. This discussion was by no means only theoretical. Throughout the Middle Ages and until the Elizabethan age, the Augustinian anecdote was able to capture the de facto political and legal situation of maritime violence in the context of European seafaring, and thereby assumed additional substantiation as an "apt and true" summary of the legitimacy dilemma faced at sea. For example, Thomas Heebøll-Holm goes so far as to use the distinction between Cicero's and Augustine's perspectives on piracy to create alternative classifications of historical maritime piracy, distinguishing, in his words, "the 'Ciceronean paradigm' where pirates and piracy are objectified as inherently criminal. . . . a category created by a hegemonic and durable regime in a region with the power to define right and wrong and where the pirate is cast as the enemy of the commonality" and the "Augustinian definition" of the anecdote itself, which emphasizes the "subjectivity" of the pirate charge and which is "especially applicable for regions and epochs with no clear and uncontested hegemonic power" (*Maritime War*, 3–4). Heebøll-Holm proceeds to argue that this "subjective" understanding of piracy has been used since Hellenic times "to facilitate the mobilization and motivation to fight this enemy [or elsewhere in the passage, "this inhuman criminal"] with all available resources" (ibid., 4–5).

Indeed, such an explicitly relativistic, "subjective" element of piracy has been consistently emphasized in historical analyses of piracy charges that occurred throughout the Middle Ages and well into early modernity (see, for example, Earle, *Pirate Wars*; Gerassi-Navarro, *Pirate Novels*; Heebøll-Holm, *Maritime War*; Risso, "Cross-Cultural Perception"). It has also been reflected in famous and often-quoted maxims, such as Samuel Taylor Coleridge's remark on the topic of Francis Drake: "No man is a pirate, unless his contemporaries agree to call him so" ("Genius Feminine," 2:26).

An anecdote is not a concise definition, so it is worthwhile to consider what happened to the Augustinian anecdote once it was used in a context that ran counter to its original argumentative basis in *The City of God*. Modernity approached the anecdote from a radically different perspective —and perhaps necessarily so. Marxist and poststructuralist scholars in particular have emphasized the structural centrality of perpetual war and perpetual accumulation for Western modernity (Foucault, *Society*, 43–64; Harvey, *Neoliberalism*, 137–82; Reid, *Biopolitics*, 1–17). Western colonialism and capitalism are, in Augustine's understanding, deeply predatory and therefore illegitimate regimes.

How did early modern writers react to the obvious contradictions they encountered as they tried to naturalize and legitimate a regime based on military expansionism, the division and compartmentalization of labor, and the generation of surplus value from within a philosophical tradition that identified such a regime as the epitome of injustice? The narrative strategies used to achieve this balancing act tell us much about the attributes that would be linked to the hostis humani generis fiction in the early modern European context and, later, in the American frontier model of civilization. These reinterpretations have especially led to the increasing redefinition of the pirate as an unwitting pioneer of legitimate Western expansion, as the next chapter suggests.

[2]

CHARLES JOHNSON: *A GENERAL HISTORY OF THE PYRATES*

THE TENDENCY TO RENDER invisible the exploitation of innocents external to the rule of law is generally typical of treatments of the pirate-emperor in modernity. Augustine's unambiguous moral condemnation of conquest contradicts the practices of colonialism, imperialism, and strategic redistribution that constitute modern regimes. An interesting change in the Augustinian anecdote's narrative pattern thus emerges with the rise of imperialism, as the anecdote now has to be harmonized with the claim that conquest and the economic exploitation of Other neighbors are not only legal (at least among European empires), but also just and even virtuous (Fisch, *Europäische Expansion*, 183). The pirate-emperor of the City of Man and the legitimate ruler of the City of God are increasingly considered different varieties of the same regime: a contradiction between two separate forms of rule becomes the internal contradiction of one and the same regime. The two rereadings of the anecdote analyzed in the remainder of this part of the book constitute very different attempts to make sense of this characteristically modern contradiction.

The rereading of Augustine's anecdote discussed in this chapter was first published in 1728, at the beginning of Great Britain's decisive and systematic, but most of all successful, efforts to establish an empire primarily based on trade colonialism. The passage is taken from the British anatomy of roguery *A General History of the Most Notorious Pyrates*, the most influential work on the so-called Golden Age of Piracy (c. 1690–1730). The *General History* is a two-volume collection of pirate biographies, first published in 1724 and 1728. It focuses on pirate captains of European descent who almost exclusively operate in colonial contexts. The biographies of pirate captains are accompanied by extensive descriptions of overseas locations, legal opinions on some of the pirate cases, and the biographies of a few particularly interesting crew members, such as the female pirates Anne Bonny and Mary Read.

The entire *General History* is authored by Captain Charles Johnson, a pseudonym that has never satisfactorily been linked to an existing person. It is by no means clear whether the two volumes of the *General History* were written by the same person, or even whether several persons were involved in writing individual pirate biographies.[1] The *General History* covers the two pirate generations that comprise the Golden Age of Piracy in reverse order. The second volume (1728) deals with the first generation (1690–1702), which witnessed a definitive turning point in the European, and especially British, political treatment of maritime violence in colonial space; the first volume covers the second pirate generation, after the War of Spanish Succession (1714–30).

Historically, both generations, but especially the first, can be seen as symptoms of a change in eras. Before the Golden Age, rogue privateers in colonial realms could usually rely on their status as freelance agents of a larger imperialist effort. Especially the so-called buccaneers in the Americas, though organizationally independent, were considered valuable assets in expansive imperial outreach in defiance of dominant imperial rivals (most importantly, Spain). English buccaneers such as Henry Morgan purposefully capitalized on the generous conflation of privateering and exploration in English history (as epitomized by historical characters such as William Drake and Walter Raleigh), and suggested that their raids were not to be considered piracy at all. Morgan even sued Alexandre Exquemelin for libel when his former fellow buccaneer wrote about Morgan as a captain of pirates (Cordingly, *Black Flag*, 53).

The English, and later British, authorities moved from an attitude of leniency to a zero-tolerance policy in the course of only two decades. Pirates of the Golden Age's second and last generation, such as Edward "Blackbeard" Teach, were already considered primitive rebels in Eric Hobsbawm's sense (*Primitive Rebels*): they were threats to the survival of the empire, and drastic measures were taken against them, but their threat was by no means existential; most of all, they were considered entities that violently tried to uphold an old social order in the overwhelming presence of the new. As if to affirm this assessment, they even presented themselves as moral and social deviants and clear-cut criminals.

The white, Christian, privateering-derived, colonial piracy that the Golden Age stood for was virtually exterminated by 1728, the result of increasingly coordinated military intervention by the European powers along the major deep-sea trade routes (Earle, *Pirate Wars*, 205–7). By the time the *General History*'s second volume was written, the outcome of the shift from strategic lenience to ruthless persecution of pirates had been completed. It is feasible to assume that the retrospective characterization of this shift almost necessarily focuses on its construction as a turning point in British history. The different bases of legitimate violence that have to be negotiated are thus not presented as mutual contradictions, but as different stages of an inevitable sequence, leading toward overall imperial triumph.

The *General History*'s second volume, which focuses on the first pirate generation, differs significantly from the first volume, which is renowned for its relative historical accuracy. In contrast, the second volume is often inconsistent in style, featuring a number of fictional accounts (notably the biography of Captain Misson) and intertextual references that indicate that a pirate's life is already viewed allegorically to a considerable extent. A pragmatic reason for this greater fictionalization may very well lie in the limited availability of reliable sources on the volume's protagonists at the time of writing; if several writers were involved, perhaps not all may have had the same research ethos. Finally, it was a second volume that was primarily geared at repeating the great success of the first, so other parameters than accuracy may have mattered in the production and publication phases. It is this second volume that contains the passage I will discuss here. It is taken from the biography of Samuel Bellamy and is a very well-known passage conventionally referred to as the Free Prince speech:

> I can't pass by in Silence, Captain Bellamy's Speech to Captain Beer. "D—n my Bl—d," says he, "I am sorry they won't let you have your Sloop again, for I scorn to do any one a Mischief, when it is not for my Advantage; damn the Sloop, we must sink her, and she might be of Use to you. Tho,' damn ye, you are a sneaking Puppy, and so are all those who will submit to be governed by Laws which rich men have made for their own Security, for the cowardly Whelps have not the Courage otherwise to defend what they get by their Knavery; but damn ye altogether: Damn them for a Pack of crafty Rascals, and you, who serve them, for a Parcel of hen-hearted Numskuls. They villify us, the Scoundrels do, when there is only this Difference, they rob the Poor under the Cover of Law, forsooth, and we plunder the Rich under the Protection of our own Courage; had you not better make One of us, than sneak after the A—s of those Villains for Employment?" Captain Beer told him, that his Conscience would not allow him to break thro' the Laws of God and Man. "You are a devilish Conscience [conscientious] Rascal, d—n ye," reply'd Bellamy, "*I am a free Prince, and I have as much Authority to make War on the whole World, as he who has a hundred Sail of Ships at Sea, and an Army of 100,000 Men in the Field; and this my Conscience tells me*; but there is no arguing with such sniveling Puppies, who allow Superiors to kick them about Deck at Pleasure; and pin their Faith upon a Pimp of a Parson; a Squab, who

neither practices nor believes what he puts upon the chuckle-headed Fools he preaches to" (Johnson, *General History*, 587; emphasis in original removed; quotation marks added; emphasis added)

The Free Prince speech essentially narrates the story of a failed seduction. Bellamy has captured a merchant ship and speaks to its master, Beer. Bellamy attempts to convince Beer to give up his employment for a life of piracy and is rebuffed by a reference to Beer's impeccable conscience. Bellamy, in an enraged attempt to regain moral high ground, refers to his own conscience, which dictates to him the Augustinian anecdote. Then he triumphantly dismisses Beer as a puppet of the rich and ends the conversation. In this passage, Bellamy is presented not as the antagonist of Beer, but of "the rich" who have employed Beer. Not only are the rich chosen as the antagonist in Johnson's reading of the Augustinian anecdote, but the entire narrative scenario of seduction, and the generous space devoted to the topic of the rich in the pirate's monologue, suggest this change in the pirate's addressee.

In my analysis of this passage, I will restrict myself to the discussion of three aspects: first, the characterization of the pirate as an antagonist and equivalent of the rich instead of the emperor, and Beer's complex position within this constellation; second, the distinction made between a rule of law and a rule of courage earlier in the passage, its intertextual foundations, and its implications; and third, the Enlightenment philosophy that sees the origin of man in a state of nature, which underlies the perspective encountered here and is central to any change in use of the Augustinian anecdote.[2]

The pirate and the rich must be addressed first, because it is on the basis of a specific historical discourse that the anecdote's reformulation must be understood. In particular, the direct link between Enlightenment philosophy and imperialism that is exhibited in the context of piracy must be placed in its historical context before it can be addressed. Bellamy and the rich, in this passage, are not mutually independent warlords whose confrontation helps dramatize similarities in their motivation to violence, as is the case in Augustine. In Johnson, they are part of the same imperial regime and represent different forms of organizing legitimate maritime violence within this regime.

Bellamy represents the older institution of privateering warfare. Throughout the Middle Ages and well into the eighteenth century, the privateer was the central maritime entity used by any war-waging power at sea. While the specific forms of legitimation varied over time, among sovereigns, and between wartime and peacetime, the general principle of privateering is this: A privately equipped man-of-war is hired by a sovereign to molest the sovereign's enemies and the enemy's allies at sea, while the sovereign's subjects as well as his allies must remain unmolested by the privateer. The privateer may keep the bulk of the booty acquired in these engagements but has to give a certain percentage to his sovereign. It is a profitable institution for both sides: the privateer secures access to ports where he is free from persecution, can make repairs, sell the booty, and so on. In turn, the sovereign does not have to pay for maritime warfare but in fact generates income for the crown (through the percentage of the booty) as well as his subjects (who may be investors who help equip the man-of-war, who buy the privateer's booty comparatively cheaply and sell ship material and provisions to him, or who make money through the privateer's shore activities).

It was generally difficult to distinguish between legitimate and rogue privateers, because the legitimacy of privateering was not based so much on procedural correctness at sea but on success in terms of the generation of profit. All privateers tended to overstep the lines of the privateering contract at least occasionally, but they could expect to do so with impunity if the financial returns for the sovereign were good. All members of the privateering crew collectively profited from the institution even though theirs was an extremely hard and dangerous trade. They were paid a percentage of the booty, so rich takings could at least potentially make a common sailor rich as well. Also, hierarchies aboard were comparatively flat. Since the privateer's principle was that of "no prey, no pay," each sailor had a manifest interest in making prey, and crews often pressured captains who did not deliver enough booty to be more aggressive.

In contrast, the rich represent the system of the merchantman that developed in parallel to the system of privateering. Privateering remained the central institution for maritime warfare until the establishment of the first European navies in the mid-eighteenth century and continued to exist for at least a century afterward. However, with the increasing stabilization of colonial rule and the establishment of the Atlantic trade system, the merchantman had replaced the privateer as the central maritime entity in European imperial seafaring by the beginning of the eighteenth century. The merchantman system emphasized stable and stark hierarchies on board, predictable routes and shipping schedules, and profit maximization through cost reduction. The absolute rule of captains and the violent and financial exploitation of sailors, attributes that are conventionally associated with early modern seafaring today, are specifically attributes of the merchantman system, and for these reasons, this system was unloved and widely contested at the time of transition. Golden Age pirates like Bellamy epitomized the critique of the merchantman system for many of his British contemporaries. At the same time, it was widely recognized that the merchantman system was the maritime system of the future, especially when it came to the integration of colonial spaces into the empire.

In the context of piracy, the rich thus stand for the trading companies profiting from colonial trade in a rapidly stabilizing system of mercantilism. During the Golden Age, the trading companies were powerful and extremely visible representatives of the merchant community, and they tended to represent the paradigm shift in imperial maritime politics that mercantilism entailed. The companies were also at the forefront of antipiracy measures. Especially after 1695, they aggressively, creatively, and eventually successfully promoted an end to lenient European attitudes toward piracy (Ritchie, *Captain Kidd*, 127–59). The knowledge in retrospect that the companies will eventually be successful in the removal of pirates like Bellamy informs the understanding of the passage's central conflict: Johnson's contemporary reader saw the pirate still fighting but already knew that he would lose. All of Johnson's piratical protagonists of the second volume were dead or presumed dead by the time that volume was written.

It is at this point that Enlightenment philosophy can be linked to the debate, because that philosophy generally postulates the assumption of temporally progressive human development. For instance, Gotthold Ephraim Lessing took his idea of a perpetually civilizing world from Joachim of Fiore's millennialist notion of three ages that lead to the replacement of imperfect law with perfect justice. Gradual human improvement can occur, according to Lessing, because of civilization's ever more perfect reliance on reason (Eusterschulte, *Trinität*, 13), a philosophical orientation that is indicated in Johnson's piratical economic man who hates to sink a useful vessel, as well as in the rationalist merchantman system as a whole, which was decried as ruthless. Beer, in turn, foreshadows the more civilized regime that must eventually follow both reasonable rogues, the pirate and the company.

While the millennialist tradition emphasizes the notion of a gradual evolution toward civilization, the Enlightenment notion of a state of nature adds the dimension of the forceful replacement of one stage in the civilizing development by a successive stage. This notion of forceful replacement is central to Johnson's reading of piracy, because it allows the spatial interpretation of a temporal claim. If temporal development is translated as spatial expansion, it is plausible to suggest the parallel existence of several stages at the same time but in different spaces. Around the time of the publication of the *General History*'s second volume, it was an accepted fact that the Golden Age pirate was a figure of the past which could be addressed from a retrospective, philosophical viewpoint.

It is at this point that the pirate became a decidedly modern metaphor of rule. Rather than being a metaphor for bad rule, as he had been in Augustine, he became a metaphor for original rule in arguments based on the fiction of the state of nature. In Enlightenment discourse, the state of nature constitutes humanity's prehistory, from whence humanity as a whole has developed, or is still in the process of developing, into civilization. What this state of nature looked like, what it was characterized by, and what was to be derived from it were the great questions of early modernity because the answer to these questions would reveal the true nature and fate of humankind. Ingo Berensmeyer pointedly speaks of a "Ciceronian Moment" at which point European culture begins to imagine human nature not as inherently social and political, but rather claims that "society and civilization . . . emerge through a radical break with what precedes them (as 'nature')" (*Contingency*, 178; my translation; see also Thornton, *State of Nature*). Early modern writers introduced the state of nature as the origin of political rule and derived political legitimacy directly from the way the state of nature was imagined (Berensmeyer, *Contingency*, 178–79; Kucklick, *Das unmoralische Geschlecht*, 40). In this sense, colonial Golden Age pirates could provide firsthand empirical evidence on the likely construction of the state of nature. They offered a way to observe stages of the law prior to the European way of organizing law and legitimacy, and thus helped affirm or discount prevailing assumptions of the origin of humankind and civilization. Joel Baer writes:

> Interest in stories of the [Golden Age] pirate was fueled not only by their atrocities, courage and treasure, but also by the discovery that pirate communities recapitulated the evolution of law in "legitimate" societies. Readers of Plato, Hobbes and Locke were alerted to the philosophical value of pirate biography in prefaces and reviews of the two primary compilations.[3] . . . While some genteel readers might have been appalled to discover a kinship with pirates, the more philosophical would have welcomed new proof of Locke's thesis "that man is by necessity a law-making and law-obeying animal." (*British Isles*, 208–9)

Locke's notion of a "law-making animal" corresponds with Hobbes's notion of war as the natural context of humanity (*Leviathan*, 111) in the sense that they both naturalize the Augustinian pirate-emperor as the founding father of human civilization. The link to Locke is particularly important in the context of hostis humani generis, since the second of his *Two Treatises of Government: In the Former, The False Principles, and Foundation of Sir Robert Filmer, and His Followers, Are Detected and Overthrown. The Latter Is an Essay Concerning the True Original, Extent, and End of Civil Government* (1689) even includes a paraphrase of the Augustinian anecdote in which Locke completely agrees with Augustine's analysis of the conqueror (Locke, "Second Treatise," 385–86).

In part 2 of this book, I will discuss the importance of Locke in greater detail. Here, it is most relevant to note that the state of nature argument creates significant overlap between the notions of illegitimate rule and original rule. The colonial pirate was not primarily an illegitimate invader to Britons, who had long sympathized with the buccaneers' conquests. Instead, and most importantly, the pirate was deprived of Christian order and sovereign rule and lived, to all intents and purposes, in a state outside order itself (Baer, "Plot of Piracy"). This absence of order in the imperial margins made pirates into men in the state of nature, and the state of nature itself could be studied in the contemplation of pirates. A simultaneous reference to Locke could be made through the pirates' well-ordered distribution of booty that was considered the pirates' most characteristic feature and that confirmed Locke's naturalization of property in the "Second Treatise": "everyone [of the pirates] seemed to have his property as much secured to himself, as if he had been a member of the most civilized community in the world," a 1699 preface relates with a clear sense of respectful amazement (quoted in Baer, *British Isles*, 208). In this sense, the illegitimate law of the band that Augustine condemns as inherently unjust is now rewritten as the defining property of any order, including a civilized one. As Baer suggests, the social order based on conquest and distributive justice is "empirically confirmed" as natural by the existence of the pirates, an amoral rather than immoral feature of worldly rule (ibid.).

Nevertheless, Enlightenment thinkers did not suggest that humanity was eternally doomed to be ruled by pirates and the rich. Instead, humanity was assumed to be collectively evolving into stages that would eventually render conquest superfluous. This notion, too, seemed empirically confirmed by the history of colonial piracy. The swift end of the Golden Age of Piracy was in no small part the result of the concerted legal and military effort of European empires to regulate colonial ports, courts, and waters. But pirates were not the only ones who felt the results of increasingly concerted imperial rule. The colonial structures established by trading companies also experienced considerable pressure to change and adapt. The original reader of the *General History*, well aware of the pirates' practically achieved pastness, was routinely confronted with reports on the severe shortcomings of the companies' representation of the empire overseas. This strongly suggests that Johnson expects "the rich"—that is, the autonomous trading companies—to share the fate of the pirate as a transitional entity that will vanish as progress toward a perfect order continues. The rich necessarily have to enter into a kinship with the pirate to populate the colonies, Johnson suggests, but once they have created a preliminary and primitive order, they may be replaced by worthier successors—namely, the imperial state that obeys the law of nature more perfectly, and that is evoked by Beer's normative use of the law of God and man. In that sense, the end of piracy must naturally lead to the equally complete replacement of the rich by the legitimate empire.

For Johnson's contemporary readers, it made sense to consider the rich and the pirate as two aspects of the same thing and to assume that both would be swallowed up by the establishment of stable imperial rule.[4] At the same time, the question arises as to how a passage with premises so different from those of Augustine's anecdote could use that anecdote to support quite different Enlightenment conclusions. The use of the anecdote clearly helps establish the illegitimacy of these early stages in the sense that they would have to be replaced eventually, but it does not in and of itself characterize them as entities that can at least temporarily be recognized as legitimate.

As in Augustine's (presumable) treatment of Cicero's original anecdote, Johnson's treatment of Augustine's is based on a subtle reinterpretation of the figure of Alexander the Great. Augustine rejects the affirmation of Alexander as an ideal emperor that had most likely informed Cicero's writing; Johnson, in turn, rejects Augustine's notion that Alexander is the embodiment of endless warfare. The difference between the rich and the pirate in Johnson (but not in Augustine) boils down to a difference in understanding the principle of distributive justice: the rule of wealth versus the rule of courage, referring to different claims to legitimacy based either on traditional status or personal achievement.[5] The struggle for the origin of legitimacy in the vocabulary of wealth versus courage is a stock reference associated with piracy in the eighteenth century. The construction of this struggle can be referred back to Homer's *Iliad*, which, like many antique texts, was frequently cited in the eighteenth century. While the Augustinian anecdote requires that the two entities share a normative orientation that renders them both illegitimate (the love of conquest), the Homeric reference postulates that they represent two fundamentally different claims to the legitimacy of leadership over a specific band.

The subtle narrative combination of Augustine and Homer is in no small part possible because the characters of Alexander and Achilles overlap. Both are ambiguous heroes. While both are famous for their brilliance in battle, their bravery is often characterized as shortsighted; both are considered to have rash, impulsive, and brutal natures, and to be unable to accomplish anything that is lasting or substantial. These shared characteristics that allow an overlapping narrative reference to both Augustine and Homer allow for an effective change of narrative emphasis in the Free Prince speech. While the Augustinian pirate is arrested in eternal potentiality by his comparison to Alexander, Achilles is a transitional figure; he is defined by defying Agamemnon, but he dies in a battle whose victory Agamemnon will eventually claim.

The *Iliad*'s narrative revolves around a disagreement between Agamemnon, the leader of the Greek army because of his supreme nobility, and Achilles, the army's best fighter. After a battle, Agamemnon has to return an enslaved Trojan to his enemies, though he had previously claimed the captive as a spoil for himself. Thus deprived of a spoil of war, he claims a slave from Achilles as a replacement, arguing that the noblest man of the army should never receive less than a full share. Achilles refuses, arguing that he plays a central role on the battlefield and thus is more important to the war than Agamemnon is. The disagreement results in Achilles's famous grudge and is the central moment in the development of the epic. Joachim Latacz has shown that the quarrel over the spoils of war dramatizes the constitutive question of the *Iliad*: who is allowed to rule, the noblest or the best? ("Ilias," 117) In the Free Prince speech, this classic conflict is between the surrogates of wealth and courage instead of between those of nobility and skill.

In posing the question in this way, Homer's *Iliad* naturalizes the very origin of the law of conquest that Augustine condemns on general principle. Both Agamemnon and Achilles are members of the same army, although they are rivals in their different claims to rule it; neither poses a challenge to the general concept of a rule by conquest that the army as such represents. The slave Agamemnon and Achilles fight over is a prototypical Augustinian innocent. Her ownership does not contain a personal element of justice, such as the question of who had defeated her in battle; rather, she is simply an unlucky captive whom the army had come across in enemy territory, and who was thus considered a spoil comparable to, say, a horse. She enters the legal sphere of the army only as a spoil of war—a fact that is acknowledged even by the Trojan enemies who have to argue for extraordinary circumstances to have her returned. In other words, Agamemnon and Achilles represent different systems of distributing spoils like her, but the notion of distributive law based on the exploitation of the innocent is presupposed and affirmed by both.

The Free Prince speech draws very close to this core assumption. Bellamy explicitly does not challenge the right of the rich to exploit others; he merely argues that there is a different system of exploitation that has proven to be more advantageous for him and might also prove more advantageous for Beer. The narrative reference to the *Iliad* also explains Beer's centrality as an object of seduction. If the rich and the pirate are equivalents to Agamemnon and Achilles, they struggle over the domination of the same band. In the Free Prince speech, this band is represented by the merchant sailor, who is both the core employee of the rich and the primary candidate for pirate recruits (Rediker, *Villains*, 38–59). Both require him to affirm their ultimate legitimacy, which firmly excludes the legitimacy of their rival, and both call for Beer to decide between them. Since the rich and the pirate both represent predatory and recruitment-based regimes, Bellamy argues that the only open question is: if there is only the choice between the two, whom should the sailor obey, the courageous or the wealthy? The actual victims of their conquest—the native peoples who live in conquered territories and are subjected to the imperial project, as it is they who produce trade-based colonialism's spoils of war—are completely removed from the discussion. The innocent, in this passage, are invisible. The Free Prince speech is not about mercy but exclusively about distributive law.

At the same time, the insertion of the *Iliad*'s dispute between wealth and courage adds a meaning to the Augustinian anecdote that helps incorporate into it Enlightenment constructions of order as a genuinely progressive development. In Augustine, both the good, legitimate, fatherly ruler and the bad, illegitimate, predatory pirate-emperor can and do exist in parallel, as their normative orientations (and, thus, the individual bases of their rules) are independent of each other. In the *Iliad*, however, the question of a better or worse emperor is explicitly linked to a certain moment during conquest. Homer offers a clear temporal hierarchy between the two opposing regimes of rule. The courageous, brilliant Achilles manages to operate exclusively on his own terms, but he does not reap any benefit from doing so. He dies before Troy is even taken. The rich, noble Agamemnon remains the leader of the army and returns home as the victor who has conquered the city. In the *Iliad*, the regimes represented by Agamemnon and Achilles are not analogies of each other, as they are in Augustine, but necessary complements of each other. True, Johnson suggests, the rule of Agamemnon will always bring victory, while Achilles will always just die in battle—but this does not mean that a piratical Achilles is useless to the imperial Agamemnon in his struggle to win a colonial Troy; he is an important early asset. His self-interested life, as well as his violent death in battle, is for the greater good of conquest and expansion in general. Just as Achilles was able to kill Hector, the leader of the Trojan army, the pirate is able to break Spanish dominance in American waters (Beeching, introduction, 16–17).

In short, the *Iliad* reference achieves to several important things for the Free Prince speech. It establishes the notion of a pirate-emperor as a transitional entity by evoking parallels between Alexander and Achilles, which causally derives the pirate from his antagonists in the sense that it creates a hierarchy between them: the pirate paves the way for his antagonists just as Achilles paves the way for Agamemnon. The *Iliad* reference furthermore refocuses demands for justice by concentrating on the demands of band members rather than on those of the victim of conquest at large, which helps naturalize both conquest and a law based on distributive justice. In the Free Prince speech, the exploitation of the innocent is naturalized, and the imperial regime's overall justice is instead measured by the way it treats band members.

While the *Iliad* helps pinpoint the specific construction of pirates and emperors as parts of the civilizing process in early modern discourse, the Augustinian anecdote obviously remains the most visible and most important intertextual reference in the Free Prince speech. Johnson uses this specific passage for a reason— namely, to balance out the claims to legitimacy made by the pirate and the rich. The rich are acknowledged as lawful representatives of the national interest by Beer, while Bellamy's claim to legitimacy is explicitly rejected as immoral both by Beer and by the narrative voice. Bellamy's own reproach of the rich, however, is given considerable force and room. It is eloquently delivered, citing accepted facts of the day such as the exploitation of merchant sailors and the factual sovereignty of trading companies in at least some colonial spaces. While Johnson uses different dialogue strategies than Augustine, the fundamental challenge of the anecdote remains the same: the conflict between the pirate and the rich is a conflict of exchangeable entities.

At this point, the specific construction of Captain Beer in the passage must be addressed once more. As mentioned above, the pirate in Johnson does not meet his opponent face to face, as he does in Augustine. Instead, their antagonism is expressed in the proxy war of seduction, of attempts to lure away the other's followers. The merchant sailor constitutes a convincing common ground for such a proxy conflict, as he has a relationship of recruitment to both. However, Beer subverts both attempts at his seduction; he integrates the more serious implications of Augustine's philosophy into the Enlightenment context.

As a Golden Age pirate, Bellamy originally started out as a merchant sailor like Beer, and he wants Beer to follow his example. It is appropriate for both to question their conscience on this matter, because turning or not turning pirate is a normative question that they both have or had to answer from the perspective of the common sailor in the merchantman system. Bellamy's speech is characterized by his expectation that anyone will be most convinced by an argument focused on personal benefits, just as he was and as the rich are. The speech describes the piratical regime as superior to the merchantman regime because it offers the common sailor a better chance to make a profit. Bellamy especially emphasizes that the pirate system respects the band member instead of systematically and predatorily defrauding him, as the rich will do. In other words, Bellamy's central argument is the offer of a more legitimate system of distributive law for the band member.

Confronted with Beer's evocation of "the Laws of God and Man" that keep him from leaving the service of the rich, Bellamy's reference to his own conscience destabilizes the common ground between Beer and the rich by questioning the rich's sincerity in positioning themselves as faithful to the laws of God and man. Although they pretend to be the representatives of legitimate rule, the piratical argument goes, the rich are in fact like the pirate: intent on establishing a kind of autonomous subregime whose only purpose is parasitical enrichment. This regime is not primarily derived from a just control over territory but from unpunished practices of exploitation. According to Bellamy, the laws of God and man are a travesty that has long lost any proximity to justice, precisely because the rich have transformed these notions into a mere cover for their ulterior motives: to systematically increase both their own security, power, and wealth, and their own detachment from the rules they claim to maintain and represent. Beer does not, Bellamy suggests, obey the laws of God and man—he obeys the interests of the rich. Correspondingly, Bellamy's sole personal attack against Beer's character is not a charge of malice but one of naivety.

But compelled to decide between two explicitly exploitative regimes, Beer chooses neither. Instead, his reference to the laws of God and man positions him as a prototypical Augustinian Christian soldier who agrees to do worldly, even unjust, work not as a matter of choice but because God dictates that he owes loyalty and respect to worldly regimes (Mattox, *Just War*, 57). Importantly, however, the worldly regime whose unjust work must be done for the sake of the greater good is not sovereign in this case—it is the regime of the rich. This implicitly positions imperial sovereignty as the equivalent of God, in the sense that the empire is available as a legitimate successor regime from within the logic of the Free Prince speech. Once the pirate and the rich are replaced, Beer suggests, a truly legitimate and lawful imperial regime can come into existence.

In this way, the Free Prince speech suggests two aspects that are absolutely crucial for the genesis of the pirate construction in modernity: first, the emperor (here, in the form of the rich) is externalized as normatively and structurally separate from the state; and second, the state can therefore represent just rule. Bellamy cannot acknowledge these distinctions because the normative reference system represented by the pirate does not consider right and wrong, but only profitability and unprofitability. Bellamy, and by implication the rich, are portrayed as unable to see beyond the realm of the economically advantageous and immediately useful, and to consider the moral dimensions of loyalty and lawfulness as integral parts of the greater imperial interest. Yet even though they are blind to this core interest of the empire, they nevertheless serve its genesis.

As mentioned above, the link between Achilles and Agamemnon, which eventually produces Agamemnon as the enduring ruler and Achilles as a heroic asset, is in great part accomplished by a temporal construction that renders the emperor a transitional phenomenon. In the anecdote's late antique context, Augustine argues on the basis of a structurally similar premise, which Beer specifically cites. The Christian soldier acts on the premise that a state of justice will eventually arrive, and that his own attempt to act justly will be affirmed and rewarded once the legitimate ruler establishes his reign. Both the pirate-emperor and the Christian soldier are therefore constructed as figures whose role is fully understood only in retrospect, when legitimate rule has in fact established itself. This parallel temporal construction is evoked in the Free Prince speech by the complementary construction of Bellamy and Beer as the only figures present during the telling of the anecdote. Once legitimate imperial rule has been established, Bellamy will not have been a criminal, but a pioneer; Beer will not have been naive, but a model subject whose faith in justice has been rewarded by the establishment of a better reality. Both premises are based on a repositioning of the legitimate ruler as the worldly result of progress, rather than the divine decision to end worldly time.

In summary, the Free Prince speech uses Augustine's anecdote to evoke something like a transitional phase of illegitimate yet necessary rule that, in the long run, will lead to the establishment of a legitimate empire when the process of economically minded appropriation is concluded. The modern metanarrative of progress represents the most prominent new strategy for circumventing the legitimacy problems that Augustine raises. Aggressive conquest carried out by the pirate and the trading company is accepted as a regrettable yet integral early aspect of the imperial project. Because of their pursuit of private rather than public interests, these figures do not actually represent the imperial sovereign but can be externalized as the separate representatives of early stages that must eventually make room for ever more mature versions of colonialism, inevitably culminating in a regime that will be fully civilized. In this view, the naturalization of distributive law within the band of civilization becomes a universally accepted standard of justice in modernity.

As is obvious from today's perspective, the eventual conclusion of expansion into the establishment of a static, fully civilized empire never materialized. Instead, the system of mercantilism grew into various stages of capitalism, and the modern Western person was increasingly imagined as a void defined by the need for appropriation and consumption (Berman, *All That Is Solid*, 67–71). Concerning the pirate specifically, certain aspects of the constellation of the early eighteenth century already indicate why the pirate would remain stuck in his role of a scornful reflection of imperial injustice—why he should, in fact, come to serve as a literary shorthand to help reveal the hypocrisy of imperial power structures especially during the late nineteenth century, the peak of British imperialism (Harty, "Playing Pirate"; Lutz, "Pirate Poet").

The central problem for the pirate figure in modernity lies in a paradox within the idea of the state of nature—namely, that such a concept is dependent on the construction of a central moment of fundamental transition. In all concepts of a state of nature, there is a basic shift between an inherently static and an inherently dynamic state, one of which represents the precivilized state of nature and the other the state of order. The problem faced by the Augustinian/Homeric constellation in the Free Prince speech is that it is based on the assumption that a dynamic state of pre-order (represented by the pirate and the rich) will eventually be replaced by a static state of order (represented by the anticipated future empire).

However, this constellation was soon reversed in dominant philosophical discourse. Central Enlightenment thinkers such as Rousseau, Kant, and Hegel turned the tables and argued that, rather than the dynamic state being replaced by the static state, the static state would be replaced by the dynamic state (Kucklick, *Das unmoralische Geschlecht*, 68–69). In this increasingly dominant version of the state of nature fiction, the idea was that imperial progress was perpetual and would never be replaced by any substantially different regime, because it had itself replaced a prehistoric, static state of precivilization. In the context of pirate fictions, however, this development meant that the order that would separate the legitimate ruler from the pirate would never arrive, and that the pirate would always remain the evil twin of the various versions of imperial order he encountered.

The replacement of the pirate-emperor stage with the stage of legitimate imperial order had been the key feature that allowed the modern pirate to be anything other than a metaphor for unjust rule in Augustine's sense. But if the pirate's claims remained permanently "apt" (Augustine, *City of God*, 101) to challenge modern claims to imperial legitimacy, the pirate as a figure became a perpetual reminder of a gaping void in imperial justice. The pirate as well as the illegitimate rich could be humiliated, defeated, and replaced, but the rich could never disappear completely as the true epitome of modern civilization in European discourse.

The adaption of the Augustinian anecdote to imperial needs thus failed because the state of nature fiction, which enabled this adaptation, changed after the discursive positioning of the pirate vis-à-vis modern rule. The pirate was established as a representative of an illegitimate element of modernity, and what he represented could no longer be replaced by an alternative. It thus became impossible, from within the British discourses of legitimate violence based on the state of nature, to delink imperial violence from the implications of the pirate as the European empire's permanent evil twin. From within the structural premises of the conversation, any modern claim to imperial violence must remain contestable. To render modern rule legitimate, the conversation about legitimate violence would have to be structurally changed.

[3]

CHARLES ELLMS: *THE PIRATES' OWN BOOK*

WHILE EUROPEAN, AND ESPECIALLY British, discourse never persuasively resolved the dilemma presented by the pirate figure, a discourse that emerged in the United States did. The final rereading of Augustine's anecdote that I will analyze here exemplifies this resolution and indicates an interesting discursive maneuver in the United States that will inform much of my discussion of hostis humani generis in this study. In the rereading of Augustine in the early nineteenth century, a simple yet effective twist is performed: the United States is squarely defined as the realization of the legitimate civilized state that is anticipated in British discourse, and the entire history of European imperialism takes the place of a static, precivilized state of nature.

The passage I will discuss here is taken from Charles Ellms's *The Pirates' Own Book*, published in Boston in 1837. *The Pirates' Own Book* has been widely reprinted as one of the classic publications on Western piracy, and it is especially famous for its rich body of illustrations. Charles Ellms was a stationer who gave up that profession to write popular books and almanacs on maritime topics. While not much else is known about him, his location in Boston indicates some of the reasons for his topic as well as his perspective: the city has an extensive piracy-related history and was also a hotbed of American phrenology in the early nineteenth century. *The Pirates' Own Book* strongly reflects both of these contexts.

During the Golden Age of Piracy, Boston could boast of being one of the most important colonial spaces for antipiracy measures. Many of the Golden Age pirates covered by Johnson were tried and executed there, Cotton Mather had preached his pirate sermons there, and booksellers there had traditionally made small fortunes from descriptions of pirate trials and pirates' dying confessions. In *The Pirates' Own Book*, Ellms refers to this history by often inserting texts originally written by Captain Charles Johnson, William Blackstone, and other central sources on piracy into the chapters, copying texts extensively and verbatim.[1] Other passages in *The Pirates' Own Book* from British sources are interwoven with the text and often greatly revised from their original versions. I see this use of key texts on piracy as an attempt to come as close as possible to an authoritative account of the history of piracy. Indeed, the texts incorporated by Ellms represented a cultural consensus about piracy in the nineteenth-century United States. Ellms may have attempted to summon and summarize the most important historical documents on piracy to contextualize the actual focus of his publication, the pirates of the early nineteenth century. I will return to this aspect in a moment.

First, the second reason for the importance of Boston must be addressed, as it heavily influences Ellms's perspective on piracy. As noted above, Boston played an important role in the American history of phrenology, a discourse that structures the entire text of *The Pirates' Own Book* and is explicitly mentioned in the rereading of the Augustinian anecdote I will discuss below. Phrenology essentially argues that the character of a person can be determined by the shape of his or her head. The theory assigns special meaning to certain "bumps" and their prominence—for instance, the bump of destructiveness that informs piratical behavior. Phrenology is largely dismissed today as a racist and sexist pseudoscience, and indeed it contributed to the progression of scientific racism, to the naturalization of dichotomist gender constructions in American society, and to the social exclusion of disabled citizens. The hierarchy of heads in phrenology clearly favors white, able-bodied men as the ideal that is superior to all others, and because of this position these men become a standard of civilization.

The mainstream popularity of phrenology in the United States began with a series of lectures given by Charles Caldwell in the 1820s, one of which notably was in Boston. In 1832, five years before the first publication of *The Pirates' Own Book*, one of the fathers of phrenology, Johann Gaspar Spurzheim, came to Boston during a lecture series and fell victim to a deadly fever. His funeral was a very public event that may help illustrate the great popularity of phrenology in the city. In the course of the funeral ceremony, a cast of Spurzheim's head was made, his corpse was publicly dissected in front of as large an audience as the anatomical theater allowed, his brain and skull were removed as artifacts for the Bostonian phrenological society, and his burial was attended by approximately three thousand people (Oehler-Klein, *Schädellehre*, 340–41). Considering the visibility of such events, it is not surprising that Ellms was aware of the long-lived phrenologist community in Boston. His own deep familiarity with phrenological discourse suggests that he was an active part of that community. For instance, almost every chapter of *The Pirates' Own Book* ends with a detailed physical description of the protagonists. These descriptions, which are complemented by the book's famous illustrations, appear as postscripts with no apparent narrative connection to the rest of the chapter. Their only function is to add important phrenological information such as a person's beauty, disfigurement, and other meaningful physical characteristics.

In the passage discussed here, impressions are reviewed from the trial of Benito de Soto, one of the most famous, bloodthirsty, and glamorous Latin American pirates of the early nineteenth century. In 1820 and 1830s, after the Napoleonic wars, there was a spate of particularly vicious pirate crews in Europe and, more importantly for the United States, in Latin America. As Peter Earle notes, many of the features associated with Golden Age piracy in the United States today actually stem from the post-Napoleonic period that Ellms lived in and wrote about. Americans were extremely aware of these contemporary waves of piracy and were kept informed by newspapers throughout the nation (Earle, *Pirate Wars*, 216–20). Because of the prominence of Latin American pirates in US discourse, Ellms devotes the greatest portion of his book to the pirates of his own day and their phrenological interpretation. Here, too, he makes free use of trial documents and other primary sources. The passage that refers to the Augustinian anecdote reads as follows:

> Indeed, when I saw him [Captain Benito de Soto] in his cell and at his trial, . . . he still exhibited strong traces of what he had been, still retained his erect and fearless carriage, his quick, fiery, and malevolent eye, his hurried and concise speech, and his close and pertinent style of remark. He appeared to me such a man as would have made a hero in the ranks of his country, had circumstances placed him in the proper road to fame: but ignorance and poverty turned [him] into the most ferocious robber, one who might have rendered service and been an honor to his sunken country [Spain]. I should like to hear what the phrenologists say of his head; it appeared to me to be the most peculiar I had ever seen, and certainly, as far as the bump of destructiveness went, bore the theory [of phrenology] full out. *It is rumoured here that the skull has been sent to the savans* [*sic*] *of Edinburg* [*sic*]*; if this be the case, we shall no doubt be made acquainted with their sage opinion upon the subject, and great conquerors will receive a farther assurance of how much they resemble in their physical natures the greatest murderers.* (Ellms, *Own Book*, 99; emphasis added)

In this rereading of Augustine, the narrative construction is very different from the previously discussed examples. Whereas Augustine and Johnson had used the similarity between pirate and emperor as a dramatic way to shatter certain existing claims to legitimacy, the figures' relationship in Ellms is characterized as neither surprising nor problematic. It is merely a "farther" affirmation of a long-established scientific fact. At the same time, it is noticeable how much effort Ellms devotes to associating the emperor with Europe rather than the United States, as the repeated remarks about de Soto's "country" or even "his sunken country" indicate.

The most obvious indication of a vilification of Europe is the reinterpretation of a prototypical remark in eighteenth-century British discourse on piracy—namely, the lament that the pirate might have been of great service to the empire if circumstances had been different. In the context of Captain Edward "Blackbeard" Teach, who was at least as glamorous a pirate as de Soto, Johnson had observed that "here was an End of that courageous Brute, who might have pass'd in the World for a Heroe, had he been employ'd in a good Cause" (*General History*, 82). Johnson suggests that a brute might be a hero, indicating, however, that his superior courage is the decisive aspect in that assessment—a nod to the Achilles-like qualities that the eighteenth century attributed to the pirate. Ellms uses a very different formulation: "ignorance and poverty turned [him] into the most ferocious robber, one who might have rendered service and been an honor to his sunken country." In this sentence, Ellms highlights the structural shortcomings of European societies and identifies the lack of education and economic opportunity as the main causes of piracy. He not only replaces "courageous" with "ferocious," but he also formulates the reference to heroism as a parallel construction to "the most ferocious robber." He suggests that being a despicable and exceptionally cruel criminal and being "one who might have . . . been an honor to his sunken country" are virtually synonymous. The famous and widespread British lament about Blackbeard is no longer used to conceptualize a legitimate "us" but an illegitimate "them."

The two categories of pirate and emperor are thereby collapsed before Ellms even evokes Augustine, and they are collapsed specifically as the common properties of Europe. The state of the pirate who bears mere "traces of what he had been" as he awaits his execution mirrors the decay of the "sunken country" he might very well have served. Ellms uses famous and recognizable turns of phrases from the context of piracy—in this case, the combination of Johnson's lament about Blackbeard and the Augustinian anecdote itself—but never uses the word "pirate." Instead, he uses much more obviously derogatory characterizations such as "robber" and "murderer," thus underlining the unambiguous illegitimacy that he assigns to both pirate and (European) emperor. Pirate and emperor no longer constitute a vexing paradox of imperial expansion, but pathologies of the past, regrettable social anomalies that are the direct product of the pirates' European origin.

The age of the legitimate empire that is both heralded and postponed in Johnson is no longer a state of the future in Ellms's writing. Rather, it is a state that has long been achieved—not in Europe (which still battles with the dilemma of being imperialist invaders and narrative equivalents of the pirate) but in the United States (which, according to Ellms, had never been imperial in the first place). In terms of territorial expansion, citizens of the United States are portrayed in a completely defensive light throughout the book, and the US westward (and, significantly in the context of Ellms's topic, southward) imperial expansion is rendered as invisible in *The Pirates' Own Book* as is the fate of the external innocent victims in the Free Prince speech. Instead, Ellms suggests that the foundation of the United States is nothing less than the fundamental turning point that British texts such as the Free Prince speech anticipated—a securely achieved state of civilization from which one can review the follies of an earlier developmental stage with scientific rationalism and moral disinterestedness.

In my analysis of this new position, I will focus on two larger points. Most important, I will discuss Ellms's position in the debate about abolitionism. This point is important insofar as Ellms's take on phrenology is directly linked to the legal use of the hostis humani generis fiction that addresses, for the first time, a crime other than piracy. Some fifteen years earlier, piracy law had been amended to criminalize the deep-sea slave trade as one additional form of piracy. Thus, in Ellms's time, the slave trade was considered a crime committed by enemies of all humankind. But first, I will discuss the impact of Ellms's use of the discourse of phrenology in this passage, and how this discourse helps naturalize the United States as an absolute representative of legitimate rule.

Phrenology, seen as a science, attempts to empirically identify and differentiate personalities by physical features and to create verifiable standards to measure any person's true nature, character deficits, and likely future behavior. Early phrenologists tended to focus on criminals and other problematic segments of the population—an obvious example being Ellms himself, who writes about pirates. Phrenology's founder, Franz Joseph Gall, originally promoted a deterministic analysis of a person's personality bumps. The American tradition almost immediately deviated from this and allowed that people may gradually change their own skull's bumps and also may encourage change in the bumps of others. Spurzheim in particular argued that Gall's main fault lay in his focus on ideal character types who represented only one property, such as "the emperor," instead of attempting to identify an ideal equilibrium of features—in other words, the normal state—from which extreme types deviated, and to which they should be led back (Tomlinson, *Head Masters*, 84–86). In this sense, the American phrenological tradition explicitly affirms the modern invention of the normal as the new standard of human behavior (Hacking, *Taming of Chance*, 160–69) and emphasizes the notion of the criminal as a curable deviant.

Even though phrenology relied on a blatantly hierarchical structuring of humanity that remained deterministic in its core assumptions and helped naturalize these assumptions as scientifically proven facts of life (such as the inherent superiority of white over nonwhite), American phrenologists believed that favorable social conditions, education, and the willingness to improve could change the bumps of an individual person for the better: "Once instructed by phrenology, individuals [were considered to have] both the means and responsibility for self-improvement" (Cynthia Hamilton, "Man and Brother," 175). Because young bones were especially capable of changing, the all-important reliance on the self-help tradition was accompanied by the second pillar of the American phrenological movement, a decided focus on pedagogy (Tomlinson, *Head Masters*, 265–85) that drew on Locke's and Rousseau's reasoning that the education of a child determined the character of the adult. Furthermore, the scientific, empirical results of bump analyses were used to argue for the improvement of various underprivileged populations' station in life. After all, as Spurzheim had argued, every human being was considered to consist of good parts and bad parts that needed only to be balanced to create a good nature. Such transformations could occur even in those who were otherwise deemed hopelessly lost and wicked. Social justice was necessary to facilitate skull transformations toward a normal equilibrium: following this reasoning, phrenologists opposed physical punishment and the death penalty in the legal system and argued for the more humane treatment of the mentally ill who were housed in asylums (Oehler-Klein, *Schädellehre*, 335–36).

Even though most strands of phrenology clearly helped usher in scientific racism, the discourse was also sometimes used to oppose African American slavery. For instance, an abolitionist pamphlet of 1839 compared the heads of Africans, American slaves, and American freedmen, deducing that the Africans (who had never been exposed to Western notions of order) stood at the lowest level and the freedmen (who had been exposed to the Western order but not reduced to slavery by it) stood at the highest level in the hierarchy of heads (Cynthia Hamilton, "Man and Brother," 181–82). *The Pirates' Own Book*, too, is structured by a pronounced abolitionist argument (see especially Ellms, *Own Book*, 82).

In Ellms's reading of the Augustinian anecdote, the discursive basis of American phrenology helps clarify the role implicitly attributed to the United States in the text. Like Spurzheim in his critique of Gall, Ellms refuses to read the pirate and the emperor as ideal types who represent a form of rule, as in Augustine, or externalized early stages of civilization, as in Johnson. Instead, Ellms reads them as individuals who reveal the flaws of a less than ideally organized regime. Their extremity does not render them archetypes. Rather, they are considered warning signs that a given regime cannot maintain an environment for its citizens that allows them to develop normally. As indicated by the equating of the ferocious robber and the European hero in Ellms's rereading of the Augustinian anecdote, the central property of Europe is the reducing of entire classes to ignorance and poverty. Not only did the social conditions of Europe push European citizens into violent extremes, but they even celebrated such personal degradation as heroic. It is in light of this that Ellms understands the special legitimacy of the United States—namely, as an environment that encourages people to develop freely and to achieve personal and collective happiness. Here, he agreed with the Fowler brothers, perhaps the most famous American phrenologists and Ellms's contemporaries, who wrote: "In this land of plenty and equal rights, conscious of its liberty to exercise any and all of its powers, the human mind marches forth unfettered and free" (Fowler and Fowler, *Phrenology*, iii).

Both the Fowler brothers and Ellms saw the free and natural development of the mind as the central ideal represented by the United States, but they also indicated that violent and decadent excesses might result from such freedom. The Fowler brothers continued: "Here, then, if anywhere, we might expect to find, not only the greatest variety [of human characters], but, also, the greatest extremes" (*Phrenology*, iii–iv). This is hardly a completely positive statement in a discourse that emphasized the virtue of tranquil normalcy. In Ellms, therefore, American judges and officials are the most virtuous characters because they wisely regulate the undesirable extremes represented, in this case, by criminal pirates. In the numerous trial scenes in the book, but also in included documents such as letters from the US president and assorted military leaders, US officials represent the ideal of fatherly tranquility that welcomes and supports any credible attempt to improve oneself after previous bad conduct (*Own Book*, 41–43). At the same time, they sternly defend the law and citizens against those who continue to resist betterment (ibid., 68). The evocation of extremes in the American nation-state is a starting point for an individual to either become better or be excluded from the nation. The stage of this society, in other words, is not determined by the characters that live there but by the ideal of a national character to be striven toward. This ideal, Ellms argues, serves as the basis for the United States' supreme legitimacy, because those who already represent and reproduce these ideals are at the same time the direct representatives of US statehood.

The Pirates' Own Book contains one chapter (33–48) that is an interesting elaboration of this basic premise, and I will include it in this analysis because it helps specify the role of the United States in the text more generally.

The chapter in question revolves around Jean Lafitte, the pirate who had helped defend New Orleans against British forces in the War of 1812, and who had therefore gained the status of a regional American folk hero. Ellms does not share the romanticized view of Lafitte. In *The Pirates' Own Book*, Lafitte's heroic entanglement with the United States in the defense of New Orleans is described as a mere episode in his life that helps demonstrate both the tragedy of his deeply rooted wickedness and the desirability of being an American citizen.

In Ellms, Lafitte has lost his American citizenship due to his piratical activities before the beginning of the chapter and desperately seeks a chance to win it back. When the British attempt to win his assistance in the invasion of New Orleans, he turns his back on their generous offer in exchange for a second chance to be an American citizen. After the successful defense of New Orleans, he and his men are indeed rewarded with renewed citizenship. In Lafitte's decision to defend standards rather than to be recruited for money, the pirate has taken up the role of Captain Beer, who answers the economic argument of a low, amoral pseudosovereign with a normative answer that evokes his allegiance to a legitimate ruler. The representatives of the US government respond justly and grant him a second chance within the nation.

As indicated by Ellms's use of the Augustinian anecdote, however, the United States is the legitimate rule that succeeds, replaces, and justly condemns European predatory rule as well as its piratical counterparts. Lafitte fails to live up to American standards. He soon returns to his piratical activities and reestablishes pirate ports just outside of United States territory (Ellms, *Own Book*, 46). These specific ports are also associated with historical practices of slave trading (Exnicios, "Jean Lafitte," 41). In consequence, Lafitte loses his citizenship once more, this time forever. This story indicates that the externalization of the pirate not only lies in his predatory economic practices but also retains a pronounced territorial component: piracy can occur only outside of American territory.

Lafitte's second failure proves that the pirate, even at his best, is an anachronistic figure in American society; indeed, this is one of Ellms's major points throughout the book. A pirate is an individual so deeply entangled with precivilizational, illegitimate structures that his betterment in the spirit of phrenological logic is impossible. Failure ensues not because some human natures are naturally unfit to better themselves, but because they have been too fully exposed to un-American influence in the skull-defining years of their youth. As Lafitte's reestablishment of alternative community structures indicates, he does not feel comfortable in a society that is good for his nature but chooses to remain in an environment that brings out the worst in him.

He is imperial, predatory, and culturally European—he continues to lose his citizenship because he is simply not enough of an American to keep it.

Lafitte's story substantiates Ellms's suggestion to treat de Soto's skull as a scientific proof that emperors and pirates are alike. It is even a fitting gesture in this context to suggest sending the skull to Europe, since the gesture not only pays tribute to the widely acknowledged Scottish expertise in phrenology at the time but also allows the pirate's skull to be in an environment that can provide the skulls of emperors to compare to the pirate's. The United States as a state, Ellms suggests, is the completion of the modern project and therefore necessarily free of emperors; the United States is the natural heir and successor of the "sunken countries" of Europe and will gradually but necessarily remove the scattered piratical relics of earlier colonial times.

In this sense, Ellms's perspective and Augustine's perspective on the pirate-emperor problem are direct inversions of each other. They argue for the existence of two cities (one just and one unjust) and emphasize the same characteristic of the unjust regime (namely, that it is based solely on the law of conquest). Neither city is hermetically sealed off from the other; both Augustine and Ellms allow for the parallel existence of just and unjust individuals in each city or regime. However, Ellms's central premise is the exact opposite of Augustine's. Whereas Augustine presupposes the impossibility of any just regime on earth, Ellms presupposes that the United States constitutes just such a regime, and already exists. In Augustine, the just are marginalized and are engaged in a futile struggle to better a world that cannot be saved as such. In Ellms, the unjust are marginalized deviants who will necessarily be expelled from the just regime because they cannot live up to its standards.

This rearrangement of Augustinian elements is stabilized by an approach that has been mentioned before in the context of the American discourse of phrenology—the self-help tradition. Ellms renders piracy as a symptom of an individual failure to better oneself. It is in this sense that the emperor and the pirate return to what they were in Augustine—namely, metaphors of a flawed state of mind. Rather than failing to strive to attain the City of God, these flawed characters now fail to strive to reach the City on a Hill. The American nation takes the place of a promised legitimate kingdom that fulfills Christian dreams of a utopia. The imperfections of this legitimate nation are due merely to the imperfection of its individual citizens, not to the national character that in fact represents precisely the paternal, merciful rule advocated by Augustine. In this spirit, the United States in Ellms is characterized by the perpetual willingness of its citizens to better themselves, combined with a regime that allows and encourages them to do so. This personal as well as structural devotedness to the ideal of a just nation are positioned in sharp contrast to the situation in Europe, which systematically produces degenerated men and rewards them for their viciousness.

Both pirate and emperor are structurally as well as individually characterized as un-American or pre-American entities: for the first time in this discussion, the Augustinian anecdote is used to demonstrate where both pirate and emperor inherently fall short in comparison to the systemic virtues of national statehood. In contrast to Augustine and Johnson, Ellms uses the pirate to mark the territorial—that is, national—limits of an achieved just regime by placing him always just outside of the United States. The spatial location of pirate communities marks territories that have to be dissolved into the United States or be vanquished by it in self-defense (*Own Book*, 37). This territorialization of an achieved state of order is directly and constitutively linked to the notion of race, even though the American, the European, and the pirate are all marked as white. The notion of race is used to identify the innocent as distinct from all three, as in Brown's gendered state, and thus as an entity that stabilizes the claim to legitimate US rule. Augustine's innocent neighbor, dependent on mercy rather than a flawed idea of justice, appears as the enslaved African in Ellms. This is why Ellms's topic of piracy and his abolitionist argument mesh so well.

Augustine had repeatedly suggested that motivation was central to determining the justice of violent intervention. He contended that a defense of the Christian faith was the only cause that could render violence just. Sovereign violence was allowed to coerce enemies into submission only if this intervention also forced these enemies to consider the superior wisdom of Christian faith, which would inevitably result in their eventual acceptance of its truth. John Mark Mattox explains Augustine's reasoning at this point by analogies of a shepherd who uses the stick to usher straying sheep back into the safe fold and a doctor who forces an unwilling patient to take the medicine that will eventually save his life. The normative orientation of Christianity is assumed to be universally valid, because even enemies are expected to acknowledge its truth if they look at it without prejudice. Then they can acknowledge that war against them is ultimately for their own good, and violence is only the last resort to achieve the actual goal—namely, to better them (Mattox, *Just War*, 68–71). This argument directly corresponds with phrenology's assertion that a just regime is defined by its practice of enabling individual betterment and its resolution to defend its institutions against the incorrigibly wicked.

In my discussion of Augustine above, I mentioned that the meeting of the pirate and the emperor necessarily evokes two other entities, the legitimate ruler and the innocent. The innocent is the constitutive victim of the pirate-emperor who must be protected by the Christian, who in turn represents the only truly thinkable legitimate ruler, God. In Ellms's usage of the anecdote, the nation replaces God as well as the anticipated stable empire, so the nation has to mercifully defend someone who is systematically victimized by Europeans and pirates alike.

A specific and continuously evoked American order that represents such an alternative to the illegitimate pirate-emperor entails the need for an equally specific and tangible innocent who must be protected to actualize American legitimacy. In Ellms, those innocent are African slaves. He frequently reminds the reader that the United States can claim to be really just only if the humanity of every human being is acknowledged, including that of slaves. Like the innocent in Augustine, African slaves in Ellms are not active agents but merely the recipients of merciful acts that substantiate the Augustinian characteristics of the American nation-state. The interests of African slaves may be represented by American courts, but the slaves themselves are almost never acknowledged as parties in Ellms, which is consistent with contemporary legal practice (Martinez, *Slave Trade*, 73).

The African slave as a figure in Ellms's narrative is as external to the United States as the pirate is. For example, Ellms ends the chapter on de Soto with the following scene: "The black slave of the pirate stood upon the battery trembling before his dying master to behold the awful termination of a series of events, the recital of which to his African countrymen, when he shall return to his home, will give them no doubt, a dreadful picture of European civilization" (*Own Book*, 101). The African slave here is decidedly a foreigner to the just nation. He has been wrongfully removed from his native home and will now return to it; this is made clear when Ellms uses the adventure topos of the sole survivor to frame the slave's perceptions of events. The evocation of this topos allows Ellms to ignore the structural links of the slave trade and the institution of US slavery in his own review of "events" and allows him to muse instead on the bad reputation given to Europe by being linked to practices of piracy and the slave trade. It is in this sense that the innocent reenter the picture in the form of African slaves who must be rescued from the exploitation of an illegitimate Europe and given neighborly assistance by the just American nation. Violent acts by the United States against Europe are therefore inherently legitimate because they are carried out in defense of the innocent.

Importantly, it is the entire continent ("country") of Africa that is assigned the role of a passive, innocent victim in the economy of the slave trade. There is a territorially discernible nation-state (the United States) taking the place of the legitimate ruler and a territorially discernible "country" (Africa) taking the place of the innocent. This territorialization in Ellms emphasizes the most extreme poles of a legitimate spectrum: first, an achieved just order understood as a fulfilled Augustinian sovereignty that, in its supreme legitimacy, is equivalent to a sovereignty directly carrying out the laws of God and nature; and second, a passive, faultlessly victimized territory that represents pure innocence. The pirate-emperors of Europe are considered outsiders to both of these spaces and are marked as illegitimate as soon as they interfere with either legitimate territory. Space, in other words, becomes constitutive in resolving the dilemma posed by the Augustinian anecdote, especially its modern variety presented by Johnson. The innovations in Ellms are that legitimacy is specifically discussed in terms of normalcy and deviance and that normalcy is linked to the specific definition of the American nation. *The Pirates' Own Book* portrays pirates as the brothers of slave traders because both represent illegitimate economic infrastructures that victimize the innocent continent of Africa and are punished by the just US nation-state. The United States and Africa as the spatial equivalents of the legitimate ruler and the innocent stabilize a perception of all other regimes that exist in the world as inherently illegitimate and predatory.

Ellms suggests that the history of European and Latin American piracy is a history of barbarism that does not go back to the European privateering tradition, but (somewhat inconsistently) to the history of the North African Barbary States of the Mediterranean (*Own Book*, 24). This representation resonates with the writing of later abolitionist authors (for example, Du Bois, *African Slave Trade*). While the most famous English privateers roaming the Americas (such as William Dampier, Francis Drake, Henry Morgan, and Walter Raleigh) are completely missing from Ellms's account, the Vikings and the Barbary corsairs are included and portrayed as the true forefathers of eighteenth- and nineteenth-century colonial pirates. This repositions the pirate as the heir not of daring pioneers but of cunning and brutal invaders and slave traders. This is an important narrative deviation from the British context, especially when considering the dilemma of the British tradition that acknowledged a structural kinship with white, Christian Golden Age pirates. As Ellms's selection of his contemporary pirates' roots indicates, pirates were redefined as white predators engaged in a nonwhite tradition of piracy and slave trading.

Even potentially problematic tendencies, such as US warfare against Native Americans, can be rationalized as legitimate in such constructions. Even though, as I have mentioned, Ellms does not address the question of US territorial expansion in the Americas, it makes sense to suggest that he would have characterized this kind of expansion as a continuation of the legitimate US project of removing threats to the national ideals, exemplified by Lafitte's removal from the nation and the destruction of Lafitte's pirate colony just off the coast of the United States. Indeed, this differentiation between Native

American Others and African slaves is substantiated by phrenologist discourse's general racialized naturalization of this difference (Fowler and Fowler, *Phrenology*, iv). In part 2 of this book, I will offer a more specific discussion of a narrative that naturalizes warfare against Native Americans on related grounds in my analysis of a novel of Ellms's time, James Fenimore Cooper's novel *The Deerslayer* (1841).

At this point in the argument, however, it is more interesting to explore why Ellms's construction of the inherent legitimacy of the United States would help expand the hostis humani generis fiction—which until the early nineteenth century had been limited to piracy—to encompass the slave trade. Initially it was Great Britain, not the United States, that most loudly condemned the slave trade. At the same time, it is important for this study's argument to understand on what grounds this position was embraced in the United States.

At first glance, the equation of pirates and slave traders does not completely hold up. Pirates of the Golden Age regularly preyed on slave traders. For example, archaeological research has shown that the historical Samuel Bellamy used a transformed slave ship for his piratical enterprises (Christopher Hamilton, "*Whydah*"). In the second volume of the *General History*, a utopian pirate kingdom is evoked that abolishes slavery and accepts former slaves as the brothers of pirates because they, too, have been abused by tyrannical, profiteering merchants (Johnson, *General History*, 403–4). At the same time, however, historians strongly affirm that the historical practices of piracy and the slave trade were interwoven on many levels. On a structural level, Michael Kempe argues that in the seventeenth century "the members of the 'Pirate Round' at the back of international trade relations helped to connect the economic realms of the West Indies and Eastern Asia. This was especially true for the slave trade. Pirates indirectly helped to open or expand new markets for the international slave trade by their 'wild' enslavement of Eastern Africans in the Indian Ocean" (*Fluch der Weltmeere*, 203; my translation). The tendency of slavers to employ sailors with a shady past soon created an overlap between people engaging in piracy and people engaging in the slave trade. It was an open secret that "the crews of [nineteenth-century] slave ships were generally made up of 'suspicious and dangerous characters,' some of whom were also engaged in piracy" (Martinez, *Slave Trade*, 77).

In the United States in the early nineteenth century, piracy was connected to the slave trade because both established predatory economies. Ever since the merchantman system came to dominate the Atlantic region, trade had been considered equivalent with peace, and a strict separation of war and trade had been emphasized as a core feature of the modern world order

(Kant, *Frieden*, 33; see also Rodger, *Wooden World*). In legal discourse, it was because of the aspect of predatory economies that slave traders were defined according to the standards of piracy. The importation of slaves into the United States was abolished in 1808, and the US law against piracy was amended to also cover the slave trade in 1820. In any maritime context, "if any citizen of the United States, . . . seize any negro or mulatto, not held to service or labour by the laws of either of the states or territories of the United States, with intent to make such a negro or mulatto a slave . . . such citizen or person shall be adjudged a pirate" ("An Act to Continue in Force," 2). Congress enacted the law in 1823, which established a firm link between the two crimes' definitions in US law that remains in effect. The abolition of the slave trade indicated the US investment in the notion that predatory economic infrastructures were disruptive of peaceful international trade, which the nation depended on.

The slave trade, in contrast, was not considered a part of peaceful trading structures. It was based on the violent abduction of Africans from their homelands, and—more important, for writers like Ellms—it destabilized sovereign claims to a legitimate monopoly of force in national territories. Seen from his perspective as a citizen of the United States, the cases of Latin and South America demonstrate this destabilization. When the slave trade was abolished in the United States but not in major American slave trade markets such as Cuba and Brazil, wild inter-American trade infrastructures immediately emerged and allowed the increasingly intertwined businesses of smuggling, slave trading, and piracy to continue in Latin America and US coastal regions (Exnicios, "Jean Lafitte," 39; Howard, *American Slavers*, 49–56; Labaree, *Boston Tea Party*, 52–57). The mutually beneficial presence of slave traders and pirates in connection with the Latin American pirate wave after 1820 rendered this informal economic infrastructure increasingly problematic for the United States, as Ellms's pirate portraits in *The Pirates' Own Book* generally affirm. The abolition of the slave trade was also already contextualized by the decade-long efforts to abolish privateering as the institutional backdrop of piracy, efforts that came to fruition in the mid-nineteenth century (Stark, *Abolition of Privateering*).

As Ellms's use of the discourse of phrenology indicates, the inherent illegitimacy of these predatory infrastructures could be substantiated by emphasizing the degeneration of the customs and practices associated with them. After all, the Latin American pirates of the early nineteenth century were renowned not only for their ability to develop unaccountable infrastructures, but also for their excessive cruelty (Earle, *Pirate Wars*, 218–20). Ellms thus emphasizes the reliance of both piracy and the slave trade on excessive violence in connection with their illegitimate usage of space. In the international legal discourse of the early nineteenth century, the slave trade had already been explicitly characterized as "a 'crime against humanity,' putting that term into legal use more than a century before its more famous debut at Nuremberg" (Martinez, *Slave Trade*, 114). In the more specific US context, Ellms states that "the regard for human life is one of the most prominent proofs of a civilized state of society. . . . You will ever find that the more a nation becomes civilized, the greater becomes the regard for human life. There is in the eye, in the form, and heaven-directed countenance of man, something holy, that forbids he should be rudely touched" (*Own Book*, 82). In Ellms, the condemnation of both piracy and the slave trade serve to secure the ability of the United States to exist peacefully, and at the same time to substantiate the nation's normative claims to legitimacy in Augustinian terms.

However, the inherent illegitimacy of the slave trade remained restricted to its comparison with legitimate international trade in the maritime realm. Therefore, the slave trader as hostis humani generis also remained firmly restricted to the international maritime context, while slave traders in the United States remained excluded from the definition. In addition, the identification of slave traders was directly derived from the existing regulations concerning piracy, indicating that the legal fiction's new usage still considered the undisturbed sovereign rule over space, rather than the protection of a universal humanity, as a central legitimating factor.[2] Pirates were commonly recognized by their attacks on other ships; in contrast, slave traders were more than eager for a calm, swift, and discreet passage. It was thus impossible to identify them as enemies of all humankind without at the same time breaching the rights of all legitimate traders. After a treaty was signed between France and Great Britain in 1831 that granted the countries mutual rights of search when slave trading was suspected, the United States remained the last major maritime power whose flag granted slave traders protection from British search on the high seas. Despite its comparatively early criminalization of the slave trade as piracy in domestic law, the United States refused to allow international enforceability of punishment for the crime until 1862, a date that corresponds with the end of the Western slave trade as a whole (Martinez, *Slave Trade*, 79). The bitter disputes about the right of foreign navies to search trade ships directly originate in this close definitional analogy between piracy and the slave trade (Soulsby, *Right of Search*, 28–33). In the nineteenth century, this aspect of the slave trade helped establish the more general Western understanding of piracy as a practice of exploiting legal loopholes.

In this sense, it has become obvious that especially this final rereading of the Augustinian anecdote operates on a basis of its transfer to crimes other than piracy, which introduces a new understanding of the humankind that the enemy of all humankind attacks. In the classic case of piracy, the enemy of all humankind is defined as such because he randomly attacks all vessels he encounters; in the derived case of the slave trader, the enemy of all humankind attacks the very "regard for human life" that would later re-emerge as the philosophical essence of human rights law. The rise of this new understanding of humankind is why the legal fiction could henceforward be separated from the crime of piracy and reinforce the ability of the hostis humani generis constellation to formulate legitimate violence much more fundamentally than before.

[II]

RACE, SPACE, AND THE FORMATION OF THE *HOSTIS HUMANI GENERIS* CONSTELLATION

WHILE PART 1 MADE a general point about the centrality of legitimacy in modern constructions of piracy, part 2 specifically addresses the history of hostis humani generis as a constellation. It will put the constellation in its imperial context and demonstrate that the constellation relies on the assumption of a racialized conflict between three different figures in a specific form of space. The conflict takes place between white representatives of civilization, nonwhite representatives of a collectivist hostile bloc of Otherness (whom I call praedones), and white individualist renegades who adopt nonwhite behavior and turn against civilization (whom I call piratae). According to the constellational logic analyzed here, these three figures always appear together in an ambiguous, sea-like in-between zone. Praedo and pirata are not necessarily allies, but they are constructed as complementary figures within the constellation. The role of the representative of civilization in this constellation is essentially determined by the relationship of praedo and pirata toward each other.

Many of the aspects that the discussion of Ellms in part 1 touched on become understandable as general properties of the hostis humani generis constellation. This especially concerns the intimate link between discourses that rely on an essentialist understanding of race (such as the discourse of phrenology) and the structuring of territorial spaces as discernible realms of inherent justice and injustice, or the understanding of white figures such as the slave traders as adopting behaviors that are themselves understood as characteristically nonwhite.

The first chapter in part 2 discusses the historical roots of the praedo-pirata constellation in early modern English and Scottish (and, later, British) law. It establishes the terminology that will be used to discuss the structural properties of the hostis humani generis constellation in the remainder of this book and pinpoints the source of the racialized split in the constellation's original legal context. This chapter focuses on the European—mainly English and Scottish—assessment of the Barbary States of North Africa and of Barbary corsairdom in the Mediterranean.[1] The chapter sketches the defining properties of praedo and pirata, how the two are structurally linked, and which discursive history has informed these connections. In conclusion, it becomes evident that the praedo, pirata, and representative of civilization always appear together whenever the hostis humani generis fiction is used successfully in a modern text.

The second chapter in part 2 remains in the now-British context as it dissects the narrative implications of William Blackstone's definition of hostis humani generis in the context of eighteenth-century British colonialism in America. In addition to a discussion of the narrative constellations of conflict in Blackstone's commentary on the legal fiction, this chapter resumes part 1's discussion of the state of nature, which Blackstone explicitly names as the most important contextual factor of the hostis humani generis constellation. While the general importance of the state of nature fiction for Enlightenment thought has already been outlined in part 1, the discussion of Blackstone shows the theoretical centrality of the Lockean state of nature fiction, and the role that the notions of race and space play in the hostis humani generis constellation on this basis.

The final chapter of part 2 focuses exclusively on the context of the United States in the nineteenth century and discusses how Americans attempt to adopt European discourses of civilization to substantiate their own claims to legitimacy. As mentioned above, I focus on a novel by a contemporary of Charles Ellms, James Fenimore Cooper, and use this discussion to show that the application of the hostis humani generis constellation not only begins to extend beyond the crime of piracy at this time but also is used beyond the maritime context, which is not yet the case with the legal conceptualization of the slave trade. As in Ellms, in Cooper this expansion of the constellation's thinkable application is closely associated with the attempt to legitimate violence on behalf of a nation-state. This chapter discusses the American historical novel as the genre that, more than any other, begins to offer itself for a translation and development of the hostis humani generis constellation into what R. W. B. Lewis called "the American myth" (*American Adam*, 1). I discuss Cooper's novel *The Deerslayer* as a particularly interesting literary interpretation of the narrative constellations of praedo and pirata used, in this case, to interrogate the notions of race, space, and territorial expansion into the American wilderness.

[4]

PIRATAE AND *PRAEDONES*: THE RACIALIZATION OF *HOSTIS HUMANI GENERIS*

THIS CHAPTER DISCUSSES the first construction of hostis humani generis as a constellation in early modernity. As I emphasized in the introduction, the pirate—who, at the time discussed in this chapter, was still the only representative of the fiction—was already a highly ambiguous figure. In law, piracy could encompass the activities of a whole range of maritime entities. Rogue privateers, privateers acting in the name of enemy sovereigns, predatory coastal communities, and small independent pirate states were already part of the pirate discourse in early modernity. Why, then, is there a need to redefine the pirate in the specific terms provided by hostis humani generis?

The reason lies, somewhat unsurprisingly in the context of this study's focus, in the imperial expansion of European empires into the Atlantic region and the new constitutive centrality that was necessarily assigned to the maritime realm that connected the distant spheres of emerging imperial influence. For centuries, the central maritime antagonists of all European states had been the Barbary States of the Mediterranean (primarily, but not exclusively, Algiers, Tunis, and Tripoli). The Barbary States were autonomous city-states of the Ottoman Empire; in Europe, they were often conceptualized as wholly independent entities. This was due to the Barbary States' specialized predatory economies, which largely rested on the combined enterprises of maritime warfare and the slave trade. Barbary corsairs conducted raids along the coasts of Europe as far as the British Isles, enslaving and selling European villagers, sailors, and travelers. From *Don Quixote* to *Robinson Crusoe*, European epos and literature reproduced a construction of the corsairs and the Barbary States as an impenetrable, faceless evil, the nemesis of Christian sailors who could flee their captivity but could never triumph over the captor. Institutional responses were also widespread across Europe. Entire religious orders were formed on the slaves' behalf, and slave funds that helped organize the release of captives from Barbary slavery constituted long-standing insurance institutions in coastal regions (Clark, "Barbary Corsairs," 23). The picture was not, of course, wholly black and white. For instance, European sovereigns also made use of European slaves bought in Barbary ports to man their galleys. The galley was a favorite in the Mediterranean because it could accelerate quickly during battle and maneuvering was possible even in a lull. Its popularity was one of the great reasons for the maritime slave trade as conducted in Barbary ports (Earle, *Corsairs of Malta*, 49–49 and 168). Still, the fear of Barbary corsairs remained a constitutive European sentiment for centuries.

In the altered context of an increasingly colonialist world order, the role of the Barbary States as a defining violent Other was complemented in Europe with the Otherness of colonial peoples. In the context of European imperial states' rising economic, military, financial, and cultural importance since the onset of early modernity, the Barbary States became only one of many influential non-European sovereigns. After the invasion of Algiers by the French (1830) and the Ottoman Empire's abolition of privateering in the Declaration of Paris (1856), the Barbary States would eventually be subsumed into a general racialized category of nonwhite, non-Christian, and non-European inferiority and would henceforward disappear from all mainstream accounts of European history.[1]

In early modernity, of course, the Barbary States were far from decline and constituted a central military antagonist for the rising European empires. At the same time, these young European empires were eager to define themselves by their overseas activities and to create unified bodies of law that would address the core question of legitimate maritime violence in a way that would facilitate, as well as legitimate, imperial expansion anywhere. Early modern imperial law was preoccupied with the question of what kind of maritime violence should always be criminalized as piratical, and what kind should always be naturalized as legitimate imperial outreach.

In the context of legal studies, the discursive link between the Mediterranean and the Atlantic regions has long been a topic of research. The facts that the Atlantic and the Mediterranean regions were so vastly different yet both so essential in the development of colonial and international law resulted in major efforts to establish common ground between them in the sixteenth and seventeenth centuries. The central concern of many legal scholars of these centuries was to formulate universally applicable laws (for an excellent overview and analysis of the history of these debates, see Fisch, *Europäische Expansion*).[2] After all, consistent legal approaches and instruments had to be in place so that all extrasovereign spaces could be addressed in an equally meaningful way, and thus the very premises of sustainable imperial rule could be established. The early modern conceptualizations of legitimate violence in the Mediterranean and the Atlantic region were thus formulated in conversation with each other.

The Mediterranean still provided the richest context in Europe for a discussion of maritime legitimate violence, and it also provided the basic model of space used for the hostis humani generis constellation, along with the original properties assigned to early modern corsairs. However, the Atlantic region allowed a fundamental redefinition of the categories that had already moved the model beyond its core example of the Barbary corsairs. The notion of race as it is used in the constellation, then, is a central contribution of the Atlantic discursive context, and it eventually replaces the importance of territorial shorelines and a specific cluster of political antagonists.

If the history of hostis humani generis had relied on the Mediterranean context alone, it would not have been so necessary to make essentialist racialization a core property of the hostis humani generis constellation. As in the messy case of the galley slaves mentioned above, European sovereigns of the seventeenth century were still willing to side with Muslims against each other in the struggle of Catholics versus Protestants, and they did not use just one aspect of Otherness, such as race, to argue for their own difference from the Barbary States. Since the medieval period, the difference between Europeans and Turks in the Mediterranean had been established by a whole cluster of properties: pigmentation, religion, regional origin, and cultural and political backgrounds were all included into these discourses, but typically not differentiated from each other (Loomba, *Shakespeare*, 24–27 and 70–71).[3]

Because of the vast variety of unfamiliar political entities in colonial spaces, however, a very general conceptual distinction between European and non-European became necessary, and the notion of race was gradually identified as the smallest common denominator of the non-European Other. The early modern period began to structure these differences systematically and to insert conceptual hierarchies. Intertwined and increasingly overlapping notions of religion and race eventually came to be the core means to define inherent difference from an increasingly normalized image of white, male, European supremacy (Loomba, *Shakespeare*, 24–27). In this vein, a variety of "noncivilized" nations were collapsed into one "nonwhite" race (Haselstein, *Gabe der Zivilisation*, 19; my translation).

In other words, the rise of colonialism in early modernity introduced two important notions into European discourse on legitimate maritime violence that directly informed the formulation of the hostis humani generis constellation: first, the notion of Europeans' difference from, and already latent superiority to, all other peoples they encountered; second, the claim that one legal definition had to be able to apply to all violent maritime antagonists that were described as illegitimate. Hostis humani generis was designed to suit both the establishment of a model of space that would help legitimate expansionism and the corresponding model of race and racial deviance that would define the Other's inability to make legitimate claims to a contested space.

The European, and especially English and Scottish, legal debate on the nature of civilization as the core justification for legitimate expansive violence is therefore central. In early modernity, the notion of civilization is a comparatively unsophisticated construction and boils down to "us, by definition." This lack of sophistication stems from the fact that in these early discourses of imperialism, civilization was synonymous with the sovereign who claimed it, or, if applied in the context of a racialized Other, with the larger group of Christian rulers. Especially in the context of European expansionism, the notion of civilization was an extremely flexible construction that was only really relevant for Europeans when they were confronted with someone who was not European.

In the sixteenth and seventeenth centuries, the period that this chapter addresses, this Other was not actually inferior in any immediately discernible way. The Barbary States were strong enough to dictate terms in the Mediterranean and to invite complex political maneuvers that sometimes included them as allies. The situation was not very different in the Americas, where Native American nations were deemed serious potential partners as much as potential rivals (Colley, *Captives*, 162–67). The open questions regarding power relations in non-European spaces are the reason why the European construction of civilization became central to any discussion of the imperial project, and why a comprehensive and overarching definition of civilization was rarely part of the conversation.

In the introduction to this book, I mentioned that two main models of civilization dominated these conversations in early modernity, both of which addressed the properties and expected development of the Other rather than of civilization. The traditional mode of defensiveness against the Barbary States explains why it was the essentialist model of civilization—the model that assumed an inherently hostile Otherness that demanded the Other's removal or even extinction—that remained overwhelmingly dominant in English and Scottish assessments of the Mediterranean context and that informed the development of the hostis humani generis fiction in law. The essentialist model of civilization, with its tendency to imagine essentialist blocs of irresolvable antagonism, drew on the geographical context of Mediterranean shorelines. Civilization and an Other controlled opposing shores and encountered each other in the Mediterranean, a territory that was inherently beyond rule or possession (Muldoon, "Sea"; Bynkershoek, *Domino*

Maris, 88). Because the Barbary States' significance as Others was based on corsairdom, the sea—the specific, discernible, and locatable zone in between civilization and Otherness—was treated as the central locus of civilizational negotiation. The Other, barbarous or uncivilized, always lurked beyond this neutral zone of contact.

However, the sea was not merely neutral: it was believed to have its own effects on both the contractual and moral situation of Britons. The sea had long been considered an inherently transformative space in European legal traditions. This status had been indicated by the medieval establishment of the institution of privateering as a form of state-supported violence that did not automatically lead to war—a sea-derived institution, in other words, that supplemented but did not extend the sovereign's reach, and was therefore able to strategically destabilize property relations otherwise secured by enemy sovereigns (Rubin, *Law of Piracy*, 31). In his discussion of these fundamental destabilizations performed by the sea, Daniel Heller-Roazen has suggested that the transformative effect could sever not only property relations but also vows of loyalty such as marriage vows (*Enemy of All*, 75–76).

Although most early modern writers tended to condemn these rather more serious implications of the sea's transformative nature, the possible destabilization of allegiance was nevertheless obvious to many European observers due to the Barbary States' massive recruitment of European privateers into their service. It is here that the central racialized differentiation within the hostis humani generis fiction takes its historical root. The main reason for an internal racial differentiation of pirates was that captives and slaves were not the only Europeans who entered the Barbary States on a mass scale; a substantial number of early modern Barbary corsairs themselves were renegades from Europe (Earle, *Corsairs of Malta*, 35). Paul Baepler even claims that at times, two-thirds of the Barbary fleet was captained by Europeans, accompanied by an even larger estimated number of unknown common sailors (introduction, 42).

The fact that so many of the Barbary corsairs were European renegades is a significant historical detail in the development of the hostis humani generis constellation. The conspicuous mix of native and renegade Barbary corsairs required a differentiated legal position toward the phenomenon of privateering-derived piracy at large. After all, it was conceivable for Europeans that someone who acted loyally in the name of his native faith and sovereign (even if faith and sovereign were not deemed civilized) should be treated differently from someone who had treacherously abandoned his native faith and sovereign and turned against them (at least if these original allegiances were European and had been abandoned for a barbarous alternative). The result was a more formalized acknowledgment of what might be called cultural treason, combined with an increasingly firm and explicit rejection of the idea that treason actually achieved a successful change in allegiance. European—especially English and Scottish—philosophy increasingly insisted that certain allegiances were too inherent to man even to be transformed by the sea.

As to the native and renegade corsairs specifically, Hugo Grotius makes their differentiation explicit in his first major work, *Commentary on the Law of Prize and Booty* (originally published in 1604), a work that attempted to harmonize the various legal positions toward the different conflict-ridden maritime spaces of his time, notably including colonial maritime spaces (van Ittersum, introduction). Grotius identifies four different forms of illegitimate maritime violence, two of which are encountered inside—and two of which outside—of the civilized realm. I will discuss only the figures outside of the civilized realm at this point in my argument. In formulating the two types of violence beyond the reach of the civilized sovereign, Grotius does not mention the Barbary corsairs. However, his argument seems carefully crafted to speak to the Mediterranean situation, which was at the core of contemporary legal debates (Rubin, *Law of Piracy*, 73 and 86). Grotius writes:

> For, in the first place, that gain is dishounorable [*sic*] which is acquired by individuals who despoil others through privately exercised force and without urgent reason for so doing. To such individuals we give the name of "piratae" when their activities take place upon the sea. Secondly, the same criticism applies to acquisitions made by persons who without any legitimate cause usurp authority to wage public war. For example, it is recorded that in earlier times whole peoples—such as the Cretans, the Cilicians, and even the Greeks themselves (according to the testimony of Homer), as well as the Germans and the Normans—engaged openly and publicly in the practice of despoliation without so much as an appropriate pretext. To despoilers of this kind we refer (and not unjustly) as "praedones." (Grotius, *Law of Prize*, 447–48)

The English translation used here in fact translates "pirata" as "pirate" and "praedo" as "freebooter." In this quote, I have maintained the Latin terms originally used by Grotius because his characterization of these entities is the basis for the terminology I use in this chapter. Because the discussion of Grotius that follows will eventually lead to an abstraction of these two key terms into the terminology I use throughout the book, a few signposts that anticipate this change might be helpful, and indeed, necessary.

My own usage of the terms praedo and pirata in the remainder of this study will not refer to specific groups of enemies and/or criminals, but to the positions of any kind of figure in any given text that uses the hostis humani generis constellation to establish a claim to legitimate violence. For example, the pirate is a figure with a vast and multifaceted legal, cultural, and literary history that is linked to the identification of someone or something as distinctly piratical. The praedo and pirata, in contrast, are figures that appear only in the hostis humani generis constellation. As we shall see, neither figure necessarily has to be a maritime or an economically oriented actor: the terms refer to each figure's position as a node in the constellation.

I find the Latin terms offered by Grotius useful for a number of reasons. First, I use the terms used by his translator (especially "pirate") in other capacities in this book, and I hope to avoid confusion by visibly differentiating them. Second, the less familiar Latin terms are not burdened with the cultural associations we have with terms such as "pirate," "freebooter," and "privateer," and they can be more easily and more fully identified as strictly analytical terms. Third, the terms, once established as recognizably analytical terms, still clearly betray their origin in pirate law—as indeed the hostis humani generis constellation as a whole does, even when it is most clearly abstracted from its original context. Fourth, Grotius, in his specific use of these terms, describes precisely the relationship between these constellational nodes that I find central for an understanding of hostis humani generis in general.

Grotius's differentiation between praedo and pirata in the passage is appealingly clear. The difference between these entities is primarily achieved by their fundamentally different normative reference points as entities. The praedo is the representative of an entire predatory culture. He is thus fairly congruent with what Michel Foucault describes as a barbarian, "someone who can be understood, characterized, and defined only in relation to a civilization, and by the fact that he exists outside of it. There can be no barbarian unless an island of civilization exists somewhere, unless he lives outside of it, and unless he fights it" (*Society*, 194). Still, Grotius allows that in the context of the praedo's own people's laws and customs, he acts for legitimate public ends. Even though causing maritime mayhem itself is not legitimate, Grotius acknowledges that in the case of the praedo, the desire to serve a common good lies behind his actions, and that his raids can even support the existence of a whole society such as the Cretans or the Normans. It is only because the general structure of these societies is inherently barbarous that the actions of the praedo are unjust.

The pirata, in contrast, commits violence for private ends. He is an expressly individualized figure. The notion of abandonment is the central aspect of the pirata's characterization in Grotius. If the praedo's crime is to support a pseudosovereign's attempt to "usurp authority" to wage war, the pirata's crime is the abandonment of any collective cause, legitimate or illegitimate. The emphases on individuals and private ends indicate that a community of piratae is not a community brought together by a cause that reaches beyond them, but merely an unstable, strategically motivated group of individuals who simply happen to pursue the same ends—namely, each member's personal enrichment.

In the context of English law, these motivation-based differentiations remained implicit rather than explicit in the use of the hostis humani generis fiction. By the seventeenth century, the conflation of praedo and pirata had become a common practice in English courtrooms. The reason is perhaps best stated by the Italian-English jurist Alberico Gentili, who was mentioned briefly above. For Gentili, the difference between praedo and pirata was irrelevant. What made a sovereign legitimate, in Gentili's view, was the acknowledgment of that legitimacy by England, and thus a sovereign whose status as civilized was undisputed. It did not matter whether an illegitimate sovereign (for instance, a Barbary State) officially commissioned a ship to plunder, or whether the crew plundered without any commission at all. Both were automatically and equally illegitimate from Gentili's perspective. In the political, economic, and legal climate of European states that struggled hard to find a satisfactory position toward the Barbary States, as well as toward the rapidly expanding rest of the world, Gentili's sweeping conflation of piratae and praedones in the course of an essentialist reading of hostis humani generis was quickly absorbed as a general practice. Even scholars like Grotius who otherwise fundamentally disagreed with Gentili shared his basic view on conflict lines in pirate law (Rubin, *Law of Piracy*, 70).

Even though English law thus treated hostis humani generis as a broad category, differentiations remained that suggested an implicit acknowledgment of the distinction between praedo and pirata made by Grotius. The large numbers of European renegades in Barbary service kept all parties in English courts, including Gentili, acutely aware of the difference between a native and a renegade Barbary corsair. The former was the faithful representative of a culture that was at the same time feared, reproached, and envied; the latter was the despicable, self-interested traitor to civilization who dared give in to godless Barbary temptation. As a result, the qualitative difference between pirata and praedo remained an important implicit feature of the early modern pirate discourse. While legal language insisted on the figures' conflation as mere varieties of the same threat, the rising discourse of racism began to insert itself deeply into the hostis humani generis fiction and became the discourse-defining carrier of qualitative difference between praedo and pirata. The structural vehicle of this differentiation was the contractual basis of privateering law.

Put simply, a legal privateering contract requires two parties: the representative of a privately equipped war ship (the privateer to be) and a legitimate sovereign. A privateering contract is voided if either party's status as sovereign or privateer is illegitimate, and this voiding of the contract marks the piratical transgression. For this reason, the pirata is originally understood as a privateer who acts outside of his commission and thus loses his status as a legitimate man-of-war.[4] The praedo, in contrast, fully satisfies these standards and would normally be a legitimate privateer, if not for his reliance on an illegitimate sovereign. Here, it is the commissioning entity that has assumed a rightful sovereignty that does not exist, and as a result this entity does not have the right to create privateers in the first place—meaning that this sovereign's privateers can be charged with piracy. The contractual dimension of hostis humani generis maintains the notion of two inherently different, but structurally complementary, entities within pirate law. This is a kind of constellation that could be racialized comparatively easily.

The hostis humani generis fiction was especially suited to incorporating structures of racism because the historical positioning of the fiction's subcategories of pirata and praedo already relied on the notion of religion and conversion. In the larger essentialist discourse of civilization in Europe, Islam had come to serve as a cultural shorthand for the illegitimacy of all Barbary corsairs (Rubin, *Law of Piracy*, 39–40 and 72–74). In the more specific context of the hostis humani generis constellation, the reference to Islam served as a second pillar, in addition to that of contractual legitimacy, for the establishment of a distinction between native and renegade Barbary corsair as praedo and pirata. According to the contractual logic alone, all Barbary corsairs, native or renegade, would count as praedones. However, the religious notion of conversion allowed the application of the individual-collective divide to this context. Whereas the native Barbary corsair was collectively Muslim, the renegade Barbary corsair had to convert individually. Native Barbary corsairs could claim to represent a cultural collective that was larger than themselves and epitomized by Islam; they could claim to represent a common public cause and were imagined as culturally homogeneous, a collective bloc of Otherness. Not so the converting renegades, who were solely compared to other converts to Islam and thus legally grouped with other individual, isolated transgressors like them: people who were originally European and Christian but acted as if they were not, and who did so only because they wanted to serve their private ends of personal profit.

The reference to Islam therefore established an internal hierarchy between praedo and pirata. The native Barbary corsair and his features always remained central in the popular imagination of the Mediterranean conflict.

This hierarchy was a direct result of each figure's position in relation to Islam: the native Barbary corsair truly represented Islam, he was the real agent of moral bankruptcy and the actual taster of forbidden fruit (Matar, *Turks*, 109–27). Even though the treacherous renegade's employment by the Barbary States and his assumption of the Muslim faith were strongly condemned, the renegade only imitated the native and thus remained a sideshow to the central, gruesome antagonist: the native Barbary corsair, the "king of evil" (Crowley, *Empires*, 45).

Indeed, in judging the otherwise exchangeable performances of these corsairs at sea, English law increasingly emphasized not the renegade's present status of allegiance but his original allegiance. The origin and original faith of the corsair at hand were used to determine his status as pirata or praedo. Treason and conversion became simultaneous acts, the political and religious sides of one and the same abandonment. The renegade was not considered a Muslim corsair, but a Christian privateer who had turned against his homeland (Baepler, "Barbary Captivity"; Earle, *Corsairs of Malta*, 30; Rubin, *Law of Piracy*, 72–74). This simultaneous conversion and treason could not undo Christian Europe's enduring claims to these privateers' loyalty and could not stop it from attempting to enforce them. This essentialization of origin is illustrated in this extract of a 1624 ballad on renegade Barbary corsairs:

> Those halfe-Turkes and halfe Christians, who now ride
> Like sea-gods (on rough billows in their pride),
> Those renegadoes, who (their Christ denying)
> Are worse than Turkes, Turkes them in heart defying . . .
> ("Lamentable Cries," 344)

In this ballad, renegades are presented as hybrids whose natures are torn between Christian and Turkish aspects. It is fairly clear how these conflicting natures manifest themselves: the Muslim aspect of the renegades is that of activity and performance—they roam the sea to attack their own countrymen and deny their own God—yet both the Christian God and the home country remain at the core of their properties as figures. In all formulations of the ballad, the Christian aspects are deemed inherent to the renegades' natural selves, while the denial of these natural allegiances is characterized as sinful ("proud") and insolent. Their Muslim aspects of the renegades are, in this sense, characterized as falsehoods against themselves and their better natures as well as crimes against their innocent victims. Even in the last line of the extract, which directly relates renegades and native Barbary corsairs, these two are treated as completely separate entities. Renegades act like Muslim corsairs although they are Christian privateers. From an English perspective, essentialized identity is more important than transgressive performance both legally and culturally, even though this differentiation is not explicitly spelled out in pirate law.

Christianity and Europeanness—the two central categories that, according to Ania Loomba, began to be distilled into the notion of whiteness in early modernity (*Shakespeare*, 45)—were defined as the unchangeable characteristics of a person in treason-based pirate law, even if that person had become a Muslim Barbary corsair in practice. Birthplace and original religion were treated as the features that continued to define a person despite all contrary experiences and practices. In this sense, the conviction of European Barbary corsairs as traitors can be called the first racializing act of Western pirate law. The element of treason in pirate law had the primary effect of isolating the renegade as a pirata and denying him the ability to assimilate into the community of praedones. Instead, a new form of community was imagined for him: a recruitment-based, unstable and ad hoc community that was based not on a common cause, but on the fact that all members happened to have the same individual cause.

The complementarity of praedo and pirata quickly became the central characteristic of the hostis humani generis constellation in the Anglo-American tradition. The substitution of a simple contractual differentiation with a nuanced characterization of Mediterranean corsairs came at a time when legal scholars were becoming increasingly unwilling to accept the idea that the allegiance to a sovereign, let alone to civilization, could be voided. The construction of renegades as piratae insisted that English civilization was and always would be the normative center of the world for any Englishman regardless of his choices, as well as for the members of any other people that could only either barbarously defy or progress toward this superior civilization.

The basic spatial structure of the Mediterranean, along with the unnatural convert status of the renegade as a defining additional feature of the basic essentialist antagonism, became the defining feature of the hostis humani generis constellation. Precisely because the convert status of the renegade is so central, it should be mentioned that the colonial context contributed to this figure's enduring presence in the fiction and helped shape his properties well before the Golden Age of Piracy as Great Britain's problem-defining example of pure piratae who were converts only to their own individual cause and were characterized by a radical "legal and spiritual isolation" (Baer, "Plot of Piracy," 10–11).

As I emphasized at the beginning of this chapter, the hostis humani generis constellation has a long tradition of use in comparatively arbitrary pirate charges against any given maritime antagonist—European or not,

Christian or not, and privateer or not. Empires' expansion into the colonial realm of the Americas was routinely accompanied by charges of piracy against their equally Christian and European rivals. Indeed, Grotius himself uses the discussion of pirates, freebooters, and robbers as the basis for an expanded argument on the derived evils of inter- and intra-imperial illegitimate seizure. He requires the discussion of unambiguously illegitimate seizures by pirata and praedo to prepare the ground for the much less clear-cut problem of illegitimate violence within the realm of civilization. I will briefly return to this problem in the fourth part of this book.

At this point of my argument, it is notable that the routine interimperial accusation of piracy assumed a racialized dimension in early modernity that directly cited the Mediterranean situation of the renegade traitor-convert. In her discussion of Spanish-English rivalries in early modern America, Nina Gerassi-Navarro draws attention to this dimension. For example, when sixteenth-century English imperialists were discovered by their Spanish rivals to have formed strategic alliances with natives, the English were charged with being corruptible "traitors to their own race" whose greed detached them from civilization (Gerassi-Navarro, *Pirate Novels*, 52). The Spanish argued that English cooperation with natives "infected" them with the inherent barbarism of the natives. This charge of corruption through natives was meant to legitimate the claim of Spain to the colonial space in question. This fairly early episode affirms the general logic of an internal racialization of hostis humani generis, as well as the hierarchies and forms of influence ("infection") assumed between pirata and praedo.

As is immediately obvious in the example provided by Gerassi-Navarro, imperialist struggles in the colonial realm underscored the importance of race as a category for discussing piracy. In the hostis humani generis constellation that was to bring all conceivable spaces together, however, the Mediterranean model dominated for two main reasons.

First, the construction of space and legitimacy was clear there, whereas colonial space was still a legal no man's land with too many unknown properties. Piracy had always been a space-related crime, in the sense that piracy was something that took place by uncommissioned entities outside of the sovereign realm. But how was an imperial power to conceptualize non-European space in early modernity? Was such space the sovereign space of a native nation or even an imperial rival, was it nonsovereign space, or was it one's own sovereign space? Any answer would have far-reaching political implications that exceeded the reach and authority of pirate law as only one of many legal frameworks that were able to speak to the issue of non-European space.

The Mediterranean, in contrast, was a clear-cut case, especially in the context of the essentialist model of civilization that dominated the construction of the modern hostis humani generis fiction. At the same time, this case had a long history of leaving room for even the starkest political contradictions, transformations, and readjustments. In its legalist abstraction, the Mediterranean realm was divided into one shore dominated by civilization and another shore dominated by barbarism. These shores, firmly and enduringly inhabited by legitimate good and illegitimate evil (often translated as Christianity versus Islam), were divided by a transformative sea space within which all contact between the realms—friendly, hostile, or neutral—occurred in all its broadness and complexity. The sea that divided good and evil was defined as a liminal in-between zone, a buffer zone that allowed civilization and its Other to coexist in an existential antagonism, but left sufficient leeway for political maneuvers that deviated from this core premise.

Second, even though the sea (or the later conceptualization of precolonial space as sea-like) radically expanded the possible forms of contact by being a space beyond all sovereign rights, there was something that the sea could not do: it could not undo race, which primarily meant the ties of origin and religion. Here, the Mediterranean context helped specify categories. In the Mediterranean context of renegade Barbary corsairs, the charge of race-based treason was more serious than in the colonial context because in the former context it was not just noisy political saber rattling by imperial rivals. The Barbary renegade had proven to be greedy and corrupt by taking Barbary employment for his personal benefit; he had proven to be a traitor to civilization by his indiscriminate attacks against Europeans, and even more so by his explicit spiritual abandonment of the Christian God. He was a true renegade to barbarism for the entire world to see. Therefore, he could become the prototype of the pirata, the epitome of civilization-abandoning degradation that imperial rivals only cited in their accusations against each other.

It is in this context that the Mediterranean realm assumes the greatest importance: it is there that the notions of race and space are combined for the hostis humani generis constellation. While the constellation of civilization versus barbarian can easily be established anywhere by virtue of racial categories, the barbarian will become a praedo only if there is also a pirata, and the pirata can meaningfully exist only in a zone in between clear blocs of mutual essentialist antagonism. The Mediterranean context provided a model for the way such a zone was internally structured. It thus contributed greatly to the conceptualization of precolonial space as empty and transformative, as well as the conceptualization of the inhabitants of such space as entities against whom violence was always inherently legitimate.

[5]

JOHN LOCKE, WILLIAM BLACKSTONE, AND THE INVADER IN THE STATE OF NATURE

THE BRIEF INTRODUCTION TO the historical genesis of the two most defining elements (pirata and praedo) of hostis humani generis and the sea-like space in which they are imagined to operate largely rests in the immediate context of pirate law. The discussion of these basic relations within pirate law does not yet explain how these two complementary figures became associated with the fundamental negotiations of legitimate violence in the Augustinian anecdote. To understand the source of this connection, it is helpful to start out with the most authoritative and comprehensive definition of hostis humani generis to date and to work our way backward to trace this definition's philosophical and historical origins.

William Blackstone's *Commentaries on the Law of England* (first published in 1765–68), which contains this authoritative definition, is generally considered fundamental for British law as well as for the establishment of United States law (Holdsworth, *Historians*, 55 and 59). While Blackstone's is not the only definition of hostis humani generis in English or British law, it is the most interesting and by far the most frequently cited one. Blackstone writes:

> Lastly, the crime of piracy, or robbery and depredation upon the high seas, is an offence against the universal law of society; a pirate being, according to Sir Edward Coke (*Third Part*, 3 Inst. 113) hostis humani generis. As, therefore, he has renounced all the benefits of society and government, and has reduced himself afresh to the savage state of nature, by declaring war against all mankind, all mankind must declare war against him; so that every community hath a right by the rule of self-defence, to inflict that punishment upon him which every individual would in a state of nature have been otherwise entitled to do, for any invasion of his person or personal property (*Commentaries*, 2:71).

The noteworthy aspects of this definition become obvious when compared to the definitions of hostis humani generis offered a century earlier. Coke and Charles Molloy had both explicitly stated that the enemy of all humankind was a robber and operated at sea. Coke, who is referred to in Blackstone's definition, had primarily rendered the pirate an enemy of all humankind because he considered piracy a form of treacherous conspiracy (Coke, *Third Part*, 113); Molloy added that the community made up by the pirate was generally not a lawful society (*Iure Maritimo*, 71). Blackstone remains in the tradition of these assessments, but in contrast to his legal predecessors, he elaborates what it means to be an enemy of all humankind. This elaboration is more than a specification of the crime of piracy; instead, and for the first time, the pirate is *subsumed* under the larger category of hostis humani generis. This hierarchization in fact constitutes the basis for the numerous uses of the legal fiction to conceptualize crimes other than piracy and spaces other than the sea.

While it differs in quality from the descriptions in previous legal commentaries, Blackstone's understanding of hostis humani generis is not original to him. It is Locke who actually speaks in this passage,[1] with Blackstone simply paraphrasing Locke's words as a straightforward description of an enemy of all humankind. In Blackstone's definition, the enemy of all humankind is essentially equivalent to Locke's invader in the state of nature ("Second Treatise"). This figure of the invader, therefore, is central to the discussion in this chapter. Indeed, when we study the invader in Locke, it becomes apparent that Blackstone's choice of this invader figure as a prototype of the enemy of all humankind is not incidental: Locke himself was influenced by the traditions of piracy law when he constructed the invader figure. This chapter will thus briefly outline Locke's relation to the Augustinian anecdote, then discuss the invader figure, and finally discuss the consequences of this transfer for the definition of hostis humani generis in Blackstone.

Locke's usage of the Augustinian anecdote in the "Second Treatise" is remarkably nuanced, and it is integrated into the context of a larger argument in a way that rivals Augustine in its theoretical complexity. When it comes to legitimate violence, Locke rereads Augustine just as Augustine rereads Cicero. While most other rewritings of the anecdote in modernity exclude the argumentative context in Augustine to give the pirate-emperor constellation a radically new meaning, Locke acknowledges the rather more serious questions about the possibility of just rule raised by Augustine, which directly lead him into an argument on legitimate violence as foundational violence that is crucial for the role played by hostis humani generis in modernity, especially in the United States.

The "Second Treatise" engages in a debate on legitimate violence in ways that are somewhat comparable to *The City of God*. Augustine attacks traditional Roman values in defense of the value system of Christianity, a faith that was rapidly growing in popularity and whose value system was becoming increasingly accepted. Locke engages the defenders of hereditary monarchy such as Robert Filmer, whose arguments he challenges directly in the "First Treatise." The main disagreement that Locke has with scholars such as Filmer is that they claim there is a natural sovereign right to domination over the people of the respective territory—a right whose defense permits legitimate violence against both those people and external enemies. In contrast, Locke claims that the sovereign and the population have entered into a contract, and that this includes the right of the governed population to reform and even to resist and overthrow the sovereign, if the sovereign is not just. The contract is specified in Locke's discussion of the state of nature and the law of nature.

The state of nature is not part of a terminology in the sense that it is strictly defined; it merely describes a precivilizational state that reflects the truly general and natural properties of humanity. These properties have to be considered as the bases of any order that claims to be appropriate to humans, but the state of nature also draws attention to tendencies in human nature (such as destructive desires) that have to be neutralized by any order that claims to be just. The state of nature, Ingo Berensmeyer explains, is a fiction used across the political spectrum in early modernity because it "fulfils a compensatory function by serving as a homogenizing communicator of a generalized sense of normativity in a society increasingly characterized by rapid change and increasing heterogeneity" (*Contingency*, 179; my translation). Locke, like Augustine, essentially claims the existence of eternal and universally applicable norms in a world characterized by turmoil and uncertainty.

In the "Second Treatise," the original state of nature is a tranquil state of plenty characterized by friendly, neighborly relations. In contrast to other Enlightenment thinkers such as Hobbes or Rousseau, Locke considers the state of nature a largely positive backdrop to contemporary civilized human life. His state of nature is neither brutish and terrifying, as in Hobbes, nor prehuman to the point of incomprehensibility, as in Rousseau. The state of nature in Locke is characterized by the condition of absolute freedom, and life among humans is informed by the "great Maxims of *Justice* and *Charity*" (Locke, "Second Treatise," 270). Locke argues that these maxims are dictated by the law of nature:

> The *State of Nature* has a [divine] Law of Nature to govern it, which obliges every one: And Reason, which is that Law, teaches all Mankind, who will but

> consult it, that being all equal and independent, no one ought to harm another in his Life, Health, Liberty, or Possessions. . . . Every one as he is *bound to preserve himself*, and not to quit his Station wilfully; so by the like reason when his own Preservation comes not in competition, ought he, as much as he can, *to preserve the rest of Mankind*, and may not unless it be to do Justice on an Offender, take away, or impair the life, or what tends to be the Preservation of the Life, the Liberty, Health, Limb or Goods of another. ("Second Treatise," 271)

Locke's state of nature is a state of peaceful cohabitation without any mediating institutions. Humans operate in an environment common to all, and human actions are only geared at securing the immediate well-being of the individual, his family, and his cooperative community. Unlike some scholars today (see, for example, Gray, "Hunter-Gatherers"; Rancière, *Dissensus*, 27–44), Locke does not assume from this that the maintenance of egalitarian collectivism can be the principal objective of political practice. Instead, Locke's main objective is to conceptualize the legitimate protection of the inherent human "double Right: First, A Right of Freedom to his Person," and "Secondly, A Right, before any other Man, to inherit, with his Brethren, his Fathers [*sic*] Goods" ("Second Treatise," 393–94). The first right is central because it points to the freedom of every human to preserve himself and thus establishes a definition of defensive violence as legitimate violence, since the right to self-defense is the birthright of every man (though not every human). The second right is central because property is constructed by Locke as a natural extension of the individual (white male) body into the world. Importantly for his debate with Filmer, Locke's understanding of the right to property as a natural birthright establishes claims to the land by the people who cultivate, rather than rule, it. According to Locke, one can generally distinguish the characteristics of a society by the way property is managed. The only just political society is the one that leaves property to the disposal of the individual who makes it property by labor in the first place, rather than having a sovereign who controls all of the property while his subjects control none of it (Locke, "Second Treatise," 384).

In Locke's original state of nature, the invader who disregards the natural rights to life and property and who amasses the property of others by violence inspires both the formation of political order and the explicitly formulated expression of the law of nature as the law of society. The argument in the "Second Treatise" about the invader is directly derived from the discourses on piracy and legitimate violence discussed in part 1. Locke himself draws explicit parallels between the invader and Cicero's and Augustine's respective treatments of the pirate: "That the *Aggressor*, who puts himself into the state of War with another, and *unjustly invades* another Man's right, can, by such an unjust War, *never* come to *have a right over the Conquered*, will be easily agreed by all Men, who will not think, that Robbers and Pyrates have a Right of Empire over whomever they have Force enough to master; or that Men are bound by promises, which unlawful Force extorts from them (Locke, "Second Treatise," 385)."

In this passage, the pirate is not only mentioned as a specific example, but Cicero's central distinguishing feature of the pirate—namely, that it is legitimate not to keep a promise made to a pirate—is taken up as a defining feature of the invader that underlies the all-important right to resist him in defense of the law of nature. The despotic sovereign, Locke suggests, is to be treated like the Ciceronian pirate. Thus, it does not come as a surprise that in the same paragraph, the Augustinian anecdote is paraphrased as an integral part of Locke's argument: "The Injury and the Crime is [*sic*] equal, whether committed by the wearer of a Crown, or some petty Villain. The Title of the Offender, and the Number of his Followers make no difference in the Offence, unless it be to aggravate it. The only difference is Great Robbers punish little ones, to keep them in their Obedience, but the great ones are rewarded with Laurels and Triumphs, because they are too big for the weak hands of Justice in this World, and have the power in their own possession, which should punish Offenders" (Locke, "Second Treatise," 385–86).

Locke takes up the argumentative context of Augustine's anecdote and comes to the same conclusions about the nature of the pirate-emperor who violates divine right, though he substitutes for the mediator of divine will; instead of Christianity and the church, reason and the law of nature are the central normative orientations that allow each individual man to commit violence legitimately. This possibility is dramatized by the encounter of peaceful people who obey the law of nature in the state of nature with the invader who threatens their lives and property. People in the state of nature react to invasion with defensive violence and the simultaneous formation of law and order: they organize to defend themselves against a collective threat and, in the process, distill the divine, unwritten, universal law of nature into a specific body of positive law. The invader thus emerges as the all-important catalyst that ends the state of nature, since his attack makes explicit that the protection of life and property are the main functions of both rule and law. Defensive violence creates social organization and the law itself.

In this way, the claim to legitimate violence in Filmer is directly inverted by Locke—not only the sovereign but every individual carries within himself an inherent potential to commit legitimate violence in the name of the law of nature. The invader can be either a pirate (Locke, "Second Treatise," 385) or a sovereign who abuses "his" population. The invader is thus already, in the truest sense of the word, a pirate-emperor; and because this figure occasions the replacement of nature with order, Locke's law of nature is made most visible, and most explicit, by the exercise of legitimate violence against the invading pirate-emperor. It is worth quoting some of the respective passages in full:

> In transgressing the Law of Nature, *the Offender declares himself to live by another Rule, than that of reason and common Equity*, which is that measure God has set to the actions of Men, for their mutual security: and so *he becomes dangerous to Mankind*, the tye [*sic*], which is to secure them from injury and violence, being slighted and broken by him. *Which being a trespass against the whole Species, and the Peace and Safety of it, provided for by the Law of Nature, every man upon this score, by the Right he hath to preserve Mankind in general, may restrain, or where it is necessary, destroy things noxious to them*. . . . Besides the Crime which consists in violating the Law, and varying from the right Rule of Reason, *whereby a Man so far becomes degenerate, and declares himself to quit the Principles of Human Nature, and to be a noxious Creature*, there is commonly injury done to some person or other, and some other Man receives damage by his Transgression, in which Case he who hath received any damage, has besides the right of punishment common to him with other Men, a particular Right to seek Reparation from him that has done it. . . . And thus it is, that every Man in the State of Nature, has a Power to kill a Murderer, both to deter others from doing the like Injury, which no Reparation can compensate, by the Example of the punishment that attends it from every body, and also to secure Men from the attempts of *a Criminal, who having renounced Reason, the common Rule and Measure, God hath given to Mankind, hath by the unjust Violence and Slaughter he hath committed upon one, declared War against all Mankind, and therefore may be destroyed as a Lyon or a Tiger, one of those wild Savage Beasts, with whom Men can have so Society or Security*. (Locke, "Second Treatise," 272–74; emphasis in original removed; emphasis added)

I have highlighted some of these passages to draw attention to the direct parallels between the characterizations of the Lockean invader and the construction of hostis humani generis in Blackstone quoted above:

> Lastly, the crime of piracy, or robbery and depredation upon the high seas, is an offence against the universal law of society; a pirate being, according to Sir Edward Coke (*Third Part*, 3 Inst. 113) hostis humani generis. *As, therefore, he has renounced all the benefits of society and government, and has reduced himself afresh to the savage state of nature, by declaring war against all mankind, all mankind must declare war against him; so that every community hath*

> *a right by the rule of self-defence, to inflict that punishment upon him which every individual would in a state of nature have been otherwise entitled to do, for any invasion of his person or personal property* (Blackstone, *Commentaries*, 2:71; emphasis added).

Blackstone's definition of hostis humani generis thus positions the confrontation with any enemy of all humankind as the confrontation with an invader who tests the very normative foundations of civilized society (designed to protect both life and property) and once more occasions the law of nature to become explicit in positive law.

However, the invader in Locke carries some concealed analytical baggage that is important for a further analysis of Blackstone's definition. The replacement of the state of nature with a state of order in Locke is clearly the prerogative of white Europeans. Characteristically for Enlightenment thought as a whole, Locke singles out the wilderness of North America as an example of a state of nature that is still in place. Locke presupposes an inherent difference between Europeans and non-European Others on this basis, using Native Americans as an exemplary people still arrested in the state of nature (see, for example, "Second Treatise," 277, 287, 294, 296, and 339; see also the critique of Mills, "Racial Liberalism"). Locke was not alone in this assessment of Native Americans. For instance, Hobbes unambiguously shared his perspective and, in accord with his own characterization of the state of nature, cast Native Americans as inherently hostile and brutish (see, for example, *Leviathan*, 85; see also Eggers, *Naturzustandstheorie*, 34–35).

This link between the state of nature and the notion of race, which is still comparatively implicit in the "Second Treatise," is significantly developed and substantiated during the Golden Age of Piracy. The pirates of the Golden Age replaced Mediterranean corsairs as the historical core example of hostis humani generis in law and of piracy in the popular imagination. The Golden Age begins approximately a year after the publication of the "Second Treatise" and colors the interpretive history of the invader figure in the years leading up to Blackstone's definition. This shift in emphasis away from the Mediterranean standard of maritime violence and toward Golden Age piracy reflected a more mature stage of the oceanic revolution as described by Thomas Bender: previously marginal European states subverted the cultural, economic, and political dominance of the Ottoman Empire by orienting themselves toward other, more remote spaces (*Among Nations*, 20–27). Ottoman imperial power, concentrated in the Turkish control over the Mediterranean, was replaced by European imperial power, concentrated in the Atlantic and the Indian Oceans. The trade routes exploited by Golden Age pirates and the goods stolen by them constituted the lifelines of this new regime of European colonialism, and the normative questions raised by the existence of Golden Age pirates were questions about the inner logic and developments of European imperialism in general, regardless of specific nationalities.

Even though the Golden Age pirate was from and of European civilization, he openly defied the trade system that was the backbone of the imperial project—and, like the Barbary States, he recruited great numbers of seafaring Europeans into his service, causing them to abandon their sovereigns in the very spaces where imperial power was weakest.

In British discourse, fundamental questions were thus raised about the nature of seafaring men who constituted both the pool from which this kind of threat emerged and the group most vulnerable to the threat. What was the nature of common sailors—were they most appropriately viewed as monsters in disguise, slaves to be broken for the prevention of revolt, innocent subjects to be protected, citizens to be respected, or even sovereigns in the making? When the pirate, a former mercantile worker, broke away from the empire, what kinds of communities did he found, and what did these communities explain about the nature of the mercantile worker and humanity in general? When the pirate was seen as an opportunistic parasite of colonialism, what kind of malfunctioning structures of colonialism did he expose, and what were his positions on money and trade? What did his crime consist of, and when was he not a criminal? How did he interact with space, representatives of European rivals, and natives? How did he interact with God and the notion of family? Was he lost or evil or free? Was he primitive or visionary? All of these questions were only superficially questions about the Golden Age pirate. They were really cultural and philosophical negotiations of a new system of expansive imperialism. That system was, to some extent, prepared to incorporate the parasitical colonial pirate into its normative logic and official history.

While the previous chapter focused on the construction of praedo and pirata as racially divided allies, this chapter is interested in a later, more mature version within the project of imperialism: a construction of praedo and pirata that does not imagine them as allies who necessarily operate in concert, but as organizationally and racially separate entities whose complementary existence is mediated only by their common existence in sea-like, transformative spaces beyond the reach of imperial power.

The native Other remained the most serious, unreadable threat of precolonial spaces. Encounters with Native American nations and the Barbary States were unambiguously established as variations on the same struggle of white, European civilization versus a barbarous, nonwhite, collectivist bloc of Otherness (Baepler, "Barbary Captivity," 228). In these discourses, the Native American is constructed both as a fragment of the wilderness (when he is arrested in the state of nature and merely exists somewhere) and an illegitimate aggressor (when he is a praedo who represents a barbarous culture and engages in war with Europeans). Hobbes in particular claimed that contracts with any (non-European) antagonist do not have to be honored (Griffin, *American Leviathan*, 26; Kempe, *Fluch der Weltmeere*, 155–56).

It was certainly conventional to conceptualize war with Native Americans as an essentialist clash of good Europeans versus evil Others, but to claim that the Native American was a praedo combined this routine charge with a new possibility for legitimating a claim to precolonial space. Where Native Americans and European imperialists clashed as praedones and representatives of civilization, one could speak of a clash in sea-like territory—that is, in empty, unruled, and unpossessed space. Land had not previously been conceptualized in this manner, but the advantages of attributing sea-like qualities to the precolonial wilderness were obvious. After all, an inherently empty and unpossessed territory could, by right, be claimed by Europeans without raising the charge of illegitimate conquest. However, a pirata figure was still required to complete the constellation and turn an argument about contested land into one about empty land.

The Golden Age of Piracy may have become such a discursively constitutive period and may have been able to absorb previous as well as later pirate waves almost completely, because these pirates were the perfect pirata complement to a Native American praedo on land. The white Golden Age pirate was a renegade in pursuit of his own interests, and with his peers he formed independent, unstable brotherhoods of economic parasites. Golden Age pirates were deemed so radically beyond allegiance that not even the familiar notion of simultaneous treason and conversion could properly describe them (Baer, "Plot of Piracy"). To his contemporaries, instead of religious or cultural conflict, the Golden Age pirate began to stand for the existential questions of Enlightenment philosophy that were already raging within Europe. With the pirate as a problem-defining example, central issues about the nature of the human being could be addressed.

The state of nature that is later evoked by Blackstone is primarily characterized by the absence of enforceable sovereignty. The explicitly mentioned high seas are defined as inherently nonpossessed at a very early point of modernity, so it is clear that they constitute a central example. However, Blackstone's enemy of all humankind explicitly relies not on his presence at sea, but on his presence in the state of nature. Whereas the legitimate defender against the invader only acts as if he exists in a state of nature, enemies of all humankind do exist in that state. As mentioned above, arrestedness in the state of nature is a characteristic that Locke and especially Hobbes unambiguously assign to Native Americans, but the great visibility of the

Golden Age of Piracy requires that these pirates are described similarly. In part 1 I touched on the ways in which the Golden Age pirates' distribution of property, in particular, was considered proof of a (white) state of nature capable of developing into an (imperial) state of order in precolonial space. But only in combination could the Native American and the still-maritime Golden Age pirate support the larger point of these characterizations, which was the construction of the American continent as an unpossessed quasi sea.

Blackstone's definition obviously speaks only of one enemy of all humankind. However, the figures of praedo and pirata, who are already latently complementary in customary pirate law as well as in Locke's original, are made visible in Blackstone by the conflation in the definition of two very different premises of conflict. These premises are a construction of good versus evil, and a construction of the norm versus deviance. Although these premises seem to be related to one and the same figure—the enemy of all humankind—the premises' narrative implications are vastly different from one another, and even mutually exclusive to some extent. Their intertwined nature affirms that hostis humani generis encompasses two kinds of figures rather than just one, and furthermore it allows certain deductions about the specific quality of the state of nature they operate in.

The construction of good versus evil is immediately obvious in the passage. In Blackstone's definition of hostis humani generis, civilization and savagery, or humanity and its Other, are divided into two incompatible blocs, one of which represents an illegitimate aggressor while the other is a legitimate defender of "society and government"—or, indeed, of humanity itself. Quite in line with Locke's argument, the invader somehow exists outside of humanity.

The defender's mission in this struggle is to establish or reestablish a stable legitimate sovereign rule in a lawless zone of conflict. The inherent antagonism in this construction of good versus evil locks Blackstone's figures into a constellation of essentialist struggle. Civilized humanity opposes an inhuman, barbaric invader. Whoever loses will perish, and if civilization loses, humanity will fall back into a terrifying state of permanent war (Locke, "Second Treatise," 400). Unsurprisingly, the existential struggle is the one I assign to the praedo in Blackstone's reading of hostis humani generis. In her analysis of narrative constructions of existential conflicts, Eva Horn has aptly characterized this sort of conflict as a "war of two races" ("Enden des Menschen," 107; my translation), which emphasizes once more that this construction has a long tradition of being associated with the understanding of race discussed in this book.

As noted above, a construction of the norm versus deviance is also apparent in Blackstone's definition. This form of antagonism describes a transformative movement based on the notion of weakness and corruption: an individual "renounces" civilization, then "reduces" himself to a state of nature, and eventually "declares" war on civilization. This is the process that the pirata—a figure originally informed by the Barbary renegade—goes through. However, as the pirata in particular assumes a different and more important role in the context of the Golden Age of Piracy than previously, I will discuss this notion at greater length here.

To understand the narrative logic of deviance that is at work here, it is worth considering the Anglo-American tradition of the captivity narrative at least very briefly. The captivity narrative constituted the genre within which the renegade corsair appeared in his most fully formed relation to England or Britain; indeed, this body of texts helped inform the pirata's original legal position. The Barbary captivity narrative (accounts of white sailors who were captured and enslaved by Barbary corsairs and wrote of their experiences after their safe return) provided constructions and characterizations of spaces and antagonists in the Mediterranean that were eventually transferred to the American context in the American captivity narrative (Baepler, "Barbary Captivity," 219; see also Carroll, *Rhetorical Drag*). In the Barbary captivity narrative, the praedo traditionally represents the larger core antagonism of civilization and barbarism. The pirata, in contrast, is set up in direct structural contrast to the captive who narrates the account. The reason for this is based on the context of these narratives' publication in England, as Nabil Matar argues:

> [The pronounced and widespread] anxiety about the returning captive in seventeenth-century England suggests an identity insecurity. To have been among the Muslims did not necessarily mean that the English/British/Christian identity had been preserved. Rather, it had been tested, and there was no foregone certainty that it would have passed the test successfully. Long before the Stockholm syndrome was identified, communities worried that a captive would have started to identify with the captor—especially at a time when becoming Muslim might have led to advancement and financial gain. To have been among the Muslims was not just to have been a prisoner of war, but a prisoner of temptation too. And many of the prisoners reported on compatriots who had succumbed to Muslim allure and settled among the Muslims. (*Turks*, 72)

In response to these anxieties, Matar continues, former captives presented themselves as spies for England who offered their writings as strategic reports from within the enemy fortress. These reports also served as testimonies of their detachedness from the Muslim Other: former captives presented themselves as particularly devout Christians who, in contrast to others, had passed the "test" of captivity. In other words, the genre of the captivity narrative structurally relies on a near-essentialist separation of the virtuous captive and the pirata renegade who yields to the temptations offered to him. The weak, sensual compatriot who succumbs to the call of preferment and the promise of advancement—the pirata—is the ideal complement of the Barbary captivity narrative's hero because he makes explicit what the protagonist represents as unthinkable for himself. Without the pirata's transgression, the genre's retrospective construction of the steadfastness of the representative of civilization is meaningless (Colley, *Captives*, 82–98).

In the Golden Age of Piracy, this structure of complementarity is adopted in the construction of honest sailors as the counterparts of pirates that even identify themselves as pirates. These self-assured outlaws are perfect examples of conscious deviance. A good illustration of how the process of renunciation, reduction, and declaration in Blackstone functions is the story of Bartholomew Roberts, one of the most famous pirate captains of the Golden Age of Piracy. The following passage is part of Charles Johnson's attempt to construct Roberts as the prototypical pirate:

> In the Beginning he [Roberts] was very averse to this Sort of Life, and would certainly have escaped from them [the pirates], had a fair Opportunity presented it self; yet afterwards he changed his Principles, as many besides him have done upon another Element, and perhaps for the same Reason too, *viz.* Preferment,—and what he did not like as a private Man he could reconcile to his Conscience as a Commander. . . . Roberts was accordingly elected [captain], tho' he had not been above six Weeks among them, . . . and he accepted of the Honour, saying, that since he had dipp'd his Hands in muddy Water, and must be a Pyrate, it was better being a Commander than a common Man. (*General History*, 194–95)

This passage features the elements of renunciation of civilization, reduction to a state of nature, and a subsequent declaration of war against the law of nature. In the passage, it appears that the renunciation of benefits is still a neutral rather than a hostile act. It is achieved through Roberts's voluntary removal to remote spaces where sovereign power over him becomes difficult to maintain without his explicit consent. This may still be the act of an honest sailor. The removal from the imperial center is intensified by his abduction to a pirate ship that is beyond "society and government" (Blackstone, *Commentaries*, 2:71) and is itself capable of representing the state of nature (Baer, *British Isles*, 208–9). The removal to this state of nature directly exposes Roberts to the danger of being infected or, in Blackstone's words, "reduced." At this point, his presence aboard is still only a form of captivity, as in the example of Captain Beer (discussed in part 1), who finds himself in a very similar situation. In his analysis of the pirate in the captivity narrative, David Johnson has rightly pointed out that the captive, faced with a situation such as Roberts's, has no option but to transform himself, either into a purer version of what he had previously been (an honest sailor, a Christian, and so on) or into the monstrous, soiled Otherness of the pirate ("Limits of Culture," 366). In an essentialist model of civilization, a third option does not exist. The parallel reading of the figures of Beer and Roberts illustrates this fact very clearly.

Roberts's reduction to pirata savagery is established by the corruption that has generally been emphasized in the context of the enemy of all humankind in a colonial setting—the awakening of sensual "Preferment" for the life of a wild beast, which results in an acceptance of his situation and smothers his desire to return to order. Roberts's eventual election as pirate captain features the official declaration of his transformation, "that since he had dipp'd his Hands in muddy Water, and must be a Pyrate, it was better being a Commander than a common Man" (C. Johnson, *General History*, 195). The greatest weight of his statement here is not carried by his acceptance of the position of captain (even though it is offered as a partial explanation) but by the acknowledgment that his transformation into a pirate necessarily results from his awakened "preferment." The "muddy Water" on Captain Roberts's hands is as fatal as the blood on the hands of Lady Macbeth: after six weeks of exposure to a ship's company in the state of nature, a transformation has taken place after which he cannot turn back but has to be an aggressive deviant.

As the conflict of a good captive self and a bad pirate self in Captain Roberts as well as Bellamy's Mephistophelian hailing of Beer indicate, the British merchant sailor and the pirate are systematically constructed as inversions of each other in the eighteenth century (Rediker, *Villains*, 51, 86, and 136). Confronted with the twin hail of threat and seduction, the merchant sailor is always urged to prove himself and reveal his colors as a truly honest man (such as Beer) or as a lurking pirata in disguise (such as Roberts). In other words, pirata and merchant sailor are no longer different shades of gray in European privateering practices; instead, they constitute clearly delimited identities defined in contrast to each other just as clearly and inversely as pirata and praedo. Knut Weibust relates a much-quoted anecdote of the teachings of an experienced hand on a merchant ship that summarizes this dichotomist view: "There is no justice or injustice on board ship, my lad. There are only two things: duty and mutiny. . . . All that you are ordered to do is duty. All that you refuse to do is mutiny" (*Deep Sea Sailors*, 372).

Within the essentialist, racialized framework that already informs hostis humani generis in the eighteenth century, this allows the creation of a unique position for the pirata in the larger discourse of the essentialist model of civilization. The pirata and the praedo act in the same way but are racially different, while the captive or sailor and the pirata are racially the same but act differently. In other words, the pirata illustrates the essence of both Same and Other, and civilization and barbarism, by personifying their unnatural conflation. He is able to combine these incompatible elements because the entire dramatization of the essentialist relationship occurs in any sea-like zone in between, and because a completed transformation into the Other is deemed impossible in the essentialist model that informs early modern pirate law based on treason.

These relations had already existed in the context of the Mediterranean simultaneous treason and conversion; now, however, their possible application is significantly expanded. Not just sea space, but any space, is thinkable as an in-between zone. Praedones do not necessarily represent an Other sovereign, but an Other humanity. Piratae do not necessarily cooperate with praedones, but are simply cast as deviant Europeans who—like the praedo, but not necessarily in cooperation with him—invade European order.

This is, of course, precisely the point at which I break with previous scholarship on the enemy of all humankind. As I mentioned above, the assumption that there is always only one enemy of all humankind instead of two informs virtually all analyses of hostis humani generis available to me. From such an alternative perspective, one might argue that Roberts as a representative deviant does transform himself into a full-fledged antagonist and thus occupies the positions of pirata and praedo at different times. If that were so, the two narrative positions of the enemy of all humankind that I have introduced as separate would instead be successive. For three reasons, I am not convinced that such an argument holds.

First, much of the possible confusion about the topic of one enemy of all humankind may stem from the already discussed fact that Blackstone uses a generic "he" to discuss hostis humani generis. But if Blackstone's distinctions are indeed informed by Locke, we must acknowledge that his use of the generic "he" in the state of nature suggests extremely ambiguous and multifaceted notions of agency. We furthermore have to consider that the praedo and the pirata are entities whose actions at sea are exchangeable and who have a discursive history of cooperation. If we also consider that the racialized split in hostis humani generis has always been implicit rather than explicit in legal practice, it is obvious that the fiction can easily apply to a parallel variety of representative persons of extremely different properties without rendering the usage of the singular "he" nonsensical.

Second, the constructions of good versus evil and the norm versus deviance that clearly coexist in the passage in Blackstone evoke different narrative implications. While both constructions evoke antagonism, the first contrasts good with something inherently other than itself, while the second contrasts good with a treacherous element of itself. There is a substantial difference between conceptualizing an antagonist as an unreadable Other who invades from elsewhere for unknown reasons, and conceptualizing that antagonist as the direct answer to and product of one's own civilizational priorities and shortcomings. On the basis of mere description, these two structures may be interwoven so as to prevent an easy recognition of their difference—which Blackstone's definition certainly does—but their narrative implications cannot be reconciled so easily, and will necessarily lead to internal contradictions if the separation of pirata and praedo in the constellation that I have suggested does not take place. As the narrative choices of the Barbary captivity narrative and of Charles Johnson's eighteenth-century *General History* have demonstrated, this problem was appreciated and addressed by contemporary writers.

The third reason is, as I have repeatedly suggested, that the hostis humani generis fiction has historically been inserted into the larger discourse of an essentialist model of civilization and derives much of its meaning from this discursive context. It is this context in particular that renders the idea of a temporal transformation from deviant to antagonist unconvincing. In terms of the praedo, the link to the essentialist model of civilization is straightforward: the essentialist model of good civilization and an inherently evil Other is directly duplicated by the narrative construction of the barbarous praedo in Blackstone, a figure that invades representatives of civilization (as well as the innocents whom such representatives have to defend and protect, in Wendy Brown's sense in *States of Injury*).

The deviance of the pirata requires the essentialist approach primarily because the figure and its development are unthinkable in the alternative framework of the progressivist approach. Even though the pirata's development mirrors the progressivist approach's basic structure—someone crosses over from one camp to the other, or at least attempts to do so—the pirata "reduces" himself to savagery instead of rising to civilization. He cannot be conceptualized within the progressivist framework because his development fundamentally contradicts this approach's central premise of civilization as the universal objective of any personal and societal development. In the context of the progressivist approach, the pirata as a descending entity is utterly nonsensical.

Of course, the pirata also remains somewhat alien to the essentialist approach because the notion of transformation is not inherent in a concept that assumes two stable blocs of antagonists. In the end, it is the racializing internal split of the invader figure and the pirate figure that offers a justification of the pirata's existence within the essentialist model. The pirata's transformation can be conceptualized as an attempted rather than an actual transformation—despite all efforts, the deviant remains unable to merge with the Other because he must always remain on his side of the racialized divide. What loyalty to the homeland and faith to God cannot achieve, an essentialist argues, the natural fact of racial incompatibility establishes. This way, the pirata does not challenge the inherent difference presupposed by the essentialist approach and can be tolerated as a figure explicable by the logic of the model. Precisely because of this narrative context, the pirata begins to move into the position of perpetual potentiality that I outlined in chapter 1 as a pronounced, defining feature of the pirate in modernity. His movement is not in fact a transgressive crossing over but a kind of loop, as if the pirata were an orbiting satellite of civilization that, despite all lack of communication and coordination, is unable to escape civilization's gravity. The pirata is civilized, however like a savage he acts.

All of this is important for a discussion of the notion of space because the specific nature of the racial narrative split with the hostis humani generis fiction explains the properties of space presupposed by the fiction in Blackstone—properties, indeed, that this definition helped establish for colonialist law more generally.

Thus far, the discussion of this chapter has three implications. First, all constellations identified within hostis humani generis are mediated by space rather than by time. If praedo and pirata are divided by race rather than by developmental stage (as they would be if they were indeed one), their complementarity is the exact reflection of a pirata-captive constellation. While the captive and the praedo respectively represent civilization and Otherness in an in-between zone, the pirata represents the sea-like in-between zone itself—primarily its ability to transform behavior and allegiance, though not racial identity. When the in-between zone is not identified as such by its own materiality (for example, by being a sea), it is successfully identified as an in-between zone only if a pirata exists to specify the other two figures' struggle as taking place in a zone that is beyond predetermined boundaries of order and legitimacy.

Second, when all three figures are present, an existential state of war between civilization and barbarism (represented by captive and praedo) exists, which is in turn indicative of a state of nature. However, not all three figures are in this state of nature—it is restricted to the two figures that can be described as enemies of all humankind. The praedo is inherently caught up in the state of nature, and the pirata explicitly attempts to reduce himself to it by his praedo-like behavior. The pirata's deviant behavior generally indicates the dilemma of the representative of civilization in the essentialist model. In this model, civilized man is defined not by positive traits but only by his refusal to behave like a savage. If any representative of civilization were truly in a state of nature, he would automatically be transformed into a pirata. Blackstone acknowledges this problem when he carefully distances the representative of civilization from any such implication: the representative of civilization defends himself only "as if" he existed in a state of nature, which "otherwise" would entitle him to employ any means necessary against an "invasion" such as that of the enemy of all humankind. The state of nature is forced on him by the existence of enemies of all humankind; his defense is not only against an immediate attacker, but primarily against the state of nature itself.

In fighting praedo and pirata, the representative of civilization defies the absence of legitimate order. No matter which means of violence he employs, the explicit end of a defense of the sovereign order at its margins justifies all of his means. The enemies of all humankind had originally been derived from the spatial properties of the sea, but now the existence of a state of nature is derived from the presence of enemies of all humankind. In other words, Blackstone suggests a dialectical relationship between the identification of enemies of all humankind and the characterization of the space within which they are encountered.

Third, if the state of nature represents the absence of order, and the presence of the pirata indicates a zone in between the blocs of civilization and barbarism, the dialectically identified space can be located in specific historical situations. It is significant, at this point in my argument, that Blackstone is writing in the mideighteenth century. At this point, British colonialism is already a comparatively well-established system, and the existence of piracy has already been rendered a phenomenon typical of colonial space. In such a context, the legitimacy of appropriating land must be secured, and this is precisely what legal scholars of Blackstone's age attempt to do.

In the Americas specifically, the main apple of discord between Native Americans and European settlers was the question of who could legitimately claim to be the ruler of American territory: the natives, who had an ancient claim of use, or the Europeans, who—by their own definition—constituted the civilizational peak of human existence? This had always been the core question of colonialism, since British law did not traditionally admit to a legitimate right of conquest and annexation.[2] In 1758, only a few years before the publication of Blackstone's *Commentaries*, Emer de Vattel had famously postulated the establishment of infrastructure as the foundation of European claims to the American continent and had established the notion of space itself as a vehicle for imperialist claims. Vattel writes:

> The cultivation of the soil deserves the attention of the government, not only on account of the invaluable advantages that flow from it, but from its being

> an obligation imposed by nature on mankind. The whole earth is destined to feed its inhabitants; but this it would be incapable of doing if it were uncultivated. Every nation is then obliged by the law of nature to cultivate the land that has fallen to its share; and it has no right to enlarge its boundaries, or have recourse to the assistance of other nations, but in proportion as the land in its possession is incapable of furnishing it with necessaries. Those nations (such as the ancient Germans, and some modern Tartars) who inhibit fertile countries, but disdain to cultivate their lands, and choose rather to live by plunder, are wanting to [*sic*] themselves, are injurious to all their neighbours, and deserve to be extirpated as savage and pernicious beasts. There are others, who, to avoid labour, choose to live only by hunting, and their flocks. This might, doubtless, be allowed in the first ages of the world, when the earth, without cultivation, produced more than was sufficient to feed its small number of inhabitants. But at present, when the human race is so greatly multiplied, it could not subsist if all nations were disposed to live in that manner. Those who still pursue this idle mode of life, usurp more extensive territories than, with a reasonable share of labour, they would have occasion for, and have, therefore, no reason to complain, if other nations, more industrious and too closely confined, come to take possession of a part of those lands. Thus, though the conquest of the civilized empires of Peru and Mexico was a notorious usurpation, the establishment of many colonies on the continent of North America might, on their confining themselves within just bounds, be extremely lawful. The people of those extensive tracts rather ranged through than inhabited them. (*Law of Nations*, 35–36)

In this passage, Vattel, too, visibly draws on Locke when he argues that the use of land is the foundation of any sovereign claim to territory, and that nomadic and predatory[3] uses of land are the two most obvious thinkable ways to void such a claim. The characterization of the Native American as a nomad who must make room for "more industrious" (that is, civilized) peoples had found its way into law especially through Vattel[4] (even though the assumption of Native American nomadism had existed in Europe for at least a century, as Hobbes's use of the same notion indicates). The land-use argument associates the European as the inherent representative of civilization with the "industrious" use of "the earth," "the soil," the land," "territories," and "tracts." The colonial conflicts discussed by Vattel in this passage do not simply occur in space, they are mediated by it.

Vattel's evocation of an imposing, obligating "nature" thus has a double sense. Primarily, the term "nature" is a straightforward reference to human nature and, more specifically, to the law of nature: Vattel claims that the land-use argument constitutes a universal rule of human conduct.

In a passage discussing the earth as a normative centerpiece of sovereign rights, however, a more literal interpretation of the term "nature" can be added to its Lockean meaning. The nature that "imposes" a certain form of possession can also be interpreted as the specific wilderness of the American continent. The wilderness can be understood as an imposing "nature" in the sense that it is a space in which, by virtue of its properties as a space, the state of nature occurs. Such an assumption achieves something important: the act of taking possession is the act of introducing the land to the legal sphere in the first place.

According to Vattel's logic, Europeans cultivate the wilderness according to civilized needs—namely, the needs of European empires. The representative of civilization, then, is the person who settles in colonial space and associates himself with the imperial interest. Vattel's contention that Native Americans are nomads renders them praedones eternally existing in the state of nature; a pirata would either be someone white who is both nomadic and associated with Native Americans (Paul and Hein, "Fugitive," 230) or someone who settles but delinks himself from some imperial project, such as the oft-cited Golden Age pirate kingdoms (Baer, introduction, vii).

In this way, the American continent becomes the eighteenth-century precedent-setting space for a mature modern understanding of hostis humani generis, which uses the state of nature—rather than the much narrower concept of the sea—as the main resource for understanding the in-between zone. In Blackstone's definition of hostis humani generis, the inherently hostile natural space allows a broader reading of the constellation as applying anywhere that features an untamed and uninhabited space.

In an explicitly imperial framework, the hostis humani generis constellation and the fixed relations encountered in it thus help establish the notion of the imperial margin. After all, colonial space is transformative only due to its spatial distance from legitimate sovereign rule. Eighteenth-century piracy continuously supported this notion by providing impressive examples. The farther away from the homeland, the more mutinies occurred (Rediker, *Villains*, 136), the more sailors decided to desert and to live as brothers or kings of natives (Kohl, "'Travestie,'" 95; C. Johnson, *General History*, 62), and the more standard reports of marooned or lost wild white men in the colonial woods became (Exquemelin, *Buccaneers*, 55–57; Seidel, *Robinson Crusoe*, 36–46). Transformative space was thus considered a force unto itself that would completely replace the political notion of the nonwhite "kings of evil" in the context of hostis humani generis. The space in which the praedo was encountered and that produced the pirata became the margin both of the empire and of the wilderness as a bloc elsewhere.

This significantly broadened application of hostis humani generis was possible because of two central discursive changes that occurred in the course of the eighteenth century. These were the increasing merging of the progressivist and the essentialist approach to civilization and the solid establishment of binary identity difference as a core feature of European approaches to human nature in general. As applied to the Barbary States, the hostis humani generis fiction's inherent reliance on the essentialist approach severely limited its cultural explanatory potential. After all, the progressivist approach offered a powerful alternative that relied largely on the missionary charisma of Christianity. During the eighteenth century, however, the progressivist approach drew nearer to the essentialist model. For instance, the notion of Native Americans as inherently inferior was an increasingly conceivable position even in the progressivist approach. By the end of the eighteenth century, the progressivist position had strongly deemphasized the possibility of a full crossing over to civilization in the unfolding larger context of imperialism, a notion that is especially evident in the view of natives as eternal children (Lehmkuhl, "Kolonialismus," 45).

In North America, progressivist and essentialist characterizations of the Native American Other by European settlers had existed in parallel for a long time. This parallel existence was due to significant regional differences, since the concrete experience of specific settlers with specific Native Americans informed the discourse chosen to characterize the relationship. Settlers who had friendly relations with their Native American neighbors tended to express progressivist views that often included missionary efforts and the hope for the Other's conversion;[5] settlers who tended to have less peaceful experiences with their neighbors emphasized the essentialist antagonism between brave, civilized settlers and wild, bloodthirsty savages. Nancy Shoemaker writes of the situation by the end of the eighteenth century:

> It is easy to see how imperialistic desire drove European settlers to believe themselves different from Indians, but more importantly, imperialistic desire also shaped the design of those differences. Across a wide spectrum of cultural attributes, Europeans classified Indians as inferiors. They made proper use of the land; Indians did not. Europeans had kings for leaders; Indians had chiefs. Europeans could write; Indians could not. European men behaved with civility; Indian men behaved like animals. Casting Indians as inferiors, as incarnations of a primitive past, Europeans saw no need to treat Indians as equals in diplomacy, no need to invite them to peace treaties held at Utrecht and Paris, no need to recognize their governments or territorial claims as legitimate.
>
> Underlying the belief in Indian inferiority, one question remained: could Indians change or was Indian inferiority as immutable as skin color? (*Strange Likeness*, 142)

Shoemaker suggests that this central question was eventually decided in favor of the essentialist perspective. According to her, colonists and Native Americans were strongly convinced of their "intransigent differences" by the end of the eighteenth century (*Strange Likeness*, 141), a conclusion that considerably changed the function of civilizational approaches in the American context. Because of the increasing agreement on the existence of an essentialist divide between the races, the hostis humani generis constellation could insert itself into virtually all discourses on encounters with the Other, provided these encounters took place in a marginal zone that could be read as a sea-like in-between zone.

But it was not only the notion of race that became more important in imperial discourse—the notion of binary identity difference generally began to dominate all imperial relations as a central category. Leo Braudy suggests that hierarchical gender constructions that had rendered captives of both genders in America exchangeable versions of each other were replaced by a two-part model that assigned inherently different meanings to male and female representatives of civilization in the wilderness. While woman in the wilderness was reduced to her sexuality and either remained chaste (which maintained her status of an idealized representative of civilization) or not (which sullied her forever and rendered her lost in the wilderness), man in the wilderness was able to act as a representative "subject of a secular political philosophy, [and] a contradictory compound of all these elements, single but collective, private but public" (Braudy, *Chivalry*, 202; see also 199–214). It was therefore not least the construction of all enemies of all humankind as unambiguously male that allowed the constellation to remain philosophically relevant.[6] The importance now assigned to the masculinity of all enemies of all humankind and the pirata's whiteness, which was much more developed than many other figures' racialized position, emphasized these figures' roles of philosophical representation. At the same time, the notion of the captive as a representative of civilization was gendered, and thus the captive as a figure was removed from the more aggressive representative of civilization in the American context. Man in the wilderness explored and tamed, while the American captivity narrative conventionalized captivity as a specifically female experience. The notion of passive captivity, then, was also factored out of American applications of the hostis humani generis constellation in the wilderness.

In summary, the hostis humani generis constellation premises a stable and unquestioned antagonism between civilization and Other in a marginal zone in between empire and a nonwhite wilderness, inhabited by praedones insofar as they represent the wilderness itself rather than a specific political entity. As we have seen, furthermore, the margins as spaces are most clearly narrated and negotiated by the white male figures that operate in these zones and who make existential decisions there—they either become purified as better versions of themselves (that is, they become true defenders of the innocent) and thus turn into representatives of civilization, or they degenerate and become piratae. This specifically colonial constellation of civilizational representative, pirata, and praedo in a state of nature in between blocs of civilization and wilderness allows a simultaneous negotiation of civilizational space, British identity, and imperial legitimacy within the expansive framework of mercantile expansionism.

This basic constellation with its muddled philosophical and legal history was ready by the early nineteenth century to be used as a solid basis for imagining contexts other than piracy. The extension of the legal fiction to conceptualize the slave trade as a crime is one of these examples, but it may be the least illustrative one when it comes to the potential of the constellation to negotiate the question of legitimate violence anew. It is at this point that literature becomes a particularly helpful site to trace the significance of hostis humani generis as a constellation that structures the meaning of violence in deliberately unspecific contexts of violence.

[6]

HOSTIS HUMANI GENERIS AND THE AMERICAN HISTORICAL NOVEL: JAMES FENIMORE COOPER'S *THE DEERSLAYER*

NOT LONG AFTER the publication of the legal opinions of William Blackstone and Emer de Vattel discussed in the previous chapter, the United States of America declared its independence from Great Britain. As Kathryn Preyer has observed, "the new forms of government at the time of the American revolution required new concepts of sovereignty; gone were doctrines and institutions that had derived historically from the theoretical structure of the Crown as sovereign" ("Jurisdiction," 186). In the formulation of a radically new form of legitimate sovereignty, Americans originally relied on British models to substantiate their own claims to legitimacy. Blackstone and Vattel were especially well known among the members of the republican elites, and their ideas were used to develop and support the American position within the world. It is not surprising that such a positioning should also incorporate the hostis humani generis constellation as an important resource to make sense of an unprecedented form of sovereign rule. After all, it had helped formulate the margins of the British Empire that, for Americans, suddenly became core territory. Also, it was a constellation that could be used as a resource to successfully claim the right to exercise inherently legitimate violence, which was of course one of the most central claims for a newly founded sovereign power and had to be established both inside and outside its borders. Hostis humani generis has a history of being used to characterize the European enemies of the United States in the republic's early political discourse. Echoing the familiar colonialist uses of the fiction to deny each others' claims to legitimate sovereignty over the American territory, Americans and Britons routinely called each other pirates and *hostes humani generis* during the United States' struggle for national independence. A particularly notable example from the American side is Thomas Jefferson's original draft of the Declaration of Independence, which strongly suggests parallels between Barbary corsairs and British enemies ("Declaration of

Independence"; see also Hawke, *Honorable Treason*; Lee, "Florida Blanca," 2:209).

Especially during the first half of the nineteenth century, the *hostis humani generis* constellation played an important role in US narratives. This conscious incorporation—which leads to the use of civilizing narratives, the state of nature, and hostis humani generis as central structural elements in American literary fiction—is due to the particular historical situation indicated by Preyer. Peter Schneck (*Rhetoric*, 120–24) has argued that in the first half of the nineteenth century an independent American way of interpreting law and conducting legislation was systematically formulated. He points out that it was a period that many legal scholars continue to consider a golden age and a pioneering epoch in American legal discourse. Because legal concepts and priorities were fundamental to the future identity of the United States as a nation, public discussions about the law were widespread at the time across cultural levels and means of expression. A particularly important voice, Schneck continues, was that of literature, which often relied on the fiction of the wilderness as a central and ever-present alternative state of possibility. The existence of the wilderness, especially in historical novels, allowed characters in these novels to step out of prevailing legal orders adopted from Europe and to interrogate them. It was thus possible to dramatize alternative forms of legal conduct and organization in the historical novel while still following the European model closely.

In the early nineteenth century's cultural negotiation of what the United States as a nation-state should stand for, the structural link between American literary discourse and hostis humani generis is often surprisingly explicit. This is not only the case with writers such as Charles Ellms, who openly uses the legal fiction's recent expansion to encompass the slave trade in an attempt to suggest the rise of inherently legitimate American civilization in the wake of the decline of European empires. Even in many historical novels set in explicitly land-based contexts, the maritime pirate makes a guest appearance that gestures toward the constellation (see, for example, Cooper, *Deerslayer*, 2:205; Hawthorne, *Scarlet Letter*, 198–99 and 208–9; see also Marr, *American Islamicism*, 231–33).

Indeed, the two wars between the United States and the Barbary States (1801–5 and 1815) made the dialogue between the US interrogations of the wilderness and the British Barbary captivity narrative particularly explicit. However, the early nineteenth century was also when the difference between piracy and hostis humani generis became a relevant one in legal discourse (due to the expansion of the fiction's use to deep-sea slave trading). In this context, the explicit basis of hostis humani generis on the writing of Locke permitted it to be used to address other spaces than maritime ones. The historical novel serves as a particularly interesting example of the results of such spatial transfer on the basis of a state of nature argument.

In accord both with Blackstone's definition of hostis humani generis and the Barbary captivity narrative, the protagonist in these historical novels tends to be an untainted representative of civilization who resorts to violence only as a means of self-defense. The male American protagonist's often considerable use of violence is meticulously legitimated in this peace-loving and peace-defending fashion. Indeed, the protagonist of the historical novel is decidedly more active than the original Barbary captive is. His resourcefulness is not used to allow him to escape from a hostile realm that cannot be usurped but instead to tame the wilderness into submission. His treatment of the space and the enemies of all humankind that he encounters is truly more sovereign that that of the Barbary captive. The predicament of captivity was instead negotiated by genres such as the American captivity narrative featuring a female protagonist and the slave narrative.

In the American wilderness of the historical novel, there is still a pirata who serves as the protagonist's evil twin—perhaps even his nemesis—and who succumbs to the temptations of the wilderness. This pirata is often cruel, lecherous, and generally defiant of all boundaries; the protagonist, in contrast, is defined by civilizing boundaries that are set by the law of nature cited by Locke and Vattel, for instance. As the anxieties evoked by the spatial setting of the wilderness indicate, the pirata chooses the easier and more pragmatic way to respond to the wilderness, while the protagonist chooses a harder, often quixotic, way that nevertheless anticipates the rise of an order that constitutes the American reader's present. As in Ellms's construction of Lafitte, the historical novels of his contemporary James Fenimore Cooper suggest that the pirata is a relic of Europe, whereas the real protagonist of the novel is a model American. The retrospective construction of a protagonist reminiscent of Captain Beer, who hails the specifically American present, is an example of the United States' claim of inherent legitimacy.

In the first half of the nineteenth century, the American historical novel was a particularly suitable genre for dramatizing the assumption of the wilderness as a spatialized state of nature. The novel combined the three dominant interpretations associated with the state of nature as the origin and mirror image of civilization. As Daniel Eggers has suggested, the state of nature as a concept has always been seen in a "historical," a "legal," or an "anthropological" light (*Naturzustandstheorie*, 30; my translation), meaning that interpreters of the concept tend to understand it as a recounting of an actual precivilizational past, a fiction that helps clarify the fundamental nature and function of the law by contrasting it to a hypothetical state of the absence of law, or a statement on the universal (often predatory) nature lurking in the depth of any human heart.

Literature has always claimed to show in its characters, as well as to inspire in its readers, universally human feelings and reactions. What Eggers somewhat awkwardly terms the "anthropological" view of the state of nature is, in a way, the idea of a universal human nature that is also cited in the contemporary abolitionist arguments on behalf of slaves' equal dignity. The representation of a universal human nature is the project of the novel in particular, which exhibits a "totalizing" tendency that often amounts to a complex yet coherent "model of the world" (Engel, "Roman," 1670). In the specific case of the nineteenth-century American historical novel, the two other views of the state of nature are also clearly presented. Not only did the historical novel explicitly discuss the past, but its specific construction of the past also inherently presupposed the existence of a state of nature.

Winfried Fluck has explained that the narrative pattern established by Sir Walter Scott, which underlies the genre of the American historical novel, was generally based on the state of nature fiction: "In drawing on theories of the Scottish Enlightenment, a philosophy that conceived of history in terms of a sequence of states from savagery, barbarism, and a pastoral, agricultural state to modern commercial society, the central drama Scott saw at work in history was the conflict between different stages of social development" ("Historical Novel," 121). The American historical novel thus relied on the fundamental structural dichotomy of civilization and its Other and—within the limits of possible meaning production that these models allowed—dramatized possibilities of contact and negotiation. Regarding the particularly American contribution to the genre, Fluck sees the most important "modification of Scott's narrative pattern" in the inherent racial separateness that is maintained in the American case: "the culture conflict formula does not end in reconciliation or integration but remains forever arrested in violent conflict and struggles of survival" (ibid., 127). In other words, the American historical novel was especially rigid in its assumption of an essentialist construction of civilization—particularly of the American past.

The legal dimension, too, is a classic element of the novel as a genre. Fluck argues that the novel as a genre is capable of fundamentally interrogating institutional interpretations of justice. According to him, the novel can complement the law in offering an alternative mode of conceptualizing the relationship between individual and society. In their respective narratives of individual fate, both the law and the novel tend to formulate general concerns about social and political organization and power structures in their representation of an otherwise irreducibly specific situation. In its aesthetic and narrative treatment of conflict, the novel "is the placeholder of a sense of justice that cannot be guaranteed or enforced by the law" (Fluck, "Fiction," 35) and the site for alternative formulations of concerns that are discussed by the law. Indeed, a case can be made that the American historical novel, with its predominantly male cast and its decidedly essentialist outlook, was particularly likely to claim that the worlds it created presented a sustainable alternative to systems of European imperial justice.

To substantiate and illustrate these claims, I will now discuss in detail James Fenimore Cooper's novel *The Deerslayer* (hereafter abbreviated as DS in the citations) as an example of the American historical novel's use of the hostis humani generis constellation. My analysis will focus on two points. First, I show the existence and function of the hostis humani generis constellation of representative of civilization, praedo, and pirata in the novel's plot. Second, I discuss the conceptualization of space that is indicated by this deeply racialized constellation. After all, as I argued in the case of American precolonial space, the hostis humani generis constellation establishes a characterization of space that produces enemies of all humankind. This presence of praedones and piratae, then, requires the taming of this space by the representative of civilization in Blackstone and in Cooper. Cooper, however, adds some interesting elements to this process of taming that I focus on.

The Deerslayer is the concluding novel of Cooper's *Leatherstocking Tales*, five novels that focus on the character of Natty Bumppo as the archetype of the American frontiersman. The series is viewed as consisting of foundational works of the Western genre (B. Brown, "Reading the West," 33). Furthermore, the series, and this novel in particular, are also frequently cited as key texts that represent "the American myth" (R. Lewis, *American Adam*, 103) or as texts that formulate "a metaphor and theory of nationhood" (LeMenager, "Frontier," 533). In *The Deerslayer*, Bumppo is portrayed at his youngest in the entire series: he encounters love and war for the first time and successfully defies the temptations of both lust and cruelty. Quite in line with the Barbary captivity narratives, *The Deerslayer* does not tell a story of heroic transformation but one of heroic purification. The opinions that Bumppo expresses in the beginning of the novel, but cautiously qualifies because of his lack of experience, are all proven to be authentic expressions of his true nature and affirmed as virtuous positions (see, for example, 2:500–501 and 595–602). In contrast, figures that have indeed undergone a transformation—especially Tom and Judith Hutter, a former pirate and his sexually adventurous daughter—are killed cruelly or disappear, facing a dismal future.

The novel takes place in the region surrounding a lake called Glimmerglass. The territory is claimed by—yet is allowed to remain beyond the control of—

both the Native Americans who use it as a meeting place and the king of England who claims possession but does not enforce these claims (DS 515). Instead, Glimmerglass is permanently inhabited by Tom Hutter (also known as Floating Tom), who has lived there for fifteen years with his two daughters, Judith and Hetty; his wife has recently died. Judith is beautiful and intelligent but also reckless and vain; Hetty's "wits are . . . small" (DS 516), but she is of incorruptible—even otherworldly—virtue. Bumppo (also known as Deerslayer) arrives at Glimmerglass in the company of Henry March (also known as Hurry Harry), a cruel, reckless, and handsome frontiersman who is in love with Judith and wants to visit her. Bumppo, in contrast, plans to meet his Delaware friend Chingachgook at the lake; the two are in pursuit of a party of Huron warriors who have abducted Wah-ta-Wah, Chingachgook's betrothed. When the Huron also appear at the lake, Bumppo and Chingachgook join forces with the whites in the area and experience war for the first time. The protagonists spend most of their time on the water, in Tom Hutter's "castle," and on his "ark" (DS 514–15). The Huron antagonists dominate the woods until they are massacred by a British regiment, an intervention that somewhat abruptly concludes the novel. The nonwhite antagonists in the novel are the bloodthirsty Huron (also called Mingos and Iroquois), while the supposedly good side features four men who are divided into two pairs: the virtuous Bumppo and Chingachgook and the villainous frontiersmen March and Hutter.

The Deerslayer is a particularly straightforward example of a work containing the twin structures that help negotiate discourses of essentialist civilization in the historical novel. Several characters have more than one explicit partner, whether in terms of an allegorical construction of character (for example, Bumppo and Hetty are detached and virtuous, and March and Hutter are incorrigible villains), a parallel social situation (for example, Judith and her mother, who are both fallen women; and Judith and the Huron woman Sumach, who hope to marry Bumppo but are presented as not worthy of him), or the dynamics of the narrative (such as the parallel friendships of Bumppo and Chingachgook and of Hetty and Wah-ta-Wah, or the rivalries between authenticity and glamour represented by Bumppo and March and by Hetty and Judith, respectively). These partnerships are particularly important in the case of Bumppo and March. They enter the novel as twin protagonists, a strategy that is typical of the *Leatherstocking* series (Smith, *Virgin Land*, 69). Bumppo and March are presented as fellow privateers in the sense of having been commissioned to do the work of the empire outside of the empire's reach. They represent different approaches to this inherently ambiguous form of warfare (DS, 2:526 and 551). Within the gray zone of representative warfare in an in-between zone, Bumppo represents faith in the spirit of the law (the superiority of whiteness over redness, to use the terminology of the novel), whereas March is barely faithful to the letter of the law in his indiscriminate destruction and/or exploitation of everything in the wilderness in exchange for monetary rewards.

Bumppo's and March's respective characterizations in terms of race are related to discourses surrounding European privateers in the Mediterranean. Barbary renegades had been charged with acting against their own nature because they sought a life among people who did not belong to their true faith and race. In a civilization structured by race, Bumppo, like a faithful and steadfast privateer, acts outside of the realm of civilization and is quite evidently alienated from it, yet he never forgets what his natural duty is—namely, to represent white civilization and to fight for it whenever necessary (DS, 2:551). March, too, nominally serves the British king in the wilderness, yet March's conscious decision to go against his better nature for financial benefit is carefully portrayed. He knowingly teams up with Floating Tom Hutter, a pirate who represents the limits of legitimate violence in the in-between zone, and he repeatedly battles an inner voice attributed to his human nature that "accused him of sundry lawless acts against the Indians," which he reacts to by even greater ferociousness against Native Americans (DS, 2:538 and 802). March's characterization in particular clearly evokes the traditional characterization of Barbary renegades.

Both Bumppo and March are tested but remain true to their original positions throughout the novel, positions that lead to heroism in Bumppo's case and to shattered dreams in the case of March. We might assume that this particular twin construction, which so explicitly evokes a maritime context, already indicates the use of hostis humani generis constellation as the plot's structural framework. In the remainder of this chapter, I will test this assumption by analyzing the plot's structure.

The plot is subdivided into a war plot and a love plot, as war and love are the areas in which Bumppo is tested and proves his virtue. The war plot dominates and is also more central to this book's focus. The love plot essentially comes to nothing. It is structured by the different ways in which the sisters Judith and Hetty deal with their unrequited love for Bumppo and March, respectively. Judith passionately attempts to win Bumppo's favor and even proposes to him (DS, 2:901–3), while Hetty virtuously keeps her benevolent love for March a secret, even on her deathbed (DS, 2:1016). The only couple that comes together in the end is the couple that was engaged even before the beginning of the novel. I will thus treat the love plot as an element of the war plot in my analysis, because the love plot only supports the elements and priorities of the war plot without bringing about the typical transformations of a protagonist's status through marriage.

The most important element used to divide the belligerent men in the novel is race, as it is understood by the essentialist model of civilization. Within the novel, race is negotiated via the presupposed notion of "red gifts" and "white gifts," (DS, 2:599–600) meaning those races' respective natural properties. In my analysis of the novel, I will use the terms "red" and "white" without further marking them as borrowed from the novel's own language; they should be understood in this vein, however, and my use of these terms as analytical ones is restricted to the analysis of this novel.

In *The Deerslayer*, the main difference between good and evil characters is that the virtuous pair, Bumppo and Chingachgook, are aware of their respective "gifts" and act according to them, while the villainous pair, March and Hutter (as well as the Huron), do not. This difference becomes most obvious in the context of violence. Generally, red and white forms of violence, as well as other racially marked behaviors, are only neatly and consistently distributed along color lines in the pair of Bumppo and Chingachgook. The white villains and the Huron are not identified as allies in the plot—they remain mortal enemies throughout the novel—but they are united by their primary reliance on red gifts, their mutual disregard for white gifts' superiority, and their constant attempts to subvert the racialized divide. In other words, a harmonious separation of races (represented by the friendship between Bumppo and Chingachgook) is contrasted with forms of invasion and violence that blur the lines of racial difference. The white villains' dangerous abandonment of civilization is not so much a matter of political treason and transgression, as was the case in the Mediterranean context, but a matter of adopting customs that may establish traditions inherently alien to civilization. The adoption of red violence, Cooper suggests, opens up the way to degeneration and confusion rather than to the purer civilization represented by Bumppo, who insists on white forms of violence—even against the orders of the English king.

White violence, as it is represented in the novel, corresponds directly with traditional definitions of legitimate violence: it is always born of necessity and ends with fulfilling the necessity. This approach is manifested by the encounter with the first man Bumppo ever kills. Bumppo refrains from shooting his Huron opponent in the back but encounters him instead in an open duel over the possession of a strategically important canoe. Afterward, and despite his opponent's repeated exhibitions of deceit, boastful sarcasm, and cruelty, Bumppo refuses to scalp him to receive a bounty. Instead, he brings his dying enemy water and allows him to die peacefully (DS, 2:595–602). "[Bumppo's] innocent vanity on the subject of colour" dictates a disinterested, chivalrous, and modest form of violence that achieves no more than the removal of hunger when directed against animals and the removal of danger when directed against humans (DS, 2:600). It is a kind of violence that explicitly negates a craving for power (DS, 2:929), even though it always insists on its own "natural" superiority (DS, 2:623 and 986). To some extent, this approach to violence is duplicated by the British regiment nearby—which, although a problematic entity in *The Deerslayer*'s love plot, is likewise a fortress of white masculinity that does not conquer but pacify, and that stoutly serves as a generally just and benevolent outpost of civilization in the wilderness (DS, 2:1011). Even when the white regiment defeats the Huron at Glimmerglass, they do not take up command there but leave the place as they found it after they have restored peace (DS, 2:1030).

In contrast, red violence in *The Deerslayer* is characterized by vengeful blood lust, merciless cruelty, and bravado. These elements are derived from a general craving for honor (DS, 2:654), which is perverted by the Huron into a craving for expansion and domination. Significantly, the "good" Native Americans in the novel are deprived of meaningful military force. The Mohicans have already "been broken up by the increase of our own [white] colour" Bumppo explains at one point (DS, 2:612), while the Delaware, who have assumed the role of a home tribe for Bumppo and Chingachgook, are ridiculed as a toothless tribe throughout the novel (DS, 2:500, 867, and 934). The Huron, in contrast, are determined to increase rather than to vanish. They invade Glimmerglass and thus act with a kind of entitlement that is deemed unsuitable to them (DS, 2:880); they also maintain the "unnatural" custom of integrating whites into their communities (DS, 2:969). Huron torture includes a significant portion of psychological warfare that serves to demonstrate the tribe's excessive cruelty and lust for power even by red standards (DS, 2:917 and 974). Moreover, the Huron party encountered in the novel is a representative segment of a ferocious people that constitutes a threat even after the conclusion of the novel,[1] even though they no longer attempt to conquer Glimmerglass (DS, 2:1021). The structural link of the Huron to the notion of praedones can be made in several ways.

First, the two Huron chiefs, Rivenoak and Panther, represent the classic elements of Other rulers who are able to destroy as well as to corrupt. While Panther embodies ferocious, vengeful, and cruel violence, Rivenoak uses his eloquent cunning to corrupt whites into red behavior and company (DS, 2:954–56). The two chiefs together assume a position specifically characteristic of praedones. They represent an illegitimate public interest by representing not only the larger Huron tribe but also red culture generally, which is indicated by the fact that their party consists of cruel warriors and loveless families.

The notion of oppressive Native American families is considered self-evident in the novel. As a case in point, Bumppo and Hetty both urge Chingachgook not to be cruel to Wah-ta-Wah, even though his "red gifts" would normally lead him to abuse her (DS, 2:935–36 and 1015). Such assumptions reflected prevailing US attitudes toward Native Americans (Pearce, *Savagism,* 84). In the novel, the significance of these appeals to Chingachgook is heightened by the narrative context of being both figures' deathbed wishes. Bumppo is captured by the Huron and is temporarily released to settle his affairs among his friends and allies before returning to be tortured. His visit to the ark at this point functions like a deathbed scene. Hetty, in turn, is shot during the regiment's victory over the Huron and is the center of an actual deathbed scene. Because of the context of such scenes, Bumppo's and Hetty's shared concerns about Chingachgook's treatment of Wah-ta-Wah are particularly serious appeals. This general assumption about Native American families in the novel is important to note because the loveless warrior family constitutes an important marker of inherently illegitimate community and legacy. This notion also becomes important in terms of March's failed plan to marry Judith, but it is most glaringly represented by the Huron men in the novel, who bring women and children as part of their war party and use marital politics as an element of expansionist warfare.

Second, the Hurons' general movement in space also supports the notion of praedones. The narrator relates that Hutter has built a solid castle whose architecture becomes continuously more sophisticated (DS, 2:517–19), while the Huron content themselves with shifting camps. All actively belligerent characters constantly move around in the novel, white quasi privateers as well as nonwhite quasi corsairs; the important difference is that for the Huron, perpetual movement is considered integral to their red nature. Being nomads as well as predators, they clearly constitute the warfaring representatives of illegitimate sovereignty in the state of nature.

Third, the characterization of the Huron as praedones is made explicit by the inclusion of a classic renegade scenario that is nonsensical except as a gesture toward this larger discursive context. Near the end of the novel, there is a brief and somewhat artificially inserted scene that directly echoes the Mediterranean constellation in the form of an adopted Delaware who has turned Huron and is exposed as a traitor by Wah-ta-Wah, another Delaware. The episode might make sense as the answer to the question of how Wah-ta-Wah could be captured by the Huron in the first place; however, the reader is entirely unprepared for the scene, the question of the logistics of Wah-ta-Wah's abduction is never raised anywhere else, and the scene is useless for the further development of the plot since directly after it virtually all of the Huron, including the renegade, are killed (DS, 2:1000–1003). However, this direct intertextual reference to the Barbary captivity narrative helps underline the Huron's role as praedones within the novel.

As is to be expected, the hostis humani generis constellation in the novel is most explicit in the characterization of the piratae. Indeed, the imposing illegitimate entitlement of Huron praedones is recognizable as part of this specific constellation only by Cooper's purposeful construction of the two white villains' greedy and selfish cruelty. Hutter is an actual retired pirate (DS, 2:502), while March is a "rover" whose principal characteristic is restlessness (DS, 2:549). Though not always allies, they are constructed as a single entity in the novel. "Old Tom and I," March retrospectively summarizes, "fitted each other as remarkably as a buckskin garment will fit any reasonable-built man" (DS, 2:883–84).

The two villains are unmistakably white, and in fact much more openly racist than Bumppo. March, like Hutter, considers Native Americans "a sort of natural competitor, and not unfrequently [*sic*] as a natural enemy" (DS, 2:527); he believes them to be savages who are "only a slight degree removed from the wild beasts that [roam] the woods" (DS, 2:802–3). Because he puts "the whole family of red men, incontinently, without the category of human rights" (DS, 2:538), he is capable of acts of "unthinking cruelty" against them (DS, 2:802). I emphasize these characters' pronounced insistence on their own whiteness to determine more clearly the locus of their racialized transgression. Indeed, they are solely criticized as being nonwhite in terms of cruelty in war and lovelessness in family matters—the same two notions that generally help characterize Native Americans as red in the novel (notably including Chingachgook and Wah-ta-Wah).

Hutter's and March's deviance can be traced quite neatly along the lines of war and love, which are the main sites of the figures' character testing in the novel. In terms of war, both Hutter's and March's principal "cravings" are greed and revenge (DS, 2:703, see also 734, 742, and 784). Their vicious cruelty toward their enemies is constantly emphasized. In addition, they never seek open battle with a worthy opponent but always engineer sneak attacks against the weakest possible victim. The cruelty and cunning apparent in these designs link them to the notion of red violence embodied by the Huron chiefs Rivenoak and Panther.

Likewise, March's and Hutter's notions of family are an imitation of Native Americans' allegedly loveless and cruel dynasties that include adoption as a central feature (DS, 2:894). Hutter has been an unloved, tyrannical, and constantly drunken husband, and he is now an unloved father whose principal merit is protecting his adopted family from a fate even worse than living with him (DS, 2:835 and 895). March exhibits an obvious potential for duplicating Hutter's domestic tyranny and violence (DS, 2:573). Correspondingly, unlike the markedly white-natured Bumppo, who shuns Judith for not having been chaste in the past, March shows as little regard for his desired wife's past as Hutter had shown in the case of his wife (DS, 2:504–5 and 894)—or, for that matter, as the Hurons would show (DS, 2:969). Even the mixture of family and war, which is indicated by the women and children who accompany the Huron men on the warpath, is reproduced by both villainous figures. While Hutter uses his daughters to rally support in the conflict with the Huron (DS, 2:560), March conditions his help on Judith's willingness to consider his proposal (DS, 2:801).

In the end, both Hutter's and March's attempts to solidify their adopted red lifestyle in the manner of dynastic reproduction are prevented by Judith. When Hutter confesses that he is not, in fact, the biological father of his two daughters (DS, 2:837), Judith receives his confession with joyous relief and bans Hutter from the family memory as completely as she has rejected March's marriage proposal earlier in the novel (DS, 2:851–52 and 1020). Had Judith remained Hutter's daughter and become March's wife, the white dynasty of Glimmerglass would constitute a perfect analogy of what Cooper presents to the reader as a prototypical red warrior family: Glimmerglass would, in a sense, become a pirate kingdom.

If Bumppo is a creature between worlds because he refrains from any human contact that exceeds the realms of "friendship and sarvices" (DS, 2:746), Hutter and March are creatures between worlds in the sense that they are white and act red. Hutter's "nature [is] of that fearful mixture of good and evil" that directly results from a long exposure to the wilderness (DS, 2:568); he is quite explicitly "neither white, nor red" (DS, 2:775). March is described as a "creature equally of civilization and of barbarism" and even as a "handsome barbarian" (DS, 2:802–3). Their joint attempts to take women's and children's scalps for bounty—along with the notions of cruelty, treachery, greed, and lust for revenge implied by their designs—are often and explicitly problematized as imitations of a red nature that is not theirs, and that constitute sinful offenses against their own white nature (DS, 2:528, 550, 563, 566, 602, and 734). It should be added that in this kind of transgression, they are duplicated by "the French," who are repeatedly called savages and are mentioned as equivalent to Native Americans in the context of their intra-European war with Great Britain (DS, 2:522 and 526).

It has become evident from these examples that the hostis humani generis constellation indeed appears in the historical novel to interrogate and substantiate the antagonisms presupposed in the essentialist model of civilization. Based on the essentialist divide of red versus white, and the possibility of whites who act red, piratae and praedones in *The Deerslayer* serve to represent a double threat to civilization (a civilization that is, in this case, epitomized by a specifically white law of nature). Because of the novel's obvious focus on race, praedones and piratae no longer need to operate in military alliance to achieve complementarity. While red families and red violence generally threaten white racial purity as well as white claims to land, the second threat is posed by a corruptible whiteness that embraces shunned behaviors identified as red in the novel. The characters who adopt such behaviors are irrevocably isolated from (white) civilization, but they still remain white. They thus represent the threatening possibility that whiteness may not in fact be equivalent to virtue. Both of these complementary threats are rendered moot by the end of the novel. The Huron are massacred; Hutter dies, unmourned by his surviving family; March, humiliated, has been shown to be an inferior coward and drifts out of the narrative; and Judith—who, after all, has hindered the establishment of a corrupted pirate kingdom at Glimmerglass—is presented as the ghost of a ruin on the last pages of the novel (DS, 2:1029).

To make this discussion of the novel useful for the argument in the following parts of this book concerned with the rewriting of civilization in the late nineteenth century, let us return to the notion of space and the state of nature and, in this context, to Cooper's characterization of Hutter. Even though Vattel had considered the notion of space only as a way to legitimate the British imperial project, his land-use argument had some important implications that the novel's characterization of Hutter helps explore. The primacy of superior land use theoretically subjects the white settler, as well as the Native Americans, to the threat of replacement by even more advanced followers. This is an especially interesting point in the case of settlers like Hutter, who are not portrayed as representatives of civilization. Instead, his piratical presence, along with the Native American custom of using Glimmerglass as a general meeting point (DS, 2:516), define Glimmerglass as the spatialized site of a state of nature. As a pirata, Hutter operates for private—that is, individual—ends; this is where his claim to Glimmerglass begins and ends. In his actions, he is not representative of whiteness or civilization, yet the fact that he is a white man who establishes infrastructure in the wilderness places him under the umbrella of industrious whiteness and sets in motion the civilizing process discussed by Vattel.

When characters such as Hutter are eventually replaced by others more civilized than themselves, however, the usefulness of their industrious selfishness is exhausted. Instead of them, the space they have begun to cultivate is recruited for the project of white advancement in the wilderness. In Cooper, this process of absorbing space rather than figures into the civilizing project is achieved through the characterization of the twin protagonists, Bumppo and March, who represent two different possible futures for Glimmerglass as a space. While March threatens to continue Hutter's piratical use in defiance of white civilization, Bumppo saves Glimmerglass from this fate by planting a desire for virtue in Judith and thus hands the space over to its later, civilized use in the nineteenth-century reader's present.

When reading the white villains encountered in *The Deerslayer* against the backdrop of Hobbes's state of nature in particular, it becomes apparent that these villains do not actually represent life in a state of nature. They certainly are engaged in extralegal existential antagonisms, and they do exhibit the human properties that make a state of nature possible (the desire for glory, the desire to compete, and the tendency to compare themselves to others—especially, March with Bumppo). But when seen as a collective (both as a pair and within the white, or good, group at large), they represent something far more interesting—namely, the final stage of the state of nature. Hobbes imagines the transitional entity of the defensive alliance as a form of community within the state of nature that foreshadows and leads up to the establishment of legitimate sovereign rule. As this alliance is directly formed against the backdrop of the state of nature, it encounters situation-specific problems that are all evident in The *Deerslayer*'s plot:

> And supposing how great a number soever of men assembled together for their mutual defence, yet shall not the effect follow, unless they all direct their actions to one and the same end; which direction to one and the end is that which . . . is called consent. This consent (or concord) amongst so many men, though it may be made by the fear of a present invader, or by the hope of a present conquest, or booty; and endure as long as that action endureth; nevertheless, by the diversity of judgments and passions in so many men contending naturally for honour and advantage one above another: it is impossible, not only that their consent to aid each other against an enemy, but also that peace should last between themselves, without some mutual and common fear to rule them. (Hobbes, *Elements of Law*, 101–2)

The characterization of defensive alliances in Hobbes is extremely reminiscent of the construction of the colonial pirata in British imperial discourse, and it corresponds more generally with Enlightenment readings of premodern pirates as historical presocieties, on the verge of leaving the state of nature before entering the stage of late Greek and Roman civilization (see Montesquieu, *Spirit of Laws*, 362–64). In *The Deerslayer*, the notion of defensive alliances is directly associated with the figures of Hutter and March, who repeatedly move in and out of the larger group of whites. These figures' motivations are a mixture of all three possible ones given by Hobbes: "the fear of a present invader, or . . . the hope of a present conquest, or booty." The Huron are a superior enemy that has invaded Glimmerglass; because the plot is contextualized by the French and Indian War, Hutter's and March's attacks on the Huron are instances of imperial conquest; and the promise of booty in the form of scalps is a prominently discussed motivation of their adventures.

At this point it is interesting to compare the position of the white villains in the state of nature to that of Bumppo in the state of nature. Bumppo represents a different form of final stage: that of bourgeois civilization turning into a civilization based on Rousseau's state of nature rather than that of Hobbes. Rousseau's man in the state of nature is extremely different from Hobbes's man in that state. While Hobbes basically imagines the state of nature to host modern man in unmediated circumstances, Rousseau imagines man in the state of nature as a decidedly prehistoric being; he even speculates on the possibility of imagining primitive men as apes (*Inequality*, 222). Bumppo corresponds to another philosophical figure introduced by Rousseau: the man who turns his back on the present and allows his soul to unite with a universal and sublime sense of justice in nature. Rousseau argues that in civil society, the impulses of man are contradictory—the primitive man wants what is best for himself, while the citizen wants what is best for his community. Because civilized man is hopelessly torn between these two fundamental impulses, he is neither truly a man in the state of nature nor a citizen, which is why the existing order is also torn and must always fall short of true justice. Complete alienation from human society, then, can paradoxically achieve the restoration of unity in man: a harmonious order can be established. In this third stage after both the state of nature and existing order, man "is not *whole* as he was in the state of nature, but neither is he divided and disunified as he was in previous civil society" (Campbell, *Rousseau*, 61).

Bumppo's main characteristic is virtue, a property Rousseau explicitly excludes from the state of nature as too directly tied to civil society. At the same time, it is precisely the notion of virtue and perfectibility that can bloom only when man turns his back on civil society and allows his soul to be educated by nature (see Cassirer, "Rousseau," 70–72; Plattner, *State of Nature*, 78–79). Bumppo himself emphasizes the notion of the soul's divine education in nature, and he does so in a context that highlights the paradoxical nature of the American wilderness as the proper site for unfeeling Hobbesian defensive alliances and for Rousseauian divine education both (DS, 2:514). The representation of space in *The Deerslayer* thus creates a kind of time loop in terms of civilizational stages represented by white characters. The American wilderness features both a whiteness that is just in the process of rising from the state of nature, and a whiteness that has already transcended the state of order and returns to the wilderness as a site of divine education and potentially utopian society. It is the interaction between these two stages that makes the existence of an inherently legitimate nation in American space conceivable. In this sense, Rousseau's reachable utopian final stage replaces the unreachable Augustinian divine kingdom and thus helps substantiate the notion of achieved civilization in the present of the nineteenth-century reader.

Judith Stinson May has commented that Cooper's novel frequently "unifies the past and the present in a striking manner" (*Family and Aggression*, 381). After invoking a history of evil and crime that has long been forgotten, Cooper devotes the last words of the novel to a present "world of transgressions and selfishness" within which "gleamings of the pure spirit in which likeness man has been fashioned, are to be seen" (DS, 2:1030). The present, while still influenced by characters like March, Hutter, and Judith, can envision a future that is foreshadowed—indeed, guided into existence—by Bumppo. Had Bumppo not changed Judith into a person who would prefer personal and spiritual ruin over marriage to March, Glimmerglass might have remained pirate territory. But since Judith sacrificed herself to bring an end to the piratical dynasty, the territory could become the civilized national space familiar to the nineteenth-century reader.

These treatments of characters in terms of temporality are, of course, central to their relationship to space. The future-embodying Bumppo remains fleeting in his spatial manifestation of presence; indeed, he takes pride in leaving spaces in a way that does not testify to his former presence. The villains—in particular, Hutter—are different from Bumppo in this respect. Because Cooper generally allows his characters to transform themselves only once, Hutter can be treated as an epitome of piracy regardless of his present situation, just as Judith serves as the epitome of fallen femininity regardless of her behavior over the course of the plot. Hutter is a man who has already fallen and is already a firm part of the continent's criminal past in Charles Ellms's sense. At the same time, the characterization of Hutter directly evokes the discursive history of white colonial piracy as free princes and potential sovereigns (Pringle, *Jolly Roger*, 202). The lake Hutter has chosen as a home is firmly located in a no man's land, and even Bumppo acknowledges that Hutter alone enjoys sovereign rights there (DS, 2:501 and 550).

Hutter is largely indistinguishable from the infrastructure he has built. The ark hints at his piratical past and suggests that it still shapes his present conduct; the castle is named Muskrat Castle after his nickname among Native Americans (DS, 2:517). Cooper's characterization of this infrastructure borrows from the gothic register to emphasize its inherent pastness. While Hutter's daughters each have a specific place in the castle (their respective sides of a shared bed), the entire castle as a space is associated with Hutter. Not only has he obsessively planned and overseen every aspect of its architecture, but he has also stored his pirate chest in its taboo-ridden heart and center—a symbolic charging of the house that is typical not only of the gothic but of the romantic tradition at large. The gothic register becomes especially apparent in the final chapter of the novel. Here, a long description of "a picturesque ruin" (DS, 2:1028) along with forgotten evil, lost graves, and decaying structures is melancholically visited by its history's sole survivors. This end of Muskrat Castle and its inhabitants directly reproduces the fate of the majority of villains and their castles in the gothic tradition of Cooper's day (Fisher, "Poe," 75).

Glimmerglass remains deserted after the complete removal of the Hutter family: "it was probable the lake had not been visited, since the occurrence of the final scene of our tale" (DS, 2:1029). The reader understands that the regiment's interference has permanently ended all Native American use of the lake region, and the ruins of the last stages of a white state of nature are narratively removed into the pastness of "a century" (DS, 2:1030)—which once again uses the reader's present as a reference point to evoke the space's history after the conclusion of the novel. The state of nature is transferred to the past precisely by the removal of both piratae and praedones. The empty space, in contrast, remains a potentially civilized space.

In her discussion of the American frontier as a cultural construction, Stephanie LeMenager has argued that "in its fantasies of the settler becoming 'native' without reproductive sex or the crossing of blood, the Leatherstocking series betrays the deep wishes and fears of a settler culture faced with unthinkable facts, such as its own violence. The desire to think outside of history is most fully satisfied by Cooper in the exceptional figure of the scout Leatherstocking [Bumppo]" ("Frontier," 520). While I largely agree with LeMenager's reading of Bumppo, it is worth pointing out that the ahistorical and timeless protagonist evoked by her is necessarily complemented by the gothic representation of white villains that draw on European literary formulas of the completed past. The castle in the European gothic narrative tends to refer to the assumed monstrousness of the Middle Ages, which was eventually replaced by Enlightenment humanism, and at the same time to evoke the fear that gothic human relationships may not be so easy to shed (Lacôte, "Gothic Architecture," 201–2). Cooper's white villains, who represent a stage in-between the state of nature and achieved civilization, take up a similar temporal position of completed yet still consequential historical pastness.

To construct the history of the American nation, the importance of maintaining the purity of racial whiteness, even in the wilderness, is complemented by the white villains' establishment of an infrastructure that changes the wilderness even before civilization arrives. The emptiness of Glimmerglass at the end of the novel emphasizes the specific importance of piratical infrastructure in this sense. While red history remains invisible in space, and European white history withdraws along with the intervening British regiment, the ruins of villainous infrastructure serve as evidence of a nonmilitary, nonimperial white history in the wilderness, and thus of the legitimate civilized ownership heralded by Bumppo.[2] The ideas that the future of the territory is reserved for whites (of the United States) and that the infrastructure built by exiled villains is key to their claim are most forcefully spelled out in a passage attributed to Hetty, the female equivalent of Bumppo. She is the most inconsistently written character of the novel, alternating between being an epitome of white, female virtue and being a comic sidekick whose good intentions constantly cause her to jeopardize her companions' plans. The following passage is perhaps the clearest example of her function as an epitome of white virtue in the novel:

> "The Hurons can't understand the difference between white people and themselves," she said, "or they would n't ask Judith and me to go and live in their villages. God has given one country to the red men and another to us. He meant us to live apart. Then mother always said that we should never dwell with any but christians [*sic*], if possible, and *that* is a reason why we can't go. This lake is ours, and we wo'n't leave it. Father [*sic*] and Mother's graves are in it, and even the worst Indians love to stay near the graves of their fathers. I will come and see them, again, if they wish me so, and read more of the bible [*sic*] to them, but I can't quit father's and mother's graves." (DS, 2:880)

In this passage, the implications of a white history of crime that is represented by piratae become clear. The parents Hetty refers to are a pirate and a fallen woman—two characters who have irrevocably transgressed the norms of civilization. Nevertheless, they remain both Christians and white. Despite their crimes, they are a spearhead of civilization, as well as the beginning of a legitimate dynasty of whites with a right to a space. Even in a context that evokes family dynasties rather than race dynasties, the race context is used to legitimate Hetty's claim to possessing Glimmerglass. Whites just like "Indians love to stay near the graves of their fathers"; because Hetty's father's grave is here, it follows that Glimmerglass is legitimately part of the white country that Native Americans may not frequent. The knowledge of her parents' invisible graves in the lake functions in the same way that the starkly visible ruins of Muskrat Castle do. Villainous infrastructure—rather than the villain himself—constitutes the spark of civilization that sets the civilizing process in motion, in this case resulting in the US nation of the nineteenth-century reader.

Because the villains' achievement of transforming space is as important a legacy as the hero's demonstration of white superiority, the representative of civilization and the pirata can serve as complementary figures in an overarching effort to civilize the wilderness. They can even, to some extent, gesture toward the two different models of civilization that had long ceased to be mutually exclusive by the time of Cooper's writing. The progressivist approach had firmly incorporated the essentialist's basic premise of white superiority over red and translated this into the construction of a good red way and a good white way. As Cooper's novels demonstrate, the white way is always inherently better than the red way, but each includes a separate range of conceivable behaviors, and therefore a separate horizon of possible individual betterment. At the same time, what few unique qualities remained of the essentialist approach—such as its decided emphasis on violent antagonism between races—could be criticized as excessive and inhumane and be attributed to villains.

Still, the harmonization of the two civilizational approaches is by no means complete in Cooper. The twin protagonists of Bumppo and March only grudgingly cooperate and do not exhibit any respect for each other. They tend to accuse each other of irresponsible unmanliness and never make peace with each other; they eventually part coldly, each maintaining his original position. While both contribute to the rise of the civilized present, they do so while opposed to each other, and therefore they do not help construct a unified origin of the nation as it presents itself in the early nineteenth century: white, industrious, just in its institutions, and removed from the illegitimate violence of Native Americans and European empires alike.

In the course of the nineteenth century, the increasing proximity of the two models of civilization would culminate in the creation of a third, specifically American, model. This would take up the central premise of narratives from the early nineteenth century—namely, that the United States constituted a national state of civilization that had risen beyond piratical European imperialism. Johannes Voelz argues that this model would incorporate the notion of "a liberal individualism that came to replace the humanist ideal of republican virtue." According to him, in the midnineteenth century "a new sort of moral personality" begins to be constructed as representative of the United States, a personality or "character" that "demonstrat[es] to others that one shares values such as autonomy, independence, and self-reliance. . . . Thus, the new culture of liberal individualism at once espouses an economic individualism and equips the new order with a moral dimension to be realized by the self" (*Resistance*, 64). In this assumed shared national character in the United States the state of nature assumes importance in a different way. Indeed, as the next part of this book will demonstrate, a specifically American state of nature is identified as underlying and legitimating these new forms of "moral personality" in the United States.

[III]

THE AMERICAN CIVILIZATION THESIS: INTERNALIZING THE OTHER

IN *THE DEERSLAYER*, James Fenimore Cooper presents two protagonists who represent the essentialist and progressivist approaches to civilization, but he does not offer a solution to the differences that remain between the two approaches. Bumppo's and March's positions cannot be harmonized by the end of the novel. As Cooper's meticulous balancing of their position in terms of historical memory and space indicates, however, there is a serious national desire for discursive harmonization behind the seemingly trivial problem of quarreling protagonists. Only in harmony can the two discourses of civilization help legitimate specifically US claims to civilization and the North American continent. After all, if Americans do not constitute the unified, industrious nation that replaces Native Americans, they themselves must be considered the rugged and transitional piratical sovereignty that will eventually be replaced by legitimate European powers. The European, at the time of Cooper's writing, still is the inherent definition of a representative of civilization, while Americans can still be conceptualized, at least to some extent, as deviants faced with European charges of illegitimate sovereignty.

To establish a specifically American perspective that was able to rebut these charges and that rendered the United States fully civilized, the two European approaches to civilization had to be merged. As scholars like Roy Harvey Pearce, Nancy Shoemaker, and Richard Slotkin have shown, the necessity for this lay in the history of European settlement in North America: the two rival approaches had consistently been used in parallel to conceptualize American relations with Native Americans. To decide in favor of one model while dismissing the other meant to discard half of America's early settler history as uncivilized. By the end of the nineteenth century, this basic question of American civilization seemed ripe for an answer.

A hundred years earlier, as Shoemaker has noted, settler Americans and Native Americans were considered inherently and naturally different on the basis of race. But by the end of the nineteenth century, the marginalized, scattered, militarily insignificant tribes that constituted the ideal Native American in Cooper's characterizations of the Delawares had replaced the political notion of the racialized Other as a belligerent, barbarous entity represented by praedones. The Native American as a significant political entity had virtually "vanished" from the American continent.

Fredric Jameson notes that "the prototypical paradigm of the Other in the late nineteenth century . . . is the other imperial nation state [*sic*]." According to Jameson, these imperial rivals were now characterized as "the quintessential ogres and bogeymen of childhood nightmare [*sic*], physically alien and terrifying," images that had been adapted from older characterizations of "the more radical otherness of colonized, non-Western peoples" who were now deemed inherently inferior and dependent, rather than invasive and threatening ("Modernism," 49).

The characterization of the other imperial nation-state as a quasi-racialized Other and the dismissal of nonwhite Others as naturally inferior was based on a discourse of naturalizing certain categories of difference. "By about 1890," Gail Bederman writes, "the discourse of civilization had taken on a very specific set of meanings which revolved around three factors: race, gender, and millennial assumptions about human evolutionary progress. . . . [B]elievers in civilization described evolution working in history to perfect the world. Instead of Christians battling infidels, they envisioned superior races outsurviving inferior races. . . . The most advanced, civilized races—that is, the white races—would be perfected. . . . This millennial vision of perfected racial evolution and gender specialization was what people meant when they referred to 'the advancement of civilization'" (*Manliness*, 25–26).

Because the advancement of civilization was exclusively reserved for white men, other agents—such as the representatives of nonwhite peoples—could be categorically factored out of any discussion of legitimate violence, while the internal differentiation of white men and white nations as insufficiently civilized, perfectly civilized, or even "overcivilized" (Bederman, *Manliness*, 186)—became a defining concern related to the question of legitimate violence.[1]

The first chapter of this part of the book discusses Frederick Jackson Turner's frontier thesis. Turner's "The Significance of the Frontier in American History" (1893) was almost immediately celebrated as a text of central importance for US culture, and it retains this status for good reason. As the first chapter of this part shows, Turner's essay does nothing less than formulate a new model of civilization, which uses the hostis humani generis constellation to construct the United States as the new locus of civilization. Turner's main contribution to the discourse of legitimate violence in the United States lies in combining the two previous models of civilization into a third one, which is characterized by perpetual self-civilizing disruption within the territorial borders of the nation-state. Due to the defining role of national boundaries, the frontier model's self-civilizing disruption is dependent on changing the context of the constellation's figures from the appropriation of territorial space to a progressive self-actualization within the institutions of a delimited nation-state. In this model, the pirata plays a radically altered role: rather than being a renegade or an unwitting, problematic pioneer, he emerges as the foundational figure that sets civilizing self-actualization in motion. The pirata is the central figure in all the constellations discussed in this part of the book, while the praedo and the representative of civilization step into the background and simply help place the pirata's violent actions in a national (here, primarily institutional) context.

The second chapter in this part of the book discusses the development of a corresponding understanding of civilization not as an inherent property of an expansive regime, but as a body of ideals that perpetually have to be reactualized in the nation-state. This logic is used increasingly in the early twentieth century, as European claims to inherent civilization become questionable after World War I (1914–18), and as the foundation of the Soviet Union in 1922 marks the rise of a model of post-European civilization that rivals the frontier model. This chapter discusses the ways in which US constructions of civilization adapt to these changing circumstances. To illustrate these developments, the chapter includes a brief discussion of Dashiell Hammett's novel *Red Harvest* (1929), which draws attention to urban space as a new in-between zone that helps hone the frontier model's constellational logic.

The third chapter in this part of the book discusses the redefinition of representative agency after the introduction of the frontier model of civilization, which goes hand in hand with a redefinition of the status of the innocent. This redefinition is due to the usage of hostis humani generis to define totalitarianism in the twentieth century—that is, as a regime that rests on the violent oppression of the innocent by praedones in representation of an evil ideology. In this context, the institutions of the law emerge as an explicit site for negotiating the legitimacy and illegitimacy of violence in the United States. The discourse of agency and oppression in the context of legal institutions indeed becomes the defining context for the frontier thesis's civilizational reading in the United States.

The interpretive shifts formulated in the third chapter constitute the basis for the discussion of the fourth and final chapter of this part of the book, which offers an analysis of Richard Wright's 1940 novel, *Native Son*. In this novel, an African American man serves as the pirata in a particularly nuanced application of the hostis humani generis constellation as it appears in the frontier model of civilization. The context of novel's protagonist is racially segregated urban space, and the consequences of the pirata's intervention are explicitly linked to the ideological and legal underpinnings of the nation-state. This chapter concludes the argument on an interesting shift that the frontier model of civilization, somewhat paradoxically, makes possible: by universalizing whiteness and therefore removing race as the distinction between the representative of civilization and the praedo, the model enables African American figures to be recognized as genuine representatives of national character and African American writers as serious commentators on the legitimacy of violence.

One important feature of the frontier model of civilization must be kept in mind. The frontier model never operates wholly independently of the essentialist model. Civilizing self-disruption inside the nation can be recognized as a legitimate use of violence only in the context of unambiguous binaries of good and evil outside the nation. The frontier model's dependence on the essentialist model becomes a challenge in the twentieth century—especially after World War II (1939–45), when the United States outgrows its reliance on civilizational dichotomies formulated by European powers and formulates its own set of essentialist binaries for the world. This issue will be discussed at length in part 4 of the book.

[7]

THE FRONTIER THESIS AS A THIRD MODEL OF CIVILIZATION

IN 1893, WHEN the westward expansion witnessed by James Fenimore Cooper was completed, Frederick Jackson Turner proposed the frontier thesis as a uniquely American perspective on civilization and American space ("Frontier"). The thesis is well known: it imagines a spatially expansive progression of civilization into the wilderness of the American continent. In the process, Europeans are exposed to the wilderness and are transformed by it; they become Americans through their experiences on the frontier, which are highly individual experiences of conversion but are shared by all. The experience of the frontier that all Americans share sets them apart from Europeans in their various countries of origin and connects them to each other: the individualizing frontier, according to Turner, is the perpetual birthplace of the American nation as a unified whole.

The frontier is a zone in between the imperial civilization of Europe and the untouched (that is, Native American–controlled) wilderness. Unlike Cooper, Turner does not recognize racial transgression as a threatening element of the margin, or the frontier. Turner's thesis presupposes racial integration as unthinkable from the start. The spatial progression of settlers into Native American land is constructed as a topography of racialized blocs, one of which vanishes and another of which emerges. Just as Hobbes might have argued that war with European settlers was an incidental result of a more general Native American state of nature, Turner argued that war with Native Americans was an incidental result of Europeans' transformation into Americans.

Harold Simonson has commented that the elements Turner used in his thesis had been influential in US thought long before him, but that Turner added the important claim that "the frontier *explained* America" (Simonson, *Beyond the Frontier*, 16). This formulation summarizes the two central reasons for the frontier thesis's discursive success: it "explained" America as a civilizational entity that was inherently separate from Europe, and it was able to do so only by arguing from within the logic of existing European discourses of civilization. The frontier thesis accepted European discourses of civilization as the fundamental basis of any discourse of US civilization and accepted that they had helped legitimate the original appropriation of what was now national space. Yet at the same time when economic success as an exporter of capital and an international creditor allowed the United States to assume a position of power among the "industrious" peoples (Bender, *Among Nations*, 214) and when the colonial project of appropriating space was increasingly being replaced by the neocolonial project of opening markets worldwide, Turner postulated that US success in this changing world order signified nothing less than a wholly new stage of civilization.

The discursive harmonization of the essentialist and progressivist models can be considered the frontier thesis's first objective. This is especially apparent in the management of the thesis's internal contradictions, which are carefully restricted to the realm of definitions (Turner, "Frontier," 38). The American continent is at the same time defined as empty land and as Native American land; westward expansion is at the same time a peaceful natural progression and an inherently military enterprise; conflict with Native Americans is at the same time offensive and defensive; and civilization is at the same time essentialist (as in metaphors of water versus land) and progressivist (as in metaphors of wavelike development). The contradictions in the images and examples of the frontier thesis have frequently been pointed out in scholarly criticism and are freely admitted by Turner himself, who cautions his readers not to expect sharp or exhaustive definitions of his central terms ("Frontier," 39). However, if the goal is to harmonize the at least apparently incompatible, the main emphasis must necessarily be on a constellational harmonization—even at the cost of abandoning categorical consistency. Just like Blackstone in his influential definition of hostis humani generis, Turner uses categories big enough to contain unevenness and outright contradiction.

Indeed, the frontier thesis has become a very useful instrument for cultural and literary (rather than historical) analyses of America because it completely harmonizes the two models of civilization that had separately informed virtually all previous European and settler American assessments of settlement in America. It is in this sense, too, that the frontier thesis can indeed "explain" all earlier interpretations of westward expansion: after all, at least one of the two models of civilization had always been used to frame encounters with the Native American Other and with the space of North America. If the frontier thesis incorporates both models along with their implications, the contradictions between the earlier two models can henceforward be understood as the individually varying elements of a common frontier experience. In terms of the more specific categories and concerns addressed by this book, the frontier thesis contributes three essential elements to the discussion of hostis humani generis.

First, Turner establishes an alternative to the classic notion of a state of nature situated in prehistoric time (by implication, a time preceding recorded history in Europe). Instead, he renders the state of nature a recent period in the history of America. Instead of being a remote and perhaps hypothetical starting point of history (Hartmann, "Matriarchatsidee," 6) or the dark challenge of the imperial margins (Loomba, *Shakespeare*, 31–32), the state of nature is characterized by Turner as an unrepeatable state of historical origin on the margins of European empires. If European history started with a generic and general state of nature, the frontier provides an alternative locus for the beginning of US history specifically. By situating the state of nature on the North American continent, the beginning of history becomes equivalent to the beginning of national history.

Second, because the state of nature is specified as the wilderness of North America, the spatial direction of the imperial civilizing movement is deflected and reversed. According to European models, civilization originates in Europe (which itself originates in a historical state of nature) and expands toward the margins of the world. European civilizers transform space by either destroying rivals or by molding them in their own image. In any case, Europeans can legitimately claim space by virtue of their transformative, cultivating influence in Emer de Vattel's sense. Turner proposes a model that absorbs this imperial movement toward the margins and redefines the cultivating movement of Europeans in American space as the rebirth of these Europeans as Americans. By radically severing the imperial outward movement into precolonial space, Tuner automatically redefines the position of the pirata in the hostis humani generis constellation. Rather than being a half-accepted, half-condemned pioneer who facilitates imperial expansion by incorporating the margins into the economic sphere (Baer, "Plot of Piracy," 25), the pirata is relocated to the center of constructions of national identity. This disruptive redefinition of the categories of civilization and wilderness in space becomes the core of the American character for Turner. He suggests that the pirata embodies the birth of the nation and thus assumes a role in the constellation that is sharply distinguished from those of the praedo and the representative of civilization.

Third, the notion of civilization itself is redefined. European models of civilization had imagined the European as stable in his civilized character, even though he was flexible in his specific incarnation in practice. The essentialist model emphasized this inherently legitimate representative of civilization's military expansion in space, while the progressivist model emphasized his pedagogical mission to help others catch up with him. Turner unites both notions: the radical restructuring of space indicated by the essentialist model sets in motion an internal, ever-maturing civilizing progress within national institutions (rather than across races).

In this way, Turner adds a characteristic of civilization that truly distinguishes the American model from its European predecessors. Civilization, according to Turner, is a normative ideal that informs national institutions rather than representative figures. The figures are relevant to the discussion of legitimate violence only because they initiate (the pirata) or realize (the representative of civilization) institutional maturation and change, or because they attack or pervert institutional integrity (the praedo). For civilization to exist, institutions must be established, mature, and be continuously disrupted by civilizational rebirth. Self-referential disruption becomes the defining property of civilization in a nation organized by institutions.[1]

By absorbing and harmonizing the central assumptions of the two European models of civilization, the American model is able to replace both of those models. Americans are quite literally Europeans who, like Natty Bumppo in Cooper's *The Deerslayer*, learn from the wilderness and are transformed into people for whom utopian forms of social organization are conceivable. The acknowledgment of a European basis for the frontier thesis maintains the most important presuppositions of the former models, such as the superiority of white Christians and the general desirability of technological progress, scientific objectivity, and logistic efficiency.

In the remainder of this chapter, I discuss how Turner's reading of the state of nature and the pirata help conceptualize this alternative model of civilization. Central to this reading is Turner's repeated reference to the "germ theory" ("Frontier," 38–39 and 42). According to the germ theory, European nations had developed from a stable center, where a historical state of nature was situated; this was the germ from which the flower of civilization would grow. According to the logic of continuous growth, these civilized empires had expanded from the European center, the locus of the germ, toward the margins, pushing their civilizing influence into the world. These expansive movements had been accompanied by transformations in law that served to minimize their internal contradictions that resulted from imperial outreach—for instance, via reconceptualizing the legal status of precolonial space in Vattel. Turner isolates this widely accepted vehicle of space as a separate reference point and establishes a new civilized entity—the United States—that is solely legitimated by the reference to space. The strategy was supported by the fact that much of British colonial law used American space as a precedent, which gave that particular local context a certain claim to universality.

Turner accepts the germ theory as a basis for his argument, yet he proceeds to argue that European imperialism is only a first step, and furthermore a step that has been insufficiently described. Turner agrees that European civilization expands in the manner described by the germ theory, but he emphasizes that European influence on the spaces it expands into is not, at first, cultivating. Instead, it is primarily disruptive of a local equilibrium, although Turner does not render this disruption illegitimate in and of itself. Instead, the notion of disruption and turmoil allows him to suggest the establishment of a new state of nature in a space confronted with European imperialism—a state of nature that is, as I established in part 2 of this book, recognized as such by the presence of piratae and praedones. Representatives of every European nation, who had originally risen out of the state of nature, are now exposed and reduced to a second state of nature by the space of the wilderness (Turner, "Frontier," 39). However, as they rise once more from this state and do what their inherently industrious nature dictates (namely, cultivate the land), they establish a new legitimate germ outside of Europe. The confrontation with the wilderness overwhelms Europeans, severs them from their original European allegiance, and even forces them to embrace a Native American lifestyle (ibid.). It is the completed pirata cycle of alienation, degeneration, and transformation that allows them to be reborn as people who inherently belong to the land they have settled on and removes them from the implied illegitimacy of Lockean invasion. By virtue of being piratae, they have conflated the inconflatable: they have become civilized fragments of American space. Pirata figures like Hutter, who merge with the space they gradually cultivate, can be reinterpreted as nation-affirming founding figures rather than as gothic villains who leave a criminal legacy that threatens to subvert legitimating claims to inherent national virtue. Here, Turner makes use of the only element of status transformation available in the hostis humani generis constellation. The pirata had always been able to be transformed from a representative of civilization into a representative of the in-between zone; only transformation into the praedo was denied to him. This loophole was now used to by Turner to invest limited transformation with foundational meaning.

The reference to Hutter raises an important question, however. How could Turner avoid the charge that his piratical American germ would necessarily grow into an inherently illegitimate nation? For a writer as sensitive to discursive shifts as Turner, much of the answer again lies in the historical context of his argument. As mentioned above, Turner's thesis was formulated at a time of substantial national and international restructuring that allowed him to change the reference point for the hostis humani generis constellation. Imperial rule over colonial realms had become largely uncontested, and privateering warfare had been dead since the Declaration of Paris in 1856—which the United States, though not a signing party, respected during both the Civil War and the Spanish-American War. Privateering-derived pirates no longer threatened the sovereign monopoly of force at sea. All Western states, including the United States, maintained professional navies. In fact, at that historical moment, the American navy was already ten years into a process of fundamental restoration and modernization. The new navy featured modern technology and standardized professionalization that would garner it fame in the maritime warfare of the early twentieth century, substantiating the rapidly increasing American dominance in the international military realm.

Next to this general shift in the role of the nation-state as the possessor of a stable monopoly on force, the previously all-important notion of race lost its defining influence on models of civilization. The analysis of Cooper's *The Deerslayer* in chapter 6 has shown that the essentialist and the progressivist approach had already been brought together as variations of each other by the midnineteenth century. In accord with the essentialist model, racial mixture or transgression was deemed impossible, while at the same time, progress within each racial group, as well as "friendship and sarvices" (DS, 2:746) between the races, was considered possible and desirable. During the second half of the nineteenth century, this position was maintained until a tipping point was reached—roughly corresponding to the time Turner proposed the frontier thesis—after which both models of civilization were increasingly dismissed from the conceptualization of Other peoples in American scholarship. For instance, scholars such as Franz Boas began to reject the notion of racial hierarchy on general principle (Hegeman, *Patterns*, 49). If different races had inherently different ranges of progress, different priorities, and different forms of refinement, and if they, by nature, wanted different things, yet friendship was possible on the basis of these nonconflicting goals and desires, why must any relationship between the races be one of violent rivalry, as the classic essentialist approach insisted was the case? Conversely, if central racial attributes would never change because racial transgression was not possible, why still use white civilization as a standard for assessing inherently Other formations, and why insist on its imitation by Others, as the progressivist approach did?

The decreasing importance of imperial expansion and the growing importance of the stable territorial integrity of nation-states generally allowed a conceptualization of civilization and its Other in spatial terms that were more clearly delineated. Cultures were separate from each other because they occurred in different territories. Different cultures' internal developments were imagined as analogous to the sovereignty of nation-states

(Hegeman, *Patterns*, 38). The two classic models of civilization and the assessment of racialized Other collectives were thus separated from each other in anthropological scholarship, which freed up the models for alternative uses—including their bold harmonization as descriptive of all-white figures in Turner.

At the same time, Turner remains wary of the traps that accompany the use of the pirata as a central entity, and he attempts to neutralize the most immediate delegitimizing implications. Two aspects seem particularly important here. First, Turner avoids the figure of the emperor. He dismisses the very notion of conquest by insisting that Native American land is free land, empty land, even "public" land (Turner, "Frontier," 42). Americans do not conquer, they cultivate. The villainous frontiersman is not a representative of the American past, informed by European-style conquest and illegitimate expansion, as in Charles Ellms and Cooper. Instead, in Turner, the frontiersman becomes a representative of his own future—namely, the farmer, the businessman, and the statesman. In the decontextualizing argument of the frontier thesis, the villainous frontiersman can be explained by the political order he brought to the wilderness, not by the rulers that have exiled him there.

Turner's argument is supported by the fact that the privateer never embodied the United States as he had the British Empire. Instead, potentially unruly frontiersmen can become the founding figures of a new regime and constitute its main characteristics as perpetually disruptive and regenerative, and always as explicitly national. The frontiersman as a figure is much more closely and directly linked to the national project than the privateer had ever been: rather than being the gallant and reckless servant of a farsighted sovereign, the frontiersman of the frontier thesis embodies the birth and rebirth of a civilized national order. The vast difference in the understanding of violence in contexts related to hostis humani generis—either as the expression of rule or as representing order—fundamentally underlies the re-reading of hostis humani generis in Turner.

This narrative move of Turner's is supported by a careful inclusion of existing strategies of legitimation that work in favor of his theory. In Ellms's discussion of Lafitte, the most powerful argument against US illegitimacy had been the exclusion of the pirata as a relic of the European past. Turner takes up this notion in the larger context of his thesis. Much like Cooper, Turner constructs a nostalgic double past: the recent past of the state of nature, which is inherent in the frontier and that informs everything that is developed on it, and the recent conclusion of the westward expansion, which occasions the formulation of Turner's thesis. "And now, . . . the frontier has gone, and with its going has closed the first period of American history"

("Frontier," 62). The claim of the frontier's conclusion ends the essay and follows Ellms in the narrative removal of villainous conduct into an inaccessible past. The present is already in the realm of the refined; the past cannot be repeated because the free land that can be obtained without conquest is now fully settled. At this crucial point, the authentic American character (which relies on westward movement into the American wilderness) can exist only as a citable ideal, not as a potentially problematic political reality.

Once again, the narrative strategy is aided by the contextualizing discourses surrounding the publication of the thesis. In contrast to Ellms and Cooper, Turner has the discourse of evolution at his disposal. Ellms and Cooper had to draw clear lines between the pirata and the American nation because, as we have seen, piracy and illegitimate sovereignty had an obvious history of collapse and overlap. Every suggestion that the United States had originated in piratical conduct was an invitation to render it an inherently illegitimate nation. This is a problem Turner does not have to the same degree as his predecessors. Even if the United States had been born as the practice of piratae, the discourse of evolution allows him to presuppose that once development had been set in transformative motion, the United States could never fully return to its original stage. Furthermore, the discourse of Manifest Destiny supports Turner's argument. This discourse is characterized by the assumption that the natural expansion of the United States is virtuous, and that legitimacy is obtained through industrious superiority. This discourse indeed belongs to the conversations that Turner's scholarly argument draws on and contributes to (Grimm, "*Imaginary Indian,*" 79; Weeks, *Continental Empire*, 61).

In Turner, the frontiersman, by adopting the lifestyle of the Native American, conforms to the specific praedo-pirata relationship established in Cooper's fiction. As we have seen in the analysis of *The Deerslayer*, people who were "white" but acted "red" were considered closest to the Hobbesian state of nature.[2] Cooper had to consider such figures problematic because his central concern remained with the fragile racialized divide between "red" and "white." To Turner, the clichéd Native American properties used in the frontier thesis merely help underline the notion of a white regression into a state of nature. Because "red" behavior in Cooper's sense is no longer threatening, early infrastructures, like those associated with Hutter, are not complex constructions of previous exiled whiteness but straightforward evidence of first-wave American cultivators. The dangerous transformation indicated in Hutter's and March's adoption of Native American lifestyles is even viewed positively by Turner. In the thesis, he quite explicitly refers to the discourses coined by Cooper and his contemporaries who had established a characterization of villains as exiles lost between civilization and wilderness—characters who were "white" but acted "red." This is most explicit in a lengthy quote Turner includes in his essay that, in the context of an English debate, warns of frontiersmen's transformation into "hordes of English Tartars" that take over the government in America and may dislodge Great Britain ("Frontier," 59).

Unlike the founders of the United States, who had vehemently rejected such suggestions in American-British diplomacy (see, for example, Lee, "Florida Blanca," 2:209; see also Spahn, "Cruel War"), and much later writers such as Ellms and Cooper, who viewed those suggestions ambivalently, Turner does not deny the provocative construction of Americans as enemies of all humankind. On the contrary, he embraces and expands on it, and he suggests a positive rereading of villains as the first true Americans. After all, such "English Tartars" represent the very "disintegrating forces of civilization" that become the germ of something new (Turner, "Frontier," 45 and 51). The way to integrate them is to include them in an American nation of people who, despite their strictly institutional refinement, still have a historical knowledge and understanding of the piratical experience. It is only the European empire that cannot contain them, because Europeans and Americans have not originated from the same state of nature. In Turner, piratical unruliness becomes evidence of the separateness of the United States in general.

Correspondingly, when Turner lists the properties of his first authentic Americans, they seem inspired more by figures like Hutter and March than by those like Bumppo. While frontiersmen's lives are socially based on family structures (a notion not unfamiliar to Cooper's white villains), Turner most famously argues that "the frontier is productive of individualism. . . . The tendency is anti-social. It produces antipathy to control, and particularly to direct control" ("Frontier," 56). He concludes:

> From the conditions of frontier life came intellectual traits of profound importance. . . . [T]hese traits have, while softening down, still persisted as survivals in the place of their origin, even when a higher social organization succeeded. . . . That coarseness and strength combined with acuteness and inquisitiveness; that practical, inventive turn of mind, quick to find expedients; that masterful grasp of material things, lacking in the artistic but powerful to effect great ends; that restless, nervous energy; that dominant individualism, working for good and for evil, and withal that buoyancy and exuberance which comes with freedom—these are the traits of the frontier, or traits called out elsewhere because of the frontier. (Turner, "Frontier," 61)

Such descriptions evoke the coarse, inventive mind of Hutter and the restless strength of March, along with their common concentration on the material, their emphasized mobility, and their focus on their own advantage. Even the more specific practices of "evil currency" at the frontier that Turner points out ("Frontier," 58) are reminiscent of Hutter's and March's plans to fraudulently pass off the scalps of women-and-children as those of enemy warriors (DS, 2:564). The characteristics of Bumppo, however, are found in descriptions of how the East attempted to regulate and integrate the West, chiefly by promoting "educational and religious activity" (Turner, "Frontier," 60). These efforts represent the maturing process in American society, which involved softer rather than higher stages of civilization that turn back to the more primitive versions of themselves in an attempt to raise the latter to their own standards.

As in the European progressivist approach, the primitive and the refined share some basic features. In Turner's model, however, these common features are national instead of human in general. The greatest and most pronounced difference between Turner's model and the European progressivist approach, however, is that the primitive and the refined reverse their value in the frontier thesis. Even though the refined continues to shape the primitive, it is the primitive that constitutes the true basis of national character. The refined does not better the primitive—it softens it, waters it down. American authors had used the metaphor of increasing softness to describe American separateness from Europe long before Turner,[3] but Turner is especially radical in his claim that an increase in complexity and refinement comes at the price of decreasing a specifically American authenticity ("Frontier," 57). This reversal makes sense when institutions are included as relevant factors. Characters like Bumppo inform the spirit of American institutions, which secures their civilizational potentiality; but it is the task of individual Americans to continuously test the civilizational authenticity of established institutions. This is why violence within the nation can be legitimate even though it disturbs the peace.

As we have seen, Turner does not understand authenticity in a Rousseauian sense of a return to the human being's true nature—indeed, the analysis of Cooper's two protagonists, Bumppo and March, has allowed us to appreciate the vast difference between Rousseau's and Turner's respective agents of rebirth. The notion of villainous intervention as pure and authentic is instead one of the most important, and also one of the most unsettling, new implications of the frontier thesis. Turner sets forth a model of civilization that essentially explains America as the Other civilization: civilization because America can be explained in the language of prevailing European models, and Other because America is defined by the struggles and development usually associated with the praedo in previous models. The frontier model of civilization solely describes the successive internal development of civilization—namely, the birth (from the essentialist model) and maturing (from the progressivist one) of American national character within the territory and institutions of the United States. Rebirth can take place within each wave, at any moment, through a citation of a specifically American state of nature that is produced by using the hostis humani generis constellation to dramatize the civilizational necessity of violence.

What kind of space is national space, if the pirata figure takes center stage in the moment of birth or rebirth of the nation? Turner uses the white man with a tomahawk and the hordes of modern Tartars as powerful and suitable metaphors for Americans. For the second stage of civilization to occur, Turner reasons, there must be wilderness: the praedo is an integral part of this wilderness, and it is important that he is there because the pirata cannot be a pirata without the presence of the praedo. Because the Native American praedo is hidden as an unreadable fragment of space in Turner, the pirata plot of deviance remains the only narratable plot that the hostis humani generis constellation can provide for Turner's model. Only with a pirata who is disintegrated and lost in cruelties, alienated from himself, hostile to his civilized fellows, but still industrious in space can we identify a wilderness existing around him, and imagine a rebirth of civilization that can be channeled through him. It is in this sense that Richard Slotkin rightly speaks of "regeneration through violence [as] the structuring metaphor of the American experience" (*Regeneration*, 5).

However, what I want to argue here is that the pirata's violence, as emphasized by Slotkin, is in fact incidental to the American experience as described by Turner. Violence helps demonstrate the actualization of the hostis humani generis constellation and thus helps identify the pirata as a pirata, but violence alone does not automatically make the pirata's experience an American one. Instead, it is the cultivation of infrastructure and institutions that ties the violent, villainous birth and the softer maturing process together as elements of a new model. The progress of civilization does not depend on the pirata as any specific individual or collective entity; instead, it depends on his manipulation of space that changes the meaning of space. It is this manipulation that allows the two notions of violent birth and soft maturity to interact meaningfully, which is why only the radical restructuring of space will allow the frontier thesis to explain the violence committed in the process. Only when the pirata changes the meaning of space can he represent the pioneering center of civilization. If space is not fundamentally restructured in its meaning, the pirata is only a thug, and his violence cannot be explained by the frontier model.

Turner's reliance on national space as a site of civilizational development, based on the perpetual actualization of the hostis humani generis constellation, has important implications for the construction of national space. After all, the pirata as the new foundational figure of the United States is necessarily linked to his presence in an in-between zone, and a case can be made that Turner is the first to suggest that the national territory of the United States is such a zone. Such a conceptualization of national territory is, indeed, the condition for perpetual internal rebirth to occur.

What of the other figures, the praedo and the representative of civilization, in Turner's model? Turner does not discuss them extensively; their mention is simply required to indicate what kind of conflict the pirata replaces. This solution works well enough in Turner's short essay that introduces the frontier thesis. Later and longer texts that adopt Turner's use of the constellation consider the problem of these two other figures more extensively. The distribution of figures into a foreground and background structure is a more complex spatial image than that of figures meeting on the plane of the sea. A more systematic use of the metalevel of textual architecture evolves as an appropriate way to translate such a rearranged constellation into an effective literary composition (we will see early versions of this in the discussion below of Richard Wright's *Native Son*, first published in 1940, and especially in the discussion of Kurt Vonnegut's *Mother Night*, first published in 1962).

In addition, the significance of Britons for the United States was more complicated than the frontier thesis suggests. For example, Theodore Roosevelt's four-volume *The Winning of the West*, first published between 1889 and 1896, still resorts to the race argument familiar from Cooper to distinguish Americans from Britons. Roosevelt suggests that "the American race was not the same as the English race, since it had been reconstituted of new racial stock in the act of winning a new and virgin continent. Americans were literally of a different blood than the British" (quoted in Bederman, *Manliness*, 178–79). Turner's creative use of hostis humani generis leads him to a similar conclusion, but his construction of a specifically American way of committing legitimate violence via hostis humani generis allows him to move the question of race to the sidelines and thus render invisible any international or even "imperial dimensions of his founding paradigm" (Kaplan, "'Left Alone,'" 5).

To illustrate the enormous implications of the innovation that the frontier thesis represented, it is instructive to compare the British Victorian traditional use of the hostis humani generis constellation to Turner's. The British use is based not on the nation but on the empire. In such a context, the motherland is ontologically separated from the colonial realms it rules; the empire contains realms of inside and outside that are always meticulously distinguished from each other. Yet these two separate internal realms have a long history of being used to make sense of each other, and colonial struggle is often used as a metaphor in discussing conflicts in the motherland (see Turley, *Rum, Sodomy and the Lash*, 40–43). The pirate example in Victorian literature offers a good idea of the general tendencies in these constructions of space. When George Gordon Byron introduced the notion of the pirate as a melodramatic, seductive rogue gentleman in 1814, his corsair was still a fundamentally maritime entity, operating in the Mediterranean. When Turner proposed his frontier thesis in the late nineteenth century, the idea of maritime pirates in the colonial realms of the British Empire had been transformed into a metaphor for antisocial practices in the motherland. As Sean Grass observes, in the British Victorian period, the existence of a traditional pirate figure in colonial space was necessary to stabilize and support the characterization of piratical behavior in the motherland ("Piracy," 190). In the motherland, the pirate was used as an analogy to characterize mercenary and aggressive female characters undeserving of romantic love (Lutz, "Pirate Poet," 23–24), the speculative financier (Reade, *Hard Cash*; Grass, "Piracy"), and the US publisher who commits copyright infringement (for a characterization that depends directly on the premise of a traditional colonialist structuring of global space, see Fredriksson, "Globalisation"). Even the most famous Victorian pirate novel of the late nineteenth century, Robert Louis Stevenson's *Treasure Island* (first published in 1883), imagines its archpirate as the prototypical exploiter of loopholes. This archpirate, Long John Silver, is always successful when he operates unseen and from inside civilizational structures, but he fails miserably as soon as he begins to lead his pirates openly—that is, in the way colonial pirates were originally imagined to have done. After his failed attempt to gain power, Silver is returned to civilization and immediately manages to outsmart everyone again. It is only Stevenson's emphasis on Silver's deceitful smoothness that allows him to create a meaningful pirate figure in the context of Victorian literature, a context that emphasizes hypocrisy and the exploitation of loopholes as central characteristics of the pirate. As a classic maritime figure, however, the pirate in British literature appears increasingly anachronistic and even comical—hence the figure's increasing inclusion in the realms of satire and children's literature (most famously in James Barrie's *Peter Pan*, published first as a play in 1904, and as a novel in 1911).

In other words, in Britain in the late nineteenth century, piracy had explicit intracivilizational associations, largely through the use of allegory and metaphor. The civilized quasi pirates imagined in the core realm of civilization are perfectly integrated into British society and are often characterized as charming and successful. They are not primarily violent but simply take ruthless advantage of existing structures. The characters' insistence on taking liberties, even at the expense of others, becomes the hallmark of piratical behavior in Victorian literature; this is why the very rich and very successful are often characterized in this fashion. The pirate figure exposes certain types of exploitative behavior that cannot yet be punished as lawless even though they are considered semicriminal. The explicit use of metaphor helps maintain the separation between inside and outside in these colonialist constructions. These Victorian works of literature do not use the hostis humani generis constellation on the plot level precisely because their civilized quasi pirates are not imagined to operate in an in-between zone.

In the American case, the nation-state is also contextualized in a two-level relationship, but a different one. Here, the distinction of the national and the international is constitutive, since American writers since in the early nineteenth century had made a relentless case of the qualitative separateness of the United States as a nation-state. The relationship between the national and the international is thus not well expressed by metaphors of loopholes. The different function of the defining but separate international "outside" with regard to the US nation-state is thus negotiated differently on the plot level, and in the late nineteenth century, Turner's theoretical use of the constellation served to structure such later narrative negotiation. In the American context, it becomes possible to encounter an in-between zone, traditionally associated with the imperial margins, within the nation, as the space constitutive of national character.

"After 1875," Slotkin writes, "many of the most popular new dime-novel series abandoned Indian-war settings in favor of conflicts between 'outlaws' and 'detectives,' preferably set in the complex urban space of New York" (*Gunfighter Nation*, 127). Considering the Western genre's prototypical heterotopian location of "far away and long ago," then-contemporary city space at first seems like a surprising site in which to reinvent the genre. Cities such as New York constituted the epitome of civilizational advancement, different not only from the cities of Europe but also from rural America (Hegeman, *Patterns*, 24–25). But it was indeed urban class conflict that spurred the increasing conflation of Communism, workers, and Native Americans in the United States by the time that Turner formulated his thesis (Slotkin, *Fatal Environment*, 338–45).

If rioting workers became the equivalent of illegitimate Native American praedones, the peacekeeping forces that opposed them were almost necessarily cast as the representatives of civilization. Institutions as the possible embodiments of civilization take form in this context. As Robert Cover has observed, "keeping the peace is no simple or neutral task" ("Nomos," 163). According to Cover, keeping the peace generally requires the continuous maintenance of a normative metanarrative that underlies the interpretation of the law as well as the centralized use of violence to maintain the dominance of this particular interpretation (ibid., 139–42). National state violence, in other words, is ideological by design, especially when it is actively and explicitly directed against its own citizens. According to Cover, the nation-state's monopoly of force and its monopoly of legal interpretation constitute two sides of the same coin. Michel Foucault has added that, in the context of political and legal institutions, collective struggles for access to the monopoly of force—such as the workers' struggles described by Slotkin, as well as the struggles against political exclusion and for civil rights by women and nonwhites of any gender—tend to be informed by an essentialist formulation of political perspectives that formulate concepts such as "class" in the language of race. Any legitimate claim to have a monopoly on force goes hand in hand with the defense of a very specific metanarrative of history at the expense of Other rival metanarratives (Foucault, *Society*, 79). Nevertheless, if institutions are assigned inherent civilizational value, such a defense is based not on the idea of unsurpassable difference between rivals but on "competing understandings of the good and how the good is grounded and legitimated. These understandings are reflected in competing moral visions of collective life and the discourse sustaining these visions" (Hunter, "Culture War," 15). In particular, questions about the American national claim of the equality of all people created "a society that [is] struggling with the question of whom to include within the imagined [civilized] community of U.S. American society," and on what grounds to include them (Markus and Moya, "Doing Race," 53).

Hazel Rose Markus and Paula Moya ("Doing Race," 24) make a particularly important point about the specific situation of the United States—namely, that collective political action for normatively grounded institutional change took place in a nation-state that viewed individual agency as the central resource for actualizing the civilization that national institutions stood for. For this reason, the collective exclusions that did take place had traditionally been translated into an individualist framework (Voelz, *Resistance*). Individual bodies were categorized from birth to represent a given race, gender, or other supposedly natural property, in this human being's dealings with national institutions. The resulting difference in the institutional treatment of white able-bodied American men from that of all others informed political interventions on behalf of excluded populations. Activists accepted institutional constructions of their own natural Otherness to define the collectives they, as individuals, could legitimately speak for. In other words, this political strategy used the ability of each individual excluded body to epitomize the fact of a much more general institutional exclusion. Each individual encounter with exclusion could be construed as a case in point of a structural injustice (Markus and Moya, "Doing Race," 24 and 77). For instance, Ralph Ellison, consistently uses the frontier thesis as a backdrop to his extensive writings on the African American contribution to American cultural life and national identity (*Territory*, 134, 148, 165, 179, 213, 223–24, and 236). Drawing on these arguments, any African American who interacts with the nation is, in an important sense, always also all African Americans who interact with the nation. At the same time, the agents of oppression that an African American struggles with are as unspecific and generalized as the praedones are in Cooper, and as incidental to the institutional space of the nation as Native Americans are to the space of the wilderness.

This observation is helpful in reading the political power struggles within the nation as struggles that take place in an in-between zone. After all, in such a zone, the central property of individuals is their ability to represent legitimate and illegitimate collectives as a whole: their individual violent confrontation actualizes a much greater normative conflict. This conflict is clearly no longer one between different normative frameworks (such as civilized versus savage structures of community), but rather one between different interpretations of a shared normative framework (for instance, the US Constitution). The exclusion of certain populations from participation in the nation sets in motion a conflict not of regimes of violence, but of regimes of interpretation, and it is the urgency of this interpretive conflict that is now described via the hostis humani generis constellation.

[8]

THE DEMOCRATIC FRONTIERSMAN AND THE TOTALITARIAN LEVIATHAN

IF AMERICAN NATIONAL SPACE is an in-between zone, questions immediately arise about the nature of representation and the derived narrative conditions for claims to legitimacy. Which elements of the nation-state can be presupposed to be civilized and to constitute resources for a softening process toward civilization, and which elements can—or must—be transformed because they represent fragments of the wilderness that have to be removed? During World War I and the interwar period, important early concepts were developed that help answer these questions.

Especially in urban space, the notion of spatial restructuring was influential, and as a result the frontier model of civilization was often applied to urban space. By the 1930s, urban restructuring was routinely called for with references to "urban frontier" in Frederick Jackson Turner's sense (Duffus, "Waterfronts"; Silzer, "Super-Port," 668), and such language thus informed the spatial manifestation of industrial development in the city. In this context, the relationship between collective violence and the law soon emerged as the most important site for the hostis humani generis constellation's production of illegitimate Other collectives as political factions. This becomes evident in the First Red Scare in the aftermath of World War I (circa 1919–21). The First Red Scare marks a period of upheaval and civic unrest in the United States that "accompan[ied] American industrial development" (Gage, "Terrorism," 87) and that associated communism with domestic violence carried out by excluded groups, especially within the American urban population. "Native Americans, blacks, Catholics, immigrants—all, at one time or another, embodied the threat of internal subversion," Ellen Schrecker explains, and she adds in reference to the First Red Scare: "By the twentieth century, the American 'Other' had become politicized and increasingly identified with communism, the party's Moscow connections tapping in conveniently with the traditional fear of foreigners" (*McCarthyism*, 10).

The usage of hostis humani generis to describe domestic urban conflict was accompanied and strongly reinforced by international developments during the same period. As has been widely recognized among scholars,

> World War I produced two unforeseen events with profound implications for the rest of the twentieth century, including the cultural wars of our historical epoch. The first was the Russian Revolution, which sparked communist revolutions and revolutionary movements from Mongolia to Germany and then around the world. The second was the national liberation movements of the colored peoples in the colonies and neo-colonies of the great empires. . . . During World War I, what Africans and Asians, as well as American "Negroes," saw in the great cradle of "Western civilization" was an insane orgy of mass murder and devastation on an unprecedented scale, as the hallmark of this civilization, its miraculous technology and vast production, was used to turn portions of Europe into poisonous wastelands. (Franklin, *Vietnam*, 117–18)

As Bruce Franklin notes, the classic European notion of inherent civilization is fundamentally shattered by World War I, especially because the war was largely waged in Europe itself. As my discussion of pirate figures in Victorian literature has indicated, European discourses of civilization still depended on the assumption that Europeans and European space were inherently civilized. European discourses of civilization were not able to explain the war's "insane orgy of mass murder and devastation" in any way that allowed Europeans to continue to insist on their inherent civilization. Indeed, it seemed that either Europe was civilized (in which case, World War I should not have occurred) or it had degraded into savagery (which would explain the war but was deemed an unacceptable notion). World War I thus occasioned the widespread formulation of alternative models of civilization in Europe that could restore the lost premise of inherent civilization. These discourses borrowed from the American frontier model, especially in their references to the constitutive importance of transformative revolution and the premise of national space as an in-between zone that was the site of a perpetual civilizing effort.

At the same time, new European discourses abandoned the centerpiece of all three existing civilizational models (essentialist, progressive, and frontier)—namely, the notion of origin in a state of nature. The frontier model could hold onto that notion by respatializing it in an explicitly American territorial context; Europeans could not reinvent the state of nature in a similar way because the original state of nature had been the product of European philosophy in the first place. Instead, the alternative concepts of civilization that emerged in Europe postulated that civilizational problems of legitimacy were rooted in the concept of the nation-state itself, and that European-style civilization (that is, inherent civilization) could be regained only in the aftermath of the nation-state.

Regimes based on such a premise would come to be known as totalitarian regimes in the United States, a category that gradually came to replace that of the barbarian in US discourse of the twentieth century. Totalitarianism, in this emerging understanding, held that the massification of populations in twentieth-century Western nation-states required a new form of political organization that responded to, and was thus theoretically based on, the notion of atomized masses. Such masses were to be justly governed by a state that loosely combined Hobbes's idea of the Leviathan with Rousseau's idea of social progress. The totalitarian Leviathan, representative of all, was also endowed with a coherent will that corresponded directly to the collective will of the masses. The totalitarian state was to be a living and constantly self-purifying body, made up of all the humans within it. Because of the oneness of state and human, the totalitarian state always legitimately acted on behalf of "its" humans. The nation-state merely constituted a necessary larva for such a totalitarian Leviathan to rise from and to rule the masses. The Soviet Union, founded in 1922, was the first nation-state to be conceptualized as a mere transitional state that would establish a just, inherently civilized order in its own aftermath. The totalitarian regime did not, in this sense, represent its territory, nor did it represent its people; it represented a people and a territory of the future that, to legitimate the state's existence in the present, had to be molded by the state in the first place (Peters, *Torture*, 127).

In this sense, totalitarianism can be described as an attempt to resolve the difficulties of European states in renewing a claim to inherent civilization. The totalitarian solution echoes the notion of a future legitimate order presupposed by the Augustinian anecdote but also assumes that the arrival of this legitimate order can be expedited. According to the totalitarian solution, if the future is to arrive soon, all aspects of the present have to be ended, and every failure of the future to arrive legitimates increasingly aggressive efforts to end the present, all in the name of awakening the totalitarian Leviathan.

Americans were acutely aware of the ideological challenges posed by totalitarianism and sought to address them from within the frontier model of civilization, which presupposed that existing national institutions were the proper place for an anticipated full realization of civilization. As early as 1916, Randolph Bourne discussed the contradictory nature of the German culture that had produced the philosophical and cultural pillars of inherent civilization but that now constituted an antagonist in hostile and disruptive defiance of civilization. How, Bourne asked, was one to react to such a paradoxical status transformation, and how was one to conceptualize the notion of civilization in response to it? The solution for the United States, he argued, was to be mindful of its own unique civilizational origin: "Our ideal we can only find in our still pioneer, still struggling American spirit. It will not be found in any purported defence of present 'democracy,' 'civilization,' 'humanity.' . . . It will have to be in terms of values which secure all the vital fruits of the German ideals, without the tragic costs. It must be just as daring, just as modern, just as realistic. It must set the same social ends, the realization of the individual through the beloved community" (quoted in Hegeman, *Patterns*, 60).

Bourne firmly rejects the notion that any nation-state, including the United States, can make any claim to inherent civilization or can legitimately defend itself on this basis. This does not mean that the nation-state is inherently uncivilized, as a totalitarian argument might suggest. It simply means that civilization must be understood in Turner's sense—namely, as a movement of perpetual institutional actualization of foundational ideals that are indeed inherently civilized, and that must be considered universal as well as national values. The nation-state, understood as an in-between zone, is the proper place for such perpetual actualization because it delimits the "beloved community" that can strive to actualize these values in collective political practice.

This reading of the frontier model of civilization became especially widespread in the 1930s and underpins the importance of Turner's thesis in American discourse of the twentieth century. As Susan Hegeman points out, the formulation of an "American Way of Life," which appears for the first time in the 1930s, is used to render the mythic nationalist idea of America as a sturdy ideological framework that embraces and affirms the continuation of the democratic nation-state, in explicit contrast to "totalitarianism" (*Patterns*, 4 and 105–6). In 1939, Peter Drucker pointedly argued that "Western democracies have to realize that totalitarian [ideology] . . . can only be overcome by a . . . concept of a free and equal society" (*Economic Man*, 227).[1]

Civilization in this sense always already exists in nation-states, even though it exists only as a citable ideal, and the civilizing mission consists of the internally disruptive effort to recruit all members of the national community to participate in this mission. The call for "equal" inclusion in the democratic regime of the United States directly responds to the problem of massification. The notion of freedom has been conceptualized as the "individual and collective human development in terms of . . . the individual's progressive liberation from a malignant regulatory regime and its incorporation into a benign one" (Slaughter, *Human Rights Inc.*, 9).

Totalitarianism and the frontier model of civilization share the assumption that destruction and resurrection are foundational aspects of the civilizational future in the present, and they both rely on the existence of the nation-state as a spatially delineated site on which to formulate the future fate of civilization. Since neither assumes the nation-state to be a de facto civilized space, both models postulate that the nation-state constitutes the site for a civilizing movement in the spirit of certain specified values. These values are diametrically opposed to each other in the two models due to the implications of the foundational figures that each model identifies as its core civilizing reference: whereas the totalitarian state imagines a collectivist Leviathan of the future, the United States imagines an individualist frontiersman of the past. The implications of this difference are especially well described in the realm of the law.

The frontiersman represents a recognizable American spirit that may express itself in a variety of incarnations inside and outside national institutions, and it is this American spirit that becomes the "spirit of the law" (Waldron, "Torture," 1748). It became an expression of civilized institutional conduct for the United States to grant each citizen a transparent, accountable rule of law that emphasized a reliable, reciprocal relationship between the people and the law. Rather than keeping its citizens in a state of perpetual existential insecurity, the United States claimed to offer a society that helped liberate each citizen to pursue individual happiness. The existence of civilization is increasingly deemed equivalent to the institutional inclusion of populations previously excluded from equal political and legal representation: "the true subject of democracy is not simply material well-being but the extension of the democratic process in the direction of perfecting itself" (Ellison, *Territory*, 110).

Such an expansion of institutional participation on the basis of equal legal treatment, which has been demanded by various civil rights movements, can be seen as a civilizing premise only when contrasted with totalitarianism. Hannah Arendt, whose work is central to US understandings of totalitarianism, emphasizes "that legal stability and a totalitarian movement [can] not be reconciled" (*Eichmann*, 186; see also 176) because of totalitarianism's inherent orientation toward the future. Arendt generally foregrounds the importance of movement and fluidity for totalitarian regimes, which forbids any legal protection for the status quo and thus reinforces the idea that a totalitarian state is a larva of the Leviathan, destined to be outgrown. She suggests that in totalitarian regimes, the entire population is always suspected of potential (that is, future) rather than actual crimes against the rise of the Leviathan, and that any person charged with such a crime can bring to his or her defense only "a number of factual details which naturally [lack] the consistency of the fictitious, logical, possible crime" (*Totalitarianism*, 427; see also 430).

These differences between totalitarianism and frontier civilization are a matter of degree rather than of kind, as scholars have regularly pointed out. For instance, Jeffrey Goldfarb remarks that in states that rely on institutions as well as the primacy of interpretive ideology, the difference between atomized subject and liberated individual seems somewhat artificial (*Cynical Society*, 32–39). However, Jeremy Waldron argues that different normative interpretations of comparable phenomena do in fact make a substantive difference for the law because interpretive traditions, rather than the phenomena themselves, serve as the bases for political and legal customs and standardized procedures. Central cultural interpretations of human communities such as frontier civilizations and totalitarian states, Waldron suggests, inform an entire network of legislative, judicial, and administrative decisions that respond to the underlying ideological logic represented by the relevant foundational figure (the frontiersman of the past or the Leviathan of the future) and make it possible to experience the underlying civilizational logic in a wide variety of situations and cases ("Torture," 1721–26). The ideological spirit of the law in the United States and totalitarianism could be constructed as diametrically opposed on the basis of their foundational figures.

The frontier model and the totalitarian model share the core assumption that civilization is something that must be continuously implemented in the nation-state. Because the sovereign use of its monopoly on force is directly informed by the model of civilization involved, the question of which model is chosen for the nation-state is, almost by default, translated into a discourse of legitimacy. The frontier model, which presupposes a fluid diversity of life and the stable equality of rights, is read in the United States as the most legitimate interpretation of a general human civilizing mission. Much of this legitimacy is derived from the contrast with the illegitimacy of the totalitarian model, which presupposes stable homogeneity of life and a fluid, situation-specific law.

It is not surprising that the frontier model's interpretation of the nation-state itself became associated with the notion of legitimate statehood in the United States, which explains the great importance of the US use of totalitarianism as a way to characterize nation-states with a different outlook (Jung, *Nürnberger Prozesse*, 135; Minow, "Introduction," 7–9). International bodies such as the League of Nations, founded as a result of World War I, likewise approached the idea of international criminal law using specifically American premises (Jung, *Nürnberger Prozesse*, 92–96). In this sense, the importance of different interpretations of international law by the United States and the Soviet Union during the Cold War were already foreshadowed during the period between the world wars (Nijman, *Legal Personality*, 257).

The League of Nations as an international body that followed the frontier model of civilization also prepared the grounds for a massive interpretive shift of hostis humani generis as a legal fiction after World War II. The League's most important contribution to this shift is its radical and influential rereading of piracy, which completely disassociates hostis humani generis from the crime of piracy and thus confirms the constellation's importance for other purposes—namely, to negotiate the notion of legitimate violence within nations, rather than in territories whose sovereign status was still undetermined.

The crime of piracy was historically derived from the space of the sea, and in the period between the world wars—when the legal status of territorial sovereignty was strengthened everywhere, including in the postcolonial realm (Falkowski, *Indian Law*, 39)—legal scholars and lawmakers contended that piracy could occur only on the high seas. Defining maritime piracy under these circumstances was reduced to a geographical problem: did a given assault happen in or out of territorial waters? Only outside of territorial waters—and when it satisfied other severe limitations (Menefee, "Piracy," 59–61; Murphy, "UNCLOS," 163–65)—could an assault be defined as an act of piracy. The first definition of piracy as such a geographical crime is commonly associated with the League of Nations' Committee of Experts for the Progressive Codification of International Law's *Draft Provisions for the Suppression of Piracy* of 1932 (Bingham et al., "Draft Provisions"), known as the Harvard Draft Convention on Piracy. This document served as the basis for one of the first international laws adopted by the League of Nations, and then for the United Nations Convention on the Law of the Sea (UNCLOS) of 1982 with very little modification, which testifies to an extremely stable international legal perspective on piracy between the 1920s and the 1980s. Martin Murphy explains this amazing continuity by the prevalence of "two consistent assumptions that run through the consideration of piracy in the twentieth century: That it was an old problem—a problem out of history—that had largely disappeared; . . . [and t]hat the sovereign rights of states always and everywhere had precedence over the measures to prevent and suppress it" ("UNCLOS," 158).

At the same time that piracy—a normative challenge to civilization at the margins of inherently civilized and inherently legitimate empire—was delinked from any space other than the sea in its narrowest definition, national space was substantiated as an in-between zone that could be a new site in which to determine what was legitimate violence. The central interpretive break in the use of the legal fiction of hostis humani generis was enabled by the frontier model: a constellation conventionally used to construct an existential conflict between races emerged as the means of constructing an equally stark dichotomy between institutions that order a society in the legalist spirit of civilization, and lawless institutions that subject the citizen or human being to illegitimate violence (see Sarat, "Robert Cover," 260).

It is with all this in mind that I read the genre of hard-boiled detective fiction, which emerged as a mainstream genre in the 1920s and radically formulated the American city as an in-between space. In this genre, the city is a site of claustrophobic, all-encompassing lawlessness reminiscent of the Hobbesian state of nature (Cynthia Hamilton, *Detective Fiction*, 129–30). It is the unaccountable world of shadows, rather than the open landscape, that eludes and defies taming by civilization. Urban space is constructed as a specifically institutional in-between zone insofar as the proper use of institutions is never self-evident but always threatened and precarious.

I use Dashiell Hammett's novel *Red Harvest* (1929; hereafter abbreviated in the citations as RH) as an example of the growing trend of investigating legitimate violence in the national context. This canonic classic of hard-boiled detective fiction may serve as a transitional text in the construction of national space as an in-between zone. The novel is a transitional because it does not yet argue that the entire national space is such a zone. As soon as the nameless Continental Op has traveled from San Francisco to Poisonville (RH, 4), he is spatially moved from civilization to the wilderness that actualizes a traditional hostis humani generis constellation, familiar from the American historical novel. The industrialized American city of Poisonville—a functional yet nightmarish site of oppressive thug rule in the aftermath of World War I (RH, 8–10)—is imagined in the tradition of pirate nests or outlaw refuges on the American frontier. Still, the city's more specific characterization in the novel anticipates assumptions about the nation-state as an in-between zone that will become dominant later in the twentieth century.

Until the point of the Continental Op's intervention (he is based in the San Francisco office of the Continental Detective Agency), the city's history related in the novel is one of ever-increasing oppression and corruption (RH, 3–4 and 8–10) that is represented by a band of thugs who were originally invited to the city as strikebreakers (RH, 9). The hostis humani generis constellation is comparatively straightforward throughout *Red Harvest.* Unchecked greed has turned Poisonville into a highly infectious state of nature (RH, 115, 119, 154–59, and 215). The regime established by the thugs evokes prevailing characterizations of totalitarian regimes. Poisonville suffers from a general atmosphere of oppression, in which all central peacekeeping offices are held by thugs, and the murder of a journalist who sought to reveal this state of oppression serves as the catalyst of the story.

Essentialist distinctions are made between the totalitarian rule of criminal thugs and their associates and the rule of law that characterizes the

American nation as a whole, and between the unaccountable violence of the shadows and the violence of those who will eventually have to make their actions public and be accountable for them (RH, 82–83, 89, 136, 138, and 215). In this sense, only uncompromising, unbiased, disinterested, and temporally limited violent intervention from outside is able to end the thugs' rule over the city. In the end, the Op's intervention and the ensuing military lockdown of the city reinstall the monopoly of force in the proper hands, Poisonville is restored to its original name of Personville, and the Op has to legitimate his own actions through the proper channels (RH, 216). Still, the city does not cease to be an in-between zone, as is shown by the character of Elihu Willsson, the Op's client who brought the Op—and the thugs—to the city in the first place.

If the protagonists Natty Bumppo and Henry March could be described as a legitimate representative of civilization and a ruthless pirata in James Fenimore Cooper's *The Deerslayer*, Hammett's *Red Harvest* features a corresponding relationship between the Continental Op and his client. The Op is a privateer-like character who represents a legitimate institution that implicitly allows him to waive regulations for the sake of efficiency (RH, 85, 117–18). His client, Elihu Willsson, is an "old pirate" (RH, 151) who is deeply tainted by, yet also ambiguously removed from, the regime of thug rule. The characterization of Willsson directly draws on classic representations of the piratical rich in the British tradition, but the character is not described by analogy to forces outside of the nation-state. Willsson belongs to this city. He has initiated and legitimated both the thugs' and the Op's presence in the city, and acts ambiguously toward both of them throughout the novel. Before, during, and after the removal of both thugs and Op (the praedo and the representative of civilization), Willsson embodies the city and serves as its central gatekeeper (RH, 9, 84, 151, 202–3). By the end of the novel, when the Op's successful intervention and his defeat of thug rule is followed by a change in who holds the monopoly on force (RH, 216), Willsson remains unchanged in his position. His enduring presence indicates that the city will continue to serve as a perpetual in-between zone, within which the normative struggle between thug and Op will continue indefinitely.

Indeed, the most important consequence of the pirata's stabilization of city space as an indefinite in-between zone is that it renders the violence between the representative of civilization and the praedo perpetual. *Red Harvest* suggests that the representative of civilization (the Continental Op, representing the rule of law) and the praedo (the thugs, representing their own illegitimate rule) are interlocked not as successive continuations of each other, as Turner had imagined them, but as antagonists whose confrontation within city space will always remain existential. Theirs is the clash of interpretive regimes over the use of the monopoly on force, which determines whether or not national institutions can actualize their civilizing potential. For this reason, the limitation of the in-between zone to the city space of Poisonville makes sense, as it renders the rest of the United States a site of civilization that the Op, as well as the American military, can meaningfully represent without having to further specify the source of their superior legitimacy.

In contrast, Hammett explicitly characterizes the thugs as oppressive, abusive, and false keepers of the peace. For instance, the Poisonville police force concentrates on fighting the personal opponents of its chief in a warlike manner (RH, 120) and routinely resorts to torturing prisoners (RH, 99). In the course of the novel, the story of a police officer called MacSwain is related: "He had been a pretty good guy, straight as ace-deuce-trey-four-five, till he got on the force. Then he went the way of the rest of them. His wife stood as much of it as she could and then left him" (RH, 89). MacSwain is transformed beyond recognition by a system that encourages and promotes, rather than condemns and punishes, inhumane oppression. His example shows that the thug rule of Poisonville anticipates the central moral and legal question that would later be raised in the political and legal context of macrocrimes and crimes against humanity: "Indeed, can behaviors, even the most outrageous ones, be considered criminal at all if they are the expressions of a state of society out of joint, a state of society which has only made these acts possible: deeds, in other words, that are not characterized by 'deviance' but by adaption, conformity, and a 'normalcy' that can be called adequate for the situation, and that dictates the behavior of many?" (Jäger, "Makroverbrechen," 331; my translation).

Hammett answers this question in the affirmative. He suggests that such a rule can be ended and that the implicated criminals must be punished. The civilization that is anticipated by the transformation of Poisonville into Personville can retrospectively legitimate the existential clash between American civilization and totalitarian oppression within the in-between zone. At the same time, Hammett allows for an important qualification to this answer. The implications of the thugs' and the Op's violent presence are diametrically opposed, the main difference being that the Op voluntarily leaves in the end, while it requires a string of assassinations and a military lockdown of the entire city to get rid of the thugs. Still, the thugs have been brought to Poisonville in virtually the same way as the Op. By emphasizing the similarities between the thugs and the Op, Hammett implies the possibility of a future similarity between the thugs and the soldiers who perform the military lockdown. As long as Willsson remains in the city, it is by no means clear whether the city will remain on the civilizing track toward Personville or lapse back into being Poisonville.

Let us pause for a moment and consider the distinction Giorgio Agamben makes between constitutive and constituted violence (*Homo Sacer*, 42–47). Agamben argues that constitutive violence corresponds with foundational violence as it has been understood in this book, while constituted violence is institutionalized violence that refers back to foundational violence only to gain legitimacy. In other words, frontier civilization originates in constitutive violence (birth) and softens into constituted violence (maturity). Agamben suggests that in the specific context of totalitarianism, constituted violence does not exist—instead, constitutive violence is rendered perpetual (ibid., 47). If civilization is inherently characterized by disruption, communities such as Poisonville under thug rule are totalitarian because the thugs' original disruption has been installed as a permanent state of oppression. Like the Native Americans who were imagined to exist in a perpetual state of nature in the wilderness, so do the totalitarian thugs rule with their unpredictable use of institutional structures.

This, consequentially, introduces a gray area in the application of the constellation, because a specific form of political order can be characterized as a quasi state of nature. Perpetual disruption of the in-between zone can occur in the service of either democracy or totalitarianism—introducing a latent essentialism to both notions, which allows for the existence of an almost classic European representative of civilization (such as the Op), who proclaims that democracy is "us, by definition" whenever a praedo as a representative of totalitarianism is identified.

However, since both totalitarianism and democracy, following the understanding of the frontier model of civilization, are defined by the perpetual violent disruption of order, the only way to distinguish them is to measure how violence transforms space. Totalitarianism is identified as foundational violence that refuses to give way to a process of softening, and violence that maintains itself—rather than allows itself to be surpassed—emerges as a praedonic usage of the in-between zone. It is because of the importance of maintaining a specific meaning for violence *in space* that oppression becomes such an important hallmark for totalitarianism.

It is therefore important that the monopoly on force is in the hands of a regime that allows the meaning of violence to change, as well as its agents and targets to shift.

Only when the monopoly on force is in such proper hands can the frontier model emerge as a description of the internal structure of the in-between zone. Because perpetual disruption implies the perpetual risk of totalitarianism, the monopoly on force that occasions this internal civilizing process has to maintain an institutional structure that limits the scale of disruption; order can be disrupted only in certain ways and not in others. The ability to transform only in certain ways can and must be reproduced wherever the meaning of space is under violent negotiation. Totalitarianism emerges as the predatory, oppressive alternative to the genesis of civilization—an alternative that not only civilization but also the in-between zone has to be protected from. At this point, we can see how the frontier model of civilization, while internally a new concept, uses the distinction between constitutive and constituted violence to substantiate an element of inherent civilization in the nation (which can then be contrasted with the inherent illegitimacy of totalitarian uses of national institutions).

To summarize, totalitarianism in *Red Harvest*, rendered illegitimate by its oppressive rule over faceless and unnarrated (that is, innocent) townspeople, does not constitute a violent birth that is preceded by a softening process, but neither does the civilizing intervention of the Op that is followed by military lockdown. Rather than representing an intertwined foundational moment, the struggle narrated in *Red Harvest* evokes diametrically opposed orders that are irreducible to each other. During such a perpetual standoff in spatially unspecified in-between zones, the completion of the essentialist struggle becomes the necessary condition for frontier development. As Lucia Folena concludes, this construction fundamentally depoliticizes the notion of violence itself because violence is necessary to allow either interpretive regime to introduce its own notion of civilization in the first place ("Figures," 228). Violence itself is not, in this sense, legitimate or illegitimate—it is rendered neutral because only the use of violence helps distinguish, retrospectively, between a spark of frontier civilization and a first instance of totalitarian oppression, and thus between an entire regime of legitimacy and one of illegitimacy.

The frontier model requires that a claim to represent civilization be backed up by the internal meaning of violence as transformative of space, and as the beginning of a softening process. Only from within such a softening process can the meaning of constitutive violence be determined. Only then can one speak, as Ronald Reagan does in his much later remark about the Sandinista regime in Nicaragua, of democracy as an "original purpose of the revolution," which can be "restored" violently ("Remarks").

To summarize, the institutional landscape of the nation in Hammett is not qualitatively different from the wilderness in Turner when it comes to the ways in which the hostis humani generis constellation is used. This is possible because the wilderness in Turner is also more generally described as "the bondages of the past," whose revolutionary removal is realized by the frontier. "Each frontier did indeed furnish a new field of opportunity, a gate of escape from the bondage of the past," Turner writes, "and freshness, and confidence, and scorn of older society, impatience of its restraints and its ideas, and indifference to its lessons, have accompanied the frontier" ("Frontier," 62). In this sense, as mentioned above, a state of oppression as Hammett imagines it can be characterized as equivalent to the forest that may legitimately occasion a revival of the frontier in national space, and the wilderness can be redefined as an oppressive "older society" characterized by "bondage" and "restraints." In the next chapter, I discuss the theoretical conditions that underlie such a use of the frontier model.

[9]

FREE AGENCY AND THE PURE WOMAN PARADOX

THE USE OF the frontier model in national territory assigns three central components to space: the notion that a clearly delimited geographical territory is able to permanently host all figures of the hostis humani generis constellation; that opposing factions are generally segregated from each other in the national territory and only their removal from segregated realms exposes them to an in-between zone; and finally, that in the entire territory, the same law reigns and the same basic cultural reference points can be meaningfully used for legitimation. Communities in the nation are distinct groups (and may describe each other in an essentialist register), but in an important sense, their group status is insignificant when it comes to institutions understood as realms of justice and civilization. Before such institutions, each human is again only an individual, and group status is unable to privilege certain people while others are discriminated against. Such is the main legitimating claim of the American nation: the US Constitution supersedes all other law, and each citizen has free and equal access to participation in the democracy and to legal representation. The frontier thesis can be implemented meaningfully because freedom and equality are presupposed as the inalienable rights of all, and because at the same time the implementation of these rights remains uneven and incomplete in practice.

African American writers of the twentieth century in particular could draw on earlier genres, such as the slave narrative, to incorporate this dramatic premise into literary fiction. The slave narrative was loosely oriented by its relationship to the Barbary captivity narrative, which offered a formal tradition to problematize slavery; the antislavery movement of the early nineteenth century generally emphasized the parallels between white captives in the Mediterranean and African American slaves in the United States. Keenly aware of this link, authors of slave narratives, such as Frederick Douglass or Harriet Ann Jacobs, used the captivity narrative as a structural framework to establish their own perspective as a legitimate one and to dramatize the injustices and inconsistencies in official US positions on the question of slavery (Marr, *American Islamicism*, 149–50). Echoing the concerns of the Barbary captivity narrative, the slave narrative generally remained characterized by the writer's concern for self-legitimization as a Christian and American subject (Fluck, *Das kulturelle Imaginäre*, 162–63), a concern that could be addressed very fruitfully by inserting the frontier model of civilization's interpretation of the hostis humani generis constellation into the African American protest novel of the twentieth century.

Even in the slave narrative itself, one can already see how a focus on the pirata (rather than on the representative of civilization) as the protagonist of a text forms the possibility of nonwhite heroism. In the slave narrative, the praedo represents the barbarous institution of slavery in the South, a regime that is presented as an illegitimate conqueror-sovereign with an illegitimate interpretation of national institutional structures. The narrative itself is a plea to a legitimate interpreter of the Constitution to end the illegitimate impostor's destruction of the enslaved innocent. Correspondingly, the evil twin to the heroic African American protagonist of the slave narrative is not the person who turns into an aggressive entity, but rather the one who refuses to turn into a violent, rebellious entity. Leonard Cassuto has argued that in the slave narrative, the transformation into a fundamentally and normatively disobedient, even violent, figure is portrayed as a civilizing and liberating act ("Frederick Douglass," 242. The treacherous renegade is the impassive slave who allows himself to be broken and who degrades himself by forming a loving attachment to his master—a role that is especially associated with the figure of the house slave.)

The slave narrative's characterization of the praedo as an illegitimate *institutional* force serves to show that the genre had already begun to dramatize internal wrongs and actively suggest dissent and reform in the nineteenth century. The traditional example of US failure in terms of the nation's civilizing mission is the legacy of slavery after the disaster of Reconstruction and the introduction of Jim Crow laws. The African American example draws attention in particular to the questions of how oppression can be theorized in a legal framework that presupposes the structural absence of oppression, and how such theorization can in fact lead to a change in the legal framework itself. By introducing these contexts to a debate on legitimate violence, the slave narrative provided an important tradition that would eventually allow twentieth-century writers to render African Americans conceivable as committers of legitimate violence in the nation, rather than as mere passive innocents.

In this context, the inclusion of the frontier model of civilization in twentieth-century claims to legitimate violence points toward the notion of free agency as the new basis for legitimate representation and focuses on the law as a central locus of the in-between zone, where oppression is understood as illegitimate violence.

If oppression assumes such centrality, I must make quite clear how the term is understood in this book. Thus, this chapter discusses the notions of oppression and free agency at some length. In the classic Enlightenment tradition, free agency is generally defined as the ability to act according to one's free will, as opposed to actions that are the result of violence against a person or the threat of such violence. As Wendy Brown (*States of Injury*, 188–90) has suggested, the expression of free agency can assume two traditional forms that inform constructions of agency in the democratic state. Visibly remaining in the tradition of Augustine, the legitimate form of free agency, in Brown's analysis, is a representative agency that expresses its capacity of free will in the merciful protection of the innocent; the illegitimate form of free agency is invasive agency that expresses its capacity of free will in its choice of harming the innocent. Classic representatives of these two forms are the paterfamilias, who virtuously protects his family and maintains that family's means of life, and the invader, who maliciously violates the bodies and destroys the lives of the innocent. These two forms of free agency are complementary, as the legitimacy of the paterfamilias can be directly derived from his ability to protect his family from the predatory agency of the violent invader (or, as Brown puts it, from that of the "marauding warrior" [ibid., 188]). This relationship between the legitimate paterfamilias and the illegitimate invader is the basis for all other uses of the concept of free agency.

This relationship between legitimate and illegitimate agency is complicated at a very early point by the specific structural premises of the democratic state. My definition of representative agency rests once more on the philosophy of Hobbes and Locke. As indicated above, their man in the state of nature is not simply an individual human being but a paterfamilias, the representative head of a family (Eggers, *Naturzustandstheorie*, 44; Laslett, introduction, 91–97). Representative agency, in this sense, means that a representative agent's free will not only determines his own actions (as is traditionally the case of the illegitimate free agent) but also regulates the actions and relationships of the women, children, and bonded dependents who make up his family and are thus also rendered innocent in the terminology of this study. It is this position of quasi-sovereign ruler over his family that establishes the paterfamilias as a representative agent in the first place and that serves as a model for Hobbes's construction of the Leviathan. The sovereign Leviathan, in Hobbes, assumes the same position over all patresfamilias that they assume over their families: his will alone rules them and regulates their interactions, and it is because of the unquestioned and legitimate supremacy of the paterfamilias over his family that the Hobbesian Leviathan becomes legitimate as well. The family itself is notably excluded from the Leviathan's rule and remains subjected to the paterfamilias.

As Brown notes very clearly, "the family is cast as natural and prepolitical," and members of the family such as women and slaves of either gender are therefore "naturally" excluded from any claims to free agency (*States of Injury*, 181). Speaking of women specifically, Judith Butler has characterized representative agency as "a relationship between men which is, finally, about the bonds between men, but which takes place through the heterosexual exchange and distribution of women" (*Gender Trouble*, 40–41). According to the logic of the Hobbesian Leviathan, Butler's men (patresfamilias) and women (innocents) can essentially be replaced with sovereigns and representative men.

As Lynn Hunt suggests, Western democracies draw legitimacy from the notion that patresfamilias who rise up against the sovereign Leviathan reclaim access to full agency on the basis of their capacity for reason and are thus led out of the unbearable oppression that the status of an innocent had meant for them (*Inventing Human Rights*, 146–75). This is precisely the basis for the social contract imagined by Locke (Laslett, introduction, 114–15). Oppression, in other words, means the illegitimate subjection of a person to the status of an innocent. If one removal of subjection is legitimate, however, the other is as well: if representative men can dethrone the sovereign, women-and-children can dethrone the representative man.[1] It seems hypocritical from within the logic of the democratic state not to take the second step and grant the status of a free agent to previously natural innocents such as white women and slaves of any gender. Claims that previously natural innocents should be included on this basis have directly informed various civil rights movements in the United States and the formulation of human rights after World War II (Slaughter, *Human Rights Inc.*, 139).

To summarize, the establishment of the democratic state itself destabilizes the presupposed exclusion of the innocent from agency; the central internal contradiction of Western democracy is that the call for the equal right to free agency for all is coupled with the fact that the traditionally legitimate form of free agency still depends on the now-illegitimate practice of oppression (L. Hunt, *Inventing Human Rights*, 146–75). If traditional representative agency is destabilized as a legitimate form of agency, the question arises as to how legitimate free agency can be established instead. In the twentieth century, the solution is found in a reformulation of innocence.[2]

In traditional discourses of agency, there is a long tradition of narrating the fate of women who were threatened with rape by an illegitimate outside agent but who violently and successfully defended themselves, thus preventing their own rape—sometimes even killing the would-be perpetrator in the process. The problem with these women in traditional discourses of free agency is twofold. First, as Brown and Butler have both emphasized, the actions of these women contradict their status as innocents (that is, as inherently passive objects of violence); instead, their ability to successfully defend themselves against violation defines them as active subjects, a notion that contradicts their naturalized position as innocents. Second, they subvert not one but both of the traditional definitions of male free agency at the same time. Neither the legitimate nor the illegitimate free agent can define himself as an agent in relation to such a woman after her successful defense. The paterfamilias has failed to protect her and thus loses his legitimate claim to her representation, and the violent invader has failed to violate her and thus cannot constitute his agency through her.

Because such a woman thus subverts all three available positions in traditional constructions of agency (paterfamilias, invader, and innocent) and at the same time suggests herself as a violent free agent in her own right, she remains inexplicable in the traditional discourse of agency. She remains externalized from civilization even though her actions have been specifically committed to preserve the spirit of civilized values, and the injustice of her ban is usually admitted by her contemporaries. This situation of a woman who violently prevents her own rape constitutes a theoretical as well as moral paradox that I call the pure woman paradox. In its gender-specific form, and in a number of interesting variations, this paradox was discussed as a far-reaching question of legitimate violence from antiquity until approximately the nineteenth century (see Barbey d'Aurevilly, "Rache," 125–71; Exquemelin, *Buccaneers*, 201–3; Heller-Roazen, *Enemy of All*, 70–71; O'Daly, *Augustine*, 77).

It is comparatively easy to see why the pure woman paradox is an interesting vehicle to use in substantiating a discourse of oppression-defying agency. In this paradox, and only there, the oppression of women on the basis of their status as natural innocents is traditionally and consistently admitted as flawed, and oppression is recognized as a severe moral problem —a problem that cannot be resolved, however, without destabilizing the entire framework of traditional free agency.

In the American context, an interesting solution has been found. Elaine Scarry, a scholar whose work is characterized by the investigation of a dichotomy of oppression and civilization, has theorized that two intertwined aspects of torture become central in the production of a new kind of innocent in the twentieth century. According to Scarry, torture can be defined as an effort by the torturer to render the victim permanently, and thus quasi-inherently, innocent. This permanent innocence is not natural, as it is in earlier models, but actively produced through a process of fundamental defamiliarization with civilization—which, in Scarry, means an order that considers human life valuable and treats all humans equally and respectfully (which essentially corresponds with the idea of a civilized institution). Scarry devotes a large part of her argument to the observation that random objective manifestations of such a legitimate order—say, a room, a refrigerator, or a telephone—are assigned radically new meanings for the victim of torture. Instead of indicating the presence of order, these objects instead indicate the unshareable experience of torture and defamiliarize the victim from language itself. The violent, enforced subjection to an unshareable context of meaning makes it impossible for the victim to engage in those reasonable relations of exchange that Butler has described as the central attribute of free agency (*Gender Trouble*, 40–41). These relations instead become meaningless to the victim (Scarry, *Body in Pain*, 12, 45, 48–49, and 61).

The victim of this most extreme and tangible form of oppression can now be represented with full legitimacy by the opponents of oppression. This new representative position is legitimate because it can refer to the innocents it represents, yet it vocally defies the oppressive implications of traditional representation that have produced such innocents in the first place. As Avery Gordon has emphasized, this new representative position on behalf of innocence produced by violence is explicitly open to people who were previously denied free agency on general principle, such as nonwhite women (*Ghostly Matters*, 108–13).

While the victim of torture is thus assigned a permanent position of innocence, the torturer undergoes a development that ties him ever more closely to an order that, not accidentally, constitutes the opposite of civilization in Scarry. The torturer serves an order that, in her argument, constitutes a totalitarian Leviathan. In international political and legal debates about torturers since the period between the world wars, it has been postulated that normal people whose instincts revolt against torture (but who still agree to commit it out of obedience to their sovereign) can be transformed by the act into the unfeeling puppets of a totalitarian Leviathan, and as such they come to actively embrace torture (Peters, *Torture*, 179; see also Huggins, Haritos-Fatouros, and Zimbardo, *Violence Workers*). A literary example of such a transformation that has been mentioned above is MacSwain in Hammett's *Red Harvest* (89). Importantly, the torturer is transformed into an entity as devoid of will as the innocent, as he is the tool of an illegitimate regime that actualizes itself in his acts (Scarry, *Body in Pain*, 18). The torturer thus affirms the totalitarian Leviathan in two ways: by committing violence against them, he produces permanent innocents in the name of the illegitimate order, and at the same time he renders himself a mere medium of the regime that is the actual agent of his violence. The torturer emerges as the ideal representative of the totalitarian regime—a praedo on the level of agency constructions—since totalitarian rule directly expresses itself through him and toward the innocent without any resistance of the individual torturer against the state's violation of his agency.

Robert Cover affirms Scarry's general characterization of torture, and thus of the notion of innocence produced by violence, and addresses the figure of the pure woman in the form of the martyr who alone is able to resist the innocence-producing effect of totalitarianism. She is able to insist on her representative status because representation, in her case, translates not as representation of the innocent but as the representation of a norm: "Martyrs insist in the face of overwhelming force that if there is to be continuing life, it will not be on the terms of the tyrant's law. Law is the projection of an imagined future upon reality. Martyrs require that any future they possess will be on the terms of the law to which they are committed (God's law). And the miracle of the suffering of the martyrs is their insistence on the law to which they are committed, even in the face of world-destroying pain" (Cover, "Violence," 207).

Cover goes on to argue that the specific martyrdom narrated in the pure woman paradox may in fact be understood as an allegory to the American Revolution itself; he clearly understands the pure woman and the foundational frontiersman as equivalent ("Violence," 208). Indeed, the initial fragmentation of the frontiersman in the wilderness corresponds directly with the notion of defamiliarization through torture as postulated by Scarry, and the gradual subjection to abuse corresponds with a passage into the space of the wilderness. As Cover suggests, the assumption of irrevocable defamiliarization in the pure woman paradox positions the pure woman as a third entity whose normative rigor restructures the law instead of territorial space. However, as Cover plainly argues, the paradox can correspond with the frontier model of civilization only when the law is identified as originally oppressive. The pure woman then breaks the law precisely because it is an expression of oppression and changes the law into an institution that ceases to be oppressive. After all, only that which can be defied as well as transformed can serve as a wilderness in the sense required by the frontier model of civilization.

The pure woman paradox in this specific legal context can be linked to pirate law in the sense that the legally crucial genesis of the pirata also explicitly allows and even conventionalizes a transformation of innocents produced by violence (captives) into violent free agents (pirates)—as the case of Bartholomew Roberts, discussed above, illustrated. In this sense, the pure woman paradox and the history of pirate law can be linked to illuminate the formulation of legitimate violence in the context of oppressive institutions.

In trials in the Golden Age of Piracy, courts took into account the fact that not every person aboard a pirate ship was there voluntarily. The main difficulty for a court was to determine for each defendant whether or not the constitutive transformation from bonded captive (innocent) into a violent free agent (pirata) had taken place. If it had not, the defendant was deemed innocent in both senses of the word: innocent of the crime and innocent in the Augustinian sense of being a violated captive without any legally relevant agency of his own.

For a piracy charge to stick, it had to be proved that the defendant had free agency, which in this context could be demonstrated only by committing crimes. In one of the six trials of William Kidd, for instance, the judge reviewed the mitigating evidence brought forward by all defendants. "Each argument that had been raised [on behalf of the accused pirates] was dismissed as inadequate," Robert Ritchie reports, "except that of the three young servants, because 'a Pirate is not to be understood to be under Constraint, but a free Agent.' If the jury decided that these men had acted under orders from their masters, then they should find them not guilty" (*Captain Kidd*, 219). The jury reached a verdict of not guilty for all three servants, thus following a widespread legal custom that recognized bondage as a circumstance exempting a person from the charge of piratical conspiracy. In other trials, too, courts emphasized that individual pirates were "active and forward" or "brisk and lively" during attacks to prove their active and willing participation in the piratical conspiracy (Cordingly, *Black Flag*, 233). The crime of murder was accepted as especially irrefutable proof of a pirate's completed transformation from an innocent agent into a free (and therefore guilty) agent (ibid., 230).

For piratae in the renegade tradition, the committing of violence serves as a benchmark to establish the defendant's relationship to the essentialist civilization he had treacherously abandoned. In other words, the pirata's act of violence did not just establish him as a free agent; it also automatically rendered him an individual who had consciously abandoned and attacked humanity as a whole. Consider, in this context, an example from Charles Ellms's *The Pirates' Own Book*. In a chapter devoted to the white pirate Charles Gibbs, Ellms's narration of his trial includes the questioning of Gibbs's African American accomplice, Thomas J. Wansley, who has been accused of murder and piratical conspiracy. When given the chance to say some last words in his defense before the final sentence is pronounced, Wansley answers:

> I will say a few words, but it is perhaps of no use. I have often understood that there is a great deal of difference in respect of color, and I have seen it in

> this Court. Dawes and Brownrigg were as guilty as I am, and these witnesses have tried to fasten upon me greater guilt than is just, for their life has been given to them. You have taken the blacks from their own country, to bring them here to treat them ill. I have seen this. The witnesses, the jury, and the prosecuting Attorney consider me more guilty than Dawes, to condemn me—for otherwise the law must have punished him; he should have had the same verdict, for he was a perpetrator in the conspiracy. Notwithstanding my participating, they have sworn falsely for the purpose of taking my life; they would not even inform the Court, how I gave information of money being on board; they had the biggest part of the money; and have sworn falsely. (quoted in Ellms, *Own Book*, 64–65)

Wansley then specifically accuses Dawes of being the head of the conspiracy. He argues that Dawes, along with others, had pressured him into the crime by making him fear for his life, and that he was condemned to death by his shipmates if he informed others of their designs and condemned to death by the law if he participated and was found out. Stuck between a rock and a hard place, Wansley responded to the threat of his shipmates, since their threat to his life was more immediate. After this testimony by Wansley, the court hears the white codefendant Charles Gibbs. Gibbs largely affirms Wansley's charge against Dawes and the other pirate Wansley mentions, Brownrigg. Eventually, the court states its reason for upholding the death sentence for both Wansley and Gibbs.

> You, Thomas J. Wansley, conceive that a different measure of justice has been meted out to you, because of your color. Look back upon your whole course of life; think of the laws under which you have lived, and you will find that to white or black, to free or bond, there is no ground for your allegations; that they are not supported by truth or justice. Admit that Brownrigg and Dawes have sworn falsely; admit that Dawes was concerned with you; admit that Brownrigg was not innocent; admit, in relation to both, that they are guilty, the whole evidence has proved beyond a doubt that you are guilty; and your own words admit that you were an active agent in perpetrating this horrid crime. Two fellow beings who confided in you, and in their perilous voyage called in [*sic*] your assistance, yet you, without reason or provocation, have maliciously taken their lives. (quoted in Ellms, *Own Book*, 66)

Wansley argues that his deed was a result of the general oppression of African Americans, an oppression that makes him so exceptionally vulnerable to violent pressure and exploitation that it essentially renders him innocent. He suggests that his decision to kill to save his own life could not be considered malicious, regardless of the particularities of the deed. Instead, he was driven by forces that the court has not sufficiently recognized as causes of the crime, and his decision to murder the captain was based on a reasonable assessment of his options for survival. If the court disregards this argument, Wansley argues, it becomes guilty of oppression. In other words, and in contradiction to the argument of the court (Ellms, *Own Book*, 67), Wansley denies that the theoretical status of citizenship renders him a free agent in the required sense. Because the court has not actively recognized the importance of Wansley's innocence (in the sense of his vulnerability to existential pressure), Wansley claims that instead the court perpetuates his oppression, which leads him to question the legitimacy of the institutional judgment that sentences him to death.

It is significant that Wansley is charged with a double felony. He has admitted to having committed a murder, and therefore he must be punished for this undisputed crime alone. He is charged with a proved murder in unison with piratical conspiracy, a crime that is inherently relational and virtually impossible to reconstruct conclusively. In view of the situation, the court's decision on the crime of piracy can make a difference only between death and long imprisonment. In this case, since the court is openly charged with racism, the court's decision between death and imprisonment directly reflects how seriously it takes the notion of racism itself as a form of bondage, and more importantly, its own implication as a potentially oppressive institution complicit in the crime of racism.

As the judicial tradition in piracy cases presupposes, murder is by definition the act of a free agent and speaks against any recognition of the perpetrator as oppressed and, in this sense, innocent. In Ellms, the charge of oppression is therefore dismissed by the court and the author;[3] the court formally characterizes Wansley as a free agent rather than as a bonded innocent on the grounds of his acts of violence, and thus sentences him to death.

Still, the charge of racism is there, and its specific dramatization in this pirate trial constitutes an interesting predecessor to later characterizations of the pirata on trial in novels such as Richard Wright's *Native Son* (1940). In this classic protest novel, the charge of universal institutional oppression is central. *Native Son* shows the reader a murder that is the direct result of general oppression in which the court is implicit; the protagonist-defendant is subjected to oppression and threats to violence that remain invisible to the court; there is a charge of a double felony, murder and a relational crime (meaning a crime that, like piracy, can only rarely be proved by evidence and is instead determined on the basis of persuasive accounts of what has happened); and finally, the court eventually rejects the charge of oppression against it by passing a death sentence.

Considering the legal history of piracy, the question arises as to how a defendant can be unambiguously characterized as a pirata if the relational crime is not piracy, as is the case in *Native Son*. In the context of reformulated agency and oppression, the pure woman paradox not only offers an example of agency-related transformation into a new entity but also shows that rape is a crime that may, in this context, serve the same narrative function as piracy. If the pure woman who prevents her own rape is seen, as in Cover, as a foundational figure, she can also be viewed as the preferred pirata figure of the twentieth century. This figure has a long separate history of dramatizing the paradoxes of traditional agency, and her specific construction is adopted by twentieth-century institutions to inform the agency of the (usually male) foundational pirata who challenges institutions of the law to live up to their civilizational standards.

In a century fundamentally troubled by the disastrous implications of virtues such as obedience and loyalty in Nazi Germany, this foundational pirata served as a powerful model of a solitary individual whose absolute moral compass could not be confused by flawed or insufficient interpretations of the law. The foundational pirata's normative rigor could instead help expose existing institutions that failed to reflect the norms they claimed to represent. A foundational pirata is not necessarily a benevolent entity and does not have to be. As I showed in previous chapters, the pirata generally exists in a state of "spiritual isolation" (Baer, "Plot of Piracy," 11), so the foundational pirata's normative independence may take either a constructive or a deconstructive turn without any internal contradiction (see, for example, Horkheimer and Adorno, *Dialectic*, 63–93). Yet because of the distinction between constitutive and constituted violence, the foundational pirata can be retrospectively legitimated as a foundational agent that renews civilization even despite his possibly malevolent individual intentions.[4]

In this sense, as was indicated by my comments above on the wilderness as something to be defied as well as transformed, the law itself emerges as the most obvious in-between zone in which the nation may reinvent itself, and in which individual struggles are able to have the greatest normative impact on the nation as a whole. As the discussion of Wright's protest novel *Native Son* in the next chapter shows, this construction of hostis humani generis in the language of agency—which so far only includes the praedo, the pirata, and the innocent, but not the representative of civilization—assigns to the representative of civilization the role of reharmonizing the law with the foundational pirata's rigorous intervention into the institutions that structure national space.

[10]

THE FOUNDATIONAL PIRATA IN RICHARD WRIGHT'S *NATIVE SON*

RICHARD WRIGHT'S NOVEL *Native Son* was published in 1940, and it immediately became a commercial bestseller. It was the first novel written by an African American author to be a selection of the prestigious Book of the Month Club, and the novel's most severe critics were African American scholars who felt that African Americans had been misrepresented by the character of Bigger Thomas (see, for example, Baldwin, *Notes*). Wright tells the story of a young and angry African American man, Bigger Thomas, who is hired by the rich, white Dalton family to be their chauffeur. Before taking the job, he has always lived in the segregated Chicago ghetto and has rarely been near white people. On his first night on the job, Thomas kills Mary, the Daltons' daughter, thus positioning himself as a violent free agent. When her body is found, Thomas flees with his girlfriend, Bessie Mears, whom he rapes and kills. Eventually, he is caught and put on trial, which causes a spate of white violence in retaliation against African Americans. Thomas's white lawyer, Boris Max, pleads that Thomas's violence was the direct result of oppression, but, like Wansley in Ellms, Thomas is sentenced to death. *Native Son* is divided into three parts, titled "Fear," "Flight," and "Fate." The first two parts are fast paced and narrate the events that culminate, in "Fear," in the murder of Mary Dalton and, in "Flight," in Thomas's capture. The third part consists of his trial and death sentence. This part is completely different in pace and tone; it mostly revisits and renarrates the first two parts.

In 1937, Richard Wright postulated that a separate "Negro way of life" existed in America that had not been established by choice but was "forced upon them from without by lynch rope, bayonet, and mob rule" ("Blueprint," 271). Wright saw himself confronted with civilizational discourses that dismissed his own perspective as less than fully civilized, much like the early republic vis-à-vis Europe. At the time Wright wrote his novel, traditional discriminatory notions of natural innocence informed all interactions of African Americans and whites within the nation-state. In response, Wright claimed, "a new role is developing upon [*sic*] the Negro writer. He is being called upon to do no less than create values by which his race is to struggle, live, and die," but to do so within the American nationalist logic of the beloved community into which African Americans were to be integrated ("Blueprint," 271–72).

Traditional ways to claim legitimate free agency—that is, representative agency over natural innocents—remained unconvincing to Wright. The obvious reason for his reluctance to accept the paterfamilias as a suitable model was the role of the slaveholder as a supposedly legitimate representative of his slaves.[1] Another solution had to be found, one that addressed the core problem of oppression for African Americans—a discourse, in other words, that not just allowed but forced whites to accept the free agency of African Americans as equals. The general atmosphere of oppression that formed and informed "the social institutions of the Negro," Wright argued, had to be countered with a very specific African American affirmation of nationalism: "Negro writers must accept the nationalist implications of their lives, not in order to encourage them, but in order to change and transcend them" ("Blueprint," 271). *Native Son* constitutes a narrative attempt to imagine an undeniable free agency for African Americans as equals to whites, an attempt that explicitly uses the figure of the pirata and the foundational logic of the frontier model of civilization to substantiate this claim. In this sense, Wright anticipates the strategy of the civil rights movement of the 1960s that fundamentally "refused the expectation that to be full participants in the social and political order they [African Americans] needed to assimilate culturally and linguistically to a white middle-class American way of being in the world. Instead, they demanded respect for and recognition of their particular racial and ethnic identities and declared that the new era of race relations meant that nonwhite peoples in the United States would no longer have to occupy the place of second-class citizens" (Markus and Moya, "Doing Race," 57).

To integrate the affirmation of group identity with an affirmation of the nation-state as legitimate, Bigger Thomas's claim to agency in *Native Son* (hereafter abbreviated in the citations as NS) is formulated as the genesis of a foundational pure woman pirata. This position of the pirata is stabilized by the exclusion of strategies to obtain free agency that Wright identifies as unconvincing. First, he excludes the notion of traditional representative agency. The beginning of the novel characterizes the protagonist as a dependent in a single-parent household after the violent death of his father, and Thomas remains unable to make representative claims over anyone throughout the novel (Takeuchi, "Bigger"). For instance, Thomas's attempts to establish representative claims over Mears, his girlfriend and accomplice, fail (NS, 180 and 260). But before he can suffer from this failure, he decides to separate himself from her; instead of ruling her, he rapes and murders her (NS, 264–70). In the course of the novel, Thomas ceases to fail at traditional representative agency; instead, he decides to no longer seek it.

In a similar vein, Wright dismisses the African American traditions of liberation through education and of assimilation into existing institutional structures. He bases this rejection on the claim that the "Negro way of life" encompasses "two separate cultures . . .: one for the Negro masses, unwritten and unrecognized; and the other for the sons and daughters of a rising Negro bourgeoisie, parasitic and mannered" ("Blueprint," 270). In constructing this dichotomy, Wright uses the narrative tradition of the slave narrative to substantiate his construction of the hostis humani generis constellation in the novel. Like those in the slave narrative, Wright's praedones are collectively of a different race (white) and are the expressions of an explicitly institutional injustice along the lines of Elaine Scarry's characterization of the torturer (*Body in Pain*, 56–59). As in the slave narrative, the act of violence by the field slave is read as an act of liberation that is contrasted with the mute submission of the house slave (see Cassuto, "Frederick Douglass").

In *Native Son*, these two African American "cultures," as Wright calls them, are represented by the two chauffeurs in the service of the Daltons, a family whose members control much of Chicago's segregated urban infrastructure and therefore the space within which all the figures in the novel move. The representative of the "Negro bourgeoisie" who follows the path of educated assimilation is a man named Green, who does not appear in the story but who is mentioned as Thomas's predecessor in the chauffeur job. Green has gone to night school during his long employment by the Daltons and has received an education according to the wishes of his employers. Still, these same employers eventually deny him a job that is appropriate for his superior education; even though they support African American education, they generally do not hire African Americans for jobs that allow them to rise socially (NS, 86, 92–93, and 357–58).

The second chauffeur (Thomas), who represents the "unwritten and unrecognized [African American] masses," replaces Green after the latter leaves to take up an unspecified job "with the government" (NS, 86). Thomas is not interested in work ethics, piety, or education. Just as he refuses to be a representative paterfamilias to his impoverished family, Thomas refuses to be represented by the Daltons, who want to educate him (NS, 92–93), or by the "Negro institutions" that want to install piety in him (NS, 368). Because of his refusal of all legitimate paths open to African Americans, his desire for agency is necessarily expressed in the realm of illegitimate violence. He does not succumb to his mother's and his employers' wishes that he might quietly work hard and better himself to achieve unspecified goals; instead, he murders Mary, his employers' daughter, burns her body in the Daltons' furnace, and attempts to blackmail the parents into paying ransom money. He revels in his ability to control the situation, as well as to artfully manipulate the behavior of whites, who consider him incapable of reason.

His scheme collapses when he loses his nerve—as he did in his self-sabotaged plan to rob a white storekeeper early in the novel (NS, 44)—and avoids the furnace, which then draws too much smoke. Annoyed with Thomas, others attend to it, and Mary's body is found (NS, 245–47). Thomas flees and kills again in his attempt to escape, but he is eventually captured and put on trial. His transformation into a violent free agent is thus complete and can go no further; the third part of the novel, then, positions him as a foundational pirata rather than a random criminal.

The narrative construction of Thomas as a foundational pirata whose actions are a normative response to oppression is divided into two parts. While the first two parts of the novel narrate the transformative development of Thomas's piratical consciousness, the third part responds to the logic of the frontier model that requires the transformed pirata's action to have foundational consequences for the space he engages in—consequences that are independent of his actions as an agent. Two initially marginal characters become central after Thomas's capture. The first is Jan Erlone, Mary's communist boyfriend who becomes important to the plot after having an epiphany. Confronted with his girlfriend's murder, Erlone abandons all notions of proletarian revolution; he recharacterizes these early convictions as aspects of blindness to the real nature of oppression, and realizes that Mary's murder constitutes a normative disruption that can now serve as the basis of civilizing development in the sense of the frontier model. In consequence, he vows to stand by Thomas to further this more authentic disruption of American institutions (NS, 99 and 317). The second character that only takes center stage in the third part is Boris Max, the lawyer whom Erlone hires for Thomas. In court, Max presents the normative interpretation of Thomas's actions and, through his interpretation, initiates the legitimating transition from constitutive to constituted violence. It is primarily Max who works to restructure the law on the basis of the pirata's foundational disruption.

Erlone's epiphany and the character of Max as a whole have been criticized as wooden elements of an unconvincing plot twist and have essentially been dismissed as the result of bad craftsmanship on the part of the author (see Baldwin, *Notes*, 39; Menand, *American Studies*, 83). However, these much-criticized aspects of the narrative are needed to render Thomas's fate meaningful as that of a foundational pirata. During the trial, Max interprets Thomas's actions throughout the novel with an accuracy that frequently borders on narrative redundancy. While not exactly reader-friendly, renarrating these actions in the context of the law achieves something important: it allows Max to exorcise Thomas's deeds. Precisely because Max is so right about everything the reader already knows of Thomas's inner life, the lawyer's pleas and arguments meticulously separate the illegitimate acts of violence from their legitimate normative meaning. In this way, Thomas's deeds can be used to inform a restructuring of the law that may acknowledge, and eventually remove, the oppression of African Americans. Only if they constitute the foundational moment for a removal of oppression on this nonviolent legal basis can Thomas's deeds really begin to "mean" something to the nation (NS, 421).

The restructuring of the law is necessary, Wright suggests, because it is the legal oppression of African Americans that has caused Thomas's violence in the first place. In the novel, Mary Dalton's murder is the direct result of Thomas's fear of being subjected to a traditional collaboration between the criminal justice system and violent racist oppression. Wright portrays the murder in the following way: It is Thomas's first night on the job, and he drives Mary to meet her boyfriend, Erlone. Mary and Erlone urge Thomas to eat and drink with them as their equal. Unable to escape them and painfully aware of his own anxiety, Thomas fully understands for the first time that he exists in a society informed by segregation. Because Mary and Erlone are so friendly, it occurs to Thomas that segregation—although naturalized in this society—might not be natural to humankind. The friendly interaction between blacks and whites on an equal footing is described as a "No Man's Land" of unchartered consequences (NS, 98). Stepping into this no man's land during his night out with Mary and Erlone shakes Thomas profoundly because he realizes that all of his learned, naturalized behavior is useless once he stops considering whites as his natural superiors. At the end of the night, Erlone leaves, and Mary is too drunk to get to her room alone. Thomas helps her into the house and then to bed. Rather than leaving immediately after that, he lingers with the thought of molesting her; but before he can decide on a first step in any direction, Mary's blind mother enters the room. Out of fear that he might be discovered, Thomas smothers Mary, and Mrs. Dalton leaves without noticing him.

Thomas panics because an African American man cannot be found in a white woman's bedroom, regardless of his intentions, without having to expect vicious retaliation. The rape of a white woman by an African American man is a cultural topos that, for Wright, epitomizes the violent logic of oppression. "If a Negro rebels against rule and taboo, he is lynched and the reason for the lynching is usually called 'rape,'" Wright argues in a comment on the novel, "that catchword which has garnered such vile connotations that it can raise a mob anywhere in the South pretty quickly, even today" ("'Bigger,'" 7). Thomas knows this and commits violence only to remove himself from the threat of violence: the murder of Mary is thus characterized as an incidental effect of Thomas's oppression.

Nevertheless, after the fact, the murder is reinterpreted by him as a constitutive moment that proves his ability to assume the status of a free agent rather than only that of a bonded innocent. Never for a moment does Thomas admit to the somewhat accidental dimension of Mary's death; instead, he almost immediately insists that he has murdered her (NS, 135–36). After all, as we saw in the Wansley trial, murder is by definition the act of a free agent, and because Thomas is African American and assumed to have natural innocence, taking on the status of a murderer allows him to be permanently situated in a no man's land. The murder of Mary becomes the reason why he cannot be less than a free agent on equal footing with whites—after all, white law itself is now forced to recognize him as free.

At the same time, Thomas's original position of free agency through murder is transformed into the position of a pirata with the double charge of murder and rape brought against him. Rape in *Native Son* replaces piracy as a relational crime that assigns normative importance to an individual and somewhat random act of murder. For Wright, an African American man's rape of a white woman does not primarily signify illegitimate violence against women but constitutes the legitimate reaction of an African American man to white oppression in general. Rape, in the novel, is strictly a metaphor for black-white race relations, and a clear-cut case of "hommo-social [*sic*] relations" (Butler, *Gender Trouble*, 40) between the invading perpetrator and the victim's protectors. In the novel, Thomas accordingly reasons that "rape was not what one did to women. Rape was what one felt when one's back was against a wall and one had to strike out, whether one wanted to or not, to keep the pack from killing one. He committed rape every time he looked into a white face" (NS, 258). Because this metaphorical dimension of rape is the only significant one in the novel, on the level of agency it is not relevant whether or not physical rape has actually taken place.

Even though it is clear from the original manuscript of *Native Son* that "when Bigger was with Mary in her bedroom, he had rape in his heart" (Menand, *American Studies*, 80), *Native Son* goes to great length to inform the reader that the rape charge in the case of Mary Dalton is unfounded and springs solely from the imagination of white prejudice against African Americans in general. Thomas unambiguously denies the charge (NS, 378), but the fact that Mary's burned corpse cannot be examined for traces of rape is to Thomas's disadvantage, as the charge of rape cannot be disproved (NS, 337). This leads us back to Wansley and his charge of racism against the court. Just as we as readers know that Max is completely correct about his interpretation of Thomas's motivation, we also know that the charge of Mary's rape is the result of prejudice rather than evidence. The question that remained unanswerable in Wansley's case—has he acted in response to extraordinary pressure, or is he a liar trying to downplay his own malice?—is resolved from the start in Wright. The Wansley trial's underlying question—is it possible, under the conditions of racism, for a perpetrator to be considered bonded (that is, innocent)?—is brought to the attention of *Native Son*'s reader with the subtlety of a sledgehammer. It is also answered in the affirmative. While Thomas had "created a new world for himself" through murder, it is the rape charge that "utterly excluded him from the world" around him (NS, 272–73)—not least because the world around him is, to a significant degree, too racist to stand in legitimate judgment over him.

The use of rape as a metaphor—the normative violation of "their symbol of beauty" (NS, 195)—is why Thomas's acts of violence may be seen, even by his opponents, as acts of defiance against a specifically American regime of racialized oppression. It is, Wright emphasizes, white society itself that insists most on the rape charge. The state attorney who prosecutes Thomas blatantly states that the real crime for which he is on trial is not the murder of a white woman—instead, that "the central crime here is [her] *rape*!" (NS, 437). Just as white society has rendered Thomas a free agent by defining murderers in this way, it now characterizes his alleged rape of a white woman as an act of normative defiance comparable to the treason of the pirata renegade. In this sense, Thomas's position as a pirata is a position in relation to white American law itself and can—even must—be understood in this context. Consequently, it is in the realm of the law that his foundational potential in the spirit of the frontier model of civilization unfolds.

Max does not deny Thomas's violence, but he explains it in different terms than those of individual responsibility. Instead, Max argues that African Americans' violence is a natural result of their oppressed lives and that only the removal of oppression can truly pacify and simultaneously recivilize the nation (NS, 420–23). Like the trial part's redundant renarration of the two first parts' plot and character development, Max's explanation of the nature of oppression corresponds directly with the more general formulation of Thomas's feelings in the novel, thus highlighting Thomas's worthiness of such a foundational reading.

Just as James Fenimore Cooper explicitly cites the Barbary renegade plot in his writing about Native Americans, Wright refers to the model that underlies his usage of hostis humani generis in *Native Son*. In Wright's case, these citations concern the notion of territorial space that is intimately interwoven with the novel's construction of the law, and the specification of the "older society" (Turner, "Frontier," 62) as the classic European models of civilization (embodied by the parents of Mary Dalton) that are to be replaced by the frontier model. The novel's specific construction of the oppressive "older society" relies, first and foremost, on the portrayal of a spatially segregated society. This is why Thomas's normative transgression consists in his ignoring the color line, and why situations that render segregation irrelevant can be described as a socially transformative no man's land.

In all corners of the nation, Wright suggests, whites already follow the American way of life and are thus part of the beloved community, but they are generally unaware of how African Americans live and to what illegitimate extent they are excluded from the national community (NS, 101 and 318). The oppressive reality of segregation as a national condition is indicated by Wright's setting the novel in a northern city whose spatial properties mirror the segregation in the South (NS, 276). According to Wright, the segregation of African Americans naturalizes the vastly different conditions of life and the different opportunities available to African Americans and whites on a national scale.

African Americans in the novel largely remain unaware of the extent of their exclusion, simply because their lives generally do not intersect with the lives of whites. Thomas's fundamental dissatisfaction with his life at the beginning of the novel is without aim or direction because he does not know why exactly his life feels so impoverished, even though oppression already informs all of his actions. In the beginning of the novel, as mentioned above, Thomas sabotages his own plot to hold up a store with his gang because the owner is white and violence against him is unthinkable. Only later does Thomas understand that "they ruled him, even when they were far away and not thinking of him, ruled him by conditioning him in his relations to his own people" (NS, 145).

The consequences of a continuation of oppression far exceed those of the continuation of African American violence, as Max argues in the novel. Wright sees totalitarianism itself as the threatening result of the masses' oppression, and thus as a cautionary example for America if the removal of African American oppression fails to materialize ("'Bigger,'" 12–14 and 18–19). It is in this way, too, that Thomas thinks about totalitarianism—notably after the murder, when his position as a free agent is already established and now requires him to choose a direction to take (NS, 144–45). Totalitarianism is thus a consequence of oppression and not its cause. Instead, the essentialist and progressivist models of civilization are cited as the ideological sources of oppression in *Native Son*. Significantly, these models are not used to describe the American way of life enjoyed by whites, but only to explain the exclusion of African Americans from that way of life.

These two harmful European models are represented by Mr. and Mrs. Dalton. The Daltons are personally responsible for much of the oppression in the narrative universe of *Native Son*. Their role as the main representatives of illegitimate oppression is especially emphasized by their unfolding status as the victims of an attack whose pain, it is suggested, is the result of poetic justice.[2] Even though Thomas does not select his victims based on their guilt against the oppressed, the author does and, in this way, presents Thomas's crimes as redemptive actions. Of course, the Daltons are not the only agents of illegitimate oppression in the novel; representatives of the press and the judicial system also play the role of such agents, as do a private detective, various police officers and prison guards, white vigilantes, and the members of the Ku Klux Klan who terrorize Chicago's black neighborhoods (known as the Black Belt) during Thomas's trial. All of these characters combined represent an "older society" that collectively oppresses African Americans, has imprinted itself on their minds, and renders them outsiders who always relate to, but are never included in, the nation (NS, 251, 385, 412, 419, and 420). Still, all of these minor oppressive characters are derived from the characterization of the Daltons, since they interact with Thomas only on behalf of this particular victimized family.

Mr. Dalton's perspective corresponds to the essentialist model of civilization. He is heavily invested in the notion of racist segregation and economic and social discrimination against African Americans, capitalizing on the divide between African Americans and whites, reinforcing it, and encouraging its institutional reproduction (NS, 87, 184, 194, 324–25, 356–58, and 415). Mr. Dalton thus satisfies central assumptions of the essentialist approach—namely, that there is and should be a spatial separation between civilization and racialized Other, that this segregation is based on a fundamental difference in nature, and that the Other must be kept at bay by any means necessary and for the benefit of all. While Mr. Dalton emphasizes his own impartial investment in reason and justice, it is clear in the novel that the blatantly discriminatory actions of other characters and institutions can be traced back to him. For instance, the South Side Real Estate Company, which manages housing in the Black Belt and is responsible for the abominable conditions that Thomas's family lives in, turns out to be owned by Mr. Dalton (NS, 80). Racist segregation is the reason why he is able to amass a fortune independent of his wife's old money (NS, 355–57), and he consciously uses his position as a landlord to pressure African Americans into obedience (NS, 332). Also, it is his direct influence that drives the law to extremes in its punishment of Thomas for his crimes (NS, 323). Wright furthermore indicates that Mr. Dalton encourages a reproduction of racist segregation in his employment choices. This is seen not only in Thomas's job interview (NS, 83) and the discussion of his predecessor's employment history, but also in the characterization of the extreme and obvious racism and anticommunism exhibited by Mr. Bitten, a private investigator and Mr. Dalton's trusted employee (NS, 189–91). Bitten is an extension of Dalton, and so—in a weaker and more distanced form—are members of "the press" (NS, 184–85 and 229), who eventually reproduce Dalton's illegitimate prejudices (NS, 244 and 413).[3]

Mr. Dalton's blind wife represents the progressivist model of civilization. She is primarily responsible for the couple's appearance of benevolence (NS, 87). She comes from old money, whose potentially illegitimate appropriation has been naturalized and obscured by time (NS, 344–45, 355–57, and 416) and that provides a superior status reinforced by her involvement in an academically minded charity. Mrs. Dalton demands that her own values be reproduced to the letter by the recipients of her charity (NS, 77). She represents the legacy of the progressivist approach to civilization in the United States, which is destructive in its very piousness and otherworldliness. In this context, one passage is notable: in it, a preacher uses the words "wash them white as snow" (NS, 313) to refer to the kind of solution that the church offers Thomas. Mrs. Dalton and snow are linked throughout the novel; her ghostlike presence is continuously associated with the noiselessness and absolute whiteness of snow, indicating her impersonal, abstract, and hard to detect but nevertheless direct contribution to violence. Indeed, her fundamental misinterpretation of violent situations is dramatic (both in terms of the African Americans she intends to save, and the daughter whose murder she attends but does not witness). Her association with snow is most explicit in the novel's two murder scenes. Neither Mary nor Mears were killed by Thomas alone: had Mrs. Dalton not entered the room, Thomas would not have smothered Mary (NS, 116–17), and the blizzard that descends on the city during the novel freezes the not-quite-slain Mears to death (NS, 334).

Wright's choice of a married couple to represent of the essentialist and progressivist models of civilization can be viewed as a nod toward the models' traditional complementarity in American cultural history. Rather than constructing them as alternatives, as Cooper did, Wright characterizes both models as the inseparable, illegitimate products of the past that claim to represent "American civilization" (NS, 403) but in fact stand in the way of that civilization in Turner's sense (NS, 324–25). The Daltons' characterization as representative of outdated models of civilization underlines *Native Son*'s investment in the frontier model that explicitly surpasses the two older models.

Judging from the long list of white characters in *Native Son* who embrace oppression, one might be tempted to view the white American way of life as illegitimate and exclusionary by nature. When the state attorney argues that "if this fiend's life is spared because of such a [frontier model–based] defense . . . we have abandoned the fight for civilization!" (NS, 403), the novel is suggesting that the civilization he means is not worth saving—that it is in fact not civilization at all but rather a "conspiracy against rights"[4] exercised by the "older society." But the novel does not include all whites in this conspiracy, as the importance of Erlone and Max as representatives of civilization indicate. Most centrally, it is Mary Dalton, the privileged offspring of the two illegitimate perspectives, who is the chief representative of a true American way of life. Rather than duplicating her parents' perspectives, Mary represents a white America that has long been ready for racial integration, despite having been exposed to exclusionary politics for her entire life.

In contrast to her parents, Mary represents a white position toward African Americans that is characterized as legitimate and civilized in the frontier sense. She initiates Thomas's genesis as a pirata by causing him to relate to a white person for the first time in his life; meeting Mary opens up the no man's land between African Americans and whites to Thomas and allows him to maneuver in this space, thus setting in motion the characteristic stages of pirata transformation (NS, 96–98). The political statements that Mary makes before she dies mirror the underlying politics of the novel. She expresses a serious and open-minded interest in the perspectives and lives of African Americans; it is she who initiates Thomas's integration into her own circle (NS, 83 and 96), who acknowledges as well as challenges the separate experiences of blacks and whites (NS, 101), who actively—though very clumsily—tries to understand African American life and African American perspectives (NS, 92 and 108), who senses her own unwitting transgressions against Thomas and apologizes for them (NS, 103), and who is determined to integrate African Americans into the political process as equals of whites (NS, 108). Unlike Mr. Dalton, who views African Americans as innocents whose exclusion and exploitation is natural; Mrs. Dalton, who sees them as empty vessels to be filled; or Erlone, who—before his epiphany—is primarily interested in recruiting the African American masses for the revolution, Mary is willing to meet African Americans on their own terms and in the context of their own history, and to make this approach the basis of her political activism. Mary's position as a representative of the American way of life is included in the characterization of Max as Thomas's primary spokesperson: Max is first mentioned in a conversation between Mary and Erlone that suggests one of Mary's central political contributions is to finance Max's work (NS, 107). Her death is also the reason for Erlone's epiphany and his determination to imitate Mary's perspective.

The central tragedy of oppression, Wright suggests, is that it primarily kills the true Americans on both sides of the fence. On the white side, the American is Mary; on the African American side, it is the Thomas of the last pages of the novel, who has been sentenced to die at the very moment when he has completed his transformation into an American in Turner's sense and might thus begin a softening process in his own right (NS, 443–45). Both are doomed to death, but it is important that the agent of destruction that is able to become a meaningful pirata is not the white woman, but the African American man; in this way, the foundational disruption becomes meaningful in the context of race.

During the section of the novel that presents Thomas's trial, then, the oppressive hostility of the "older society" becomes fully explicit as "an attempt to throttle or stamp out a new form of life" (NS, 419), an action that follows the frontier model and helps continue the foundational history of the American nation (NS, 424–25). In this spirit, the softening process represented by Max and Erlone causes a reinterpretation of the law. Max says to Thomas's judge: "I ask you to recognize the laws and processes flowing from such a condition of [naturalized systemic oppression], understand them, seek to change them. If we do none of these, then we should not pretend horror or surprise when thwarted life expresses itself in fear and hate and crime" (NS, 417). Max renders the Thomas's motives legitimate without embracing the violence that has made these motives visible to the law. He argues that the possibility of a prison sentence for Thomas is the legitimate basis for its softening process of the law. The pirata's physical violence is thus transformed into the violence implied in the letter and practice of the law (Cover, "Violence," 203). Both forms of violence are characterized as neutral tools that can have either legitimate or illegitimate interpretation—as in Dashiell Hammett's *Red Harvest*, it is violence, rather than the oppression of innocents (W. Brown, *States of Injury*, 181), that becomes depoliticized in *Native Son*.[5] In this way, Wright can expose the rule of law as illegitimate in its service to the "older society" and still point to it as a possible way to integrate African Americans into the nation.

In the most explicit evocation of the frontier thesis as a structuring model for *Native Son*, Wright explicitly returns to the spatial dimension of segregation, which serves as the central reference for the novel's use of the hostis humani generis constellation. According to Max, Thomas's violence makes the racialized boundaries of the city visible; he points out that such segregation contradicts the national mission of America as the epitome of a second stage of civilization in the world. In the conversation between Max and Thomas that concludes the novel, Max points to the urban landscape outside the prison window and says:

> Those buildings sprang up out of the hearts of men, Bigger. Men like you. Men kept hungry, kept needing, and those buildings kept growing and unfolding. You once told me you wanted to do a lot of things. . . . What you felt, what you wanted, is what keeps those buildings standing there. When millions of men are desiring and longing, those buildings grow and unfold. But, Bigger, those buildings aren't growing any more. A few men are squeezing those buildings tightly in their hands. The buildings can't unfold, can't feed the dreams men have, men like you. . . . The men on the inside of those buildings have begun to doubt, just as you did. They don't believe any more. They don't feel it's their world. They're restless, like you, Bigger. They have nothing. There's nothing through which they can grow and unfold. . . . The men who own those buildings are afraid. They want to keep what they own, even if it makes others suffer. . . . But men, men like you, get angry and fight to re-enter those buildings, to live again. (NS, 451)

As Max's monologue indicates, foundational rebirth and the redrawing of the essentialist divide between oppressors and oppressed are translated into a fundamental reformulation of urban space; at the same time, the restructuring of that space serves as a metaphor for the more profound restructuring of the law. Max characterizes the struggle between the oppressors and the oppressed as a struggle that might, at first glance, appear to be essentialist: "On both sides men want to live; men are fighting for life. Who will win? Well, the side that feels life the most, the side with the most humanity and the most men" (NS, 452). At this point of the novel, however, this struggle has already been transferred from the realm of physical violence into the realm of the law. It is no longer fought by the pirata Thomas, who has already been sentenced to death, but by the integrated representatives of civilization Max and Erlone, who have come to understand the real reasons behind the violence and who are now able to call for political and legal reform on the basis of this understanding (NS, 318–19).

The essentialist formulation of the struggle between oppressors and oppressed has thus been transformed from a violent political confrontation into a debate about the legal interpretation of agency. The United States as a segregated realm has been translated into a universal no man's land of collective potential to overcome oppression. As Max's comments also indicate, the oppression of African Americans is just one particularly obvious and tangible form of oppression among the many in *Native Son*. While the group of "his [African American] people" remains the most explicit group represented by Thomas in the novel, his transformation into a free and normatively defiant agent engages Thomas in the discourse of "pure" legal representation (Tuitt, "Violence," 203; see also Boyd-White, "Language").

The novel renders any struggle against oppression and the American civilizational model of disruptive rebirth analogous and equivalent (excluding—ironically, considering that the pure woman paradox underlies this construction—the battle of gender equality).

The reader is called on to join Max and Erlone in their normative interpretation of Thomas's violence. This interpretation, as Wright indicates throughout the novel as well as in his commentary on it, is made possible by the conscious inclusion of any international dimension, both in the novel and in the expectations of its readership. I have suggested that the frontier model always implicitly depends on the essentialist model to be meaningful. This is because the defining foundational moment of violence cites an essentialist clash that points outside of the space of the law, as well as the space of the nation within which this law is relevant. The pirata can become an entity in an in-between zone that defines the nation, thus making perpetual self-actualization conceivable, only if the nation as a whole is situated in an essentialist struggle that formulates certain properties of civilized order as universally accepted inside the nation and that clusters an illegitimate set of properties outside it. It is only this greater, always international, and always necessarily essentialist struggle that stabilizes the normative boundaries that the pirata renegotiates inside the nation. In Turner, this essentialist struggle is waged between Europe and Native Americans. *Native Son*, published one year before the United States entered World War II, is informed by the essentialist construction of war against totalitarian regimes as a struggle taking place outside of the United States.

Only as long as the boundaries between the domestic and the international are maintained, and as long as the US nation-state can be considered only peripherally affected by the essentialist conflict that maintains it as a stable in-between zone, can the pirata assume the position of a figure that may represent a genuinely American way of life—or perhaps more specifically, a genuinely American way of interpreting the law on the basis of constitutive violence.

The US engagement in World War II, however, which went hand in hand with the widespread use of the phrase "American century," changed this precarious distinction between the national and the international. In his discussion of "American century" as a term first used by Henry Luce in an editorial in *Life* editorial in 1941, David Harvey writes: "It had long been an influential principle of political thought and practice in the United States . . . that foreign entanglements should be avoided because they would undermine democracy at home. The difficulty was to bridge the gap between this fear and the obvious fact of US global domination [especially during and after World War II]. Much as European imperialism had turned to racism to bridge the tension between nationalism and imperialism, so the US sought to conceal imperial ambition in an abstract universalism" (*Neoliberalism*, 50). Elizabeth Borgwardt adds that US security politics had always contained an element of the international, yet "traditional antinomies such as 'domestic' and 'foreign' affairs have become increasingly obsolete in the study of the politics and ideas of the World War II era" (*New Deal*, 9).

The dissolution of the national-international distinction also threatened the possibility of separating national (frontier) from the international (essentialist) constructions of civilization as an order with an inherent ability to commit legitimate violence. The problematic implications of "abstract universalism" (which went hand in hand with a covert essentialist claim to represent civilization violently) were not visible at first because the reference to universalist values had immediate democratizing effects within the United States. In respect to the "abstract universalism" in the context of the Atlantic Charter that defined the war objectives of the Allies in 1941, Borgwardt explains: "The high-toned abstractions in the Atlantic Charter, intended to contrast Anglo-American principles with those of the Third Reich, inevitably served to highlight internal contradictions and hypocrisies within democracies themselves" (ibid., 8; see also Baldwin, "Down at the Cross," 52–53 and 93).

Only because the self-evident primacy of such universalist principles and the inherently illegitimate nature of the totalitarian antagonist were uncontested in the United States could authors like Wright address these contradictions in terms of the frontier model of the civilization and be understood as the pioneers of a civil rights struggle that worked to reduce inequalities in democracies. The narrative strategies of *Native Son* (which focus on the constitutional promise of equality) anticipate the tendency of social movements to naturalize certain specific legal bodies and the "spirit of the law" that they epitomize (Waldron, "Torture," 1748, see also ibid., 1681–750) as the epitomes of civilization as well.

It is important to underline that, to sustain itself as a meaningful model of civilization, the frontier model relied on the creation of legal bodies of text that epitomized civilization: wherever they are implemented, civilization exists. The US Constitution had long been seen as such a text, and a similar status was bestowed on the "Universal Declaration of Human Rights" (Borgwardt, *New Deal*; Slaughter, *Human Rights Inc.*). In 1960s and 1970s especially, the US Constitution and the United Nations' "Universal Declaration of Human Rights" (UDHR) are read as spiritually related civilized rules set down for a humanity that has to work hard to implement them in the frontier model's sense. Even though both the Constitution and the UDHR can be altered and amended, their very existence is hailed as a sign of civilized humanity that can be relied on to formulate an inherently legitimate legal order in a future that combines the violence of disruptive piratae and the structural reforms made by representatives of civilization.

However, as the next part of this book will show, there is a crucial problem with the emerging consensus that all nations, including the United States, are not inherently civilized but only have civilizational potential, which is actualized by their perpetual rebirth within the parameters of central legal bodies of text. As the possibility of producing the innocent in Scarry's argument and Bigger Thomas's short contemplation of totalitarianism as a possible path indicate, alternatives to civilization exist: totalitarianism and, after the end of the Cold War, Islam, understood in Samuel Huntington's reductive sense of a "civilizational war" between spatialized cultures (*Clash of Civilizations*, 247).

[IV]

"IT IS UNDERNEATH US": THE PLANETARY ZONE IN BETWEEN AS AN AMERICAN DILEMMA

PART 3 DISCUSSED the frontier interpretation of hostis humani generis, which enabled the formulation of a new model of civilization that depended on perpetual self-actualization through foundational disruption—an intervention that transformed institutional, rather than territorial, space. The hostis humani generis constellation became the way in which such internal reformulation could take place. Rather than identifying barbarians somewhere near civilization along the horizontal lines of maps, the frontier model introduced a vertical imaginary, in which civilized ideals hovered as universal truths above, whereas barbarians were imagined to lurk "underneath us" (quoted in Peters, *Torture*, 147).

Yet the frontier model of civilization depended on a stark distinction between the inside and the outside of the US nation-state. The international sphere was still best understood by the civilizational logic of (horizontal) maps rather than that of (vertical) common norms and institutions, and thus it remained alien to the frontier model. Even though the frontier model's discursive success was perpetuated by the "parochial, inward nature of the two Cold War Powers" in the period immediately after World War II (Craig and Radchenko, *Atomic Bomb*, x), it became increasingly necessary to consider the international sphere in all contemplations of legitimate violence in the United States. It soon became relevant that different rules of legitimate violence applied within the nation, where only the law could make violence legitimate, than in the world beyond—a world that Americans tended to construct in essentialist terms, as Turner's frontier thesis presupposes and novels like *Native Son* confirm (see Wright, "Bigger," 15).

This inside-outside distinction was difficult, or even impossible, to maintain for a nation that ended World War II with the use of the atom bomb in 1945, an event often dubbed the first act of the Cold War rather than the last act of World War II. An important new argument about legitimate violence in terms of national statehood emerged with the mass killing of civilians as a normalized element of Western warfare. The argument was that, in the international realm, American essentialist claims to legitimate violence (which rely on the premise that the innocent are protected by violence) are no longer acceptable when Americans engage in the mass killing of innocents (Glover, *Humanity*, 69–116). Members of President Harry Truman's administration and associated commentators convinced a shocked US population of the necessity and virtue of the bombing of Hiroshima and Nagasaki as an example of "democracies beating the totalitarians at their own game" (Sembower, "Democracy and Science," 500), but the public's acceptance of these claims tended to include an element of inarticulate yet profound skepticism (see Boyer, *Early Light*; Broadhead, "Shadow").

Leo Szilard, a nuclear physicist renowned for his role both in the development of the atom bomb and its later political critique, summarizes the dilemma of legitimate violence in the atomic age: "By and large, governments are guided by considerations of expediency rather than by moral considerations. . . . Prior to the war I had the illusion that up to a point the American Government was different. This illusion was gone after Hiroshima" ("Interview").

If the difference between the United States and every other country is that the United States commits violence only according to certain moral standards, and that it allows individuals to commit violence to reactualize timeless original values for the essentially benevolent institutions of the state, and if this difference breaks down because of the use of weapons of mass destruction on Japan and Germany, the implication is clear: "Can anyone doubt that . . . [if it had been Germany rather than the United States that had dropped the bomb] we would have sentenced the Germans who were guilty of this crime to death at Nuremberg and hanged them?" (Szilard, "Interview") Interpreting the atom bomb's use as legitimate was consistently encouraged, but there was an important concern that the United States might indeed have been "Hitlerize[d]" (to use Dieter Georgi's term) by World War II (quoted in Broadhead, "Shadow," 45). The final part of this book addresses this concern. It investigates both the renegotiation of the relationship between the frontier model and the essentialist model and the increasingly widespread and successful essentialist interpretation of hostis humani generis, which is able to retain a claim of "American exceptionalism" as the root justification for American violence as legitimate violence (Pease, *Exceptionalism*, 33).

In response to the destabilization of distinct national and the international realms, a more mature interaction between the frontier interpretation and the essentialist interpretation of hostis humani generis had to develop. The essentialist Cold War apparatus and the human rights regime provided the respective platforms for a parallel use of the two models across the domestic and the international spheres: Cold War dichotomies carried essentialist distinctions inward, while the human rights regime carried the notion of perpetual civilizing self-actualization outward (Beck, "Enemy Images"; Slaughter, *Human Rights Inc.*, 156–61).

The contemplation of each domestic or international phenomenon that included claims to legitimate violence became open to a frontier interpretation and an essentialist interpretation of the hostis humani generis constellation. Irreducibly different emphases in the interpretation of figures within the constellation, rather than irreducibly rivaling models of civilization, thus began to inform the discursive divisions between neoconservatives and progressives, and between hawks and doves.

Essentialist interpretations of legitimate violence after World War II relied on the classic construction of one good entity facing two complementary evil entities. Such interpretations have been extremely successful at harmonizing the institutional rise of the human rights regime as representative of all humanity (universal human rights have to be defended against those who do not honor them) and the rise of the Cold War security apparatus, presented as the global containment of communism (the free world has to be defended against an invasive, oppressive realm), on behalf of a claim of specifically US legitimate violence. In the relationship between these two discursive patterns of claiming legitimate violence, essentialist arguments tended to use a structure that resembles William Blackstone's definition of hostis humani generis (*Commentaries*, 2:71): a praedo (a direct representative of communism or, more generally, totalitarianism) and a pirata (who, as a citizen of the globe, violates human rights anywhere) could be viewed as complementary threats to the United States as a global power. As long as totalitarianism and crimes against humanity were condemned as complementary threats to civilization (represented, again, by US institutions), the different narrative implications of each antagonist construction remained unproblematic. In this manner, the complementary use of communist praedones and anti–human rights piratae could successfully stake a claim to legitimate violence, according to an essentialist interpretation.

A good example of a text that does this successfully is the Truman Doctrine of 1947. President Truman's speech establishing this doctrine is often considered to mark the beginning of the Cold War. In his speech, Truman presupposes and affirms an intertwined use of the essentialist model and the frontier model. He emphasizes that "one of the chief virtues of democracy . . . is that its defects are always visible and under democratic processes can be pointed out and corrected" ("President Harry S. Truman's Address before a Joint Session of Congress"). He explicitly refers to the frontier model as the only right path toward civilization and embraces the institutionalized implementation of the frontier approach in the United States as a model for global civilizational becoming: "One [American] way of life is based upon the will of the majority, and is distinguished by free institutions, representative government, free elections, guarantees of individual liberty, freedom of speech and religion, and freedom from political oppression. The second [totalitarian] way of life is based upon the will of a minority forcibly imposed upon the majority. It relies upon terror and oppression, a controlled press and radio; fixed elections, and the suppression of personal freedoms. I believe that it must be the policy of the United States to support free peoples who are resisting attempted subjugation by armed minorities or by outside pressures" (ibid.). The stark contrast with totalitarianism as the frontier institutions' barbarous mirror image links the characteristics of the frontier model to the essentialist model. Because US institutions are invested in the implementation of civilization, they can be treated as inherently civilized when compared to totalitarian institutions, which are invested in the implementation of barbarism. Truman's speech in general also emphasizes American military force as a necessary unifying basis for a functioning international human rights law. This is based on the conviction that, "unless democracy and development are understood and pursued in very particular ways, their pursuit may place human rights at risk" (Donnelly, *Universal Human Rights*, 186).

While essentialist interpretations thus rely on a straightforward "one good versus two evils" interpretation of the constellation in texts, frontier interpretations increasingly rely on the conscious inclusion of form as a relevant element of an argument. Texts of the time that follow a frontier interpretation tend to be wary of giving US institutions carte blanche to make claims of legitimate state violence. This perspective emphasizes the gap between civilizational values and institutional actions in practice. The first chapter of part 4 discusses the importance of totalitarianism in the cultural and legal renegotiation of hostis humani generis after World War II and links this discussion to a reading of Kurt Vonnegut's novel *Mother Night* (1962).[1] This novel, set against the backdrop of the 1961 trial of the Nazi logistics expert Adolf Eichmann, interrogates the possibility of legitimate violence in times of human mass destruction as a normalized element of warfare. Vonnegut uses the hostis humani generis constellation to keep the novel intelligible as a moral text, a strategy that operates by separating the Hitlerizing violence of mass warfare from the more civilized force of a muscular human rights regime.

Vonnegut does not negotiate legitimate violence by foregrounding the nature of a delineated praedonic core antagonist, as Dashiell Hammett and Richard Wright do. Instead, *Mother Night* chooses sides between two parallel ways of interpreting civilization. The essentialist interpretation is constructed as an inevitably barbarous embrace of totalitarian logic that informs any industrial war and security apparatus. In this way, Vonnegut treats the American war and security apparatus like the rich, the externalized pirate-emperors of early modernity. In Charles Johnson's Free Prince speech (discussed in chapter 1), the rich had been constructed as corrupt and violent transitional entities that preceded an anticipated civilized order. In *Mother Night*, these rich would be representatives of a war machine and security apparatus that, according to Vonnegut, claim the status of representatives of civilization but cannot do so persuasively. A fully operational human rights regime, then, represents the dawn of a legitimate civilization that replaces the rich impostor.

Vonnegut tacitly agrees with Truman that it may be necessary to defend the existence of such a human rights regime violently, and that such violence is just. In *Mother Night*, Vonnegut honors historical figures such as Tuvia Friedmann, a well-known Nazi hunter who has helped bring Eichmann to Jerusalem and to justice.[2] Likewise, Vonnegut's use of the hostis humani generis constellation corresponds with the then-recent renegotiation of the constellation as a legal fiction in international law (specifically, in relation to Eichmann trial that serves as the novel's context) that not only allows but explicitly requires the praedo to represent a totalitarian state. The important difference, however, is that Americans can appear as such praedones as well. The second chapter in part 4 examines a discourse that counters such accusations of Hitlerizing and that has begun to recreate a consensus on legitimate violence from within the essentialist interpretive context. In the 1980s, the most important tool of this consensus becomes the figure of the international terrorist, who turns into a new praedo. With the help of this figure, the American citizen can be reimagined as an innocent who requires protection worldwide. The chapter analyzes two politically opposite texts of the 1980s—*Terrorism: How the West Can Win* (1986), edited by Benjamin Netanyahu, and *Pirates and Emperors, Old and New* (1986), by Noam Chomsky—and shows that this understanding of the citizen as an innocent represents an emerging new consensus that began late in the Cold War and continued after its end.

In the aftermath of the 9/11 attacks, the consensus that the international terrorist is the antagonist of the United States and of humanity as a whole is fully achieved, but it is precisely this achievement that allows new forms of criticism of essentialist perspectives. The final chapter of part 4 interprets Mohsin Hamid's second novel *The Reluctant Fundamentalist*, first published in 2007. This novel features the elusive pirata protagonist Changez, who is the protagonist and narrator—as Howard W. Campbell Jr. is both the protagonist and narrator of *Mother Night*—and who, like Campbell, is elusive precisely because he exists in a context of normalized violence largely without committing violence himself. *The Reluctant Fundamentalist* is set in the years around 9/11 and during the ensuing War on Terror. The novel links the characterization of the War on Terror to the imaginary of early modernity and the Mediterranean as the birthplace of essentialist discourse. Appropriately for the concluding chapter in this book, Hamid uses the constellation to fundamentally question whether hostis humani generis is, in fact, the right constellation to use in formulating a doctrine of legitimate violence in the first place.

[11]

THE INSTITUTIONAL FRONTIER: A NEW TYPE OF CRIMINAL

THE RISE OF the human rights regime after World War II occasions one of the central breaks in the interpretation of the legal fiction of hostis humani generis. The human rights regime rests on two bases after the war. First is the United Nations' "Universal Declaration of Human Rights," which in 1948 explicitly formulated a new consensus on what is legitimate (that is, civilized). Second is the Nuremberg trials of 1945–46, which helped specify the illegitimate Other against whom violence can be exercised legitimately. The hostis humani generis fiction was used in the Nuremberg trials and successive trials of Nazis (especially Adolf Eichmann, who was famously cast as an archetypal committer of crimes against humanity) to help formulate the link between an inherently just principle and its illegitimate Other in a single proceeding. The unobtrusive experimentations with the legal fiction in Nuremberg were a careful initial attempt to create new ways to use hostis humani generis.

The postwar international framework of human rights responded to the "crushing impact of the war [that] reconfigured two of the most enduring constructions of the Enlightenment, the individual and the nation-state" (Borgwardt, *New Deal*, 7–8). These reconfigurations were met with adaptions of the law, in particular with the establishment of the human rights regime that testified to a new "openness to large-scale institutional solutions" by the administration of President Franklin Roosevelt. There was a place for hostis humani generis in this new legal context. The League of Nations' Committee of Experts for the Progressive Codification of International Law's *Draft Provisions for the Suppression of Piracy* (Bingham et al., "Draft Provisions") had already achieved two things for the twentieth-century legal interpretation of hostis humani generis. First, it stated that the entire tradition of the enemy of all humankind as a random perpetrator of violence referred to the pirate exclusively, and not to crimes such as the slave trade or crimes against humanity. Second, the document's definition classified piracy as a crime that, in a global context defined by the universal premise of national statehood, occurs only rarely, if at all. With piracy and random attacks safely compartmentalized away—along with the implied tradition of criminals as bloodthirsty, unthinking beasts that had informed legal constructions of criminals for centuries (see Evans, *Rituals*, 365; Olson, *Criminals as Animals*)—the potential use of the legal fiction of hostis humani generis could be rethought in the spirit of the "Dignity of Man," to use Richard Hooker's term (quoted in Locke, "Second Treatise," 277; see also United Nations, "Universal Declaration of Human Rights").[1] The result was an understanding of the enemy of all humankind as a perpetrator who deliberately targets, and seeks to destroy, the human essence of his victims through crimes against humanity. The motive, and no longer the unpredictability, of the attack becomes central to the understanding of hostis humani generis in human rights law.

The crime most associated with hostis humani generis is a new addition to the catalogue of international crimes, the category of crimes against humanity. The term "crimes against humanity" was used for the first time in 1904, by Theodore Roosevelt (Borgwardt, *New Deal*, 226). In accordance with the prevailing legal properties of hostis humani generis, crimes against humanity are crimes that meet three criteria: they can occur both during war and in peacetime; they are part of a concerted, conscious effort to destroy a way of life; and their targets are the innocent—that is, people not actively and officially engaged in hostilities (Frulli, "Crimes against Humanity," 334–37). The fact that crimes against humanity were associated with crimes such as genocide, rather than with piracy, removed the obstacle of enforceability that had hampered defenses against the slave trade in the nineteenth century and allowed the construction of those who committed crimes against humanity as hostis humani generis.

While the main objective of the Nuremberg trials and the Atlantic Charter was to establish a new principle of just war, crimes against humanity took the logical next step beyond this context of warfare. And hostis humani generis was used precisely because enemies of all humankind could be encountered in wartime as well as in peacetime. In proceedings such as the Eichmann trial, it was thus a stated goal to separate crimes against humanity from war crimes (Addis, "International Community," 135).

Like piracy before the seventeenth century, "crimes against humanity" was a general category that included a long and perpetually expanding list of specific crimes, including specific crimes as different as torture, apartheid, extermination, enslavement, enforced disappearance, unlawful deportation and imprisonment, rape, sexual slavery, enforced prostitution, enforced pregnancy, and enforced sterilization. Within this large and diverse group of crimes, torture was soon to emerge as the central, problem-defining crime against humanity. As debates of the United Nation's Consultative Assembly in 1949 make explicit, UN delegates used the crime of torture to characterize crimes against humanity in general as "inconsistent with civilised society" and as "incompatible with civilization" (quoted in Peters, *Torture*, 146–47). Torture dramatized the issues of legitimacy and agency that the discussion of Elaine Scarry's work in part 3 outlined: the torturer, imagined as the inhuman vehicle of a regime, illustrated which kind of illegitimacy (namely, a totalitarian one) made torture meaningful as a crime against humanity. Acts of torture that indicated a state of oppression in a nation-state were called "offences against heaven and humanity" simultaneously committed by the torturer and the nation-state[2] (quoted in ibid., 146). The rejection of torture by the use of these terms "underlined the eternal truth which we must all remember; that barbarism is never behind us, it is underneath us. It is our task to see that it does not come to the surface" (quoted in ibid., 147–48).

In the decolonizing postwar international order, the barbarian sovereign is the totalitarian state—a nation-state, but not a democratic one. This sovereign Other to international law is exemplified by the chief beneficiaries of the Third Reich during the Nuremberg trials (Bassiouni, "Universal Jurisdiction"; Kontorovich, "Piracy Analogy"). The centrality of the totalitarian regime as a barbarous Other is illustrated by the most famous trials that used hostis humani generis to position the defendants as criminals against humanity: the aforementioned trial of Eichmann and, in the United States, the trial of Américo Peña-Irala, a Paraguayan inspector general of police who was accused of torture and convicted in 1980. The characterization of these people as enemies of all humankind is directly derived from the specific illegitimacy of the regime they faithfully and officially represented during their crimes. Eichmann in particular was made immortal as the prototypical committer of crimes against humanity because of his unquestioning acceptance of the Nazi regime's perspective, despite his knowledge of its perspective's heinous implications (Arendt, *Totalitarianism*, 360–61, and *Eichmann*, 48–49; see also Margalit, *Decent Society*, 49–50). Likewise, an important argument for the right of the US Court of Appeals for the Second Circuit to hear the case *Filártiga v. Peña-Irala* was that the act of torture committed by Peña-Irala reflected an official position of the Paraguayan government toward its citizens in general, and that through his acts of violence Peña-Irala willingly chose to perpetuate an illegitimate form of rule (Aceves, *Anatomy of Torture*, 47). The totalitarian conspiracy in these cases consists of the creation of a Leviathan whose central objective is to render significant portions of the population permanently innocent—namely, all those who, unlike Eichmann and Peña-Irala, have not undergone a praedonic transformation into an empty and violent extension of the regime.

As discussed in part 3, the understanding of totalitarianism as a category opposite to the civilization that is threatened from "underneath" was most famously established by Arendt's 1951 *The Origins of Totalitarianism* and was made more explicit in her reports of the trial of Adolf Eichmann, published as *Eichmann in Jerusalem* in 1964. In contrast to earlier commentators such as Peter Drucker (*Economic Man*), Arendt points out that the totalitarian Leviathan is not the inherent expression of any specific ideology, such as fascism (*Eichmann*, 176), but that totalitarianism instead is the realization of an ideology characterized by an "eager[ness] to generalize" (ibid., 156) and "a ruthless desire for conformity at any price" (ibid., 175). She goes on to argue that this kind of ideology is nothing less than morally evil and can render even "neutral" desires—such as to conform or, perhaps, to commit violence—acts of evil. In a radio interview with Joachim Fest in 1964, Arendt elaborated on her famous characterization of Eichmann as the epitome of the "banality of evil." In the course of the conversation, Arendt and Fest discussed Eichmann as a "new type of criminal" ("Dummheit," 38), whose motivation for crimes against humanity—the overarching desire to belong and to function efficiently—is not in itself evil but a "neutral" human motivation that is rendered evil only by the individual's unwillingness, and perhaps inability, to think beyond the immediate demands of institutional functionality. Rather than considering the justice of institutional objectives themselves, such criminals insert themselves into the regime as "fragments" of institutional space and thus refuse to consider how those subjected to institutional efficiency are affected—or even destroyed—by it (ibid., 39). It is this refusal to accept the responsibility for heinous institutional doings despite knowledge of them, Arendt suggested, that was established as criminal during the Nuremberg trials and was then identified as the basis of criminal conduct during the Eichmann trial (ibid.).

Arendt thus conceptualizes totalitarianism as an invasive regime designed exclusively for the benefit of elites and their minions who aggressively and randomly turn against other humans. While the totalitarian regime is arguably the result of revolution, the totalitarian revolution is based not on law but on the will of a regime that views humans as the malleable components of an emerging totalitarian Leviathan, rather than recognizing them as individuals. Totalitarianism, in Arendt's sense, is characterized by a theoretical separation between the illegitimate regime and the innocent populations abused by its premises. The innocent victims of totalitarianism are thus both the population that the regime claims to represent and the population that it externalizes and destroys. The Nazi regime, for instance, is separated from both the people who were tortured and murdered as a direct result of fascist ideology and the so-called good Germans, who could be viewed as the noninvolved population and whose existence was presupposed in the policies of the United States during the postwar occupation of Germany (see Lockenour, "Black and White").[3]

Totalitarianism, Arendt's reasoning continues, exploits accidents of history to establish a regime based on the illegitimate exploitation of just national or institutional structures (rather than just wars, as in Hugo Grotius) and the violent abuse of innocent populations inside national borders (rather than noncombatants across war zones). Instead of capitalizing on the imperial weakness on the margins of empire, the barbarian is thus present in the industrial nation-state as an in-between zone, threatening to rise from "underneath" the institutions that are evolving toward civilization, and misleading them toward totalitarianism (Alexander, "Social Construction," 229).

Adolf Hitler's rise to power exemplifies this vision of the new totalitarian Other to humankind. Hitler hollowed out rather than replaced legitimate state structures, to an extent that allowed him to take over the position of the sovereign, and to rely on a monopoly of force that was based on the structures of the Nazi party long before they spread to the police or the military (Agamben, *Homo Sacer*, 121–23; Baehr, *Arendt, Totalitarianism, Social Sciences*, 45; Hornung, *Das totalitäre Zeitalter*, 68–69; Jackson, "Opening Address," 1:123–25; Shirer, *Aufstieg und Fall*, xv). Hitler's rise to power, enabled by the state-within-a-state structures of the Nazi party, is a vivid example of an illegitimate totalitarian Other as a parasitical and virus-like ideological disease that may affect any nation-state. The rise of totalitarianism in the United States was not at all considered unthinkable, especially during World War II (Palevsky, *Atomic Fragments*, 128–30), and this may at least partly account for the essentialist "race war without race" waged by and within the United States after the war (Medovoi, "Race War Within," 165). This ideological struggle was informed by a "racism of interiority that constructs its target populations with reference to their creeds, thoughts, and loyalties rather than their blood, color, and physiognomy" (ibid., 168).

As I noted in the discussion of the torture debate above, the problem exemplified by Eichmann was that totalitarianism required a radically different praedo than the classic racialized barbarian. The totalitarian regime, according to Arendt's model, is able to turn parts of the captive populations into totalitarian praedones and transforms them into something permanently unrecognizably and shockingly Other. I touched on this possibility above, in the context of MacSwain's development in Dashiell Hammett's *Red Harvest*. In a discourse of human rights that systematically focuses on representing and defending innocence produced by violence, the praedo produced by violence becomes a painfully likely possibility.

Recognizing this general human ability to be transformed not just into an innocent but also into a praedo constitutes a radical innovation in the interpretation of the hostis humani generis constellation, and its importance cannot be overstated. In the course of the twentieth century after World War II, the relationship between praedo and innocent was conventionalized as one of mutually constitutive transformation. The totalitarian state was then defined by its reliance on only two kinds of subjects: praedones who commit, and the innocent who are the potential targets of, a generalized destruction of human life. This definition of totalitarianism as an inherently illegitimate order constituted one side of an essentialist divide. On the other side stood foundational piratae and interpreting representatives of civilization, who together represented a different vision of order: a sovereignty that identified violence against human beings in general as a form of undue subjection, and that relied on perpetual acts of foundational piratae's counterviolence against totalitarian tendencies around the globe. Foundational piratae and interpreting representatives of civilization together ensure the perpetual progress toward civilization in a frontier-based nation-state, and in the First World in general.

This neat division of the four relevant figures of the hostis humani generis constellation into two central relationships that define two different and existentially opposing orders can be considered an attempt to manage the overlap between the violence committed by the foundational pirata and that committed by the perpetrator of crimes against humanity. If even the most evil acts are originally neutral, it is vital to specify the kind of rule that allows people to become the source of good rather than a symptom of evil. Thus the explicit characteristic of a good nation-state, such as the United States, becomes its ability to institutionally enable a foundational relationship between pirata and representative of civilization within national territory, whereas the mass transformation of national citizens into innocents and praedones cannot be part of the national project.

The task of human rights law, which is to enable any human being on the planet to "becom[e] what one already is," (Slaughter, *Human Rights Inc.*, 26) thus assumes a consequential double meaning. Both totalitarianism and civilization allow people to become what they already are, and the distinction between them is not made easier by the normalization of mass atrocities committed against the innocent that returning war veterans, in particular, were all too well aware of. Both the best and the worst are inherent to the human being, but they are ontologically separated by the Cold War claim that US institutions always bring out the best in humans, and totalitarian regimes bring out the worst.

Kurt Vonnegut was a veteran of World War II and had been a prisoner of war in Dresden when the city was firebombed in 1945 (Klinkowitz, *Literary*

Disruptions, 36). Vonnegut made his first public mention of his personal experience with massified warfare in the second edition of *Mother Night*. That edition, published in 1966, included a new introduction that revealed Vonnegut's presence on the ground during the firebombing. The first edition of 1962, entering the market as a cheap pulp paperback, received no critical attention whatsoever and was a flop in terms of sales (Shields, *And So It Goes*, 173). Not until the second edition was published was there critical recognition of the novel. The new introduction of 1966—not to be confused with the editor's note, in which Vonnegut already appears as a fictionalized editor figure who authenticates the confessions of the narrator, Howard W. Campbell Jr.—is routinely included in later editions of the work.

Mother Night (hereafter abbreviated in the citations as MN) is composed in the form of a fictional meta-autobiography. Ralph Clare has characterized it as a conflation of "the confessional genre with a light parody of the spy genre" ("Worlds of Wordcraft," 70). With the exception of the editor's note, which is written from the point of view of a fictionalized Vonnegut, the entire novel is narrated by Campbell, the protagonist, who is "an American by birth, a Nazi by reputation, and a nationless person by inclination" (MN, 3). The text alleges that Campbell produces his memoirs in Jerusalem as a fellow inmate of Eichmann, who was being tried there at the time of the novel's writing. Campbell awaits his trial for crimes against humanity and offers his memories for the academic research on "Nazi villainy" being conducted by Israeli researchers and supported by the state of Israel (MN, 3).

The novel is divided into forty-five very short, thematically titled chapters, and moves back and forth through the various parts of Campbell's life. Campbell comes to Germany as a child; becomes a sentimental playwright; and marries Helga Noth, a German actress. The Nazis rise to power, and the Campbells rise with them. Campbell becomes a famous radio demagogue as well as a Nazi propagandist under Joseph Goebbels. Simultaneously, however, he is recruited as an American spy and uses his Nazi radio program to transmit coded messages to the Americans throughout the war. His wife disappears on the eastern front, and Campbell hides out in New York after the war. His lonely undercover life is eventually exposed by a Russian double agent. In the New York part of the plot, Campbell is idolized as an upright hero by what Philip Tew calls "a hodgepodge of American fascists" ("*Mother Night*," 17) and meets Helga's younger sister, Resi, who poses as his vanished wife. After much intrigue and confusion that exposes various characters' conflicting and overlapping allegiances to the United States, Russia, Nazi Germany, and Japan (MN, 59), Campbell is brought to Israel to await trial.

In the final pages of the novel, Campbell receives a letter from his American intelligence recruiter that confirms Campbell's unwavering allegiance to the United States throughout the war. This unexpected confirmation of his status as a US agent rebuts the charges of crimes against humanity being made against him. Campbell's reaction to the news is not triumph but suicide: "Tonight is the night I will hang Howard W. Campbell, Jr., for crimes against himself" (MN, 175). The 1966 introduction retrospectively offers an overarching interpretive motto (or, as the introduction calls it, a moral) for *Mother Night* as a novel: "We are what we pretend to be, so we must be careful about what we pretend to be" (MN, vii).

On a basic level, the novel is structured by essentialist dichotomies as they are conventionalized by the spy genre: the United States here; Nazi Germany and Soviet Russia there; and spies as the representatives of their governments in-between, with the double agent as a particularly clear-cut pirata figure. As Clare rightly notes, however, the book actually belongs to the confessional genre, which immediately undercuts the essentialist dichotomies evoked by the spy genre. In his confessions, Campbell does not focus on the difference between nations or political orders, but on paranoia and schizophrenia as interrelated states of madness that characterize an overall grotesque world. Correspondingly, the book does not focus on episodes that narrate the protagonist's character development, but instead on those that offer episodic glimpses into the multifaceted horrors and absurdities of the environments of war and alienation that dominate Campbell's life. Partly because many factors that influence his life are initially (and sometimes remain) unknown to Campbell, he admits to being an unreliable narrator, despite his stated goal of telling the truth (MN, 21, 37, and 102).

The novel was conceived after a conversation Vonnegut with a naval intelligence veteran at a cocktail party. According to Vonnegut, the veteran explained that "what you have to realize is that all these people are schizophrenics. They have to be insane . . . because otherwise they would either blow their cover or simply die of fright. He went on to say that someone ought to make a spy movie about what spies are really like. So I wrote a book about it" (quoted in Reilly, "Two Conversations," 204). As in the cocktail party anecdote, *Mother Night* does not use the terms "schizophrenia" and "paranoia" in their medical sense.[4] Instead, both terms are used to describe a continuum that ranges between an individual predisposition, which may indeed be a medical condition, and a state caused by external influences, such as a biographical and historical situation (for schizophrenia, see MN, 18, 37, 62, 116, 127, 133, 137, 146, and 148; for paranoia, see MN, 43–44, 47, 147, 160–62, and 164).

In the novel, paranoia requires the ability to believe in the natural existence of stark dichotomies and refers to the conviction that dichotomies must be violently protected and maintained. In a much-quoted passage, this paranoid condition is squarely equated with a totalitarian mind-set (MN, 145–46). "Paranoid" ideologues of all varieties—be they members of the Nazi high command, a Jewish underground fighter, a fascist activist, a capitalist engineer, a German or American policeman, an American soldier, or "the bureaucratic Genghis Khan" and "Man of the Century" Eichmann himself (MN, 8–9, 10, 17, 58–59, 64, 102–3, 111, 154–55, and 160–64)—can honestly believe in the righteousness of their deeds even when their actions are ideologically inconsistent, and when their protection of dichotomist standards causes them to commit heinous acts of violence.

Vonnegut maintains that paranoia never stops at dichotomist borders such as national borders and specific cultural allegiances, but produces these alleged borders in the first place (see, for example, MN, 103). Even though historical Nazi figures such as Hitler, Goebbels, Rudolf Höß, or Eichmann are cited as the purest epitomes of such a paranoid or totalitarian mind-set, the most developed characters of the novel that represent this mind-set are Americans: the fascist Reverend Dr. Lionel J. D. Jones (who is described as clinically paranoid and to whom the novel's famous totalitarianism passage refers) and the antifascist former soldier Bernard B. O'Hare, who captures Campbell as a Nazi criminal and who "thought of himself as St. George and of me [Campbell] as the dragon" (MN, 160).

Schizophrenia, in contrast, is described as the ability to live in a paranoid world, and to "be" or "pretend to be" many things at the same time (MN, vii). Like paranoids, schizophrenics act contradictorily and heinously, but they do so without the ability to incorporate their actions into a legitimating dichotomist mind-set. "I've always known what I did," confesses Campbell. "I've always been able to live with what I did. How? Through that simple and widespread boon to modern mankind—schizophrenia" (MN, 116). Schizophrenics, in Vonnegut's sense, survive because they radically disassociate themselves from their actions and the illegitimacy of those actions. The "schizophrenic" Campbell is able to reflect on what he has done and condemns the horrors he has committed, but his reflection does not entail any inclination to act otherwise, or indeed any possibility of doing so. This construction of a nuanced reflexivity that does not, on the whole, result in legitimate behavior, provocatively varies Arendt's theoretical focus on self-reflexive moral agency in her definition of a "new type of criminal."

Campbell's schizophrenia is described as the result of a normative orientation toward what Wendy Brown has called the "prepolitical" (*States of Injury*, 181). In the context of his marriage, Campbell refers to the love between his wife and himself as a "nation of two," whose "territory[, which] we defended so jealously, didn't go much beyond the borders of our great double bed" (MN, 30). Since this love is so self-absorbed, the lovers are capable of opportunistically inserting themselves into any context that allows them to remain together—love leads to martyrdom only when opportunism can no longer protect the lovers from paranoid persecution (MN, 29–30, 149). Indeed, the possibility of using violence legitimately exists for the schizophrenic as soon as he is directly attacked by the paranoid—the martyrdom of the female character, Resi Noth, who dies for love in the face of persecution (MN, 149), is complemented by the one moment of violence of the male character, Campbell, who successfully defends himself against a paranoid's attempt at vigilantism (MN, 163–64).

There is no dichotomist difference between paranoia and schizophrenia in *Mother Night.* Rather, they are considered to be the two major possible ways to react to an overarching experience of unspeakable horror caused by totalitarianism and massified warfare (see Broer, *Sanity Plea*; Clare, "Worlds of Wordcraft"; Tew, "*Mother Night*"). The difference between the two conditions of paranoia and schizophrenia is a degree of awareness, and these conditions are more generally tied together as complementary symptoms of war. To a certain degree, one may choose whether one is paranoid or schizophrenic, since it is possible to either close one's eyes to heinousness or to leave them open—but this is not much of a choice. Tom Marvin relates this general observation to the marginal figure of Andor Gutman, one of the Israeli guards during Campbell's imprisonment in Jerusalem and a former concentration camp inmate. In Auschwitz, Gutman had "volunteered" for the job of a corpse carrier, "whose duties were to shepherd condemned persons into gas chambers" (MN, 6–7). Like Campbell, Gutman recognizes his guilt without quite understanding his own choice to become guilty in the first place. Marvin concludes that Campbell's "story suggests that it is possible to be a victim and a villain at the same time, and this is how Campbell chooses to portray himself in his confessions. . . . Being a "victim" and an "agent" does not excuse either Gutman or Campbell, but it does suggest that conventional notions of guilt and innocence are inadequate to deal with the complexities of human behavior" ("Who Am I," 234).

Marvin's continuum of villain and victim can be tied back to this book's language of praedo and innocent, figures that centrally constitute each other in the construction of totalitarianism. The paranoid can be easily considered a praedo of totalitarian logic across ideological demarcation lines, yet Vonnegut suggests that, in contrast to the paranoid praedo, there is no easy definition of innocence. A character like Gutman is both an innocent and a praedo, as he has inserted himself as a cog in the wheels of the same institutional killing machine that seeks to destroy him. Gutman and Campbell do not have a way of capturing or even expressing the extent of their guilt because their role as praedones is determined by their *unthinking* acceptance of totalitarian orders.

Their own belief that they are nevertheless guilty points toward a strong moral position that underlies *Mother Night*. The fact that the narrative universe and all the characters in it are not only violent but also *guilty* subtly reinterprets the idea of a wilderness that is chaotic, brutish, and like a state of nature, and mixes the language of the state of nature with the Lockean idea of war as a state that is inherently illegitimate, insane, and deviant. To recognize how this underlying moral position is made accessible to the reader, it makes sense to review the few passages in the novel in which Campbell steps out of the cynical elusiveness of his schizophrenic disassociation, and makes clear value statements (see also Vonnegut, "Humanist").

> And one thing she [a fervent Nazi] did to me was make me deaf to all success stories. The people she saw as succeeding in a brave new world were, after all, being rewarded as specialists in slavery, destruction, and death. I don't consider people who work in those fields successful. (MN, 75)

> Say what you will about the sweet miracle of unquestioning faith, I consider a capacity for it terrifying and absolutely vile. (MN, 103)

> "Look at you! Came to kill evil with your bare hands, and now away you go with no more glory than a man sideswiped by a Greyhound bus! And that's all the glory you deserve!" I said. "That's all that any man at war with pure evil deserves. There are plenty of good reasons for fighting," I said, "but no good reason ever to hate without reservation, to imagine that God Almighty Himself hates with you, too. Where's evil? It's that large part of every man that wants to hate without limit, that wants to hate with God on his side. It's that part of every man that finds all kinds of ugliness so attractive. It's that part of an imbecile," I said, "that punishes and vilifies and makes war gladly." (MN, 164)

These passages reflect a clear condemnation of paranoia wherever it occurs: in the general cultural atmosphere of Nazi Germany, as in the first two quotes, or in the grandiose attitude of O'Hare, the fanatic American antifascist and the addressee of the speech in the third quote. This final passage is particularly interesting because it is preceded by an act of legitimate violence that Campbell commits in self-defense against O'Hare, and because the formulation of this lecture clearly marks the paranoid position as an essentialist one. In singling out O'Hare as the addressee of such a speech (and the recipient of a legitimate beating), the scene points to something interesting. Throughout the novel, the essentialist O'Hare speaks to Campbell exclusively as a representative of "pure evil" (MN, 163), but we also learn that only the thought of, and speech to, Campbell gives O'Hare's own life meaning (MN, 162). Only in addressing Campbell as a Nazi does O'Hare's essentialist position become recognizable, but because O'Hare is nothing more than Campbell's pathetic stalker, the essentialist perspective is exposed as a resource chosen by the desperate and damaged. O'Hare clings to Campbell by hating him. When discussing the novel in terms of the hostis humani generis constellation, then, it is particularly important to consider to whom the equally desperate schizophrenic Campbell speaks—or rather confesses.

An argument can be made that in *Mother Night*, the constellation of hostis humani generis is not laid out in the plot, as in earlier examples discussed in this study, but across the metafictional frames of the novel (Häsner, "Indexikalität," 78) that emphasize not the content but the function of Campbell's confession. Campbell's fictional confession is explicitly mediated by two gatekeepers who are both invested in the defense of human rights, not in the context of Cold War binaries but for the sake of a nuanced consideration of individual fates. The maxim in the preamble to "Universal Declaration of Human Rights"—namely, that "disregard and contempt for human rights have resulted in barbarous acts which have outraged the conscience of mankind" (United Nations, "Universal Declaration of Human Rights")—is also the defining premise of the novel. Like the declaration, *Mother Night* works to legitimate a political and legal regime designed to protect human rights. The novel essentially uses hostis humani generis as an aesthetic resource to suggest that war inevitably breeds despair, that the desperate inevitably speak, and that they either speak hatefully (like the paranoid O'Hare) or confessionally (like the schizophrenic Campbell). The human rights regime is legitimated as the proper institutional context for confession, and thus as the only constructive way of dealing with an entire generation's despair.

The first gatekeeper is the direct addressee of the book, the historical figure Tuvia Friedmann. In the novel, Friedmann's staff helps Campbell in the writing of his memoirs, doing research into his life to help make his personal memory legally and historically relevant (MN, 3). Correspondingly, the first of two relevant frames consists of the Israeli prison space as the fictional site of writing and as the contextualizing raison d'être of the text as a confession to crimes against humanity (a humanity that, importantly, includes Campbell himself).

I argued above that in *Native Son* the retelling of Bigger Thomas's story by his lawyer serves to recontextualize an act of murder as a foundational intervention calling on the legal system to return to its civilized premises. Campbell's confession to the law (MN, 122; see also MN 87, 105, 106, 117, and 137) achieves a similar civilizing effect of transforming violence into a foundational intervention. However, it is not the law that is to be transformed—it is the world that has gone mad and now has to be led back to the existing language and terms of the law.

As in *Native Son*, in *Mother Night* retelling the story of a perpetrator draws attention to the violence that informs an entire insane narrative universe that has created the already condemned protagonist. Through the mode of confession in *Mother Night*, the incomprehensible violence of a limitless and grotesque narrative universe can be made accessible to prevailing categories of legitimacy and illegitimacy and, ultimately, the law. Importantly, in contrast to the situation in Wright's novel, the crime against humanity in *Mother Night* is so elusive that its punishment can be undone by the single stroke of a pen (MN, 172–75). The protagonist, however, does not accept the possibility of acquittal because only his fatal punishment maintains the possibility that the confession will be a foundational intervention. He accordingly sentences and kills himself in his prison cell.

This conscious usage of literary form as an enabling element of legitimacy claims is made particularly explicit by the second gatekeeper, the "editor" Kurt Vonnegut who is also a fictionalized historical figure (as explained above, Vonnegut as the editor appears in the fictional editor's note that is part of the text from the start and is not identical with the retrospectively added 1966 introduction). The editor confirms that the confessions of Campbell, a writer who "admire[d] form" (MN, 119), have a specific function: to subject an insane world to the careful consideration of justice. "The demands of art alone were enough to make him lie," the editor relates, but "lies told for the sake of artistic effect . . . can be, in a higher sense, the most beguiling forms of truth" (MN, ix). If literal-minded paranoia can produce a mad world, the metafictional confession of a detached schizophrenic who accepts death for justice (rather than for love, as Resi does) can help initiate a sane world.

Two realms are constructed as distinct via the boundaries of the metafictional frame. One realm is mad and evil and is described as a cautionary example to the other, civilized realm, which must hear the confession and defy the temptation to become mad. In *Mother Night*, the contrasting realms directly correspond to contrasting approaches to violence and language. The legitimate institutional approach (the human rights regime, specifically the Jerusalem court) does not speak but institutionally enables perpetrators to confess and victims to testify. In contrast, the illegitimate institutional approach (committers of mass warfare and representatives of any paranoid security apparatus) is associated with the language of brutalizing propaganda; here, both perpetrators and victims are shouted down and condemned to silence. The civil societies of both the United States and Israel are constructed as conceivable institutional enablers of civilization because these countries adhere to the universal and international principles of human rights. Their ability to listen before they interpret is the central resource through which their transformative reactualization by a foundational pirata (Campbell) is deemed possible.

Civilization is very explicitly constructed as a civil society informed by a functioning respect for human rights, understood as a respect for nuance and complexity. It is for this reason that the structure of *Mother Night* allows Campbell to speak to the reader of a novel on behalf of the "spirit" of human rights law, in Jeremy Waldron's sense ("Torture," 1748). The protagonist becomes recognizable as a pure woman pirata because he formulates overarching civilizational values in an imperfect context of crime and punishment—whose imperfection is, in this case, not dramatized by a sentence that is too harsh but by one that is too mild (MN, 20 and 175). At the outermost frame of the novel, the reader him- or herself is included as a potential representative of civilization, who may help strengthen and uphold a legitimate human rights law that acknowledges the possibility of guilt even beyond enforceable notions of criminality. The democratic reader is called on to defy the likes of Jones and O'Hare both individually and institutionally—for instance, by positioning him- or herself against a "paranoid style in American politics" (Hofstadter, "Paranoid Style").

Campbell is a pirata not because he conflates inconflatable elements within nationalist dichotomies mapped out in the plot (even though as a double agent, he does that, too). He is a pirata because he, the repentant committer, conflates the mute violence of madness with the sane platforms for individual speech that are provided by a regime based on a humanist usage of legal and aesthetic language. Campbell remains implicated by totalitarianism yet accepts his punishment—even when it cannot be enforced by anyone other than himself.

To be such a foundational pirata, Campbell can only be "in possession of his own soul" (Broer, *Sanity Plea*, 56) at the moment when he hands his memoirs to the editor and his body to the law that has legitimate authority over him—at the moment, in other words, when his confessions are written down, and when he himself allows his speaking presence to be fully replaced by the interpreting presence of not one but two representatives of civilization (even though only one of them, "Vonnegut" himself, appears in this function within the text, and thus absorbs the role of "Friedmann" in his editorial voice). Campbell as a foundational pirata offers his entire life up for civilizational interpretation and flatly refuses to live without a civilizing judgment appropriate to the complexity of his human voice, whose misuse for conformist propaganda is also his crime (MN, 175–76).

This construction of the confessing perpetrator is contextualized by a more general shift in the treatment of the experience of violence in literature. Many US veterans took advantage of the GI bill to study creative writing in college. Literary writing, like psychotherapy, was seen as a cultural resource for formulating notions of guilt and trauma in institutionally integrated ways. After the hardening exposure to war, "the process [that the veterans] underwent on campus was one of 'softening,' a subtle transition from the silent suffering of trauma into the controlled pathos of literary recollection" (McGurl, *Program Era*, 61). It is notable that Mark McGurl, when explaining the institutional purpose and individual effect of these writing programs, speaks of "suffering" and "trauma" rather than of guilt and violence, which is a general tendency in the postwar cultural construction of the US veteran as someone who has suffered, rather than committed, the horrors of war. Later chapters in this part of the book will return to the discursive construction of such a strangely passive soldier, as the sole focus on (American) soldiers' suffering would constitute an important element of the essentialist interpretation of the hostis humani generis constellation in later decades.

In *Mother Night*, this focus on suffering alone is rejected, especially via the characterization of the self-pitying O'Hare. Instead, as Marvin pointed out, Campbell's confession explicitly combines the perspectives of the perpetrator and the victim. The centrality of the combination of the perpetrator's confession and the victim's testimony is further emphasized by the addition of the 1966 introduction, which explicitly—and, as noted above, for the first time—relates Vonnegut's personal experience of the firebombing of Dresden. In the introduction, Vonnegut expresses bitterness about the fact that mass atrocities committed by Americans were practically ignored in public discourse after World War II, even though he suggests that any reactualization of national legitimacy would require the acknowledgment of responsibility for those atrocities.

In the novel, the illegitimacy of mass warfare is transcended by the act of confession and martyrdom for offenses against the "inherent dignity" of humankind (United Nations, "Universal Declaration of Human Rights"). Campbell becomes in his confession all of what he has always been—a totalitarian praedo; an innocent produced by violence; and finally a foundational pirata whose confession opens up the possibility of the existence of representatives of civilization in the world, despite all the horrors that have been committed. However, as the belated addition of the introduction indicates, Campbell can assume this liberating role for the nation only if all of his incarnations within the constellation, not just those of the traumatized innocent and the foundational pirata, are accepted as American roles. The introduction's interpretive motto—"We are what we pretend to be, so we must be careful about what we pretend to be" (MN, vii)—does not refer to the protagonist alone; it also cautions the reader about his or her complicity in the totalitarian horrors elsewhere, and his or her responsibility to uphold the values formulated by the human rights regime.

In other words, Vonnegut uses the hostis humani generis constellation to draw attention to his claim that mass state violence of whatever nature threatens to transform people into praedones and/or innocents, and that, therefore, mass atrocities cannot be the means of legitimate violence at all. Only those who are untouched by experiences of violence and oppression and who also have a normative orientation toward human rights as a secular City of God, may remain untainted by a City of Man whose "neutral" amorality has made the institutionalized world mad and evil—whether this evil lies in the neutrality of bureaucratic functionality, of ambitious dreams of success and accomplishment, or of the very capacity to believe (see Palevsky, *Atomic Fragments*, 128–29). The entire trajectory of the novel suggests that, when faced with massified warfare, neither human nor nation can resist being transformed into a praedo and/or innocent. While it is the individual's responsibility to become a pirata who gestures toward a more legitimate future, the nation is responsible for providing the institutional grounds for reactualization by strengthening the structuring influence of the human rights regime as the proper place for a planetary representative of civilization. In other words, it is the responsibility of the nation to recognize any foundational intervention in the first place. Foundational reactualization in this form cannot take place without the willingness to engage in the meta-institutional reflection on the nation's own guilt that is demanded by Arendt and dramatized by Vonnegut.

This meta-institutional reflection on US acts of mass destruction not only remains culturally absent but is actively overridden in Cold War America, prompting Vonnegut to address this problem explicitly in the 1966 introduction. Vonnegut concludes that the United States as a nation has ceased to be different because it ignores figures like Campbell in their roles as foundational piratae. Campbell's suicide cannot offer a path toward civilization if his interpreters do not take up the responsibility of being representatives of civilization. The prophetic final words of the novel are: "Goodbye, cruel world! *Auf wiedersehen?*" (Until we see each other again?) (MN, 176; German spelling mistake in original).

The United States would indeed see Campbell again. At the time of *Mother Night*'s first publication in 1962, the Vietnam War had already been raging for seven years. Like the earlier Korean War, the Vietnam War was conceptualized as a way to contain totalitarian communism in the world. The Vietnam War demonstrated, rather than renegotiated, an already predetermined essentialist constellation: as a proxy war between the United States and the Soviet Union, it served as a symbolic actualization of a struggle of good versus evil, American democracy versus communist totalitarianism, in "Indian Country" (Greiner, *Krieg ohne Fronten*, 203; my translation).[5] Since the conventionalized use in World War II of weapons of mass destruction, space—in terms of territorial advancement along delineated battle lines—became decreasingly relevant as a measure of warfare. In Vietnam, this was true even for man-to-man combat on the ground. "In contrast to World War II and Korea," Charles Neu points out, "Vietnam was a war without a front, without any clear direction or momentum, in which progress was measured by the number of enemy troops killed rather than by the amount of territory gained. Combat had a circular quality; American units would often patrol the same territory over and over, engaging in fleeting contacts with the enemy, or take an objective and then abandon it" ("Vietnam and Transformation," 17).[6]

The identification of the enemy solely by his agency and allegiance (rather than, for instance, his position in relation to spatial battle lines) soon turned into a constitutive problem. The interpreting American soldier, exposed to a mad universe, proved unable to distinguish the praedo from the innocent. When charged with his involvement in the My Lai massacre, William Calley famously argued that the command had essentially defined the enemy as everyone who was not an American soldier: "When my troops were getting massacred and mauled by an enemy I couldn't see, I couldn't feel and I couldn't touch, nobody in the military system ever described them as anything other than Communism [*sic*]. They didn't give it a race, they didn't give it a sex, they didn't give it an age" (quoted in Glover, *Humanity*, 60).

The My Lai massacre of 1968 forcefully evoked the comparison to Nazi crimes that had been suppressed in the context of the atom bomb twenty years earlier. Especially against the backdrop of the recent Eichmann trial, the events at My Lai appeared to be a mixture of two things: the result of the unquestioning obedience of a good soldier that followed the same logic as Eichmann's infamous reasoning in his defense, and a radical degradation of American soldiers into committers of crimes against humanity, a transformation previously described as the effect of totalitarianism alone (Glover, *Humanity*, 60–63; Varon, *Bringing War Home*, 99).

As the Eichmann trial had famously established, crimes against humanity were never just the crimes of the individual perpetrator: they allowed conclusions to be made about the government in whose name the perpetrator acted.

The multiplying charges of systematic, predatory massacres of the innocent now positioned the United States government as a potentially totalitarian regime that had illegitimately usurped authority over an American civilization that stood for different values, in Leo Szilard's and Vonnegut's sense.

The counterculture movement, which is most famously associated with these interrogations of the Vietnam War's legitimacy, thus did not invent or initiate but rather revived a charge of barbarous illegitimacy against the US presidency and security apparatus. This charge had been latent since the firebombings of Dresden and Tokyo, and especially since the bombings of Hiroshima and Nagasaki. When the charge of illegitimacy was voiced in the spirit of Campbell's confessions—for instance, when American soldiers who had served in Vietnam began to present themselves as criminals in the language of the human rights regime (A. Hunt, *The Turning*, 55–76)—it mattered little that such voices were few, even within the counterculture movement. Reactions were strong because the charges were plausible according to the logic of hostis humani generis constellation, and because they were further reinforced by the "seismic shock" (Franklin, *Vietnam*, 122; see also Marcus, "Götterdämmerung," 55) of realizing that in Vietnam, the United States shared the fate usually reserved for the barbarian within the essentialist model: it withdrew from the contested territory. In a way, this end of the Vietnam War narratively rubber-stamped the construction of the United States as a potentially barbarous Other.

In response to such an enormous assault on national claims to civilization, followers of the frontier-inspired counterculture movement were identified as "un-American" domestic praedones by the rising neoconservative movement (Bader, *Neokonservatismus*, 14). As the counterculture movement's cultural impact peaked in the 1970s, the ensuing societal shifts fostered a public backlash to the counterculture movement and "generated widespread [popular] belief in evil. The popular conviction posited inherent wickedness not in actions or temptations but in specific people" (Cusac, *Cruel and Unusual*, 110). Groups that were considered nonwhite, organizationally "different," or both, were singled out as classes of "unreachables" (ibid., 123 and 125) or "undesirables" (Pateman, "Race, Sex, and Indifference," 151) in American society.

Those under attack lashed back: the 1970s witnessed increasingly widespread and articulate charges that essentialist views were at odds with "a set of [frontier] ideals based on the capacity of people to transform" (Cusac, *Cruel and Unusual*, 110). Positions hardened, and both sides of the debate accused each other of constituting an inherently totalitarian (meaning invasive, Other, and normatively un-American) threat to the nation on the basis of different interpretations of the same constellation.

Meanwhile, in international law, the frontier model of civilization remained the solid basis of any conventional understanding and use of hostis humani generis. The legal fiction had been transformed into a vehicle to link human rights law and criminal law. Because criminal law was traditionally perpetrator-oriented, human rights law used hostis humani generis (as a legal fiction) to accommodate the perpetrator requirement in its own, ultimately victim-oriented, framework. Hostis humani generis, in this context, helped identify an individual perpetrator as the representative of a collective of faceless oppressors. This was especially true for crimes against humanity, which always by definition had to be linked back to a concerted campaign of harm. The construction of specific people as praedones thus became necessary to establish a basis for the creation of representational (legal) agency on behalf of the victims. In accord with the precedents of the Nuremberg and Eichmann trials, US courts implemented this position in national law. The watershed case of *Filártiga v. Peña-Irala* explicitly rendered torturers hostes humani generis to make them liable in the United States (Kaufman, "Opinion").

Filártiga thus both provided a national precedent for the implementation of universal jurisdiction over praedones as defined by the frontier model of civilization and specified that barbarous ideology and the abuse of institutional structures are necessarily intertwined (Orentlicher, "Future of Universal Jurisdiction," 227). The interpretation of perpetrators in human rights–related cases since *Filártiga* has affirmed those American political traditions that allow for the possibility of totalitarianism within state institutions in general, but qualify that US institutions may claim to be exempt from the charge as they institutionalize human rights law instead. *Filártiga* constituted the high point of this interpretive tradition in twentieth-century American law; it seemed to create the conditions for cathartic martyrdom on behalf of an internationalist nation in the spirit of Campbell.

However, the dichotomist environment of the Cold War instead resulted in a radical rethinking of these constructions in law. The innovative legal use of hostis humani generis after World War II was fundamentally interrogated, and the search for alternative interpretations of the legal fiction began. These alternative interpretations sought to exchange the use of the legal fiction to expose illegitimate state structures with interpretations of hostis humani generis that corresponded more with the unreachables and undesirables in the nation.

[12]

WHO IS INNOCENT?: THE LATER COLD WAR YEARS

IN THE 1980s, the decade that began with *Filártiga v. Peña-Irala*, a range of discursive experiments was conducted by the neoconservative community to formulate a new type of praedo. This new praedo was no longer characterized by institutional belonging, and thus he allowed a use of the hostis humani generis fiction in law that was not vulnerable to the construction of essentialist, totalitarian, and paranoid thinking as all being synonymous. The praedo that emerged from this quest, the international terrorist, was a deliberately old-fashioned figure. The international terrorist's properties in the discourses of the 1980s explicitly referred back to the origins of the hostis humani generis fiction in early modern European law. Citing the Mediterranean example, this new praedo represented not a totalitarian state but Islam as a hostile, Other cultural realm. At the same time, the Mediterranean constellation was updated in significant ways: the barbarian represented by this terrorist praedo was not a specific political entity such as the Barbary state; rather, Islam was understood as an ideology that, like the other relevant ideologies of the time, had a spatial equivalent derived from the Cold War compartmentalization of the world. If the First World of the West constituted frontier civilization, and the Second World of the Eastern bloc under the leadership of the Soviet Union represented totalitarianism, the Third World would come to be associated with a barbarian interpretation of Islam in these neoconservative discourses.

For the terrorist figure to be used as a praedo to represent Third-World Islam, it was first necessary to arrive at a new understanding of terrorism. The most prominent terrorist groups of the 1970s, such as the Irish Republic Army or the German Red Army Faction, were nationally organized, and defense against them was satisfactorily covered by national criminal law. The conventional understanding of terrorism in the 1970s was thus affected by the same discursive restrictions as the assigning of inherent evil to the counterculture movement or impoverished African Americans: one could not disregard the national context, and thus a sense of potential institutional complicity and responsibility, in any analysis of such evil groups and their emergence. Moreover, terrorism in a national context always raised the question of the perpetrators' potential status as freedom fighters—a question that continues to rage on an international level, especially since the introduction of the international terrorist as the epitome of illegitimacy in US discourse after 9/11 (Barnidge, *Non-State Actors*, 32–33).

International terrorism was at first a subject of marginal interest to researchers—chiefly neoconservatives—in the United States. They experienced an analytical and political breakthrough in the 1980s, when Palestinian violence against Israel was increasingly systematically framed not as a negotiable conflict over access to territory, but as an essentialist conflict between civilization and its inherent Other. The administration of President Ronald Reagan was particularly important for the rediscovery of the essentialist interpretation of hostis humani generis in the United States. In terms of space, "the policy of the Reagan administration against Middle Eastern terrorism can be considered as predominantly 'globalist,' meaning one that relied on the global conceptual frameworks of the Cold War to understand regional events and to take [*sic*] decisions" (Toaldo, "Reagan Administration," 3). When it came to acts of nonstate violence against representatives of the West, which were now explicitly framed as acts of terrorism, "the [Reagan administration] viewed terrorist attacks as illegitimate acts by the Soviet Union's proxies who were intent on undermining the West" (Wills, *First War*, 22). Emphasizing the representative dimension of legitimate intervention, "Reagan was . . . very concerned for the fate of individual [innocent] victims of terrorism" (ibid., 24). In short, the Reagan administration "did not start a comprehensive new policy against terrorism [but] experimented with tools and ideas that later were incorporated into Bush's War on Terror" (Toaldo, "Reagan Administration," 2). These experiments notably included a rereading of the hostis humani generis legal fiction via the example of international terrorist as a quasi-Mediterranean corsair.

The first explicitly public connection that was made between terrorism and the legal fiction of hostis humani generis was occasioned by the *Achille Lauro* incident. In the fall of 1985, members of the Palestine Liberation Front hijacked a cruise ship, the *Achille Lauro*, to force the freeing of fifty-one Palestinians from Israeli prisons (Wills, *First War*, 143). With only one death, this incident was "remarkable less for what actually happened than for the new trends in international relations it revealed" (Cassese, *Politics*, 17).

The perpetrators in the *Achille Lauro* incident could not be described as pirates by the standards of 1985. During the course of a single criminal act, they moved into various national jurisdictions as well as international waters and airspace, which made it impossible to use the territorial definition of piracy offered by the Harvard Draft, which had been adopted without changes into the 1982 United Nations Convention on the Law of the Sea (UNCLOS). It was mainly because of the UNCLOS definition of piracy that international legal scholars overwhelmingly regarded the incident as an act of terrorism. The Reagan administration did not immediately follow suit. Instead, US officials suggested that the perpetrators were pirates—not pirates as defined by UNCLOS, but by analogy "modern pirates" (Cassese, *Politic*, 68–70).

The international legal community remained unconvinced, and the United States finally agreed that the *Achille Lauro* incident constituted an act of terrorism. Still, the attempt to define the hijackers as pirates draws attention to an interpretive pattern. Even before the *Achille Lauro* incident, officials of the Reagan administration had been extremely vocal in trying to define terrorism as a separate new variation of the hostis humani generis fiction that discontinued its use with the slave trade and crimes against humanity (Cassese, *Politics*, 69). Instead, the terrorist was going to be an explicit successor to the maritime pirate of early modernity, and the arguments made here unambiguously refer to William Blackstone's definition of hostis humani generis in their understanding of terrorism.[1] This effectively meant a reversal of the fiction's groundbreaking legal reinterpretation in the twentieth century that had informed the Nuremberg trials, the Eichmann trial, and *Filártiga v. Peña-Irala*. The reading of terrorists as hostes humani generis constituted nothing less than an attempt to reestablish an imperial interpretation of the legal fiction that identified the enemy of all humankind in the margins of states rather than underneath them—as the attackers of random victims rather than of humanity's essence.

In the 1980s, the international legal realm was the most important stronghold of the frontier interpretation of hostis humani generis. The Reagan administration's attempt to legally redefine both hostis humani generis and terrorism constituted a full-on assault not just on the frontier interpretation of hostis humani generis, but also on the legal realm as the most influential institutional interpreter of violence as legitimate or illegitimate. Unsurprisingly, a debate of such magnitude did not long remain restricted to the legal sphere. In the year after the *Achille Lauro* incident, two books were published in the United States that may illustrate the shifting grounds of the debate on legitimate violence.

The anthology edited by Benjamin Netanyahu, *Terrorism: How the West Can Win* (1986) constitutes the first concerted public attempt to define international terrorism by the use of the legal fiction of hostis humani generis in the United States. The anthology consists of forty-one very brief chapters by different authors that were assembled to form a single coherent argument. Netanyahu was Israel's ambassador to the United Nations at the time, and the anthology was a result of the second international conference organized by the ultraconservative Jonathan Institute in 1984. This institute organized only two major conferences, the first in Jerusalem and the second in Washington, D.C. These locations indicate that government officials were the main target audiences; indeed, the *Terrorism* anthology, published in the United States, was designed to serve as a policy recommendation for US officials. More than half of *Terrorism*'s forty-one contributors were high-ranking US conservatives from the realms of academia, politics, law, and the media. As the editor of the volume, Netanyahu provides an overarching definition of terrorism that all contributors share in their articles:

> What distinguishes terrorism is the *willful and calculated* choice of the innocent as targets. When terrorists machine-gun a passenger waiting area or set off bombs in a crowded shopping center, their victims are not accidents of war but the *very objects* of the terrorists' assault.
>
> I am prepared, at the risk of belaboring the point, to offer a formal definition, the one adopted in Jerusalem in 1979 [during the first international conference organized by the Jonathan Institute]: *Terrorism is the deliberate and systematic murder, maiming, and menacing of the innocent to inspire fear for political ends.* (Netanyahu, "Defining Terrorism," 9)

In this passage, Netanyahu defines a very specific terrorist figure (rather than the totalitarian state) as the invader of the innocent. The definition directly draws on the work of Claire Sterling, a contributor to the anthology ("Unraveling the Riddle"), who had written what may be called the authoritative study on international terrorism in 1981—*The Terror Network: The Secret War of International Terrorism.* Although the book has been highly controversial ever since it was published, it has informed most political and scholarly understandings of international terrorism in the West.[2] In the book, she traces the emergence of terrorism back to "a significant change in the Russians' unofficial foreign policy" that expressed itself in "an avuncular interest in terrorist 'adventurers' of every alarming shade" and a resulting spate in Soviet funding of terrorist groups (Sterling, *Terror Network*, 13). Sterling's definition of terrorism is based on a clear distinction between terror states and terror groups, a distinction that is adopted throughout the *Terrorism* anthology, albeit with variations regarding these entities' specific relationship to each other.

In Sterling's original study, as in *Terrorism,* the ultimate terror state is identified as the Soviet Union, characterized by totalitarian communism. Terror groups, in contrast, are characterized by a separate allegiance to a militant, fanatic, and antimodern Islam. "Communist totalitarianism and

Islamic radicalism" is a phrase used by various contributors to *Terrorism*, and these two barbarous ideologies correspond with the twin threat of "anarchy and tyranny" against which democracy has to be defended inside and outside national borders (see, for example, P. Johnson, "Cancer," 31; Shultz, "Challenge," 19). The legal fiction of hostis humani generis is explicitly evoked as the basis for a legitimate defense against this twin threat (Kirkpatrick, "Totalitarian Confusion," 57; Leiser, "Enemies of Mankind," 155–56).

In these arguments, Islam is introduced as a category of inherent illegitimacy that originates outside of civilization (meaning that it originates in the Third World). Compared to the secular totalitarian regime that necessarily operates from within representative statehood and thus remains an illegitimate element of an international order based on nation-states, the terror group is described as an even more inherent Other. The fundamentalist terror group as a nonstate Other is not identified along Cold War state lines, but with the help of a "discursive-intellectual binary that lines up [Judeo-] Christianity, secularism, reason, tolerance, free thought and speech on one side, and Islam, fundamentalism, submission, intolerance, restricted thought and speech on the other" (W. Brown, introduction, 14). In *Terrorism*, the terror groups' ideological outlook, and their corresponding use of violence, are constructed as too extreme and inhuman to be fully reducible to a pursuit of rational political interest, even by totalitarian states—hence the terror groups' direct association with anarchy throughout the anthology, and their specific construction as hostes humani generis in the context of an imperialist tradition that foregrounds the defense of innocent citizens against brutish, irrational, marauding nonstate actors (see especially Kirkpatrick, "Totalitarian Confusion," 57; Leiser, "Enemies of Mankind," 155–56).

Netanyahu's editorial definition of terrorism relies on precisely this distinction between terror groups and any kind of state, legitimate or illegitimate. Terror groups are specifically singled out as the most dangerous invaders of the innocent. As in the arguments of the Reagan administration related to the *Achille Lauro* incident, the characterization of terror groups in *Terrorism* clearly refers to Blackstone. If Islam is the unifying ideological reference of terror groups, the representation of Islam is by definition —indeed, by argumentative necessity—a cultural allegiance that arrests representatives in a state of nature similar to that associated with Native Americans in colonial times. Now, however, it is not the American continent that must be civilized by settlers, but the whole world, especially the Third World, that must be civilized in a way to ensure that it neither remains Muslim nor becomes communist. To protect the innocent in this way, the First World representative of civilization acts as if he existed in the state of nature, which enables him to match the inhumane anarchy that informs the illegitimate acts of his new opponent, the Third World praedo in representation of Islam.

Blackstone had legitimized unrestricted imperial violence on the assumption that there was a racialized outside to civilization in Locke (Mills, "Racial Liberalism," 1382). However, belonging to that racialized outside is a dividing line that is relevant only for violent agents. The innocent are generally not racially determined—only their defender and their invader are. In this vein, *Terrorism* implicitly defines the representative of civilization as white and Western, and the praedo as the racialized representative of Islam. They may, however, harm or protect any innocent, regardless of the innocent's race, which allows their essentialist conflict to be a truly globalist one.

These characterizations of terror groups simultaneously anticipate two predictable qualifications that informed—and continue to inform—debates on the definition of terrorism (Barnidge, *Non-State Actors*, 69, 101, and 125). The central emphasis on the innocent as the victims of terrorism discourages counterarguments based on the truism that one person's terrorist is another person's freedom fighter. Since the freedom fighter arguably operates on behalf of the innocent against an invasive oppressor, Netanyahu suggests, the terrorist as an invader of the innocent cannot by definition be considered a freedom fighter. Furthermore, by explicitly focusing on terror groups, the definition conveniently excludes any consideration of state violence's effect on noncombatant innocents.

This latter point especially has occasioned the criticism of Noam Chomsky in *Pirates and Emperors, Old and New: International Terrorism in the Real World*, an essay collection also published in 1986. In the collection, Chomsky pointedly critiques the definition of the innocent exemplified by *Terrorism* and uses the Augustinian anecdote to make his argument understood. The Augustinian anecdote, Chomsky writes,

> captures with some accuracy the current relations between the United States and various minor actors on the stage of international terrorism: Libya, factions of the PLO [Palestine Liberation Organization], and others. More generally, St. Augustine's tale illuminates the meaning of the concept of international terrorism in contemporary Western usage, and reaches to the heart of the frenzy over selected incidents of terrorism currently being orchestrated, with supreme cynicism, as a cover for Western violence.
>
> The term "terrorism" . . . has come to be applied mainly to "retail terrorism" by individuals or groups. Whereas the term was once applied to emperors who molest their own subjects and the world, now it is restricted to thieves who molest the powerful—though not entirely restricted: the term still applies to enemy emperors, a category that shifts with the needs of power and ideology.

> Extricating ourselves from such practices, we use the term "terrorism" to refer to the threat or use of violence to intimidate or coerce (generally for political, religious, or other ends), whether it is the terrorism of the emperor or the thief.
>
> The pirate's maxim explains the recently evolved concept of "international terrorism" only in part. It is necessary to add a second feature: an act of terrorism enters the canon only if it is committed by "their side," not ours. (*Pirates and Emperors*, vii)

Chomsky's assessment is a fair summary of the strategic benefits of the essentialist interpretation of hostis humani generis in the late Cold War, especially since, as he observes, the essentialist definition of "the innocent" tends to be translated as "the Western citizen" in practice (*Pirates and Emperors*, 39). Indeed, in the arguments that he attacks, defensible civilization is present in the national territory of Western states as a matter of course, but not only in the territory: it is also present in the body of each citizen, each box of cargo, each institutionalized stream of command and information that moves through the world at large—it is present in all "representatives of Western power wherever they might be" (Gage, "Terrorism," 90; see. also Policante, *Pirate Myth*; Thorup, *Intellectual History*). Every manifestation of Western influence can be actualized as a manifestation of civilization as soon as it is violated—which means, in practice, that harmed Westerners can be retrospectively characterized as innocent by default. It follows that any Western state's intervention on behalf of harmed Westerners anywhere on the globe is legitimate, even if a claim to sovereign self-defense cannot be made (Cassese, *Politics*, 67).

Throughout *Pirates and Emperors*, Chomsky argues that the concentration on Westerners as the innocent victims of terrorism hides the fact that Western states, too, rely on strategic cooperation with "terrorist 'adventurers' of every alarming shade" (Sterling, *Terror Network*, 13; see also, for example, Chomsky, *Pirates and Emperors*, 83 and 115). The United States itself, Chomsky concludes, can be considered a "terror state" in *Terrorism*'s sense—not reducible to the inherent Otherness represented by terror groups, but certainly implicated by association.

Chomsky is nevertheless careful to avoid any suspicion of endorsing those states and groups already identified as terrorist by the Reagan administration.[3] Instead, he endorses his opponents' claim that the victims of terrorism are innocent but adds that other victims, invaded by Westerners and their allies, are innocent as well. To understand what Chomsky does not do, it is helpful to compare his arguments with those of critics like Seumas Miller. Miller analyzes the antidemocratic implication of imperial constructions of Western "innocents" (*Counter-Terrorism*, 36) and suggests that Western civilians who fall victim to terrorism may never be innocent "in the required sense" (ibid., 38) because they are citizens rather than subjects. After all, the construction of the innocent as inherently Western automatically renders the citizens of democracies—which all Western states are to some degree—the state's innocent subjects instead. It is because of the antidemocratic implications of the category of innocence that Miller rejects the notion of the innocent as a workable centerpiece in definitions of anti-Western terrorism (ibid., 36–42). In *Pirates and Emperors*, however, Chomsky affirms the imperial construction of Western citizens of democracies as innocents who are wrongfully subjected to violence and simply extends this definition to every human being. Chomsky rhetorically embraces the construction of Western "emperors" and their complementary antagonists of terror states and terror groups ("enemy emperors" and "retail terrorists"). Only in this way is he even able to use the terminology of terrorism introduced by Sterling and then normalized in the debates on international terrorism exemplified by *Terrorism*. The acceptance of this basic constellation is the price to pay for being able to point out the "hypocrisy" of conceptualizing the innocent as inherently "Western," and the enemy of all humankind as anyone on the globe who attacks "the West" anywhere (Chomsky, *Pirates and Emperors*, x).

It is obvious from Netanyahu's definition of terrorism alone that the charge of totalitarianism against Western states is something that representatives of the essentialist interpretation have understood as an unavoidable element of their opponents' rhetoric, and as a problem of legitimacy that they have argumentatively moved past with their new focus on terror groups. By using the Augustinian anecdote and thus equating "retail terrorists" with pirates, Chomsky falls victim to his opponent's greater argumentative sophistication on this point, as Chomsky unwittingly affirms the very claims that his opponents make so aggressively in the first place—namely, that it makes analytical sense to render terrorists and early modern maritime pirates equivalent, and that international terrorists must be seen as collectives directly in the tradition of the early modern interpretation of hostis humani generis.

The fact that Chomsky's critique is ineffective at this level indicates that in the arguments of the contributors to *Terrorism* the relationship between terror state and terror group is not one of praedo and renegade pirata, as the notion of state-sponsored terrorism might suggest at first glance; instead, twentieth-century concepts of totalitarian states as illegitimate orders are used by neoconservative critics as a springboard to suggest a conceptualization of the racialized terror group as an Other of more inherent organizational and normative difference. The definition of the terror state may very well implicate the United States as one such state, but the terror group's potential for the formulation of claims to legitimate violence lies precisely in the idea that such a group does not actually represent any state at all.

Still, Chomsky's tacit acceptance of the pirate-emperor constellations is not naive. It serves a purpose of its own, which is, essentially, to claim legitimacy for his own voice as a critic. An element of his argument that merits closer attention is the demand that everyone on the globe ought to be recognized as innocent in *Terrorism*'s sense. To be able to render the United States an illegitimate "emperor" rather than a representative of civilization, Chomsky makes a significant difference between the "emperor," who is the US administration and its national counterparts in other Western states, and a planetary us, who are all of these emperors' innocent and misrepresented subjects. This argumentative move is consequential in its own right.

In my discussion of the Augustinian anecdote in the Free Prince speech, I drew attention to the fact that the rich did not misrepresent civilization in ways that could be remedied through reform, but that they were as inherently illegitimate and alien to civilization as pirates. This radical externalization of the rich as an equivalent to the Augustinian emperor caused a dilemma, since both illegitimate agents had to be replaced by a more legitimate one—a successor that never in fact materialized. In Chomsky's argument, we are presented with a similar problem. If even the United States, a democratic state, is defined as a totalitarian emperor in the language of the Augustinian anecdote, the other two figures of the Augustinian anecdote—the legitimate ruler and the innocent—emerge as potential alternative sources of political legitimation. Even though Chomsky's use of the Augustinian anecdote endorses neoconservative positions about the emerging figure of the international terrorist as an early modern pirate, his argument has some interesting implications because, according to his logic, the legitimate ruler and the innocent are the same people—namely, the citizens of a democracy (*Pirates and Emperors*, viii). Correspondingly, the legitimate successor to all violent states and groups worldwide is the collective of the planetary innocent, violated by pirates and misrepresented by emperors.

Any leap from this argument toward a vision of anti-imperial revolution would be hasty, however, since the innocent in this argument is still the innocent—a figure that is defined by its function of being represented. Most of the representative legitimacy lent by a planetary population of victimized innocents is absorbed by the effort of lending legitimacy to the critical voice itself—in this case, Chomsky's. After all, how can the critic claim to live (and argue) legitimately within the very structures of an imperial state that he charges with totalitarian madness and evil? In Chomsky, we the people who represent the true values of American democracy are rendered inherently innocent by a totalitarian regime structuring our lives—moreover, we share this fate with all others on the planet. We are without agency and cannot voice our position. This is why critics like Chomsky (in *Pirates and Emperors*), by drawing attention to our perilous situation, can assume legitimate representative agency over us. Such critics represent us and our civilizational values at the paradoxical price of affirming and reinforcing the idea that Western democratic citizens cannot in practice act in the role of the legitimate ruler of state institutions because their legitimacy stems from the fact that they are innocent.

Chomsky is not, of course, the only critic who represents the underrepresented innocent in this way. After the Cold War, this paradoxical construction of the innocent as the central resource of legitimate scholarly intervention has been pursued by a large number of critics. For example, Giorgio Agamben's critical self-position in his influential study *Homo Sacer* (1998) is in large measure interchangeable with that of Chomsky in *Pirates and Emperors* (see Schillings, "Privateering Critic").

First published in 1995 and translated into English by Daniel Heller-Roazen in 1998, *Homo Sacer* participates in the debate between Francis Fukuyama and Samuel Huntington, which pertained to the role of the United States as the sole remaining superpower after the dissolution of the Soviet Union in 1991. While Fukuyama envisioned a planetary transformation in the spirit of liberal democracy and the human rights regime (*End of History*, 334–38), Huntington envisioned a "clash of civilizations" with Islam as the main new adversary of Judeo-Christian civilization (*Clash of Civilizations*, 247–52). Agamben challenges both positions, insofar as he attacks their shared assumption that the United States represents civilized order (*Homo Sacer*, 38, 176–77, and 187). Instead, he suggests that any planetary order that relies on institutions exhibits inherent totalitarian underpinnings (ibid., 176). His book is explicitly devoted to a discussion of "the bare life of the *citizen*" (ibid., 9; emphasis added).

Agamben affirms Chomsky's reading of "the [American] emperor" as external to the civilization he claims to represent and identifies a no man's land of oppression that exposes any institutional sovereignty as an illegitimate emperor (*Homo Sacer*, 161). The homo sacer is, according to Agamben's definition, a figure locked in this no man's land, as he is trapped between the states of political and biological death. Echoing the assumptions of analyses of torture, the irrevocable defamiliarization from civilization is central to the status of the homo sacer. For instance, in Agamben, such status can be assigned to the surviving devotee; a person on death row; the comatose patient; and, most importantly, the concentration camp inmate. Andreas Vasilache has argued that the homo sacer, far from being a biopolitical entity in Foucault's sense, is subjected to a violence that is "exclusively breaking and not at all strategic or productive" ("'Homines sacri,'" 59; my translation). Indeed, Agamben insists on the homo sacer as a polar opposite to the sovereign, even to the extent that the homo sacer can be so broken that he moves beyond the transformative reach of the sovereign (*Homo Sacer*, 184–85).

Agamben's construction of the homo sacer as the epitome of innocence produced by violence is important for this book because he describes in detail a claim that was only sketched by Chomsky in the 1980s—namely, that only illegitimate totalitarian Leviathans and homines sacri can exist in a planetary order based on nation-states. Agamben's sovereign is understood as expansionist but replaces a "taking of land" with a "taking of the outside" of the law (*Homo Sacer*, 19). Because the totalitarian planetary hegemon is conceptualized as a single coherent body, violence on its behalf can be conceptualized as a removal of threats to the integrity of the Agambian Leviathan, a notion familiar from classic constructions of totalitarianism (see Arendt, *Totalitarianism*, 460–65; Evans, *Rituals*, 633, 649–50, and 696–709).

In the first part of his argument in *Homo Sacer*, Agamben cites a range of historical examples to help equate sovereignty and Hobbesian representative agency (105–6). This somewhat rough and sweeping equation is needed to establish the premises of the argument's second part, which constitutes the core of Agamben's argument. Here, he discusses the totalitarian state and its specific production of the homo sacer, since he conceptualizes the sovereign as an entity characterized by the refusal to acknowledge any representative entities other than itself. The totalitarian will becomes the only relevant representative will. The politicization of biological life, in this sense, subjects not only the citizens of the concerned state but potentially everyone on the planet to the representative claim of a totalitarian sovereign (ibid., 83–84 and 188). One vehicle used to enforce such a sovereign's claims to universal violent outreach may be the notion of universal jurisdiction against the enemy of all humankind. This specific development of Agamben's argument is made by Heller-Roazen in *The Enemy of All* and, in part, by Amedeo Policante in *The Pirate Myth*.

A different integration of the homo sacer constellation into a discussion of hostis humani generis is possible, though, and a historical example—that of American prisoners of war during the First Gulf War—may help illustrate how and why this can be done. After the Vietnam War, soldiers who were missing in action (MIA) had gained legendary significance as figures that retrospectively helped argue for a legitimate American cause in Vietnam. Their case provided a counternarrative to the increasingly widespread charge against the United States as an illegitimate invader that committed crimes against humanity, and against individual soldiers as hostes humani generis even in their own self-descriptions (Engelhardt, *Victory Culture*, 226). After the Vietnam War, references to soldiers who were MIA in films such as *Missing in Action* (1984) and *Rambo II* (1985) were crucial for retrospectively repositioning the United States as a good, legitimate force in Vietnam (Pease,

Exceptionalism, 62–63). Because of this importance of these soldiers in America after the war, Tom Engelhardt notes that all US soldiers in the First Gulf War were conceptualized in the spirit of those MIA in Vietnam before they even saw combat. The troops at large were framed as "America's innocent soldier boys" and as traumatized victims rather than adult agents of war (Boose, "Techno-Muscularity," 593, see also 610–11; see also A. Hunt, *The Turning*, 55–76). In a footnote, Engelhardt includes an interesting aside:

> Because the troops were already imagined as hostages, there was confusion about how to handle the small number of military personnel captured by the Iraqis during hostilities (a few of whom were shown, looking battered, on Iraqi TV). Were they heroes simply for being there or cowards for saying a few words? Either way, once released, the POWs [prisoners of war] seemed like awkward presences. In the end, they rode in a few parades and then were largely ignored. [In contrast to the Vietnam POWs, t]heir memoirs were not requested. Miniseries were not produced. It was as if, on returning, they went MIA in America. (*Victory Culture*, 288)

The ghostlike, "awkward presences" of these First Gulf War veterans who "went MIA" can be conceptualized as the presence of surviving devotees as homines sacri in Agamben (*Homo Sacer*, 97), and they point to homo sacer as a concept of exclusion that requires the broader conceptualization of innocence to become persuasive. As Engelhardt suggests, had the Gulf War troops not been conceptualized from the start as the innocent quasi prisoners of war, it would have been as easy to conceive of the victimization of actual prisoners of war in Iraq as it had been in Vietnam. In Vietnam, POWs had moved from a status of legitimate representation of civilization to the nonstatus of the innocent. But because the status of innocence was preemptively assigned to soldiers in the First Gulf War, POWs who were victimized in even more radical ways than exposure could no longer be made comprehensible according to the logic of representative agency. Therefore, they became homines sacri—a position that referred solely to their lack of any status, even that of innocents. Theirs was essentially the reverse of the traditional dilemma of the pure woman who violently prevents her own rape.

One may indeed argue that the concept of homo sacer in general describes a reverse pure woman paradox, and that this new paradox deviates from the older one in interesting and helpful ways. In its traditional form, the pure woman paradox makes the oppression of the prepolitical family visible and problematizes the construction of natural innocence by endowing the innocent with properties of agency. As Wendy Brown and Judith Butler argue, the rule of the paterfamilias is conventionally legitimated because he uses violence to protect the innocent from illegitimate violence. While the legitimacy or illegitimacy of violence is thus examined in every encounter between the two representative men, the pure woman exposes the fact that both the legitimate paterfamilias and the illegitimate free agent rely on the innocents' oppression. By rising from oppression and committing defensive (and therefore legitimate) violence, the pure woman radically renegotiates the sources of legitimacy because she questions the righteousness of her oppression; in this way, I have argued, she can evolve into a foundational pirata figure.

The homo sacer concept may well be called a reverse pure woman paradox because it is the homo sacer's very passivity, his brokenness by violence, that is theorized to be the source of his disturbing and disquieting presence. I have indicated at several points of this book that in the twentieth century, the tables are turned in terms of oppression and violence. Whereas oppression becomes a hotly debated issue that distinguishes a legitimate rule of law from an illegitimate totalitarian rule, the violence that maintains the institutions of both forms of rule is depoliticized, just as oppression is in the traditional pure woman paradox (Cover, "Violence," 203–4). The homo sacer exposes this fact.

In his construction of the homo sacer constellation, Agamben draws attention to the fact that physical violence against populations is still used by both forms of rule to establish and maintain power over populations—and, as in the original pure woman paradox, a solution to the paradox is virtually impossible to formulate from within the institutional structures whose inner logic is thus exposed. The Gulf War example highlights the fact that modern rule always relies on the violent subjection of human beings. Just as the pure woman radically questions the legitimacy of her oppression by the paterfamilias, the externalization of the homo sacer questions the legitimacy of violence in the name of any cause—even including the removal of oppression.

The radical rejection of violence as a neutral resource for formulating a transformative intervention into territorial or institutional space, as postulated by the reverse pure woman paradox in Agamben, seems at first glance to leave no feasible options for change. The traditional pure woman could become a foundational pirata because she was, after all, a new agent—but the homo sacer is a human being stripped of the capability to act in any way.

However, one figure remains as a potential source of legitimate agency: the critic who, in producing a text that draws on the hostis humani generis constellation, draws attention to the dilemma in the first place. The concept of the homo sacer suggests that no violence is ever legitimate but postulates (by posing as an expressly legitimate act of critique) that speaking itself can show a way out of the dilemma. Since the homo sacer is a mute entity and the critic assumes legitimacy by speaking on his behalf, it becomes interesting to interrogate how the act of critical speaking may actually relate to the problem of legitimate violence after the Cold War.

[13]

MOHSIN HAMID'S *THE RELUCTANT FUNDAMENTALIST* AND THE WAR ON TERROR

ON 9/11 TWO HIJACKED civilian airplanes were deliberately crashed into the World Trade Center in New York City, causing the collapse of both towers. A third airplane was crashed into the Pentagon. A fourth airplane was brought off its hijackers' course by the passengers and crashed without reaching its destination, somewhere in Washington, D.C. In the course of the attacks, approximately 3,000 people died on US soil. The Islamist network Al-Qaeda was soon identified as responsible, even though Osama bin Laden only officially announced Al-Qaeda's responsibility three years later. In response to the attacks, "countering terrorism" immediately became a near-universal national priority in the United States, and the sweeping triumph of the essentialist perspective on legitimate violence was noted across the political spectrum (see, for example, Baudrillard, "Esprit," 406; Chandler and Gunaratna, *Countering Terrorism*; Coll, *Ghost Wars*, 455–56; Harris, *Civilization*, 199; J. Lewis, *Language Wars*, 67; Mahmood, "Religious Reason," 64; Reid, *Biopolitics*, 78; Waldron, "Terrorism"). Al-Qaeda became the preferred shorthand for any kind of terror group representing Islam and opposed by a legitimate, civilized "international civil society" consisting of nation-states, and transnational, representatively organized institutions, and academic "experts" ("Princeton Principles," 20).

In terms of the hostis humani generis constellation, 9/11 led finally to the well-prepared return to an essentialist interpretation in the spirit of early modern piracy. In 2002, Georges Abi-Saab called the overall reaction to the 9/11 attacks a "shock of recognition" that changed "the collective psyche" in the United States ("International Law," 305). Two discursive results of this shock are important to mention.

First, 9/11 significantly facilitated the attempted essentialist reformulation of hostis humani generis in American interpretations of international law because the attacks could be conceptualized as crimes against humanity.

The defining characteristics of such crimes were all present: the large scale of the attack, the state of peace in the attacked territory, the concerted nature of the attack, the targeting of noncombatants who represented an entire culture and were attacked only for their representativeness. Al-Qaeda thus became the benchmark of an illegitimate nonstate organizational structure that could be assessed in terms previously reserved for the representatives of totalitarian "outlaw states" (Rawls, *Law of Peoples*, 5). The attacks of 9/11 therefore provided a strong argument for an essentialist rereading of hostis humani generis without having to risk an open break with the interpretive innovations of the twentieth century. Instead, a continuation of prevailing legal traditions could be claimed—international terrorism could become one more crime in the list of crimes against humanity.[1] However, it was immediately clear that continuity was not the objective. As early as October 2001, analysts who observed that the Malacca Straits was a bottleneck for trade and was traditionally infested by pirates suggested that a maritime equivalent of the 9/11 attacks could occur if a full tanker was steered into the port of Singapore. There were alleged reports of people who, in imitation of 9/11 terrorists' attendance at a Florida flight school, tried to learn how to steer a tanker, but not into port. In this manner, piracy and terrorism were immediately linked in the most literal possible way after 9/11 (Dali, "Malacca Strait"; see also Dillon and Selvaggi, "Stopping Al Quaeda"; Ramachandran, "Divisions"), and associated legal opinions translated this alleged kinship into a notion of universal jurisdiction against "terrorists" in the United States (for the most famous examples, see Dershowitz, *Why Terrorism Works*; Yoo, "Memorandum"). The political association of hostis humani generis with the terrorist as a modern pirate thus became politically explicit long before Charles Dragonette's term "pirate-terrorist nexus" became notorious.

Chandan Reddy draws attention to the establishment of a new national "we" after 9/11 that cuts across the divides of race[2] and other traditional markers of oppressive exclusion. This national "we" is united against the illegitimate violence of the international terrorist without reinstating the classic national-international divide. Instead, such a national configuration "produces an isomorphism between the 'hate' that defines America's enemies abroad and the 'hate' of the domestic perpetrator. . . . Within this isomorphism, any violence not sanctioned by the state is characterized either as nonpolitical or antipolitical 'hate,' both conditions best addressed by medicine, psychology, or the military (all institutions that, unlike the police, have the capacity and authority for the eradication or annihilation of the offending hate)" (Reddy, *Freedom with Violence*, 11–12). As Reddy's argument indicates, the production of broken homines sacri by US institutions is legitimized by the claim to have removed an abstract, categorically flexible, "offending hate"—a notion that visibly draws on earlier constructions of communism but is clearly designed to help establish an inhuman threat to the United States in line with the distinctions established in arguments like those in *Terrorism* in the 1980s.

Next to the triumph of essentialist constructions of legitimate, antiterrorist violence, a second "shock of recognition" was apparent after 9/11 that was qualitatively different: it was the recognition that 9/11 was, in an important sense, an unexceptional event that revealed less about the state of the US nation than it did about the realities of the contemporary world at large. For example, Dexter Filkins, a war reporter who was in New York during the 9/11 attacks, writes:

> Walking in, watching the flames shoot upward, the first thing I thought was that I was back in the Third World. My countrymen were going to think this was the worst thing that ever happened, the end of civilization. In the Third World, this sort of thing happened every day. . . . I don't think I was the only person thinking this, who had the darker perspective. All those street vendors who worked near the World Trade Center, from all those different countries, selling falafel and schwarma [*sic*]. When they heard the planes and watched the towers they must have thought the same as I did: that they'd come home. (*Forever Wars*, 44–45)

Filkins presents recent immigrants from the Third World as potential carriers of critical agency in Chomsky's and Agamben's sense. They can explain, he suggests, what it is to be subjected to a massive and unexplained violent invasion, an experience that the entire American nation suddenly shares with them—indeed, his observation reads as if only the absence of such experience had previously made the United States exceptional. Now that this wall of difference has broken down, recent immigrants, because of their more mature understanding of the experience, can spearhead the discussion on legitimate violence with an authority that Americans cannot yet claim for themselves. Indeed, the meaning of this "darker perspective" for the contemplation of legitimate violence will underlie this book's final analysis of a novel, Mohsin Hamid's *The Reluctant Fundamentalist* (hereafter abbreviated in the citations as RF).

This novel, narrated from the perspective of a temporary immigrant, claims to be based on precisely such a mature understanding. Leerom Medovoi argues that "Hamid's novel is not so much of or by, but rather *for* Americans. That is to say, America serves as the novel's geopolitical raison d'être and as the object of its rhetorical design" ("'Terminal Crisis,'" 646). Caren Irr has more generally described this rhetorical design as an example of "national allegory" in the contemporary postcolonial novel ("Postmodernism in Reverse"). Indeed, the novel deliberately uses the hostis humani generis constellation to expose essentialist US reactions to 9/11 as unsustainable and immature.

Written by a Pakistani author who has lived in the United States for a considerable length of time, the novel received enormous attention in the Anglo-American public and academic sphere after its first publication in 2007. The novel is divided into twelve chapters that span an evening's conversation between the narrator and his addressee. An American is approached by the narrator and protagonist Changez in Lahore, the Pakistani capital, and is invited for tea and dinner. During their meal, Changez tells the American the story of his personal disenchantment with America.

The novel takes the form of dramatic monologue; the narrator's voice absorbs the voice, and even the spontaneous reactions, of his addressee and all of their surroundings. Changez's extensive and detailed recollections are framed by his interpretation of the ongoing conversation; it is gradually revealed that his American interlocutor is an "undercover assassin" (RF, 209) who plans to kill him, since Changez is suspected of being the leader of anti-American terrorists (RF, 203–5)—although whether that suspicion is true is never clarified. Changez introduces himself to the reader and the American alike as a "lover of America" (RF, 1) and never admits to having participated in acts of violence.

The plot traces the life-changing four and a half years Changez spent in the United States to complete his education at Princeton and to undergo a trainee program with a prestigious international "valuation firm" called Underwood Samson (RF, 5).[3] Changez also begins a relationship with a former fellow Princeton student, Erica, who comes from New York's most elite social circles. Only months after 9/11, however, he returns to Pakistan to become a vocal critic of the United States.

As in *Mother Night*, a first-person narrator simultaneously relates his story to an informal institutional representative and to the reader of the book (see especially RF, 172–73). One can speak of a confessional mode insofar as Changez is exceptionally "open" in his recollections (RF, 105). Unlike the narrator of *Mother Night*, however, Changez does not deliver himself up for judgment. His voice absorbs and directs the voice of his listening companion; he is an unreliable narrator less in terms of the truthfulness of his recollections than in terms of his intentions toward the character he confesses to.

As in *Mother Night*, in *The Reluctant Fundamentalist* the protagonist's death after the conclusion of the novel is anticipated. In both novels, the perspective of the first-person narrator is informed by a readiness to "meet my fate" after the story has been told in full (RF, 208). But while *Mother Night* ends with an anticipated suicide, *The Reluctant Fundamentalist* ends with a fast-paced, violent scene that features an inconclusive outcome of deaths and survivals and leaves open the degree of violent participation by Changez.

The overarching possibility of everyone's death (as well as everyone's potential for extreme violence) is coupled with an even more universal assignment of victimhood. Throughout the narrative, Americans are explicitly included in a planetary population of innocents. Being "simply a university lecturer" when the narration occurs (RF, 206), Changez mimics the position of the concerned scholarly critic when he charges the post-9/11 essentialist perspective in the United States with invasive illegitimacy: "As a society, you were unwilling to reflect upon *the shared pain that united you with those who attacked you*. . . . [T]he entire planet was rocked by the repercussions of your tantrums . . . . Such an America had to be stopped in the interest not only of the rest of humanity, *but also in your own*" (RF 190; emphasis added).

This passage goes further in its endorsement of shared pain than the analyses of contemporary American critics, who tend to sidestep a thorough discussion of the committer of violence in their discussions of "shared pain" and universal innocence.[4] In this passage, in contrast, the experience of victimhood only "unites" America with the world when the notion of hate as outlined by Reddy is also acknowledged as a universal, and internally nuanced, notion that is not limited to non-Americans (or un-Americans). By threatening that America's "tantrums" will have consequences, the passage furthermore suggests that a challenge to the logic of imperial violence must necessarily be a (partly) violent one (RF, 133).

To disentangle the novel's use of the hostis humani generis constellation, the structural treatment of the essentialist interpretation must be addressed first. As in *Mother Night*, an essentialist divide clearly informs the setting of the novel but is then fundamentally complicated. Changez sits face to face with a disciplined and judgmental American soldier tasked with killing him in the context of the War on Terror. On the other side of the essentialist divide stand the anti-American terrorist personified by the waiter at the restaurant and some of Changez's Pakistani students mentioned in the conversation.[5] However, these terrorists are already much less essentialist prototypes than the unnamed American agent is. Their individual histories of victimization and subsequent radicalization are always woven into their representation in the novel (RF, 6, 45, 133, and 204).

Like the legal revisions of hostis humani generis in international law, the construction of the essentialist divide in the novel explicitly refers to the early modern history of the hostis humani generis constellation in the Mediterranean region. Changez first meets Erica on Rhodes, an island whose "cities were fortified . . . ; they guarded against the Turks . . . . How strange it was for me to think I grew up on the other side!" (RF, 26). It is no accident that, during this visit to Rhodes, Erica's deceased boyfriend, Chris, is first mentioned; his name clearly refers to the "other side" of Mediterranean divide that Changez does not, and will never, have access to.

The Mediterranean analogy informs not only the logic of the novel's love triangle but also the epiphany that causes Changez to abandon his job as an analyst with Underwood Samson and leave the United States. Shortly after 9/11, Changez is assigned to help evaluate a publishing house in Chile. The publisher, Juan-Bautista, tells Changez the story of the janissaries, "Christian boys . . . captured by the Ottomans and trained to be soldiers in a Muslim army, at that time the greatest army in the world. They were ferocious and utterly loyal: they had fought to erase their own civilizations, so they had nothing else to turn to" (RF, 172). Changez immediately makes the connection to his own situation: "I was a modern-day janissary, a servant of the American empire at a time when it was invading a country with a kinship to mine and was perhaps even colluding to ensure that my own country faced the threat of war. Of course I was struggling! Of course I felt torn! I had thrown in my lot with the men of Underwood Samson, with the officers of the empire, when all along I was predisposed to feel compassion for those, like Juan-Bautista, whose lives the empire thought nothing of overturning for its own gain" (RF, 173).

The janissary analogy, which clearly cites the Barbary captivity narrative's basic conflict lines, is interesting insofar as it turns the essentialist constellation on its head. America is portrayed as a modern-day equivalent of the Ottoman Empire as a central bearer of inherent, racialized illegitimacy. This construction of an essentialist America in analogy to an early modern Other is supported by a deliberate racialization of whiteness in the novel. As in *Native Son*, whiteness in *The Reluctant Fundamentalist* constitutes a racialized shorthand for an older society that is still supremely influential, but whose shortcomings are made glaringly obvious to the reader: whiteness, in Hamid's novel, stands for an entire "entitled and unsympathetic" culture (RF, 141) that is machine-like in its systemic indifference to any form of nuanced and respectful human interaction (RF, 47, 77, 113, 133, 157, 170, 178, and 183). White American culture is characterized as alienated from, contemptuous of, and invasive of the entire population of planet, which in turn is characterized as a large and multifaceted "color spectrum" (RF, 37; see also RF, 127).

To recall Hazel Rose Markus and Paula Moya's definition, race in this book is linked to "a narrow . . . understanding of culture as being so deeply rooted in a person, and so stable and predictable in its effects, that even important changes in a person's social environment are unlikely to make a difference in his or her values and behavior" ("Doing Race," 15). A racialized understanding of white America as a culture with "predictable effects" underlies the novel. Just as the sympathetic character Chingachgook in *The Deerslayer* is still expected to abuse his wife because he is Native American (DS, 2:935–36), the sympathetic character of Erica in *The Reluctant Fundamentalist* is likewise arrested within the limits of white behavior that "can't be helped" (Markus and Moya, "Doing Race," 15). This becomes particularly obvious in the construction of her mourning of Chris, "a good-looking boy with . . . an *Old World* appeal" (RF, 30). It is emphasized throughout the novel that Erica and Chris shared a love of adventure fiction that is explicitly set in a colonialist tradition, and that tends to characterize the nonwhite part of the world as an "exotic" site of white adventure (RF, 32, 60, 153, and 188–89). This is also a perspective, as it turns out, that Underwood Samson encourages among the firm's employees (RF, 39–40 and 72–73).

In a twist of the War on Terror's construction of Islamist terrorists, this racialization of whiteness in the novel is directly and explicitly associated with fundamentalism. This term, which in the title leads the reader to imagine the religious fanaticism of barbarous Islam, is instead used in the text to refer to Underwood Samson's guiding principle, "focus on the fundamentals" (RF, 112). It refers to an exclusive focus on financial profitability, a perspective that disconnects Changez's "native" US colleagues at Underwood Samson from the world that they shape through their interventions (RF, 77).

The recognition of the racialization of whiteness is narratively established as a threat to a gray zone of possible meaningful interaction between white America and the rest of the world; it is only this gray zone that allows Changez's initial integration into American society. The relationship between Changez and Erica that was emerging before the 9/11 attacks is based on their recognition that they both lack a "stable core" (RF, 22 and 168). It is the very inconclusiveness and instability of their identities that draws them to each other. Furthermore, the possibility of their love is explicitly linked to urban space, the prototypical in-between zone of the twentieth century. The city of New York is distinguished as a "democratically urban" space of vibrant multinationality (RF, 36; emphasis removed), and Changez pointedly observes: "I was, in four and a half years, never an American; I was *immediately* a New Yorker" (RF, 37). After 9/11, Changez tells the American: "Your country's flag invaded New York after the attacks . . . . They all seemed to proclaim: *We are America*—not New York, which, in my opinion, means something quite different—*the mightiest civilization the world has ever known; you have slighted us; beware our wrath*" (RF, 90). This "American" rather than urban perspective is characterized by Changez as "retro" (RF, 130), "classical" (RF, 133), and a "dangerous nostalgia" (RF, 130).

The attacks and the ensuing War on Terror affect Erica greatly, causing her to break up with Changez and propelling her toward her eventual suicide. "The attacks churned up old thoughts in my head" (RF, 91), she tells Changez after 9/11—specifically, old thoughts of Chris, the white boy with the supremacist Old World appeal. Erica is "pulled in" by the "spell" of this "world"—which indeed informs her entire cultural background, from her upbringing to her expectations of the future with Chris (RF, 120, 127, and 129). With the figure of Erica, the novel suggests that the logic of nostalgia combined with a fundamentalist all-or-nothing approach is ultimately suicidal. A "devout" Erica (RF, 152), who is increasingly unable to wake up from her dream of America, explains: "It's whether there's something left . . . or whether it's all already happened" (RF, 127). Erica commits suicide roughly at the time of Changez's own janissary epiphany (RF, 153, 170–72, and 184–85).

The character of Erica and the construction of the love triangle as a drama of allegiance establishes that the "devout" orientation toward a lost love generally has a direct spatial equivalent in the novel. Erica orients herself according to the realm of essentialist America. In her love for Chris, Erica becomes Am-Erica, the epitome of that America that is markedly distinct from spaces such as New York and Lahore.

After Erica's death and his return to Lahore, Changez also replaces his inner void for an unshareable "devoutness"—in his case, to Erica as his own lost love. He discovers that "it is not always possible to restore one's boundaries after they have been blurred. . . . Something of us is now outside, and something of the outside is now within us" (RF, 197). In his dreams of Erica (which are of the same consuming intensity as Erica's dreams of Chris), Changez is removed both from the association with an essentialist America, "a religion that would not accept me as a convert" (RF, 129; see also RF, 131), and from the Third World that is exposed to American intervention and that hails him to forget both Erica and America (RF, 199). He dreams of an everyday life with Erica in Lahore (RF, 195–200), and is saved from nostalgia and suicide only by never actually accepting the fact that she is dead. Changez instead becomes the representative of generic urban space, where the love between Erica and him is at least theoretically possible.

Changez's dream world is transformed into the ground for action as he starts to seek Erica's attention through America's attention. The locus of their love, multicultural and permissive urban space, becomes the site for his own engagement as an academic mentor and charismatic activist in Lahore (RF, 190, 203–6). When Changez, who can soon raise thousands of people against essentialist injustice, challenges America in the international spotlight, he confesses that he is actually trying to coax Erica back to life (RF, 207).

At the same time that Changez vocally challenges America, he acknowledges that he owes his influential position in Pakistan to his education in the United States; his leadership style is based on a notion of critical mentorship that "in no small measure modeled on that of *my* former mentor, Jim" (RF, 204–5), another reconnection with his time in New York. Changez's difference from Jim, of course, is equivalent to his difference from Erica: Jim, as a representative of Underwood Samson, is contemptuous of complexity and encourages homogeneity (RF, 43 and 110), whereas Changez emphasizes and encourages heterogeneous perspectives (RF, 45 and 204). Unlike Erica, Jim, and America as a whole, all of whom force others to live their lives according to scripts that have already been written (RF, 109–10, 120, and 131), Changez is prepared to "give people their space" (RF, 28). He therefore emerges as a genuine representative of the in-between zone where a connection between the worlds is possible, regardless of how aggressively the lines of difference are defended in it. Changez becomes the representative of those zones of interaction and conflict that make respectful unity as well as the renegotiation of legitimate violence conceivable.

When read against the backdrop of the hostis humani generis constellation, the novel cites the two important traditions—the essentialist and the frontier tradition—without embracing either one. It makes sense to briefly summarize what the novel does not do (and which derived interpretations of legitimate violence therefore cannot apply) before offering an interpretation of what the novel actually does do with the constellation.

An essentialist interpretation of the novel would consider the janissary image the defining one of the novel and argue that Changez's life in America is that of a treacherous renegade who originally and naturally is in allegiance with innocent humanity, but who temporarily acts as an invader of planetary innocents' lives with America's "economic hit men" (Perkins, *Confessions*) who are the informal "officers of the empire" (RF, 173). By removing himself from America, Changez changes his position into that of a representative of civilization who, in retrospect, narrates the story of his own catharsis and purification.

Obviously, such a reading remains unconvincing on the structural level of narration. The essentialist construction does not allow the transformation of a convinced renegade into a convinced representative of civilization. A narrative voice in support of such an interpretation would instead share the captivity narrative's focus on retrospective harmonization of past actions with present values—values that furthermore have to be shared by the narrative's addressee. Changez as a narrator does not edit the past to suggest that American culture was always suspect to him. On the contrary, he meticulously distinguishes his current position from his position while staying in the United States (see, for example, RF, 5, 73, 106, and 127). Neither does he testify to the evils of the American empire before his fellow Pakistanis. It is not a novel written in Urdu featuring, say, a Pakistani addressee who is not sure if the United States is truly evil, and who is then presented with a tale of difference between us and them. Instead, Changez's implied addressees are an American fundamentalist and an English-speaking readership.

The presence of the American agent as Changez's interlocutor and representative of an older society might instead suggest a frontier interpretation on a planetary scale. The terrorists of 9/11 could then be read as foundational piratae who commit an act of transformative violence that, on the one hand, causes deeply illegitimate calls for violent retaliation (the rise of America) and, on the other hand, occasions a representative of civilization to experience an epiphany regarding his own role and responsibility in the face of transformative violence (the janissary epiphany). Then a representative of civilization (Changez) would proceed to translate the 9/11 piratae's violent disruption of the order into the language of the law, thus restoring order. Much is to be said for such an interpretation, as 9/11 is certainly the transformative centerpiece of the novel—occasioning mass retaliation as well as individual epiphany. And the character of Changez is certainly extremely eloquent and emphasizes his own belief in nonviolence (RF, 206), which may suggest that he is a representative of planetary civilization in the frontier tradition, meaning that he delegates the use of violence to the institutions that follow as well as enforce the letter of the law.

However, *The Reluctant Fundamentalist*'s narrative universe does not rely on any explicit reference to the law, be it a national law as in *Native Son* or international human rights law as in *Mother Night*. In addition, the American addressee is not a judge passing a sentence of life or death, or another figure associated with institutions of justice. The American agent is an assassin tasked with carrying out an extralegal death sentence on Changez, which itself is a transgression of the law, both national and international (see, for example, RF, 144, 177, 202, and 207; see. also Dörr, "Gezielte Tötung"). When the law is mentioned in the novel, it is presented as biased, arbitrary, and not to be taken seriously as an institution of justice (see, for example, RF, 85, 190, and 207). This is a problem for the frontier interpretation of hostis humani generis. For the frontier representative of civilization to be a strictly nonviolent editorial and explanatory figure, there must be an assumption that some legitimate force of law will commit legitimate violence in his stead. But there is no overarching law that Changez may appeal to, nor is Changez actually characterized as a nonviolent figure (see, for example, RF, 134, 189, and 204).

Even though he never acts violently in the novel, Changez is explicitly described as a warrior type (see, for example, RF, 50 and 80), and his own insistence on nonviolent trustworthiness is undercut by his thinly veiled threats to the American agent. Changez's light, polite conversation is presented as the act of a hunter who toys with his prey before the kill (RF, 13, 137, and 140). Indeed, such anticipated violence materializes in the final passages of the novel, when Changez escorts the agent back to his hotel. The waiter and some other men, who had followed them, "rapidly clos[e] in" and gesture to Changez to detain the agent; he immediately does so by offering the agent his hand, and the agent pulls out his gun (RF, 158 and 209). The novel ends at this point. It is possible that Changez is killed by the American assassin; that the waiter and others, who are described as possible "terrorists" (RF, 209) and who are either Changez's loyal followers or convenient allies, kill the American assassin; or that a shoot-out between these two "tribal" parties (RF, 123 and 133) takes place. In any case, it is obvious from the context and structure of the scene that Changez is not an uninvolved bystander in this anticipated confrontation. But even though he is apparently in cahoots with the waiter, it remains unclear whether his intention is actually terrorist or whether he simply hopes to save himself from assassination. The novel does not offer any conclusive insights on this point.

The elusiveness of Changez's intentions and final allegiance, which is emphasized in this final scene, begins to offer a very clear idea of the interpretive tradition of the hostis humani generis constellation that *The Reluctant Fundamentalist* actually follows. The figure of Changez functions as a variation of the Elihu Willsson figure in Dashiell Hammett's *Red Harvest*. Willsson is an early American pirata figure who helped establish the American city as a transformative, elusive space. He is a vocal and supportive ally of both the evil thugs and of the good Continental Op, both of whom are characterized by their mutual violent antagonism. Willsson is neutral, not in any passive or pacifist sense of the word, but in the sense that he does not allow either essentialist party exclusively to represent his interests. He is rendered the true representative of a city as an in-between zone only through his enduring presence in Poisonville/Personville, which outlasts the presence of any essentialist committer of violence. Like Willsson, Changez is an enabling ally of various essentialist parties at different points in time,[6] but his true representation of an in-between zone (within which both parties, and many more, can operate) supersedes their conflict.

If Changez is a representative of the in-between zone, and if this zone is planetary, this also explains the necessity of the sophisticated inclusion of the essentialist and frontier models of civilization, which are both cited but eventually disabled in the novel. Hamid integrates American national space into planetary space and institutional space into space that is both institutional and extra-institutional. The simultaneous reference to the essentialist and the frontier interpretation of the hostis humani generis constellation in *The Reluctant Fundamentalist* is directly based on these interpretations' intertwined use in American discourses of legitimate violence since World War II, and makes their discursive codependency transparent by contrasting them with an inconclusive character who can be explored by both perspectives, but not explained by either.

The Reluctant Fundamentalist goes beyond characterizing America as an illegitimate totalitarian state that produces perpetrators (assassins and torturers within, national aggressors and terrorists without) and victimizes innocent populations. At no point is Changez presented as a character who can be described as a criminal against humanity or a homo sacer. Instead, the novel uses the already established position of the critic in American scholarly discourse to substantiate the position of the ex-janissary as an entity that emerges from, but does not remain confined in, either the institutional context of higher education or prevailing discourses of legitimate violence.

It is worth returning at this point to the importance of the 9/11 attacks as an act of violence that completely transforms the narrative universe. In terms of the plot, the attacks occasion Erica-America to succumb to a nostalgia that Changez characterizes as exclusionary. At the same time, the attacks make Changez aware of the planetary context of the American nation, a context that renders any dichotomy between inside and outside of America inconceivable for him. In other words, the novel traces the complementary "shocks of recognition" occasioned by 9/11 in the United States: both the recognition that the notion of unsurpassable essentialist dichotomy is available as a plausible framework for understanding the attacks, and the recognition that 9/11 exposes a kinship between the United States and the rest of the world. This kinship is relayed to America by the immigrant in Filkins as well as in Hamid, and it renders a return to essentialism unsustainable, except at the price of a suicidal exclusion of reality in general.

As a culture, Hamid's America is fundamentally interrogated by the immigrant, who raises the same kind of questions that the African American criminal in Richard Wright poses to the institutions of American law. An America that, frontier-like, "expected [immigrants] to contribute our talents to your society, the society we were joining" (RF, 4) and, essentialist-like, regards them with "unease" and "fear" when they stop playing their carefully scripted roles (RF, 181), emerges as the nostalgic incarnation of an older society in Wright's sense. In *The Reluctant Fundamentalist*, America's commitment to the scripted reality of meritocracy, in which any piece of information has only one meaning, is identified as culturally specific and dangerous as soon as it performs "a hegemonic framing of key assumptions" on humanity as a whole (Mills, "Racial Liberalism," 1382; see also Shryock, "Moral Analogies").

In accord with the double sense of "fundamentalism" in the title, the language of meritocracy is generally expanded to describe the rise of anti-imperial political dissent in the novel (RF, 203). The "ex-janissary's" gaze (or perspective) is identified as "the analytical eyes of a product of Princeton and Underwood Samson, but unconstrained by the academic's and the professional's various compulsions to focus primarily on the parts, and free therefore to consider also the *whole* of your society" (RF, 177–78). Hamid suggests that 9/11 has made the cultural specificity of America visible to the world, in the sense that these events have transformed the United States into an entity that allows itself, through its homogenizing self-racialization as white and fundamentalist, to be discussed as a comprehensive national whole—as a nation among nations endowed with a national character rather than a universalist vision for humanity.

To genuinely represent a planetary in-between zone that includes "the *whole* of your society" (RF, 178), the immigrant returns to the outside of America. The kinship of city spaces such as New York and Lahore, as well as the construction of love as a mixture of mournful representation (of Erica's and Changez's imaginary life together) and of abstracted courtship (of a United States that includes Erica as someone capable of welcoming Changez back) helps the ex-janissary distinguish an inclusive cosmopolitan spirit, which is worth saving, from an exclusionary "America" worth defying. In this way, America is rendered an analytically manageable entity for the ex-janissary. This entity can then be discussed in terms of legitimacy; indeed, it is precisely the fierce essentialist refusal of critique that enables scattered and multilayered Pakistani perspectives to develop a shared basis for their united, defensive political action—which may include concerted violent acts but does not include a shared vision of a better world (RF, 204).

In the spirit of Locke's understanding of property, which defines ownership as the direct result of intervention in the world ("Second Treatise," 286–88), interpretations of hostis humani generis throughout this book have been successful precisely when legitimate violence has been conceptualized as the power to transform: to tame an unruly territorial space, as in *The Deerslayer* and *Red Harvest*; to make a notion of universalist justice meaningful to institutions that hold a monopoly on force, as in *Native*

Son and *Mother Night*; or to create a world in which global infrastructures can be sustainably protected, as in *Terrorism* (Thorup, *Intellectual History*, 202). In these senses, transformative violence was interpreted by Locke as equivalent to the classic core case of legitimate violence among humans—violence in self-defense.

"I am a believer in non-violence; the spilling of blood is abhorrent to me, save in self-defense. And how broadly do I define self-defense, you ask?" Changez taunts the American agent (RF, 206). This question points to the modern redefinition of self-defense as the transformation of space that is assisted—indeed, enabled—by the use of the hostis humani generis constellation. The constellation relies on the notion of self-defense, but because it links self-defense to the notion of spatial transformation, legitimacy occurs precisely when acts of violence strive to change the entire world on behalf of the innocent. The United States had been able to work well with this equation of defensive and transformative violence throughout the long twentieth century because of a near-synonymous understanding of nation and civilization. What serves the interests of America also serves the interests of humankind; planetary transformative violence in the American image is therefore just. But if, as in Hamid, America is merely one nation among others rather than a universalist, visionary, holistic order—and if America's national interest is characterized as fundamentally disconnected from the planetary interest—transformative violence on behalf of this nation is an illegitimate invasion of the planet.

In direct continuation of Hannah Arendt's arguments on transformative state violence (*Totalitarianism*, 460–79), Giorgio Agamben postulates that sovereign violence, understood as purely transformative violence, is "totalitarian" (*Homo Sacer*, 10). His sovereign is defined by the power to transform a person, say, from an innocent into a homo sacer. Hamid's America is characterized as precisely such a transformative sovereign. In the expansive fundamentalism of Underwood Samson, and in the nation-state's willingness to send assassins to kill Changez in Lahore, America attempts to render the planet an in-between zone and Changez a potential homo sacer. In his critique of American "tantrums," Changez echoes the analysis of Arendt, who postulates that totalitarianism's "danger is that it threatens to ravage the world as we know it—a world which everywhere seems to have come to an end—*before a new beginning rising from this end has had time to assert itself*" (*Totalitarianism*, 478; emphasis added). The last half-sentence of Arendt's argument is precisely the leap that is never explicitly expressed by Changez as a character or the scholarly critics discussed in the previous chapter, but it is a leap that is formally specified by Changez's construction as a pirata figure.

In the construction of America as a nation at war with terrorism, the novel echoes the widely accepted notion that American arguments for planetary transformative violence are discursively akin to those of terrorists (see, for example, Baudrillard, "Esprit"; Harris, *Civilization*; J. Lewis, *Language Wars*; Reid, *Biopolitics*). In its stark dichotomies of antagonism, the construction of the War on Terror is like the struggle between the Continental Op and the thugs in Poisonville who battle for dominance rather than for a cause.

Changez is not a homo sacer, but his character, too, is informed by a reverse pure woman paradox that politicizes violence by demonstrating a lack of representative initiative. In *Red Harvest*, Willsson causes the essentialist struggle by bringing both the thugs and the Op to the city. In *The Reluctant Fundamentalist*, the essentialist struggle exists before Changez is caught up in it. Rather than actively enabling the essentialist parties' temporary transformation of city space, as Willsson does, Changez resists any claim to transformation by Americans and Islamist terrorists alike; his motives for political actions are strictly private and leave his allies their private visions as well. Whereas Hammett fundamentally depoliticizes acts of violence, Hamid repoliticizes them by not assigning his protagonist a transformative motive to violence. Changez does not formulate a "new beginning," but his stubbornly enduring presence makes room for inconclusive new beginnings.

The narrative universe of the novel is a planetary zone in which anyone's representative status, normative allegiance, and potential for violence are shifting and unstable. This is "a world where nobody is reliable and nothing can be relied upon," and thus the traditional breeding ground of totalitarianism (Arendt, *Totalitarianism*, 478). In the context of hostis humani generis, however, it is also precisely such a world that enables a fundamental interrogation of the very property that totalitarianism shares with essentialist and frontier civilization: the idea that legitimate violence is equivalent to the transformation of space.

By remaining silent even about the ends of the novel's culminating act of violence—that is, the possible transformative ends of violence beyond attempting to save a life that is threatened by an assassin—Changez becomes readable as someone who potentially commits a clear-cut act of defensive violence in the sense of the paradoxical, rather than the foundational, pure woman; he thus manages to subvert the transformative interpretations of such violence from both sides of the essentialist divide in the War on Terror. Because Changez never commits an act of transformative violence himself, the hostis humani generis constellation's major interpretive traditions are unable to make sense of his actions. As a character he is thus free to mean other things.

If the homo sacer is a reverse pure woman who exposes the depoliticized violence that lies behind both legitimate and illegitimate rule, the pirata figure of Changez draws attention to the notion that depoliticized violence must be conceptualized as boundless for another reason than the constitution of bare sovereignty. To be legitimate within the traditions of hostis humani generis, acts of violence must always strive to change the whole world. But if transformative violence is suddenly prevented from being boundless—because it is resisted, for instance, by classic acts of self-defense—the encounter of transformative violence (by the assassin) and defensive violence (against the assassination attempt) reveals that legitimate violence is not necessarily linked to the notion of transformation but could be conceptualized in other ways. Assuming that Changez is a representative of the in-between zone who uses violence to guard against transformative violence from either side—assuming, in other words, that he is a protector of the zone against any attempt to transform it into a coherent realm of legitimacy or illegitimacy—a "new beginning" in Arendt's sense is made possible by denying the legitimacy of transformative violence and by resisting its execution.

At this point, it should be noted that Changez is not a "university lecturer, nothing more nor less" (RF, 106) whose only interest is to establish the necessary conditions to develop free, innovative perspectives that transcend the notion of transformative *totalitarian* violence. After all, there is a reason for the original conflation of transformative and defensive violence in hostis humani generis. Locke, for example, renders transformative violence legitimate because factional violence—war of all against all, which characterizes the state of nature in Hobbes and the state of war in Locke—is conceptualized as transformative violence's threatening, and only, alternative. Indeed, this problem is acknowledged in *The Reluctant Fundamentalist*. The protection of the in-between zone is admitted to be incompatible with the protection of peace. Like Willsson, Changez actively invites factional conflict and even violence in the zone to maintain his own position: "I have received official warnings on more than one occasion, but such is the demand for my courses that I have until now escaped suspension. And lest you think that I am one of *those* instructors, in cahoots with young criminals who have no interest in education and who run their campus faction like marauding gangs, I should point out that the students I tend to attract are bright, idealistic scholars possessed of both civility and ambition. We call each other comrades" (RF, 205).

In this passage, a tale of creating a personal navigation of the growing conflict between university administrators and the student body is expanded into images of traditional illegitimacy, ideological indoctrination, and marauding gangs. This, of course, is the problem of the in-between zone in a nutshell: it is a space that enables the tolerant and unrestricted exchange represented by the critical scholar (see especially Arvanitakis and Hornsby, "Universities"), but it is still primarily informed by factional violence. The concept of a lawless space that defies transformation—be it the hard-boiled city that is ungovernably corrupt or a planet so rich in discursive traditions that it defies coherent interpretation and therefore a monopoly on force—is not equivalent to a genuine, alternative approach to legitimate violence or to an innovative rearrangement of the constellation (as was the case, say, in Frederick Jackson Turner).

When read as a variation on *Red Harvest*'s treatment of hostis humani generis, however, *The Reluctant Fundamentalist*'s treatment does indicate the possibility of a "beginning" of a more far-reaching reformulation of the constellation. In the early twentieth century, it was important to establish the city as an in-between zone before one could think of adapting other relations within the constellation. Only when the city had joined the sea and the margins of empire as a conventional in-between zone could writers of all genres experiment with decidedly institutional, rather than only territorial, interpretations of hostis humani generis. This has led, for example, to nuanced negotiations of legal institutions and their legitimacy as representative entities in Wright's *Native Son*.

It makes sense in the current historical moment to establish the planet as an in-between zone where it is possible to investigate the prevailing understanding of legitimate violence. The fact that one already encounters nuanced treatments of the planet as an in-between zone, as in *The Reluctant Fundamentalist*, may mean that a radical reinterpretation of the hostis humani generis constellation may just be imminent today as it was in the period between the world wars. We may soon encounter an equally consequential reinterpretation of the constellation that may reach beyond the geographical territory as well as the national institution as thinkable "spaces" to negotiate legitimate violence.

CONCLUSION

WHAT IS LEGITIMATE VIOLENCE?

This is a question that the hostis humani generis constellation helps to simultaneously address and circumvent. As this book has shown, the constellation has lasted for centuries precisely because it does not rely on timeless definitions of (il)legitimate acts, committers, or victims of violence. Instead, the constellation enables writers of texts across the disciplines to treat historically specific conflicts "as if" they captured a fundamental drama of essential allegiance, and representative figures "as if" their use of violence reflected timeless and universal principles of justice. This potential has led to two only seemingly contradictory uses of the constellation in modern text: either as a way to reinforce—indeed, naturalize—existing claims of legitimate violence, or as a way to challenge these prevailing concepts by claiming the same "natural" justice for a rival concept. In such rival concepts, one often sees the universalization of previously marginal elements, as in the categorical development of the notion of land cultivation discussed in part 2.

This book has traced the history of hostis humani generis to demonstrate the centrality of this constellation to an understanding of modern Anglo-American conversations about legitimate violence. The study of constellations allows a nuanced presentation of the problem of legitimate violence. In the case of hostis humani generis, the problem of legitimate violence is specified as a problem of defensive agency.

It is notoriously difficult to disentangle a righteous claim to self-defense from an abusive (or, at least, unfounded) claim. For example, we encounter as one end of the spectrum the unambiguous act of self-defense against direct attack, as exemplified by the pure woman who defends herself against a physical assault on her person. Such an act of self-defense has been recognized as legitimate violence for centuries, even when cultural constructions of inherently passive womanhood rendered that recognition paradoxical. In contrast, there is the example of a consciously false allegation, and the ensuing illegitimacy of so-called defensive violence based on such allegations. This danger is exemplified by the "man who persistently insults another man until everybody knows that the latter is his enemy, so that he can, with some plausibility, go and kill him in self-defense" (Arendt, *Totalitarianism*, 424). This spectrum of (un)sustainable claims to self-defense is well-known from the legal consideration of what I have called relational crimes (such as piracy and rape), but it also indicates a much more fundamental problem of claims to legitimacy in general.

As part 1 in particular has shown, any modern Western claim to legitimate violence can be considered strategic and abusive if compared with the traditions that preceded modernity. After all, the accumulative, expansionist interpretation of legitimate defense already constitutes a quite generous interpretation of the concept of defense. On the least abstract level, then, the hostis humani generis constellation helps pinpoint as well as navigate the gray zones in cultural constructions of defensive violence and helps smooth out inconsistencies or problematic implications. Thus, in modernity, an important second function of the constellation comes to the fore: the ability of the constellation to absorb contradictions and to retain categorical flexibility within the overarching framework of Anglo-American modernity.

The historicized analysis of the constellation helps us appreciate the constellation's ability to narratively integrate, for instance, a generous range of different analytical understandings of the communities to be represented and defended. In this study, the most important of these communities were the imperial civilization that claims a duty to transform the world in its own image; a national community in Frederick Jackson Turner's sense; and the abstract cosmopolitan community of innocents represented by the scholar-activist that was developed as central to the contemporary moment in part 4. Hostis humani generis contributes to an analysis of the unspoken but powerful discursive continuities that specify such diverse concepts as variations of each other via the conceptualization of the spaces inhabited, and Others encountered, by a civilizational "us."

Simultaneously, it has become apparent that widespread critical use of the constellation is, in fact, an excellent benchmark of cultural change. When the constellation undergoes significant change that is enthusiastically accepted by people at the time, it is likely that a significant shift in the conventionally accepted basis of legitimate violence is occurring. An accepted understanding of the role of violence in a culture is not easily changed. The most obvious interpretive breaks and shifts in the history of the constellation thus correspond with massive cultural paradigm shifts: the oceanic revolution, the shift from plunder-based colonialism to trade-based colonialism, the rise of industrialization and urbanization, the beginning of the postwar atomic age, and the globalized War on Terror. It makes sense to suggest, therefore, that the use of the constellation is indicative of cultural change simply because that is when legitimate violence is discussed most urgently and explicitly. In such situations, the constellation operates on a self-reflexive analytical level and provides a way to bridge the gap between old and new claims of legitimate violence.

Some moments of cultural change even had an impact on the basic interpretation of the hostis humani generis constellation itself. Until the mid-eighteenth century, the properties of hostis humani generis were developed mainly in the context of pirate law. In its early modern usage, hostis humani generis was employed to assess the margins of empire and to help formulate a claim to legitimate expansion. Violence outside of the sovereign realm was legitimated, for instance, by reference to the treasonous conversion of the renegade described in the Barbary captivity narrative. To legitimate colonialist expansion into the Atlantic region, Golden Age pirates were constructed as spiritually isolated outcasts who required European empires to end their lawless use of the wilderness.

After William Blackstone's influential definition of hostis humani generis, which constructed the pirate as only one variation of the more general figure of the Lockean invader, hostis humani generis was increasingly both actively and deliberately used as a constellation. The construction of praedo and pirata as complementary enemies of the law of nature, which then had to be defended by a representative of civilization on behalf of the innocent, were abstracted into a constellation that organized these elements into stable and enduring relations. Sea space became the model for the in-between zone, and the intertwined notions of race and space helped formulate the properties of sea space as the generalized properties of any space in which praedo and pirata were encountered (for example, precolonial, urban, and planetary space).

By the early nineteenth century, hostis humani generis was so fully formed as a stable constellation that, even as a legal fiction, it could begin to describe crimes which violated humanity in ways fundamentally different than those of piracy. Rather than merely describing the random attack of the piratical outsider on the law, hostis humani generis in law began to refer to a fundamental violation of human nature that had to be countered with legitimate violence.

These nineteenth-century innovations found their strongest expression in the United States, where the constellation was further developed in reaction to a variety of charges of US illegitimacy, originating, for instance, in the US conquest of Native American land or the nation's mutinous abandonment of the European motherland. To refute charges and challenges such as these, the United States was claimed (by Americans) to have created an order whose spirit of law corresponded directly with the law of nature: national institutions were deemed inherently capable of protecting humans from the state of war in Locke's sense. These institutions then had to be defended against subversion by praedones who distorted these institutions' inherently benevolent function. The main objective of the constellation's use in the United States, in other words, has become the actualization of the civilized essence of national institutions.

This conflation of national institutions and the idea of civilization was established by the US frontier model's wholly new arrangement of figures within the constellation. The pirata became a foundational figure rather than a renegade condemned to spiritual exile. The representative of civilization ceased to be a chivalrous avenger and became the retrospective interpreter of violence who relegated his own violent potential to institutions and who invited institutions to retrospectively absorb the pirata's violence as well. The praedo, rather than remaining the representative of a barbarous Other culture that dared to claim sovereignty, became an institutional interpreter in his own right, but one characterized by the totalitarian subversion and abuse of institutional structures. The innocent ceased to be defined as naturally passive and helpless and instead was cast as the broken victim of the praedo's oppressive violence.

In short, while the original, essentialist interpretation of hostis humani generis legitimated the expansive transformation of wild territories into civilized space, the frontier model of civilization served to narrate a perpetual purification of national structures into institutions of a perfectly civilized society. This rearrangement had unintended but far-reaching consequences.

The representative of civilization was an interpreter who relegated the commission of violence to institutions, but he also demanded that these institutions follow a coherent, accountable interpretation of legitimate violence (and, not least importantly, that these institutional interpretations of violence harmonized with his own interpretation). If a representative of civilization's interpretation of violence did not resonate within institutional structures, institutional representatives and even institutional structures themselves could find themselves characterized as un-American praedones. Examples range from the interventions of the counterculture movement in the 1970s to contemporary concepts of inherently totalitarian institutional landscapes (most notably, in the work of Giorgio Agamben). Historically a vehicle to strengthen and legitimate sovereign uses of violence, hostis humani generis was increasingly seen as enabling a critique of acts of institutional force themselves as the invasions of illegitimate impostors. The institutions of the nation-state could be made credible as deeply problematic entities by critics who expressed their disagreement by assuming the position of a representative of civilization that exposes praedones on behalf of the legitimate actualization of universalist values.

Such critics (who can be politically diverse) are enabled by one of the greatest strengths of the constellation, which is to make new thoughts defensible as serious. Hostis humani generis does not necessarily help create new thoughts, in the sense of a genuine development of new perspectives on the world. Hostis humani generis is designed, rather, to integrate such new impulses into existing patterns of thought. The constellation has become a narrative resource to formulate abstract or unpopular concerns and values in a culturally resonant way. When a conventional claim to legitimate violence is under attack, the narrative use of the hostis humani generis constellation helps make categorical problems visible, and the constellation's formal variations can open up ways to overcome them. For example, the pure woman paradox had been considered a puzzling act of legitimate violence for centuries—until, with the help of the hostis humani generis constellation, an argument that capitalized on the postulated singularity of this event reread the pure woman's violence as an act of foundational violence. Rather than being a paradoxical event without any accessible meaning, the event then began to signify a foundational purification of the law that could constitute a centerpiece of new constructions of representative agency. In Gail Bederman's words, the constellation enables the formulation of "unwelcome but unmistakable" alternative ways of seeing the world and the role of violence in it (*Manliness*, 2).

Because hostis humani generis allows new concepts to become defensible, one might leap to the conclusion that the constellation could even serve to develop the idea of implementable revolution. Indeed, revolutionary rhetoric is often linked to a narrative structure that relies on the constellation, but the forms of revolution that it makes conceivable include certain cultural assumptions that qualify the scope of thinkable innovation.

When we contemplate the question of revolution and radical overthrow, the origin of hostis humani generis as a legal fiction becomes meaningful in a more nuanced sense. Even though hostis humani generis does not operate like a conventional legal fiction in law—meaning that it is not a transitional vehicle to integrate new phenomena into the language of the law—its main function is still integration. The constellation absorbs new perspectives on meaningful belonging (and the normative limits of belonging) into a tradition of conceptualizing violence as an act on behalf of the community. The use of hostis humani generis demands a perspective that is just as invested in maintaining cultural continuity as it is in challenging selected traditional elements of a prevailing interpretation. Three cultural assumptions premised by the hostis humani generis constellation deserve to be highlighted here.

First, there is the premise that legitimate violence must correspond with a claim to represent innocents. As this book has emphasized, "the innocent" is by no means a neutral term but itself includes certain hierarchies of authority that have to be perpetually reproduced, lest the derived claim to legitimate violence becomes void. Even when the notion of natural innocence is rejected, this book's discussions of the homo sacer and related concepts of innocence produced by violence suggest that the required representation of innocents constitutes a serious analytical qualification to any claim to legitimate violence that is based on hostis humani generis.

The status of the innocent means that innocents absolutely, inherently, and permanently lack a voice within representative institutions. According to the logic of the constellation, the typical options available to the innocent (usually, a very heterogeneous group) are thus to accept their lot as passive and voiceless nonagents or to commit extreme acts of violence in the hope of becoming a variation of the pirata who, though usually an illegitimate agent, is at least accepted as an agent.[1] When we consider such a monstrous choice, it becomes fundamentally questionable whether a claim to legitimate violence made on behalf of innocents can ever in fact be in those innocents' best interest. It is at this point that the unique feature of hostis humani generis among legal fictions—namely, its claim to a permanent rather than a transitional characterization of a given conflict—assumes a problematic quality, as the static premises of the constellation prevent an inclusion of the voices of the (alleged) innocent as the primary correctives for any claim to legitimate violence committed on their behalf. Even in uses of the constellation that foreground the voice of the excluded and oppressed, there are some innocents whose subjection to violence is decidedly not constructed as an actual violation of their bodies or, in Hooker's term, their dignity. Instead, violence against them is abstracted as the symbolic violation of an illegitimate order. In *Native Son*, for example, acts of rape and murder of women somehow emerge as defensive, legitimate acts on behalf of an integrated, truly just rule.

This leads to the second point. The inclusion of innocent voices to test a claim to legitimate violence is made unnecessary, according to the logic of the constellation, by the basic assumption that legitimate violence has a universalist dimension. Hostis humani generis always serves to formulate a general principle of justice that, once universally implemented, will automatically lead to a world that is just. The claim to represent universally applicable values is inherent to all claims to legitimate violence that rely on the hostis humani generis constellation. The claim to universal applicability is why, when the constellation is used, legitimate violence is almost by default understood as expansive in modern texts. Apart from the obvious problems of such an expansive worldview, the claim to universal legitimacy constitutes a problem with regard to a phenomenon as uneven and complex as violence.

The gray zones of violence that hostis humani generis helps cut across with a clear legitimacy construction in texts never cease to exist as gray zones and will never be made fully subsumable, or explicable, by the use of the constellation. Hostis humani generis acknowledges the fact of violence's insubsumability and unknowability with the inclusion of the pirata figure—yet the constellation considerably reduces the complexity of violence as a phenomenon by its bold claim that realms of inherent legitimacy and illegitimacy exist, and that experiences of paradox and inner contradiction are primarily caused by the lawless nature of the in-between zone. The constellation encourages the use of only the most sweeping claims to legitimate violence, actively discouraging the formulation of nuanced, situation-specific claims.

Third, these qualifications do not apply only to relations among humans; they apply to spaces as well. The constellation premises that, as soon as the legitimacy of violence is fiercely contested in a space, that space can be constructed as an in-between zone characterized by general lawlessness. This points to an analytical abstraction of space that necessitates the denial of its complexities outside the context of violent interaction—and, no less importantly, of human interaction. Indeed, the constellation renders it extremely difficult to include nonhuman figures in any discussion of legitimate violence. For example, Naomi Klein's popular book on climate change, *This Changes Everything*, which makes extensive use of the hostis humani generis constellation,[2] is able to make a convincing argument only because Klein does not write about the planet at all. Instead, she uses the notion of climate change as a historical backdrop that necessitates a call for political transformation and new standards for judging the legitimacy of violence among humans. The constellation does not, in other words, easily allow a contemplation of the human being within a world that is more than a stage for interhuman relations.

These three elements alone—the facts that hostis humani generis is universalist, and that it requires the representation of innocents as well as the premise of a space without any relevant material properties of its own—firmly situate hostis humani generis in a tradition of thought that renders its usefulness for radical models of cultural change questionable. At the same time, they also point toward some of the directions of critical analysis that may indeed profit from the consideration of this constellation, if only to help circumvent unspoken core assumptions such as these.

At the same time, there is a certain instructive irony in calling for a reconsideration of the ground of legitimate violence outside of the parameters of hostis humani generis at this point of the study. The three points just made are, in essence, simply a logical development of part 4's analysis of a planetary in-between zone, and the observation of a potential new beginning—or rather, a potential structural revision of the constellation's fixed relations—at the present historical moment.

Today, we again live in a time of change and upheaval, notably including a revision of the role of institutions in Anglo-American nation-states. In many different ways, prevailing interpretive traditions of legitimate violence are currently under fundamental review. The points just raised therefore do what theorists of legitimate violence have always done with the constellation—draw attention to limits and gaps of contemporary interpretations of it and point toward realms that the existing discourse of legitimate violence still needs to charter. Such a construction of a critical outside perspective, because it is itself derived from hostis humani generis, can formulate and defend the abovementioned calls for a more nuanced treatment of legitimate violence—but it cannot escape the categorical connections made between violence and identity, transformation and legitimacy, or humanity and justice that the constellation helps establish as meaningful.

Perhaps it must suffice to conclude that hostis humani generis helps translate historically specific challenges and their historically specific analyses into actionable strategic essentialisms, which in turn are designed to make sense of violent situations that involve many unknown parameters. To study the constellation across time, space, and categories of belonging requires the tacit acceptance of a modern "condition of the subject caught up in structural repetition," to use the words of Lee Edelman (quoted in Dinshaw et al., "Queer Temporalities," 194). In the case of hostis humani generis, this structural repetition pertains to the perpetual necessity to renegotiate the nature of legitimate violence and the structural conditions that are in place to address the question. Any contemporary text that raises questions of legitimate violence is contextualized by a discursive history of the answers that hostis humani generis has helped formulate as persuasive. As long as one speaks of legitimate violence in Anglo-American modernity, one must reckon with the hostis humani generis constellation as a central cultural resource for meaning making.

ABBREVIATIONS

Page numbers cited in the text refer to the editions listed in "Works Cited."

DS	James Fenimore Cooper, *The Deerslayer, or the First Warpath* (1841)
MN	Kurt Vonnegut, *Mother Night* (1962)
NS	Richard Wright, *Native Son* (1940)
RF	Mohsin Hamid, *The Reluctant Fundamentalist* (2007)
RH	Dashiell Hammett, *Red Harvest* (1929)

NOTES

Introduction

1. Alfred Rubin discusses the case in 1705 in which universal jurisdiction was claimed against pirates. He writes that the three main conditions for a sovereign's legitimate claim to jurisdiction, according to the 1705 tribunal, are "*in loco delicti* [the place were a crime was committed] or *in loco domicilii* [the place where the criminals resided] or *in loco originis* [the place of their birth]" (*Law of Piracy*, 103–4).

2. For an excellent overview of this dazzling diversity of the pirate, see Schiedermair, "Piratenjagd."

3. Great Britain as a political entity was created in 1707, so it is the correct entity to refer to for most discourses addressed in this study. For earlier discourses, I will refer to England and Scotland instead.

1. Augustine of Hippo

1. The influence of Alexander on pirate representations is well exemplified in representations of Captain Henry Avery, especially in Charles Johnson's *The Successful Pyrate* (1713). In this play—written by an author who is not the same person as the author of the *General History*—archpirate Henry Avery is an impulsive, military-minded leader with conquest on his mind who is transformed into a legitimate king only at the moment when he begins to tame his own passions for the greater good of the pirate kingdom. This portrayal is contrasted with other contemporary characterizations of Avery as a pirate king that emphasize his resourceful, but ultimately petty, criminality (see Defoe, *King of Pirates*).

2. Montesquieu and others later interpret this to imply that all worldly kingdoms begin as pirate communities (Montesquieu, *Spirit of Laws*, 362–64; see also Kempe, *Fluch der Weltmeere*, 235), but it is more likely that Augustine is simply suggesting that a certain amount of injustice is an inherent property of every worldly rule, large or small, imperial or piratical.

3. Brown speaks of "women and children" (*States of Injury*, 181). This phrase typically describes an undifferentiated collective that helps conceptualize either form of sovereign rule as a male prerogative. In this study, I occasionally use the term "women-and-children" to indicate the phrase's function as a gendered synonym for "innocents."

2. Charles Johnson

1. The edition I use of *A General History of the Pyrates* attributes the book to a different author than I do. As mentioned, the *General History* was first published under the name Captain Charles Johnson, a pseudonym. The authorship question, especially with respect to the possibility of Daniel Defoe, has been debated for decades (see especially Furbank and Owens, *Defoe De-Attributions*; J. Moore, *Checklist*). In this study, I speak of Johnson as the author, while Manuel Schonhorn's edition of 1999 claims that the

General History was written by Daniel Defoe, listing him as the author on the title page. Schonhorn explains and defends this choice in the editor's introduction (introduction). I prefer to use the pseudonym because the authorship debate is ongoing, and because my own argument does not depend on the identity of the author.

2. This is not to say that a reading that reproduced Augustine's meaning no longer existed. Following this more traditional strand of pirate discourse, Cotton Mather characterized Samuel Bellamy's crew as predatory "Barbarous Wretches" ("Instructions to LIVING," 4:132) and used the Augustinian anecdote in an antipiracy sermon: "Be sure, the PIRATE at Sea, and so the *Robber* on Shore, is one who seeks to *get Riches and not by Right.* And here it may be complained, That while the Laws reach the lesser *Pirates & Robbers*, there are, as one of them too truly told the Execrable *Alexander*, much *Greater* Ones, whom no Humane Laws presume to meddle withal: *Monsters*, whom we dignify with the Title of *Hero's:* [*sic*] *Conquerors* and *Emperors*, but yet no other than a more splendid sort of *Highway-men*" (ibid., 4:146). Mather's vilification of Alexander the Great is reproduced in other eighteenth-century writing, thus indicating that the notion of pure conquest remained widely condemned throughout the spectrum of commentators (see, for example, Addison, "No. 31"; Swift, *Gulliver*, 214). The traditional strand of discourse notably relies on characterizations of the pirate-emperor as passionate, ferocious, and shortsighted.

3. The two "primary compilations" in this quote refer to Johnson's *General History* (both volumes) and Alexandre Exquemelin's earlier *The Buccaneers of America* (1678).

4. The idea of an imperial evolution toward civilization is illustrated by the retrospective structuring of the Golden Age as a three-generation era in many scholarly contributions on the Golden Age (see, for example, Baer, *British Isles*; Rediker, *Villains*). Historians who include the buccaneers as a separate generation of the Golden Age portray them as pioneers who end the Spanish supremacy in the Americas. I exclude the buccaneers and work with only two generations, following scholars such as Peter Earle and Hans Turley (Earle, *Pirate Wars*; Turley, *Rum, Sodomy and the Lash*). The first generation of the Golden Age is one of political and legal restructuring, but also the high point of a pirate kingdom imaginary; in the second generation, then, the pirates are relics whose communities shrink from pirate kingdoms to mere ships, as they have nothing more to expect from their existence than "a merry life and a short one" (C. Johnson, *General History*, 244).

5. Five years after the publication of the *General History*'s second volume, Fielding uses the Augustinian anecdote even more broadly, replacing the figure of the pirate with that of the thief. As in Johnson, it is the figure of the criminal who evokes the Augustinian constellation in a monologue. The notion of externalized subregimes (who, in Fielding, can even consist of only one person) and the inversion of the rich and the criminal, who differ only in organizational complexity, are reproduced and formulated even more sharply than in the *General History*: "Now we come to the second part of this division, viz., of those who employ hands for their own use only; and this is that noble and great part who are generally distinguished into conquerors, absolute princes, statesmen, and prigs [thieves]. Now all these differ from each other in greatness only—they employ MORE or FEWER hands. And Alexander the Great was only GREATER than a captain of one of the Tartarian or Arabian hordes, as he was at the head of a larger number. In what then is a single prig inferior to any other great man, but because he employs his own hands only; for he is not on that account to be levelled with the base and vulgar, because he employs his hands for his own use only" (Fielding, *Jonathan Wild*, 3:7).

3. Charles Ellms

1. The 1830s and 1840s were generally a time of extensive American translation and republishing of European writing, a practice that was also labeled piracy at the time. American laws did not recognize any copyright protection for foreign authors, so especially British texts were routinely republished and sold in the United States, generating considerable profits for booksellers (Knighton, "Wreck," 80).

2. It is notable that the League of Nations, which approached the slave trade with the prime purpose of protecting humanity as such, accordingly changed the maritime restriction in the prevailing definitions of the slave trade with the 1921 International Convention for the Suppression of the Traffic in Women and Children. In the same year, the League of Nations sponsored an international conference on white slave trafficking, thus explicitly broadening the perspective on the slave trade beyond the territorial legacy of the African slave trade (Berqôvîč, *Motherhood*, 75).

Part 2. Race, Space, and the Formation of the Hostis Humani Generis *Constellation*

1. The term "corsair" is often used to refer to pirates of the Mediterranean, but these entities are legally equivalent to the European privateer in most respects. I maintain the differentiation between corsair and privateer in this part of the book to indicate whether the entity in question belongs to a European or a Barbary state, not to suggest a qualitative difference between them.

4. Piratae *and* Praedones

1. The importance of the Barbary States for Europe was ignored by the vast majority of Western historians after the mid-nineteenth century until comparatively recently, when the 9/11 attacks spurred a search for historical models of faith-based antagonism, especially in US discourse (see, for example, Wheelan, *Jefferson's War*). This move toward a rediscovery of the Mediterranean realm was further reinforced after the first US ship fell into the hands of Somali pirates in 2009, thus evoking a popular historical parallel to that of Barbary piracy (see, for example, Phillips, *A Captain's Duty*). These developments were accompanied by a more general analytical interest in the provincialization of Europe and the United States (Bender, *Among Nations*; Chakrabarty, *Provincializing Europe*; Edwards and Gaonkar, *American Studies*).

2. In literary and cultural studies, a corresponding discussion of the Mediterranean-Atlantic link has emerged only comparatively recently, and that discussion has largely focused on the analysis of the captivity narrative. Gordon Sayre calls the increasingly pronounced analytical focus on the link between the Atlantic and the Mediterranean regions "the transnational turn in captivity studies" ("Renegades"). Important early work on a reciprocal transfer of culture in this context has been done by scholars such as Paul Baepler ("Barbary Captivity" and introduction), Linda Colley (*Captives*), and Nabil Matar (*Turks*). In a subsequent step, scholars such as Timothy Marr (*American Islamicism*) and Lawrence Peskin (*Captives and Countrymen*) have begun to expand the conversation to include narrative formations besides the captivity narrative.

3. In addition, not all inherently illegitimate sovereigns in early modernity were nonwhite, non-European, or non-Christian. A particularly important, and somewhat singular, English example is provided by Matthew Tindal in 1694. King James II, then in exile, had issued privateering commissions to conquer his own former realm, but his privateers

were defeated and arrested. In the course of the trial, a debate arose as to their status: were they the privateers of a king, or were they pirates? Tindal argued that these men should be deemed to be pirates because the sovereign they had contracted with was not in fact a legitimate sovereign but a private person, and thus did not have the right to issue a privateering contract (*Law of Nations*, 11).

4. Of course, it is conceivable that a pirata has never aspired to gain this status, as in cases of mutiny that led to the establishment of pirate crews (Rediker, *Villains*, 46–47). What is important here is that even such a mutineer's legal status as a pirate is measured by the contractual relationship between sovereign and privateer: regardless of the particulars of an individual case, the pirata is defined by his failure to comply with the standards of a privateer.

5. John Locke, William Blackstone, and the Invader in the State of Nature

1. There are also overlaps with Hobbes's state of nature, such as: "And therefore till there be security amongst men for the keeping of the law of nature one towards another, men are still in the estate of war, and nothing is unlawful to any man that tendeth to his own safety or commodity" (*Elements of Law*, 103).

2. The virtual extinction of Native Americans and the systematic marginalization of Native American sovereign rights do not allow a characterization that strays very far from that of conquest. As Dieter Dörr has pointed out, the annexation of Native American land has, for the most part, been a history of contracts. This would speak for its legitimacy and legality. However, he continues to argue that it is also a history of broken contracts, all of which were broken by representatives of European empires (Dörr, "'Savages'"). Especially in the later stages of colonialism, many contracts made with Native Americans appear to be mere legalist attempts to avoid the appearance of illegitimate conquest (Fisch, *Europäische Expansion*, 332–45; Washburn, *Red Man's Land*, 47–49).

3. As yet another example of their intimate connection in modern legal discourse, Vattel presents Native American nations and the Barbary States as two varieties of the same legal situation. The Barbary States are mentioned as the core example through the reference to "some modern Tartars" and the equally straightforward evocation of a combination of fertile hinterlands and predatory ports, which were a constitutive feature of the Barbary States' infrastructure (Earle, *Corsairs of Malta*, 23–24).

4. The Native American case was generally used as an example in European law and philosophy, and after Vattel, the land-use argument for the American case was used systematically to legitimate the dispossession of newly discovered peoples around the world (Rouleau, "Maritime Destiny," 391–92).

5. The progressivist approach strongly relied on the conversion to Christianity as a civilizing factor. The increasingly obvious failure of the Christian missionary movement in America was an additional reason why the essentialist approach to civilization had achieved dominance by the end of the eighteenth century (Slotkin, *Regeneration*, 73). Such failure was usually intertwined with the abuse of established friendly relations by settlers who arrived later and aggressively pushed westward, as the example of Pennsylvania Quakers aptly demonstrates (Pearce, *Savagism*, 35–41).

6. This is not to say that the female position mentioned here should remain without consequence for the interpretation of the hostis humani generis constellation. Indeed, this

position assumes central importance for the more sophisticated theoretical development of the constellation. In part 3, I discuss this aspect in greater detail in my analysis of what I call the pure woman paradox.

6. Hostis Humani Generis *and the American Historical Novel*

1. Huron impotence and inferiority in respect to whites are still implied in the novel. For instance, an entire tribe of Huron warriors manages to take only the scalp of Hutter, the oldest and weakest of the white men, and even accomplishes that only by virtue of trickery. Likewise, when they finally capture the protagonist, they fail to continue beyond the symbolic stage of torture (DS, 2:1004).

2. There is a hint that Glimmerglass is identical to Lake Otsego in the first Leatherstocking novel, *The Pioneers* (1823). In the last chapter of *The Deerslayer*, Cooper writes: "Chingachgook and his friend . . . held their way towards the Mohawk in silence, however, to rush into new adventures, as stirring and as remarkable as those which had attended their opening careers, on this lovely lake. At a later day, they returned to the place, where the Indian found a grave" (DS, 2:1029). Since Chingachgook dies as an old man in *The Pioneers*, the passage is likely an intertextual reference meant to close the circle between the books in the series—the town of Templeton in *The Pioneers* is also located on a beautiful lake in the New York territory. In *The Pioneers*, the wilderness had undergone the classic development of having been claimed by landowners and then been cultivated in an increasingly sophisticated infrastructure. The intertextual reference substantiates the notion of the civilizing process of Templeton as the necessary future of the Glimmerglass territory as land that is sea-like and thus ownerless in the beginning, but that differs from land in that it can be cultivated in a European spirit. It is also interesting to refer to *The Pioneers* at this point in *The Deerslayer* because the earlier novel establishes an explicit link between villains who are driven further west and their role as establishers of white infrastructure (Cooper, *Pioneers*, 1:454–55).

Part 3. The American Civilization Thesis

1. This differentiation of nation-states into legitimate and illegitimate ones echoes the logic of the older discursive tradition of normalcy and deviance that had begun in the 1800s. In this tradition, defining elements of the human being are externalized to enable the formulation of internally coherent humans who may be conceptualized as normal and contrasted with deviants. A very similar logic of externalization is at work here on the level of nation-states. However, only with the narrative combination of artificially compartmentalized properties does a discussion of the whole spectrum of violence become possible. The conceptualization of the normal requires the simultaneous conceptualization of the deviant: by definition, the normal cannot stand by itself (Glaubitz, *Mensch*, 14). The problematic implications of such compartmentalization in the context of legitimate violence will be discussed in depth in part 4.

7. The Frontier Thesis as a Third Model of Civilization

1. My characterization of institutions at this point is already colored by the premises of the frontier model, and certainly the institutions that characterize the United States today cannot be compared to those of Turner's time. In this book, the term "institution"

is arguably a category that includes a whole cluster of different entities. According to Mark McGurl, it is an "observable characteristic" of institutions "that they are understood relationally and analogically, with habitual disrespect for the distinction between public and private spheres or between 'repressive state apparatuses' (the army and police) and 'ideological state apparatuses' (schools and the media) as canonically defined by Louis Althusser." Furthermore, McGurl draws attention to the "spectrum between the institution proper and the institution as established practice" that the term relates to ("Understanding Iowa," 7).

2. Rousseau famously criticized Hobbes's model because it did not include people whose nature corresponded to the state of nature, but merely imagined civilized people in savage circumstances (Rousseau, *Inequality*, liv). However, the existence of civilized people in savage circumstances is a notion that Turner explicitly assumes in his frontier thesis when he argues that European civilization is a phase prior to American civilization. I therefore continue to refer to Hobbes's state of nature and assume it to be the basic model of the state of nature that informs the frontier thesis.

3. For instance, Nathaniel Hawthorne writes in *The Scarlet Letter*: "The age had not so much refinement that any sense of impropriety restrained the wearers of petticoat and farthingale from stepping forth into the public ways and wedging their not unsubstantial persons, if occasion were, into the throng nearest to the scaffold at an execution. Morally, as well as materially, there was a coarser fibre in those wives and maidens of old English birth and breeding than in their fair descendants, separated from them by a series of six or seven generations; for, throughout that chain of ancestry, every successive mother has transmitted to her child a fainter bloom, a more delicate and briefer beauty, and a slighter physical frame, if not a character of less force and solidity, than her own" (*Scarlet Letter*, 43). For Hawthorne, the softening of these women is very decidedly a form of Americanization. He uses the same coarseness identified by Turner as authentically American to suggest these women's English origin. The women are coarse not because of the wilderness, but because they are the contemporaries and countrywomen of "the manlike Elizabeth," steeled by "the beef and ale of their native land, with a moral diet not a whit more refined" (ibid.).

8. The Democratic Frontiersman and the Totalitarian Leviathan

1. It is notable that Drucker does not yet consider socialism totalitarian but simply distinguishes socialism from capitalism as an economic regime (*Economic Man*, 227). Only fascism is inherently illegitimate, in Drucker's view. Both socialist and capitalist societies thus have the potential to form a free and equal society. George Orwell would later contradict this assessment, reasoning that the political formations of socialism rendered it extremely vulnerable to illegitimate minority rule in a totalitarian sense. He suggests that the problem of socialism lies in the sense of collective ownership, as the power over the distribution of resources is concentrated in the hands of a few, who may claim to act the interest of all but will inevitably attempt to further their own objectives instead (*Nineteen Eighty-Four*, 159–60 and 203). I will discuss these later concepts of totalitarianism in more detail in part 4.

9. Free Agency and the Pure Woman Paradox

1. At least that logic works if one grants these natural innocents the capacity to be reasonable. This is not necessarily the case in legal practice. This problem has been addressed,

for instance, in scholarly discussions of the "reasonable person standard" (see Collier, Maurer, and Suarez-Navaz, "Sanctioned Identities"; Hayden, "Cultural Norms").

2. This reformulation is stabilized by a construction of totalitarianism as a barbarous order that is rendered illegitimate because it continues to rule through the oppression of subjects and strongly emphasizes the "natural" innocence of populations (Heater, *Theory*, 70).

3. In the text, the charge of illegitimacy against the American court system is invalidated by the constant narrative affirmation of the court and its proceedings, in combination with the more subtle characterization of Wansley as a liar. The court is presented as just and impartial, for example by twice urging Wansley to add to his testimony if he so desires. The procedure continues only when Wansley says that he is finished. Finally, in the court's explanation for upholding his death sentence, it addresses the charges of racism head on and answers them plainly (even though it circumvents addressing the charge of judicial bias). At the same time, Ellms clearly portrays Wansley as a suspicious character throughout the court scene. For instance, Wansley describes asking the conspirators very specific logistical questions about the deed but always presents these questions as "jokes"—a strategy that suggests a thinly veiled lie that the court is able to see through when it passes the sentence over him (Ellms, *Own Book*, 65).

4. In addition the pure woman pirata's affirmation of democracy, which is indicated in the rise from innocence to agency and in the emphasis on the individual, the more traditional characterization of the pirata as a maritime entity may also serve as a substantiating reference in economic terms. As the economic regime of socialism is incorporated into the construction of totalitarianism, capitalism is increasingly naturalized as an expression of civilization. It is helpful to remember here that the classic maritime pirata is conventionally conceptualized as an individualist economic man who prefers to "balance Creditor" on the side of his own greatest advancement (C. Johnson, *General History*, 244), which locates him squarely in the ideological fold of capitalism (see also Policante, *Pirate Myth*).

10. The Foundational Pirata in Richard Wright's Native Son

1. In an argument that expands on Wright's observations, bell hooks has observed that African American men have historically responded to their oppression by assuming traditional representative agency over African American women and children, thus claiming a role as legitimate free agents. Rather than helping these men to rise from their latent position of innocence, however, their establishment of a traditional "rule" over their families reinforced the legitimacy of their own oppression, since they themselves reproduced rather than challenged its general underlying logic (hooks, "Seduced," 110).

2. The special status of the Daltons is emphasized by the fact that during the trial, the families of Thomas's other two victims (most notably, that of his African American victim, Mears) are not introduced in the narrative or even mentioned by any other character, while the Daltons are granted substantial narrative space. Their emotional response to the murder of their daughter as an act beyond understanding is directly linked to their belittling of oppressive relations in the rest of the text; their grieving disbelief, in other words, is constructed as damning evidence against them (NS, 324–25 and 354–58).

3. At the same time, it is notable that Mr. Dalton understands, at least on some underlying level, the illegitimacy of his own role as an oppressor of African Americans. For example, after he learns that Thomas is one of his own overcharged tenants in the Black

Belt, Dalton voluntarily offers to pay him a larger salary to compensate for overcharging for the family apartment (NS, 79–81). There is no aspect in the scene other than the revelation of Thomas's living conditions that could spur such a willingness to raise Thomas's salary. Like Henry March in *The Deerslayer*, Mr. Dalton seems to possess a much-neglected conscience.

4. According to 18 U.S.C. § 241, "conspiracy against rights," it is unlawful for two or more persons [to] conspire to injure, oppress, threaten, or intimidate any person in any State, Territory, Commonwealth, Possession, or District in the free exercise or enjoyment of any right or privilege secured to him by the Constitution or laws of the United States." This US statute has mainly been used in the case of hate crimes or more generally oppressive acts—especially when they are committed by institutional agents of the state who have sworn to uphold the equality of rights.

5. This is further indicated by the novel's citation of the wealth versus courage construction discussed in chapter 1 of this book. The use of this construction underlines Wright's suggestion that violence is a necessary language of politics: "When men of wealth urge the use and show of force, quick death, swift revenge, then it is to protect a little spot of private security against the resentful millions from whom they have filched it, the resentful millions in whose militant hearts the dream and hope of security still lives" (NS, 430).

Part 4. "It Is Underneath Us"

1. Some of the secondary literature on *Mother Night* gives 1961 as the date of the novel's first publication, and some uses 1962. For example, Charles Shields and Philip Tew suggest it was first published in the fall of 1961 (Shields, *And So It Goes*, 173; Tew, "*Mother Night*," 11). In an e-mail message to me on September 16, 2015, Shields explained that the 1961 date is when the publisher purchased the novel from Vonnegut, but that printed copies of *Mother Night* may not have reached the bookstores until 1962. Betty Hudgens, who compiled a list of Vonnegut's first editions, lists the spring of 1962 as the date when *Mother Night* was first published (*Checklist*, 11). Donald Morse substantiates that *Mother Night* was "published as an original paperback in 1962 but with a 1961 copyright date" (*Novels of Vonnegut*, 35). In this book, I therefore use 1962 as the date of the novel's first publication.

2. In the context of the Jerusalem trial and the legitimation of Eichmann's status as a committer of crimes against humanity who may be hunted down anywhere on the globe, the legal notion of "universal jurisdiction plus" was important in establishing the notion of universal jurisdiction against committers of crimes against humanity (Addis, "International Community," 135–36). The "plus" refers to the notion that crimes against Jews were to be considered particularly grave crimes against humanity. The notion of universal jurisdiction plus is favorably mentioned in the novel (see MN, 50).

11. The Institutional Frontier

1. In his construction of the invader, Locke considers legitimate violence that punishes "a trespass against the whole Species, and the Peace and Safety of it, provided by the State of Nature" ("Second Treatise," 272). Locke specifically allows violence to be committed against such a perpetrator by outsiders who assist his victim: "any other Person who finds it just, may also joyn with him that is injur'd, and assist him in recovering from the Offender, so much as may make satisfaction for the harm he has suffer'd" (ibid.,

273). When the legal fiction was first interpreted along these lines in the early nineteenth century, only a comparatively narrow implementation of it was possible, due to the traditions of piracy law that interpreted universal crimes as random attacks. The enemy of all humankind, in the classic piracy law tradition, referred to a perpetrator who attacked others without any claim to legitimacy. The enemy of all humankind was thus associated with a random readiness to harm the virtuous and the innocent as well as the wicked and guilty. Because of this conceptualization of the enemy of all humankind as an unthinking and vicious beast, violent responses to such an antagonist depended on his attacking first, rather than on the general fact of his warfare with humankind via oppression, enslavement, and mistreatment—which were, arguably, much starker evidence of a contempt for the "Dignity of Man."

2. The fact that the barbarian is a nation-state among others, and thus enters into a kinship with civilized nation-states such as the United States, is a seeming paradox that in fact has a long tradition in claims of legitimate violence in the context of piracy. For example, in the passage by Hugo Grotius from which this book's terminology of pirata and praedo is taken, the most problematic case of illegitimate seizure is not that of the praedo, the pirata, or the robber, "but a fourth type, which can scarcely be detected save through conjectural inferences. It is the type of seizure that occurs when, in the course of a just war or a war believed to be just, someone grasps at profit in a way which indicates that he has been mindful only of profit for its own sake and not of the true objective of the war, namely, the attainments of rights" (Grotius, *Prize and Booty*, 448). If we replace "seizure" with "violence" and "profit" with "rule," we begin to see how the history of hostis humani generis could easily provide a way to conceptualize the fellow (first imperial, then national) sovereign as barbarous.

3. The characterization of the German population as an innocent victim of totalitarianism obviously does not reflect a consensus in the theoretical debate on totalitarianism. Historians of Central and Eastern Europe, for example, have almost completely abandoned the terminology of totalitarianism, precisely because it implies generalizations that are too sweeping to be helpful. However, the ontological separation between the regime and those represented by it is indicated in all characterizations of the totalitarian regime as illegitimate. Totalitarianism can be an inherently illegitimate order only if it runs counter to the humanity of those ruled by it, and it is in this sense that the regime victimizes the population. Even scholars who see the population as complicit tend to agree with this. For a more nuanced picture, see, for example, Giesen, "Trauma of Perpetrators"; Ó Dochartaigh and Schönfeld, *Representing the "Good German"*; Trutkowski, "Concepts of Totalitarianism."

4. In this study, the terms are not used in their medical sense either; I follow Vonnegut's choices regarding these terms' function in text. Scholars disagree about whether it is generally helpful to use medical terms such as "schizophrenia" and "paranoia" allegorically (see, for example, Cvetkovich, *Depression*; Mitchell and Snyder, *Narrative Prosthesis*). I thank Christina Maria Koch for drawing my attention to this debate.

5. Another feature of the Vietnam War that underlines its situatedness in essentialist rhetoric in the United States was a narrative emphasis on the role of Vietnamese allies. They were originally constructed as people of great integrity who decided to transform themselves from innocents not into praedones but into foundational piratae who wanted freedom for themselves and their country, and who thus assisted the cause against their inherently illegitimate communist countrymen (Slotkin, "Unit Pride"). These Vietnamese

allies were later used to reconceptualize the American intervention as illegitimate. In these alternative discourses, Vietnamese allies were constructed as renegades in the traditional Barbary sense—namely, as dishonorable cutthroats—who stood in opposition to their more virtuous Vietnamese counterparts, who represented stout and honorable resistance to American invasion (Neu, "Vietnam and Transformation," 15).

6. Official attempts to adapt to the irrelevance of territorial advancement while remaining within discourses of legitimacy led to contradictory and sometimes conflicting measures and criteria of "success" (Dougherty, *Limited War*, 75–76). New measures to indicate the progress of the war were introduced, most notably statistics and neutralization quotas, a measurement originally designed to make the conflicting developments in Vietnam consistent and transparent. In practice, however, the concentration on statistics fostered abuse and created "a dream world of destruction" that did not just allow but implicitly encouraged American soldiers to kill women-and-children rather than enemy soldiers (Glover, *Humanity*, 60).

12. Who Is Innocent?

1. For instance, Antonio Cassese quotes an unspecified American (probably Jeane J. Kirkpatrick) speaking in a meeting of the UN Security Council whose evocation of Blackstone could not be plainer: "The terrorist has put himself beyond the pale of civilized humanity. He should be shunned by all. . . . Every terrorist attack is an attack on the world community. Every justification offered for terrorism undermines the rule of law. Every concession to the terrorist diminishes our humanity" (quoted in Cassese, *Politics*, 70). Mikkel Thorup attributes this passage to Reagan (*Intellectual History*, 166), but he does not provide any references to support this attribution other than Cassese's study. Cassese, however, does not identify the speaker, and it is doubtful from the context of the passage that he means Reagan. He quotes Reagan several times in the chapter that contains this quote and explicitly distinguishes him from the American representative who speaks here. It is more likely that Cassese was quoting the US ambassador to the United Nations at the time. In 1985, first Kirkpatrick and then Vernon A. Walters held this position. Since Kirkpatrick vocally and explicitly supported the agenda of conceptualizing terrorists as hostes humani generis (Kirkpatrick, "Totalitarian Confusion"), and since Cassese explicitly mentions that the speech was delivered some time before the *Achille Lauro* incident (*Politics*, 69), I consider it likely that she is the person quoted here.

2. For example, Sterling's core assumption that terrorist groups are savage loose cannons sponsored but not controlled by the state gave rise to the concept of New Terrorism that was first formulated in 1986 (Zalman, "What's New"). The notion of New Terrorism spread throughout the 1990s (Juergensmeyer, *Mind of God*) and gained respectability particularly after 9/11 (see, for example, Stern, *Name of God*), even though its characteristically alarmist presuppositions had provoked severe scholarly criticism ever since its first formulation (see Crenshaw, "'New' versus 'Old' Terrorism"; Duyvesteyn, "How New"). However, the importance of Sterling's influence is better traced in the less obvious legacies of her work across the political spectrum. For instance, scholars of all political backgrounds have adopted her temporal trajectory and story of origin in defining terrorism, which means adopting her basic criteria of what terrorism stands for (see Gage, "Terrorism," 90; Hoffman, *Inside Terrorism*, 67).

3. Chomsky's careful self-positioning in this respect may be due to previous charges against his earlier, politically comparable work, especially his criticism of Zionism in Israel. For instance, when Chomsky was charged by Hawzheen O Kareem with a form of "Jewish self-hatred" after having criticized Zionism (quoted in Barsky, *Chomsky Effect*, 54), Chomsky replied with the charge that "such criticisms reflect deeply held totalitarian values" (quoted in ibid.; see also 54-60).

13. Mohsin Hamid's The Reluctant Fundamentalist *and the War on Terror*

1. Simultaneously, terrorism was established as the problem-defining example in definitions of "asymmetrical" warfare (see Pfanner, "Asymmetrical Warfare"). This strategy draws on the earlier introduction of crimes against humanity, whose introduction to law also depended on a radical reconceptualization of war (Martinez, *Slave Trade*, 156).

2. In the context of race, Mita Banerjee substantiates Reddy's assessment by drawing attention to the fact that "Arabs" were considered white prior to 9/11 and were "re-raced" as the carriers of specifically Muslim difference in the aftermath of the attacks (*Race-ing the Century*, 441). This development has important consequences, Banerjee notes, because "if a face previously deemed white can slip into racial difference, delinquency is everywhere and nowhere" (ibid., 438; see also Naber, *Arab America*, 32–33). Even in traditionally racialized discourses, then, the national "we" was fundamentally renegotiated after 9/11.

3. Underwood Samson is probably a fictional version of the New York office of the McKinsey and Company valuation firm, where Hamid, like Changez, worked to pay off his student debts after studying in the United States.

4. There are extreme voices in the United States that directly strive to deny human rights to "enemy combatants," figures defined in reference to the terrorist as hostis humani generis (Barnidge, *Non-State Actors*, 175). Critics of the War on Terror tend to single out such voices as their targets. These critics tend to focus on the victimization of the immigrant, the refugee, and the planetary citizen as classic cases of innocents transformed into homines sacri who are wrongfully excluded from humanity, while sidestepping the problem of violence that is actually committed by alleged terrorists or enemy combatants (see, for example, Butler, "Indefinite Detention"; Greenberg, "Golem," Heller-Roazen, *Enemy of All*; Kaplan, "Guantánamo"; Žižek, "Depraved Heroes").

5. In the characterizations of these minor figures, *The Reluctant Fundamentalist* plays with essentialist readings of the terrorist as a renegade as they are epitomized, for instance, in the complementary notions of "homegrown terrorism" in Western states and of "foreign fighters," Western citizens who operate as terrorists in the Third World (see, for example, Brooks, "'Homegrown' Terrorism"; Malet, *Foreign Fighters*).

6. Additional characteristics that suggest Changez's position as a quasi Willsson are the ruthlessness underneath his amiable courtesy; his disregard of the law as a regulative framework; and his aforementioned personal representation of an in-between zone, which is established by his allegiance to the absent Erica.

Conclusion

1. In "C. L. R. James, Moby-Dick, and the Emergence of Transnational American Studies," Donald Pease outlines some of the potential conditions of a transition from the innocent to the status of a representative of civilization. The main condition is that the

innocent is able to express himself in writing, and in a form that is also considered expressive of civilization (in Pease's example, academic language). As Winfried Fluck cautions in *Das kulturelle Imaginäre*, however, the adoption of an accepted language of civilization is often restricted because many of these languages' conventions already firmly rely on the categorical exclusion of the innocent's own voice.

2. For example, Klein evokes the constellation in her introductory description of a personal epiphany that led to the formation of her book's argument, which echoes the construction of Erlone's epiphany in *Native Son* and allows Klein to assume the position of a scholarly representative of civilization in Noam Chomsky's and Giorgio Agamben's sense.

WORKS CITED

Abi-Saab, Georges. "The Proper Role of International Law in Combating Terrorism." *Chinese Journal of International Law* 1, no.1 (2002): 305–13.

Aceves, William J. *The Anatomy of Torture: A Documentary History of Filártiga v. Peña-Irala*. Leiden, the Netherlands: Martinus Nijhoff, 2007.

"An Act to Continue in Force 'An Act to Protect the Commerce of the United States, and to Punish the Crime of Piracy,' and Also to Make Further Provisions for Punishing the Crime of Piracy." Accessed March 12, 2016. http://abolition.nypl.org/content/docs/text/Act_of_1820.pdf.

Addis, Adeno. "Imagining the International Community: The Constitutive Dimension of Universal Jurisdiction." *Human Rights Quarterly* 31 (2009): 129–62.

Addison, Joseph. "No. 31." *Spectator*, April 5, 1711. Accessed October 27, 2015. http://www.readbookonline.net/readOnLine/40492.

Agamben, Giorgio. *Homo Sacer: Sovereign Power and Bare Life*. Stanford, CA: Stanford University Press, 1998.

Alexander, Jeffrey C. "On the Social Construction of Moral Universals: The 'Holocaust' from War Crime to Trauma Drama." In *Cultural Trauma and Collective Identity*, edited by Jeffrey C. Alexander et al., 196–263. Berkeley: University of California Press, 2004.

Arendt, Hannah. *Eichmann in Jerusalem: A Report on the Banality of Evil*. New York: Penguin, 1964.

———. *The Origins of Totalitarianism*. 1st Harvest ed. Orlando, FL: Harvest, 1976.

———and Joachim Fest. "'Eichmann war von empörender Dummheit': Hannah Arendt—Joachim Fest: Die Rundfunksendung vom 9. November 1964." In Hannah Arendt and Joachim Fest, *Hannah Arendt, Joachim Fest: Eichmann war von empörender Dummheit: Gespräche und Briefe*, edited by Ursula Ludz and Thomas Wild, 36–60. Zurich: Pieper, 2011.

Arrian. *Der Alexanderzug: Indische Geschichte*. Edited by Gerhard Wirth and Oskar von Hinüber. Munich, Germany: Artemis, 1985.

Arvanitakis, James, and David J. Hornsby. "Are Universities Redundant?" In *Universities, the Citizen Scholar and the Future of Higher Education*, edited by James Arvanitakis and David J. Hornsby, 7–19. London: Palgrave Macmillan, 2016.

Augustine of Hippo. *The City of God*. 2nd Hendrickson ed. Peabody, MA: Hendrickson, 2010.

Bader, Tobias. *Neokonservatismus, Think Tanks und New Imperialism*. Cologne, Germany: PapyRossa, 2005.

Baehr, Peter R. *Hannah Arendt, Totalitarianism, and the Social Sciences*. Stanford, CA: Stanford University Press, 2010.

Baepler, Paul M. "The Barbary Captivity Narrative in American Culture." *Early American Literature* 39, no. 2 (2004): 217–46.

———. Introduction to *White Slaves, African Masters: An Anthology of American Barbary Captivity Narratives*, edited by Paul M. Baepler, 1–58. Chicago: University of Chicago Press, 1999.

Baer, Joel H. "The Complicated Plot of Piracy: Aspects of English Criminal Law and the Image of the Pirate in Defoe." *Eighteenth Century* 23 (1982): 3–26.

———. Introduction to *The Life and Adventures of Capt. John Avery, by Anonymous, and The Successful Pyrate, by Charles Johnson*, iii–xiii. Reprint, Los Angeles: University of California, 1980.

———. *Pirates of the British Isles*. Stoud, UK: Tempus, 2005.

Baldwin, James. "Down at the Cross: Letter from a Region of My Mind." In James Baldwin, *The Fire Next Time*, 10–106. New York: Vintage International, 1993.

———. *Notes of a Native Son*. Boston: Beacon, 1955.

Banerjee, Mita. *Race-ing the Century*. Heidelberg, Germany: Winter, 2005.

Barbey d'Aurevilly, Jules-Amédée. "Die Rache einer Frau." In Jules-Amédée Barbey d'Aurevilly: *Das Glück im Verbrechen: Drei Geschichten von Jules-Amédée Barbey d'Aurevilly*, 125–71. Munich: Winkler, 1984.

Barnidge, Robert P. *Non-State Actors and Terrorism: Applying the Law of State Responsibility and the Due Diligence Principle*. The Hague: T.M.C. Asser, 2008.

Barrie, James M. *Peter Pan*. London: Hodder and Stoughton, 1961.

Barsky, Robert F. *The Chomsky Effect: A Radical Works beyond the Ivory Tower*. Cambridge, MA: MIT Press, 2007.

Bassiouni, Mahmoud Cherif. "The History of Universal Jurisdiction and Its Place in International Law." In *Universal Jurisdiction: National Courts and the Prosecution of Serious Crimes under International Law*, edited by Stephen Macedo, 39–63. Philadelphia: University of Pennsylvania Press, 2004.

Baudrillard, Jean. "L'Esprit du Terrorisme." *South Atlantic Quarterly* 101, no.2 (2002): 403–15.

Beck, Ulrich. "The Sociological Anatomy of Enemy Images: The Military and Democracy after the End of the Cold War." In *Enemy Images in American History*, edited by Ragnhild Fiebig-von Hase and Ursula Lehmkuhl, 65–87. Providence, RI: Berghahn, 1997.

Bederman, Gail. *Manliness and Civilization: A Cultural History of Gender and Race in the United States, 1880–1917*.Chicago: University of Chicago Press, 1995.

Beeching, Jack. Introduction to Alexandre O. Exquemelin, *The Buccaneers of America*, 7–20. Reprint, Mineola, NY: Dover, 2000.

Bender, Thomas. *A Nation Among Nations: America's Place in World History*. New York: Hill and Wang, 2006.

Benton, Lauren. "Legalities of the Sea in Gentili's *Hispanica Advocatio*." In *The Roman Foundations of the Law of Nations: Alberico Gentili and the Justice of Empire*, edited by Benedict Kingsbury and Benjamin Straumann, 269–82. Oxford: Oxford University Press, 2010.

Berensmeyer, Ingo. *"Angles of Contingency": Literarische Kultur im England des siebzehnten Jahrhunderts*. Tübingen, Germany: Max Niemeyer, 2007.

Berman, Marshall. *All That Is Solid Melts into Air: The Experience of Modernity*. New York: Penguin, 1988.

Berqôvîč, Nitzka. *From Motherhood to Citizenship: Women's Rights and International Organizations*. Baltimore, MD: Johns Hopkins University Press, 1999.

Bingham, Joseph P., et al. "Draft Provisions for the Suppression of Piracy." *American Journal of International Law* 26, no. 1, supplement part 4 (1932): 743–47.

Blackstone, William. *Commentaries on the Laws of England in Four Books*. Vol. 2: *Books III & IV*. Philadelphia, PA: Childs and Peterson, 1860.

Boose, Lydia. "Techno-Muscularity and the 'Boy Eternal': From the Quagmire to the Gulf." In *Cultures of United States Imperialism*, edited by Amy Kaplan and Donald E. Pease, 581–616. Durham, NC: Duke University Press, 1993.

Borgwardt, Elizabeth. *A New Deal for the World: America's Vision for Human Rights*. Cambridge, MA: Belknap Press of Harvard University Press, 2005.

Boyd-White, James. "Reading Law and Reading Literature as Language." In James Boyd-White, *Heracles' Bow: Essays on the Rhetoric and Poetics of the Law*, 77–106. Madison: University of Wisconsin Press, 1985.

Boyer, Paul. *By the Bomb's Early Light: American Thought and Culture at the Dawn of the Atomic Age*. New York: Pantheon, 1985.

Braudy, Leo. *From Chivalry to Terrorism: War and the Changing Nature of Masculinity*. New York: Vintage, 2003.

Broadhead, Lee-Anne. "Our Day in Their Shadow: Critical Remembrance, Feminist Science and the Women of the Manhattan Project." *Peace and Conflict Studies* 15, no.2 (2009): 38–60.

Broer, Lawrence R. *Sanity Plea: Schizophrenia in the Novels of Kurt Vonnegut*. Ann Arbor: UMI Research, 1989.

Brooks, Risa. "Muslim 'Homegrown' Terrorism in the United States: How Serious Is the Threat?" *International Security* 36, no.2 (2011): 7–47.

Brown, Bill. "Reading the West: Cultural and Historical Background." In *Reading the West: An Anthology of Dime Novels*, edited by Bill Brown, 1–40. Boston: Bedford, 1997.

Brown, Wendy. Introduction to *Is Critique Secular? Blasphemy, Injury, and Free Speech*, edited by Talal Asad, Wendy Brown, Judith Butler, and Saba Mahmood, 7–19. Berkeley, CA: Townsend Center for the Humanities, University of California, 2009.

———. *States of Injury: Power and Freedom in Late Modernity*. Princeton, NJ: Princeton University Press, 1995.

Burgess, Douglas R. *The World for Ransom: Piracy Is Terrorism, Terrorism Is Piracy*. Amherst, NY: Prometheus, 2010.

Burnett, John S. *Dangerous Waters: Modern Piracy and Terror on the High Seas*. New York: Plume, 2002.

Butler, Judith. *Gender Trouble: Feminism and the Subversion of Identity*. New York: Routledge, 1990.

———. "Indefinite Detention." In Judith Butler, *Precarious Life: The Powers of Mourning and Violence*, 50–100. London: Verso, 2004.

Bynkershoek, Cornelius van. *De Domino Maris Dissertatio*. Edited by James Brown Scott. London: Oxford University Press, 1923.

Campbell, Sally Howard. *Rousseau and the Paradox of Alienation*. Lanham, MD: Lexington, 2012.

Carroll, Lorrayne. *Rhetorical Drag: Gender Impersonation, Captivity, and the Writing of History*. Kent, OH: Kent State University Press, 2007.

Cassese, Antonio. *Terrorism, Politics and Law: The* Achille Lauro *Affair*. Princeton, NJ: Princeton University Press, 1989.

Cassirer, Ernst. "Das Problem Jean-Jacques Rousseau." In Ernst Cassirer, *Ernst Cassirer über Rousseau*, edited by Guido Kreis, 7–90. Berlin: Suhrkamp, 2012.

Cassuto, Leonard. "Frederick Douglass and the Work of Freedom: Hegel's Master-Slave Dialectic in the Fugitive Slave Narrative." *Prospects* 21 (1987): 229–59.

Chakrabarty, Dipesh. *Provincializing Europe: Postcolonial Thought and Historical Difference*. Princeton, NJ: Princeton University Press, 2000.

Chandler, Michael, and Rohan Gunaratna. *Countering Terrorism: Can We Meet the Threat of Global Violence?* London: Reaktion, 2007.

Chomsky, Noam. *Pirates and Emperors, Old and New: International Terrorism in the Real World*. Cambridge, MA: South End, 2002.

Clare, Ralph. "Worlds of Wordcraft: The Metafiction of Kurt Vonnegut." In *Critical Insights: Kurt Vonnegut*, edited by Robert T. Tally Jr., 60–91. Hackensack, NJ: Salem, 2013.

Clark, G. N. "The Barbary Corsairs in the Seventeenth Century." *Cambridge Historical Journal* 8, no.1 (1944): 22–35.

Coke, Edward. *The Third Part of the Institutes of the Laws of England: Concerning High Treason and Other Pleas of the Crown and Criminal Causes*. London: Clarke and Sons, 1809.

Coleridge, Samuel Taylor. "Genius Feminine—Pirates. March 17 1832." In Samuel Taylor Coleridge, *Specimens of the Table Talk of the Late Samuel Taylor Coleridge*, edited by Henry Nelson Coleridge. 2:26–27. London: John Murray, 1835.

Coll, Steve. *Ghost Wars: The Secret History of the CIA, Afghanistan, and bin Laden, from the Soviet Invasion to September 10, 2001*.New York: Penguin, 2005.

Colley, Linda. *Captives: Britain, Empire and the World, 1600–1850*.London: Pimlico, 2003.

Collier, Jane, Bill Maurer, and Liliana Suarez-Navaz. "Sanctioned Identities: Legal Constructions of Modern Personhood." *Identities* 2, nos.1–2 (1997): 1–27.

Cooper, James Fenimore. *The Deerslayer, or The First Warpath*. In James Fenimore Cooper, *The Leatherstocking Tales*, edited by Blake Nevius, 2:485–1030. New York: Library of America, 2007.

———. *The Pioneers, or the Sources of the Susquehanna: A Descriptive Tale*. In James Fenimore Cooper, *The Leatherstocking Tales*, edited by Blake Nevius, Lance Schachterle, and Kenneth M. Anderson Jr., 1:3–465. New York: Library of America, 1996.

Cordingly, David. *Under the Black Flag: The Romance and the Reality of Life among the Pirates*. Orlando, FL: Harvest, 1997.

Coupe, Laurence. *Myth*. London: Routledge, 1997.

Cover, Robert M. "Nomos and Narrative." In Robert Cover, *Narrative, Violence, and the Law: The Essays of Robert Cover*, edited by Martha Minow, Michael Ryan, and Austin Sarat, 95–172. Ann Arbor: University of Michigan Press, 1995.

———. "Violence and the Word." In Robert Cover, *Narrative, Violence, and the Law: The Essays of Robert Cover*, edited by Martha Minow, Michael Ryan, and Austin Sarat, 203–38. Ann Arbor: University of Michigan Press, 1995.

Craig, Campbell, and Sergey Radchenko. *The Atomic Bomb and the Origins of the Cold War*. New Haven, CT: Yale University Press, 2008.

Crenshaw, Martha. "'New' versus 'Old' Terrorism." *Palestine-Israel Journal* 10, no. 1 (2003). Accessed July 13, 2013. www.pij.org/details.php?id=80.

Crowley, Roger. *Empires of the Sea: The Final Battle for the Mediterranean, 1521–1580.* London: Faber and Faber, 2009.

Curl, Ruth. "The Metaphors of Cyberpunk: Ontology, Epistemology, and Science Fiction." In *Fiction 2000: Cyberpunk and the Future of Narrative*, edited by George Slusser and Tom Shippery, 230–45. Athens, GA: University of Georgia Press, 1992.

Cusac, Anne-Marie. *Cruel and Unusual: The Culture of Punishment in America.* New Haven, CT: Yale University Press, 2009.

Cvetkovich, Ann. *Depression: A Public Feeling.* Durham, NC: Duke University Press, 2012.

Dali, Alex. "Piracy Attacks in the Malacca Strait." Singapore: ATLAS Service Partners, n.d. Accessed April 11, 2016. https://www.academia.edu/1431537/Piracy_attacks_in_the_Malacca_Strait.

Defoe, Daniel. *Robinson Crusoe.* London: Penguin Popular Classics, 1994.

Dershowitz, Alan M. *Why Terrorism Works: Understanding the Threat, Responding to the Challenge.* New Haven, CT: Yale University Press, 2002.

De Sutter, Laurent. "Piracy as Method: Nine Theses on Law and Literature." *Law and Humanities* 5, no.1 (2011): 63–72.

Dillon, Dana, and Lucia Selvaggi. "Stopping an Al Qaeda Attack in the Malacca Straits." Heritage Foundation, January 28, 2004. Accessed August 28, 2013.http://www.heritage.org/research/commentary/2004/01/stopping-an-al-qaeda-attack-in-the-malacca-straits.

Dinshaw, Carolyn, et al. "Theorizing Queer Temporalities: A Roundtable Discussion." *GLQ* 13, nos. 2–3 (2007): 177–95.

Donnelly, Jack. *Universal Human Rights in Theory and Practice.* Ithaca, NY: Cornell University Press, 2003.

Dörr, Dieter. "Gezielte Tötung erlaubt? Der Fall Osama bin Laden." *Akademie des Bistums Mainz*, no. 2 (2011): 7–25.

———. "'Savages' and International Law." *Law and State*, no. 47 (1993): 7–27.

Dougherty, Kevin. *The United States Military in Limited War: Case Studies in Success and Failure, 1945–1999.* Jefferson, NC: McFarland, 2012.

Dragonette, Charles N. "Lost at Sea." Letter to the editor, *Foreign Affairs*, March–April 2005.Accessed January 22, 2010. http://www.foreignaffairs.com/articles/60629/charles-n-dragonette/lost-at-sea.

Drucker, Peter. *The End of Economic Man: A Study of the New Totalitarianism.* London: William Heinemann, 1939.

DuBois, W.E.B. *The Suppression of the African Slave Trade to the United States of America 1638–1870.* Accessed October 14, 2013. http://www.gutenberg.org/files/17700/17700-h/17700-h.htm.

Duffus, Robert Luther. "Bringing Beauty to City Waterfronts: New York Still Must Learn How to Make Her Shoreline Attractive." *New York Times*, March 9, 1930.

Duyvesteyn, Isabelle. "How New is the New Terrorism?" *Studies in Conflict and Terrorism* 27, no.5 (2004): 439–54.

Earle, Peter. *Corsairs of Malta and Barbary.* London: Sidgwick and Jackson, 1970.

———. *The Pirate Wars.* New York: Thomas Dunne, 2006.

Eckstein, Lars, and Anja Schwarz, eds. *Postcolonial Piracy: Media Distribution and Cultural Production in the Global South*. London: Bloomsbury, 2014.

Edwards, Brian T., and Parameshwar Gaonkar, eds. *Globalizing American Studies*. Chicago: University of Chicago Press, 2010.

Eggers, Daniel. *Die Naturzustandstheorie des Thomas Hobbes: Eine vergleichende Analyse von* The Elements of Law, De Cive *und den englischen und lateinischen Fassungen des* Leviathan. Berlin: Walter de Gruyter, 2008.

Ellison, Ralph. *Going to the Territory*. New York: Vintage, 1987.

Ellms, Charles. *The Pirates' Own Book*. Boston: IndyPublish, n.d.

Engel, Manfred. "Roman." In *Fischer Lexikon Literatur N–Z*, edited by Ulfert Ricklefs, 1669–709. Frankfurt: Fischer Taschenbuch, 1997.

Engelhardt, Tom. *The End of Victory Culture: Cold War America and the Disillusion of a Generation*. New York: Basic, 1995.

Engels, Jeremy. "Floating Bombs Encircling Our Shores: Post-9/11 Rhetorics of Piracy and Terrorism." *Cultural Studies ↔ Critical Methodologies* 7 (2007): 326–49.

Esposito, Roberto. *Person und menschliches Leben*. Zurich: diaphanes, 2010.

Eusterschulte, Anne. "Die Trinität der Geschichte: Zur Geschichtstheologie des Joachim von Fiore." In *Die Zukunft der Geschichte: Reflexionen zur Logik des Werdens*, edited by Heinz Edam, Frank Hermenau, and Dirk Stederith, 11–44. Kassel, Germany: Kassler Philosophische Schriften, 2002.

Evans, Richard J. *Rituals of Retribution: Capital Punishment in Germany 1600–1987*. Oxford: Oxford University Press, 1996.

Exnicios, Joan M. "On the Trail of Jean Lafitte." In *X Marks the Spot: New Perspectives on Maritime History and Nautical Archeology*, edited by Russell K. Skowronek and Charles N. Ewen, 31–43. Gainesville: University Press of Florida, 2006.

Exquemelin, Alexander O. *The Buccaneers of America*. Reprint, Mineola, NY: Dover, 2000.

Falkowski, James E. *Indian Law/Race Law: A Five-Hundred-Year History*. New York: Praeger, 1992.

Fielding, Henry. *The History of the Life of the Late Mr. Jonathan Wild the Great*. Accessed February 14, 2013. http://ebooks.adelaide.edu.au/f/fielding/henry/jonathan_wild/complete.html.

Filkins, Dexter. *The Forever Wars*. New York: Vintage, 2009.

Fisch, Jörg. *Die europäische Expansion und das Völkerrecht: Die Auseinandersetzungen um den Status der überseeischen Gebiete vom 15. Jahrhundert bis zur Gegenwart*. Stuttgart, Germany: Steiner, 1984.

Fisher, Benjamin Franklin. "Poe and the Gothic Tradition." In *The Cambridge Companion to Edgar Allen Poe*, edited by Kevin J. Hayes, 72–91. Cambridge: Cambridge University Press, 2003.

Fluck, Winfried. *Das kulturelle Imaginäre: Eine Funktionsgeschichte des amerikanischen Romans, 1790–1900*. Frankfurt: Suhrkamp, 1997.

———. "Fiction and Justice." *New Literary History* 34, no.1 (2003): 19–42.

———. "The Nineteenth-Century Historical Novel." In *The Cambridge History of the American Novel*, edited by Leonardo Cassuto, Clare Virginia Eby, and Benjamin Reiss, 117–34. Cambridge: Cambridge University Press, 2011.

Folena, Lucia. "Figures of Violence: Philologists, Witches, and Stalinistas." In *The Violence of Representation: Literature and the History of Violence*, edited by Nancy Armstrong and Leonard Tennenhouse, 219–328. London: Routledge, 1989.

Foucault, Michel. *Society Must Be Defended: Lectures at the Collège de France, 1975–76*. London: Picador, 2003.

Fowler, Orson Squire, and Lorenzo Niles Fowler. *Phrenology Proved, Illustrated, and Applied*. New York: Fowlers and Wells, 1849.

Franklin, H. Bruce. *Vietnam and other American Fantasies*. Amherst: University of Massachusetts Press, 2000.

Fredriksson, Martin. "Piracy, Globalisation and the Colonisation of the Commons." *Global Media Journal, Australian Edition* 6, no. 1 (2012): n.p.

——— and James Arvanitakis, eds. *Piracy: Leakages from Modernity*. Sacramento, CA: Litwin, 2014.

Frulli, Micaela. "Are Crimes against Humanity More Serious Than War Crimes?" *European Journal of International Law* 12, no.2 (2001): 329–50.

Fukuyama, Francis. *The End of History and the Last Man*. New York: Free Press, 2006.

Fuller, Lon. *Legal Fictions*. Stanford, CA: Stanford University Press, 1967.

Furbank, Philip Nicholas, and William Robert Owens. *Defoe De-Attributions: A Critique of J.R. Moore's "Checklist."* London: Hambledon, 1994.

Gage, Beverly. "Terrorism and the American Experience: A State of the Field." *Journal of American History*, June (2011): 73–94.

Gerassi-Navarro, Nina. *Pirate Novels: Fictions of Nation Building in Spanish America*. Durham, NC: Duke University Press, 1999.

Giesen, Bernhard. "The Trauma of Perpetrators: The Holocaust as the Traumatic Reference of German National Identity." In *Cultural Trauma and Collective Identity*, edited by Jeffrey C. Alexander et al., 112–54. Berkeley: University of California Press, 2004.

Glaubitz, Nicola. *Der Mensch und seine Doppel: Perspektiven einer anthropologischen Denkfigur in Philosophie und Roman der schottischen Aufklärung*. Sankt Augustin, Germany: Gardez!, 2003.

Glover, Jonathan. *Humanity: A Moral History of the Twentieth Century*. New Haven, CT: Yale University Press, 2000.

Goldenberg, Naomi. *Changing of the Gods: Feminism and the End of Traditional Religions*. Boston: Beacon, 1979.

Goldfarb, Jeffrey C. *The Cynical Society: The Culture of Politics and the Politics of Culture in American Life*. Chicago: University of Chicago Press, 1991.

Gordon, Avery F. *Ghostly Matters: Haunting and the Sociological Imagination*. Minneapolis: University of Minnesota Press, 1997.

Grass, Sean. "Piracy, Race and Domestic Peril in *Hard Cash*." In *Pirates and Mutineers of the Nineteenth Century: Swashbucklers and Swindlers*, edited by Grace Moore, 181–95. Farnhame, UK: Ashgate, 2011.

Gray, Peter. "How Hunter-Gatherers Maintained their Egalitarian Ways." *Freedom to Learn*(blog), *Psychology Today*, May 16, 2011. Accessed November 12, 2014. https://www.psychologytoday.com/blog/freedom-learn/201105/how-hunter-gatherers-maintained-their-egalitarian-ways.

Greenberg, Karen J. "The Rule of Law Finds Its Golem: Judicial Torture Then and

Now." In *The Torture Debate in America*, edited by Karen J. Greenberg, 1–9. New York: Cambridge University Press, 2008.
Greenblatt, Stephen. *The Swerve: How the World Became Modern*. New York: Norton, 2011.
Greene, Jody. "Hostis Humani Generis." *Critical Inquiry* 34, no.4 (2008): 683–705.
Greil, Marcus. "Götterdämmerung after Twenty-One Years: On Nazi-Hunting Thrillers." In Marcus Greil, *The Dustbin of History*, 52–69. Cambridge, MA: Harvard University Press, 1995.
Greiner, Bernd. *Krieg ohne Fronten: Die USA in Vietnam*. Bonn, Germany: BPB, 2007.
Griffin, Patrick. *American Leviathan: Empire, Nation, and Revolutionary Frontier*. New York: Hill and Wang, 2008.
Grimm, Nancy. *Beyond the "Imaginary Indian": Zur Aushandlung von Stereotypen, kultureller Identität und Perspektiven in/mit indigener Gegenwartsliteratur*. Heidelberg, Germany: Winter, 2009.
Grotius, Hugo. *Commentary on the Law of Prize and Booty*. Edited by Martine Julia van Ittersum. Indianapolis, IN: Liberty Fund, 2006.
Hacking, Ian. *The Taming of Chance*. Cambridge: Cambridge University Press, 2008.
Hamid, Mohsin. *The Reluctant Fundamentalist*. 2nd ed. London: Penguin, 2008.
Hamilton, Christopher E. "The Pirate Ship *Whydah*." In *X Marks the Spot: New Perspectives on Maritime History and Nautical Archeology*, edited by Russell K. Skowronek and Charles N. Ewen, 131–59. Gainesville: University Press of Florida, 2006.
Hamilton, Cynthia S. "'Am I Not a Man and a Brother?' Phrenology and Anti-Slavery." *Slavery and Abolition* 29, no. 2 (2008): 173–87.
———. *Western and Hard-Boiled Detective Fiction in America: From High Noon to Midnight*. Iowa City: University of Iowa Press, 1987.
Hammett, Dashiell. *Red Harvest*. New York: Vintage Crime, 1992.
Harris, Lee. *Civilization and Its Enemies: The Next Stage of History*. New York: Free Press, 2004.
Hartmann, Elke. "Zur Geschichte der Matriarchatsidee: Antrittsvorlesung." *Öffentliche Vorlesungen der Humboldt Universität zu Berlin* 133 (2004): 1–30.
Harty, Joetta. "Playing Pirate: Real and Imaginary Angrias in Branwell Brontë's Writing." In *Pirates and Mutineers of the Nineteenth Century: Swashbucklers and Swindlers*, edited by Grace Moore, 41–58. Farnhame, UK: Ashgate, 2011.
Harvey, David. *A Brief History of Neoliberalism*. Oxford: Oxford University Press, 2005.
Haselstein, Ulla. *Die Gabe der Zivilisation: Kultureller Austausch und literarische Textpraxis in Amerika, 1682–1861*. Munich: Wilhelm Fink, 2000.
Häsner, Bernd. "Indexikalität und Indexikalisierung: Überlegungen zur literaturwissenschaftlichen Relevanz eines sprachphilosophischen Konzepts." In *Im Zeichen der Fiktion: Aspekte fiktionaler Rede aus historischer und systematischer Sicht: Festschrift für Klaus W. Hempfer zum 65. Geburtstag*, edited by Irina O. Rajewski and Ulrike Schneider, 67–84. Stuttgart, Germany: Steiner, 2008.
Hawke, David Freeman. *Honorable Treason: The Declaration of Independence and the Men Who Signed It*. New York: Viking, 1976.
Hawthorne, Nathaniel. *The Scarlet Letter*. London: Penguin, 1994.
Hayden, Paul T. "Cultural Norms as Law: Tort Law's 'Reasonable Person' Standard of Care." *Journal of American Culture* 15, no.1 (2004): 45–55.

Heater, Derek. *The Theory of Nationhood: A Platonic Symposium*. Basingstoke, UK: Macmillan, 1998.

Heebøll-Holm, Thomas K. *Ports, Piracy, and Maritime War: Piracy in the English Channel and the Atlantic, c. 1280–1330*.Leiden, the Netherlands: Brill, 2013.

Hegeman, Susan. *Patterns for America: Modernism and the Concept of Culture*. Princeton, NJ: Princeton University Press, 1999.

Heller-Roazen, Daniel. *The Enemy of All: Piracy and the Law of Nations*. New York: Zone, 2009.

Hobbes, Thomas. *The Elements of Law, Natural and Politic. Part I: Human Nature. Part II: De Corpore Politico with Three Lives*. Edited by John C. A. Gaskin. Oxford: Oxford University Press, 2008.

———. *Leviathan*. Edited by John C. A. Gaskin. Oxford: Oxford University Press, 2008.

Hobsbawm, Eric. *Primitive Rebels: Studies in Archaic Forms of Social Movement in the 19th and 20th Centuries*. New York: Norton, 1965.

Hoffmann, Bruce. *Inside Terrorism*. New York: Columbia University Press, 1998.

Hofstadter, Richard. "The Paranoid Style in American Politics." In Richard Hofstadter, *The Paranoid Style in American Politics and Other Essays*, 3–40. Cambridge, MA: Harvard University Press, 1996.

Holdsworth, William Searle. *The Historians of Anglo-American Law*. Hamden, CT: Archon, 1966.

Holmes, Robert L. "St. Augustine and the Just War Theory." In *The Augustinian Tradition*, edited by Gareth B. Matthews, 323–44. Berkeley: University of California Press, 1999.

hooks, bell. "Seduced by Violence No More." In bell hooks, *Outlaw Culture: Resisting Representations*, 109–13. New York: Routledge, 1994.

Horkheimer, Max, and Theodor W. Adorno. *Dialectic of Enlightenment: Philosophical Fragments*. Edited by Gunzelin Schmid Noerr. Stanford, CA: Stanford University Press, 2002.

Horn, Eva. "Enden des Menschen: Große Katastrophen als Biopolitische Phantasie." In *Utopie und Apokalypse in der Moderne*, edited by Reto Sarg and Stefan Bodo Würffel, 101–18. Munich: Wilhelm Fink, 2010.

Hornung, Klaus. *Das totalitäre Zeitalter: Bilanz des 20. Jahrhunderts*. Berlin: Propyläen, 1993.

Howard, Warren S. *American Slavers and the Federal Law 1837–1862*.Berkeley: University of California Press, 1963.

Hudgens, Betty Lenhardt. *Kurt Vonnegut: A Checklist*. Detroit, MI: Gale Research Company, 1975.

Huggins, Martha K., Mika Haritos-Fatouros, and Philip G. Zimbardo. *Violence Workers: Police Torturers and Murderers Reconstruct Brazilian Atrocities*. Berkeley: University of California Press, 2002.

Hunt, Andrew E. *The Turning: A History of Vietnam Veterans against the War*. New York: New York University Press, 1999.

Hunt, Lynn. *Inventing Human Rights: A History*. New York: W.W. Norton, 2007.

Hunter, James Davison. "The Enduring Culture War." In *Is There a Culture War? A Dialogue of Values and American Public Life*, edited by E.J. Dionne Jr. and Michael Cromartie, 10–40. Washington: Pew Research Center, 2006.

Huntington, Samuel P. *The Clash of Civilizations and the Remaking of World Order.* New York: Simon and Schuster, 2002.

Irr, Caren. "Postmodernism in Reverse: American National Allegories and the 21st-Century Political Novel." *Twentieth-Century Literature* 57, nos.3–4 (2011): 516–38.

Jackson, Robert H. "Opening Address for the United States." In *Nazi Conspiracy and Aggression*. Edited by the Office of the United States Chief of Counsel for Prosecution of Axis Criminality, 1:114–71. Washington: Government Publishing Office, 1946.

Jäger, Herbert. "Makroverbrechen als Gegenstand des Völkerstrafrechts." In *Strafgerichte gegen Menschheitsverbrechen: Zum Völkerstrafrecht 50 Jahre nach den Nürnberger Prozessen*, edited by Gerd Hankeland Gerhard Stuby, 325–54. Hamburg, Germany: Hamburger Edition, 1995.

Jameson, Fredric. "Modernism and Imperialism." In *Nationalism, Colonialism and Literature: Terry Eagleton, Fredric Jameson, and Edward W. Said*, with an introduction by Seamus Deane, 43–66. Minneapolis: University of Minnesota Press, 1990.

Jefferson, Thomas. "The Declaration of Independence: Rough Draft." 1776. Accessed June 6, 2013. http://www.monadnock.net/jefferson/declaration-draft.html.

Jenisch, Uwe. "Piracy, Navies and the Law of the Sea: The Case of Somalia." *WMU Journal of Maritime Affairs* 8, no.2 (2009): 123–43.

Johnson, Charles. *The Successful Pyrate*. Reprint, Los Angeles: University of California, 1980.

Johnson, Charles [Daniel Defoe]. *A General History of the Pyrates*. Edited by Manuel Schonhorn. Mineola, NY: Dover, 1999.

Johnson, David E. "Of Pirates, Captives, Barbarians, and the Limits of Culture." *American Literary History* 14, no. 2 (2002): 358–75.

Johnson, Paul. "The Cancer of Terrorism." In *Terrorism: How the West Can Win*, edited by Benjamin Netanyahu, 31–37. New York: Farrar, Straus and Giroux, 1986.

Juergensmeyer, Mark. *Terror in the Mind of God: The Global Rise of Religious Violence*. Berkeley: University of California Press, 2001.

Jung, Susanne. *Die Rechtsprobleme der Nürnberger Prozesse dargestellt am Verfahren gegen Friedrich Flick*. Tübingen, Germany: J.C.B. Mohr, 1992.

Kant, Immanuel. *Zum ewigen Frieden: Ein philosophischer Entwurf*. Edited by Rudolf Malter. Stuttgart, Germany: Reclam, 2010.

Kaplan, Amy. "'Left Alone with America': The Absence of Empire in the Study of American Culture." In *Cultures of United States Imperialism*, edited by Amy Kaplan and Donald E. Pease, 3–21. Durham, NC: Duke University Press, 1993.

———. "Where Is Guantánamo?" *American Quarterly* 57, no.3 (2005): 831–58.

Kaufman, Irving Robert. "1980. *Filartiga*, 630 F.2d 876 (June 30, 1980). Opinion." Accessed April 10, 2016. http://www.ccrjustice.org/sites/default/files/assets/files/Fil%E1rtiga%20v.%20Pe%F1a-Irala,%20630%20F.2d%20876%20(2d%20Cir.,%20June%2030%201980)%20(torture).pdf.

Kempe, Michael. *Fluch der Weltmeere: Piraterie, Völkerrecht und internationale Beziehungen, 1500–1900*. Frankfurt: Campus Verlag, 2010.

Kirkpatrick, Jeane J. "The Totalitarian Confusion." In *Terrorism: How the West Can Win*, edited by Benjamin Netanyahu, 56–59. New York: Farrar, Straus and Giroux, 1986.

Klein, Naomi. *This Changes Everything: Capitalism vs. the Climate*. New York: Simon and Schuster, 2014.

Klinkowitz, Jerome. *Literary Disruptions: The Making of a Post-Contemporary Fiction*. Urbana: University of Illinois Press, 1975.

Knighton, Andrew Lyndon. "The Wreck of the Corsair: Piracy, Political Economy and American Publishing." In *Pirates and Mutineers of the Nineteenth Century: Swashbucklers and Swindlers*, edited by Grace Moore, 79–94. Farnhame, UK: Ashgate, 2011.

Kohl, Karl-Heinz. "'Travestie der Lebensformen' oder 'kulturelle Konversion'? Zur Geschichte des kulturellen Überläufertums." In *Die andere Welt: Studien zum Exotismus*, edited by Thomas Koeber and Gerhart Pickerodt, 88–120. Frankfurt: Philo, 2000.

Kontorovich, Eugene. "The Piracy Analogy: Modern Universal Jurisdiction's Hollow Foundation." *Harvard International Law Journal* 45, no. 1 (2004): 183–237.

Kucklick, Christoph. *Das unmoralische Geschlecht: Zur Geburt der Negativen Andrologie*. Frankfurt: Suhrkamp, 2008.

Labaree, Benjamin Woods. *The Boston Tea Party*. New York: Oxford University Press, 1964.

Lacôte, Fanny. "Gothic Architecture, Castles and Villains: Transgression, Decay and the Gothic *Locus Horribilis*." In *Dracula and the Gothic in Literature, Pop Culture and the Arts*, edited by Isabel Ermida, 199–217. Leiden, the Netherlands: Brill Rodopi, 2016.

"The Lamentable Cries of at Least 1500 Christians: Most of Them Being Englishmen (Now Prisoners in Argiers [*sic*] Under the Turks) Begging at God's Hand That He Would Open the Eyes of All Christian Kings and Princes to Commiserate the Wretched Estate of So Many Captives: and Withal to Free Them from That Turkish Slavery, in Which Both Bodies and Souls Are in Danger: with a Petition to the King's Most Excellent Majesty and All Christian Princes." In *Piracy, Slavery, and Redemption: Barbary Captivity Narratives from Early Modern England*, edited by Daniel J. Vitkus, 344–46. New York: Columbia University Press, 2001.

Laslett, Peter. Introduction to John Locke, *Two Treatises of Government*, edited by Peter Laslett, 3–133. Cambridge: Cambridge University Press, 1988.

Latacz, Joachim. "Die Ilias: Inhalt und Aufbau." In *Homer: Der Mythos von Troja in Dichtung und Kunst*, edited by Joachim Latacz, Thierry Greub, Peter Blome, and Alfred Wieczorek, 114–38. Munich: Hirmer, 2008.

Lätsch, Frauke. *Insularität und Gesellschaft in der Antike: Untersuchungen zur Auswirkung der Insellage auf die Gesellschaftsentwicklung*. Stuttgart, Germany: Franz Steiner, 2005.

Lee, Arthur. "Letter to Count de Florida Blanca. Paris, December 17th, 1778." In *The Diplomatic Correspondence of the American Revolution: Being the Letters of Benjamin Franklin, Silas Deane, John Adams, John Jay, Arthur Lee, William Lee, Ralph Izard, Francis Dana, William Carmichael, Henry Laurens, John Laurens, M. Dumas, and Others, Concerning the Foreign Relations of the United States during the Whole Revolution*, edited by Jared Sparks, 2:207–10. Boston: Nathan Hale and Gray and Bowen, 1830.

Lehmkuhl, Ursula. "Ambivalenzen der Modernisierung durch Kolonialismus." *APuZ—Aus Politik und Zeitgeschichte* 44–45 (2012): 44–50.

Lehr, Peter, ed. *Violence at Sea: Piracy in the Age of Global Terrorism*. New York: Routledge, 2007.

——— and Hendrick Lehmann. "Somalia—Pirates' New Paradise." In *Violence at Sea: Piracy in the Age of Global Terrorism*, edited by Peter Lehr, 1–22. New York: Routledge, 2007.

Leiser, Burton M. "Enemies of Mankind." In *Terrorism: How the West Can Win*, edited by Benjamin Netanyahu, 155–56. New York: Farrar, Straus and Giroux, 1986.

LeMenager, Stephanie. "Imagining the Frontier." In *The Cambridge History of the American Novel*, edited by Leonardo Cassuto, Clare Virginia Eby, and Benjamin Reiss, 515–36. Cambridge: Cambridge University Press, 2011.

Lewis, Jeff. *Language Wars: The Role of Media and Culture in Global Terror and Political Violence*. London: Pluto, 2005.

Lewis, R. W. B. *The American Adam: Innocence, Tragedy, and Tradition in the Nineteenth Century*. Chicago: University of Chicago Press, 1959.

Locke, John. "The Second Treatise of Government: An Essay Concerning the True Original, Extent, and End of Civil Government." In John Locke, *Two Treatises of Government*, edited by Peter Laslett, 265–428. Cambridge: Cambridge University Press, 1988.

Lockenour, Jay. "Black and White Memories of War: Victimization and Violence in West German War Films of the 1950s." *Journal of Military History* 76 (2012): 159–91.

Loomba, Ania. *Shakespeare, Race, and Colonialism*. Oxford: Oxford University Press, 2002.

Lutz, Deborah. "The Pirate Poet in the Nineteenth Century: Trollope and Byron." In *Pirates and Mutineers of the Nineteenth Century: Swashbucklers and Swindlers*, edited by Grace Moore, 23–39. Farnhame, UK: Ashgate, 2011.

Mahmood, Saba. "Religious Reason and Secular Affect: An Incommensurable Divide?" In *Is Critique Secular? Blasphemy, Injury, and Free Speech*, edited by Talal Asad, Wendy Brown, Judith Butler, and Saba Mahmood, 64–100. Berkeley, CA: Townsend Center for the Humanities, University of California, 2009.

Mahnkopf, Birgit. "Piratenhatz am Horn von Afrika: Zur politischen Ökonomie eines Piratenkonflikts und seiner geopolitischen Bedeutung." *Internationale Politik und Gesellschaft*, no. 1 (2010): 59–81.

Malet, David. *Foreign Fighters: Transnational Identity in Civic Conflicts*. Oxford: Oxford University Press, 2013.

Margalit, Avishai. *The Decent Society*. Cambridge, MA: Harvard University Press, 1996.

Markus, Hazel Rose, and Paula M. L. Moya. "Doing Race: An Introduction." In *Doing Race: 21 Essays for the 21st Century*, edited by Hazel Rose Markus and Paula M. L. Moya, 1–102. New York: W. W. Norton, 2010.

Marr, Timothy. *The Cultural Roots of American Islamicism*. Cambridge: Cambridge University Press, 2006.

Martinez, Jenny S. *The Slave Trade and the Origins of International Human Rights Law*. Oxford: Oxford University Press, 2012.

Marvin, Tom. "'Who Am I This Time?' Kurt Vonnegut and the Film Mother Night." *Literature/Film Quarterly* 31, no. 3 (2003): 231–36.

Matar, Nabil. *Turks, Moors and Englishmen in the Age of Discovery*. New York: Columbia University Press, 1999.

Mather, Cotton. "Instructions to the LIVING, from the Condition of the DEAD: A Brief Relation of REMARKABLES in the Shipwreck of above One Hundred Pirates, Who were Cast away in the Ship *Whido*, on the Coast of New-England, April 26. 1717. And in the Death of Six, who after a Fair Trial at *Boston*, were Convicted & Condemned, *Octob.*22. And Executed *Novemb.*15. 1717. With Some Account of the Discourse had with them on the way to their Execution. And a SERMON Preached on Their Occasion." In *British Piracy in the Golden Age: History and Interpretation, 1660–1730*, edited by Joel H. Baer, 4:129–205. London: Pickering Chatto, 2007.

Mattox, John Mark. *Saint Augustine and the Theory of Just War*. London: Continuum, 2008.

May, Judith Stinson. "Family and Aggression in the Leatherstocking Series." PhD diss., University of Illinois at Chicago, 1976.

McGurl, Mark. *The Program Era: Postwar Fiction and the Rise of Creative Writing*. Cambridge, MA: Harvard University Press, 2009.

———. "Understanding Iowa: Flannery O'Connor, B.A., M.F.A." *American Literary History* 19, no.2 (2007): 1–19.

Medovoi, Leerom. "The Race War Within: The Biopolitics of the Long Cold War." In *American Literature and Culture in an Age of Cold War: A Critical Reassessment*, edited by Steven Belletto and Daniel Grausam, 163–208. Iowa City: University of Iowa Press, 2012.

———. "'Terminal Crisis?' From the Worlding of American Literature to World System Literature." *American Literary History* 23, no.3 (2011): 643–59.

Menand, Louis. *American Studies*. New York: Farrar, Straus and Giroux, 2003.

Menefee, Samuel P. "Piracy, Terrorism, and the Insurgent Passenger: A Historical and Legal Perspective." In *Maritime Terrorism and International Law*, edited by Natalino Ronzitti, 43–68. Dordrecht, the Netherlands: Martinus Nijhoff, 1990.

Miller, Seumas. *Terrorism and Counter-Terrorism: Ethics and Liberal Democracy*. Malden, MA: Blackwell, 2009.

Mills, Charles. "Racial Liberalism." *PMLA* 123, no.5 (2008):1380–97.

Minow, Martha. "Introduction: Robert Cover and Law, Judging, and Violence." In *Narrative, Violence, and the Law: The Essays of Robert Cover*, edited by Martha Minow, Michael Ryan, and Austin Sarat, 1–11. Ann Arbor: University of Michigan Press, 1995.

Mitchell, David T., and Sharon L. Snyder. *Narrative Prosthesis: Disability and the Dependencies of Discourse*. Ann Arbor: University of Michigan Press, 2000.

Moglen, Eben. "Legal Fictions and Common Law Legal Theory: Some Historical Reflections." 1989. Accessed November 12, 2015.http://emoglen.law.columbia.edu/publications/fict.html.

Molloy, Charles. *De Iure Maritimo et Navali, or, a Treatise of Affaires Maritime and of Commerce in Three Books*. London: Printed for Thomas Passinger, 1682.

Montesquieu, Charles de Secondat, baron de. *The Spirit of the Laws*. Edited by Anne M. Cohler, Basia Carolyn Miller, and Harold Samuel Stone. Cambridge: Cambridge University Press, 2010.

Moore, Grace, ed. *Pirates and Mutineers of the Nineteenth Century: Swashbucklers and Swindlers*. Farnhame: Ashgate, 2011.

Moore, John Robert. *Checklist of the Writings of Daniel Defoe*. Hamden, CT: Archon, 1971.

Morse, Donald E. *The Novels of Kurt Vonnegut: Imagining Being an American*. Westport, CT: Praeger, 2003.

Moss, Kenneth B. *Undeclared War and the Future of U.S. Foreign Policy*. Washington: Woodrow Wilson Center Press, 2008.

Muldoon, James. "Who Owns the Sea?" In *Fictions of the Sea: Critical Perspectives on the Ocean in British Literature and Culture*, edited by Bernhard Klein, 13–48. Aldershot, UK: Ashgate, 2002.

Murphy, Martin N. "Piracy and UNCLOS: Does International Law Help Regional States Combat Piracy?" In *Violence at Sea: Piracy in the Age of Global Terrorism*, edited by Peter Lehr, 155–82. New York: Routledge, 2007.

———. *Small Boats, Weak States, Dirty Money: Piracy and Maritime Terrorism in the Modern World*. New York: Columbia University Press, 2009.

Naber, Nadine. *Arab America: Gender, Cultural Politics, and Activism*. New York: New York University Press, 2012.

Netanyahu, Benjamin. "Defining Terrorism." In *Terrorism: How the West Can Win*, edited by Benjamin Netanyahu, 7–15. New York: Farrar, Straus and Giroux, 1986.

Neu, Charles E. "The Vietnam War and the Transformation of America." In *After Vietnam: Legacies of a Lost War*, edited by Charles E. Neu, 1–23. Baltimore, MD: Johns Hopkins University Press, 2000.

Nijman, Janne Elisabeth. *The Concept of International Legal Personality: An Inquiry into the History and Theory of International Law*. The Hague: T. M. C. Asser, 2004.

Ó Dochartaigh, Pól, and Christiane Schönfeld, eds. *Representing the "Good German" in Literature and Culture after 1945: Altruism and Moral Ambiguity*. Rochester, NY: Camden House, 2013.

O'Daly, Gerard. *Augustine's* City of God*: A Reader's Guide*. Oxford: Clarendon Press of Oxford University Press, 2002.

Oehler-Klein, Sigrid. *Die Schädellehre Franz Joseph Galls in Literatur und Kritik des 19. Jahrhunderts: Zur Rezeptionsgeschichte einer medizinisch-biologisch begründeten Theorie der Physiognomik und Psychologie*. Stuttgart, Germany: Gustav Fischer, 1990.

Olson, Greta. *Criminals as Animals: From Shakespeare to Lombroso*. Berlin: De Gruyter, 2013.

Orentlicher, Diane F. "The Future of Universal Jurisdiction in the New Architecture of Transnational Justice." In *Universal Jurisdiction: National Courts and the Prosecution of Serious Crimes under International Law*, edited by Stephen Macedo, 214–351. Philadelphia: University of Pennsylvania Press, 2004.

Orwell, George. *Nineteen Eighty-Four*. London: Penguin, 2012.

Palevsky, Mary. *Atomic Fragments: A Daughter's Questions*. Berkeley: University of California Press, 2000.

Pateman, Carole. "Race, Sex, and Indifference." In *Contract and Domination*, edited by Carole Pateman and Charles W. Mills, 134–64. Cambridge, UK Polity, 2007.

Paul, Heike, Alexandra Ganser, and Katharina Gerund, eds. *Pirates, Drifters, Fugitives: Figures of Mobility in the US and Beyond*. Heidelberg, Germany: Winter, 2012.

Paul, Heike, and Christina Judith Hein. "The Fugitive as an Anti-Foundational Figure:

'Going Native' in Early America." In *Pirates, Drifters, Fugitives: Figures of Mobility in the US and Beyond*, edited by Heike Paul, Alexandra Ganser, and Katharina Gerund, 229–58. Heidelberg, Germany: Winter, 2012.

Pearce, Roy Harvey. *Savagism and Civilization: A Study of the Indian and the American Mind*. Baltimore, MD: Johns Hopkins University Press, 1967.

Pease, Donald E. "C. L. R. James, Moby-Dick, and the Emergence of Transnational American Studies." In *The Futures of American Studies*, edited by Donald Pease and Robyn Wiegman, 135–63. Durham, NC: Duke University Press, 2002.

———. *The New American Exceptionalism*. Minneapolis: University of Minnesota Press, 2009.

Perkins, John. *Confessions of an Economic Hit Man*. New York: Plume, 2006.

Peskin, Lawrence A. *Captives and Countrymen: Barbary Slavery and the American Public, 1785–1816*. Baltimore, MD: Johns Hopkins University Press, 2009.

Peters, Edward. *Torture*. Expanded ed. Philadelphia: University of Pennsylvania Press, 1999.

Pfanner, Toni. "Asymmetrical Warfare from the Perspective of Humanitarian Law and Humanitarian Action." *International Review of the Red Cross* 87, no. 857 (2005): 149–74.

Philip, Kavita. "What Is a Technological Author? The Pirate Function and Intellectual Property." *Postcolonial Studies* 8, no. 2 (2005): 199–218.

Phillips, Richard, with Stephan Talty. *A Captain's Duty: Somali Pirates, Navy SEALs, and Dangerous Days at Sea*. New York: Hyperion, 2010.

Plascencia, Salvador. *The People of Paper*. London: Bloomsbury, 2007.

Plattner, Marc F. *Rousseau's State of Nature: An Interpretation of the* Discourse on Inequality. DeKalb: Northern Illinois University Press, 1979.

Policante, Amedeo. *The Pirate Myth: Genealogies of an Imperial Concept*. London: Routledge, 2015.

Preyer, Kathryn. "Jurisdiction to Punish: Federal Authority, Federalism, and the Common Law of Crimes in the Early Republic." In Kathryn Preyer, *Blackstone in America: Selected Essays of Kathryn Preyer*, edited by Mary Sarah Bilder, Maeva Marcus, and R. Kent Newmyer, 185–232. Cambridge: Cambridge University Press, 2009.

"The Princeton Principles on Universal Jurisdiction." In *Universal Jurisdiction: National Courts and the Prosecution of Serious Crimes under International Law*, edited by Stephen Macedo, 18–25. Philadelphia: University of Pennsylvania Press, 2004.

Pringle, Patrick. *Jolly Roger: The Story of the Great Age of Piracy*. New York: W.W. Norton, 1953.

Puzar, Aljosa. "Piratical Cultural Studies: Transgressive Individualism Reconsidered." *Cultural Studies ↔ Critical Methodologies* 20, no. 10 (2010): 1–12.

Ramachandran, Sudha. "Divisions over Terror Threat in Malacca Straits." *Asia Times Online*, June 16, 2004. Accessed August 28, 2013. www.atimes.com/atimes/Southeast_Asia/FF16Ae01.html.

Rancière, Jacques. *Dissensus: On Politics and Aesthetics*. Edited by Steven Corcoran. London: Continuum, 2010.

Rawls, John. *The Law of Peoples: With "The Idea of Public Reason Revisited."* Cambridge, MA: Harvard University Press, 2002.

Reade, Charles. *Hard Cash: A Matter-of-Fact Romance*. New York: AMS, 1970.
Reagan, Ronald. "Remarks and a Question-and-Answer Session with Reporters on Domestic and Foreign Policy Issues: July 21, 1983." In *Public Papers of Ronald Reagan*, July 1983. Ronald Reagan Presidential Library. Accessed August 6, 2015. http://www.reagan.utexas.edu/archives/speeches/1983/72183a.htm.
Reddy, Chandan. *Freedom with Violence: Race, Sexuality, and the US State*. Durham, NC: Duke University Press, 2011.
Rediker, Marcus. *Villains of All Nations: Atlantic Pirates in the Golden Age*. London: Verso, 2004.
Reid, Julian. *The Biopolitics of the War on Terror: Life Struggles, Liberal Modernity, and the Defence of Logistical Societies*. Manchester, UK: Manchester University Press, 2006.
Reilly, Charles. "Two Conversations with Kurt Vonnegut." In *Conversations with Kurt Vonnegut*, edited by William Rodney Allen, 196–229. Jackson: University Press of Mississippi, 1988.
Risso, Patricia. "Cross-Cultural Perceptions of Piracy: Maritime Violence in the Western Indian Ocean and Persian Gulf Region during a Long Eighteenth Century." *Journal of World History* 2, no.2 (2001): 293–319.
Ritchie, Robert C. *Captain Kidd and the War against the Pirates*. Cambridge, MA: Harvard University Press, 1986.
Rodger, Nicholas A. M. *The Wooden World: An Anatomy of the Georgian Navy*. London: Fontana, 1988.
Rouleau, Brian. "Maritime Destiny as Manifest Destiny: American Commercial Expansionism and the Idea of the Indian." *Journal of the Early Republic* 3 (2010): 377–411.
Rousseau, Jean-Jacques. *A Discourse upon the Origin and Foundation of the Inequality among Mankind*. London: R. and J. Dodsley, 1761.
Rubin, Alfred P. *The Law of Piracy*. New York: Transnational, 1997.
Rubincam, Catherine. "A Tale of Two 'Magni': Justin/Trogus on Alexander and Pompey." *Historia* 54 (2005): 265–74.
Rymer, Thomas. "The Tragedies of the Last Age Consider'd and Examin'd by the Practice of the Ancients, and by the Common Sense of All Ages. In a Letter to Fleetwood Shepeard, Esq: by Thomas Rymer, of Grays-Inn, Esquire." 1678. Accessed November 4, 2015. http://spenserians.cath.vt.edu/TextRecord.php?textsid=33632.
Said, Edward W. *Orientalism*. 25th anniversary ed. New York: Vintage, 2004.
Sarat, Austin. "Robert Cover on Law and Violence." In *Narrative, Violence, and the Law: The Essays of Robert Cover*, edited by Martha Minow, Michael Ryan, and Austin Sarat, 255–65. Ann Arbor: University of Michigan Press, 1995.
Sayre, Gordon M. "Renegades from Barbary: The Transnational Turn in Captivity Studies." *American Literary History* 22, no.2 (2010): 347–59.
Scarry, Elaine. *The Body in Pain: The Making and Unmaking of the World*. New York: Oxford University Press, 1987.
Schiedermair, Stephanie. "Piratenjagd im Golf von Aden." *Archiv des Öffentlichen Rechts* 135 (2010): 185–220.
Schillings, Sonja. "The Privateering Critic: Re-Reading the Problem of the Ban in Marie de France and Giorgio Agamben." *Krisis* 1 (2015): 30–38.

Schmitt, Carl. *Land und Meer: Eine weltgeschichtliche Betrachtung*. Stuttgart, Germany: Klett Cotta, 2011.

Schneck, Peter. *Rhetoric and Evidence: Legal Conflict and Literary Representation in U.S. American Culture*. Munich: De Gruyter, 2011.

Schonhorn, Manuel. Introduction to Charles Johnson [Daniel Defoe], *A General History of the Pyrates*, edited by Manuel Schonhorn, xi–xlii. Mineola, NY: Dover, 1999.

Schrecker, Ellen. *The Age of McCarthyism: A Brief History with Documents*. Boston: Bedford, 1994.

Seidel, Michael. *Robinson Crusoe: Island Myths and the Novel*. Boston: Twayne, 1991.

Sekulich, Daniel. *Terror on the Seas: True Tales of Modern-Day Pirates*. New York: Thomas Dunne, 2009.

Sembower, John F. "Democracy and Science Fused by the Atomic Bomb." *Antioch Review* 5, no.4 (1945): 493–500.

Shay, Shaul. *The Red Sea Terror Triangle: Sudan, Somalia, Yemen, and Islamic Terror*. New Brunswick, NJ: Transaction, 2007.

Shields, Charles J. *And So It Goes: Kurt Vonnegut: A Life*. New York: Henry Holt, 2011.

Shirer, William. *Der Aufstieg und Fall des Dritten Reiches*. Cologne, Germany: Kiepenheuer and Witsch, 1961.

Shoemaker, Nancy. *A Strange Likeness: Becoming Red and White in Eighteenth-Century North America*. Oxford: Oxford University Press, 2004.

Shryock, Andrew. "The Moral Analogies of Race: Arab American Identity, Color Politics, and the Limits of Racialized Citizenship." In *Race and Arab Americans Before and After 9/11: From Invisible Citizens to Visible Subjects*, edited by Amaney Jamal and Nadine Naber, 81–113. Syracuse, NY: Syracuse University Press, 2008.

Shultz, George P. "The Challenge to the Democracies." In *Terrorism: How the West Can Win*, edited by Benjamin Netanyahu, 16–24. New York: Farrar, Straus and Giroux, 1986.

Silzer, George S. "Making a Super-Port." *North American Review* 225, no. 844 (1928): 668–72.

Simonson, Harold P. *Beyond the Frontier: Writers, Western Regionalism and a Sense of Place*. Fort Worth: Texas Christian University Press, 1989

Skaridov, Alexander S. "Hostis Humani Generis." In *Legal Challenges in Maritime Security*, edited by Myron H. Nordquist, Rüdiger Wolfrun, John Norton Moore, and Ronán Long, 479–99. Leiden, the Netherlands: Martinus Nijhoff, 2008.

Slaughter, Joseph. *Human Rights, Inc.: The World Novel, Narrative Form, and International Law*. New York: Fordham University Press, 2007.

Slotkin, Richard. *The Fatal Environment: The Myth of the Frontier in the Age of Industrialization, 1800–1890*. Norman: Oklahoma University Press, 1994.

———. *Gunfighter Nation: The Myth of the Frontier in Twentieth-Century America*. Norman: Oklahoma University Press, 1998.

———. *Regeneration through Violence: The Mythology of the American Frontier, 1600–1860*. Hanover, NH: University Press of New England, 1973.

———. "Unit Pride: Ethnic Platoons and the Myths of American Nationality." *American Literary History* 13, no.3 (2001): 469–98.

Smith, Henry Nash. *Virgin Land: The American West as Symbol and Myth*. Cambridge, MA: Harvard University Press, 2009.

Solis, Gary D. *The Law of Armed Conflict: International Humanitarian Law in War*. New York: Cambridge University Press, 2010.

Soulsby, Hugh G. *The Right of Search and the Slave Trade in Anglo-American Relations 1814–1862*. Baltimore, MD: John Hopkins University Press, 1933.

Spahn, Hannah. "'Cruel War against Human Nature Itself': Krieg und Kosmopolitismus in der amerikanischen Revolution." In *Krieg und Frieden im achtzehnten Jahrhundert*, edited by Stephanie Stockhorst, 331–46. Hanover, Germany: Wehrhahn, 2015.

Stark, Francis R. *The Abolition of Privateering and the Declaration of Paris*. New York: Columbia University, 1897.

Sterling, Claire. *The Terror Network: The Secret War of International Terrorism*. London: Weidenfeld and Nicolson, 1981.

———. "Unraveling the Riddle." In *Terrorism: How the West Can Win*, edited by Benjamin Netanyahu, 103–5. New York: Farrar, Straus and Giroux, 1986.

Stern, Jessica. *Terror in the Name of God: Why Religious Militants Kill*. New York: Ecco, 2003.

Stevenson, Robert Louis. *Treasure Island*. London: Penguin Popular Classics, 1994.

Swift, Jonathan. *Gulliver's Travels*.London: Penguin, 1994.

Szilard, Leo. "Interview: President Truman Did Not Understand." *U.S. News and World Report*, August 15, 1960. Accessed October 22, 2015. http://members.peak.org/~danneng/decision/usnews.html.

Takeuchi, Masaya. "Bigger's Divided Self: Violence and Homosociality in *Native Son*." *Studies in American Naturalism* 4, no.1 (2009): 56–74.

Teubner, Gunther. "Enterprise Corporatism: New Industrial Policy and the 'Essence' of the Legal Person." *American Journal of Comparative Law* 36, no.1 (1988): 130–55.

Tew, Philip. "Kurt Vonnegut's *Mother Night* (1961): Howard W. Campbell, Jr., and the Banalities of Evil." In *New Critical Essays on Kurt Vonnegut*, edited by David Simmons, 11–26. New York: Palgrave MacMillan, 2009.

Thornton, Helen. *State of Nature or Eden? Thomas Hobbes and His Contemporaries on the Natural Condition of Human Beings*. Rochester, NY: University of Rochester Press, 2005.

Thorup, Mikkel. *An Intellectual History of Terror: War, Violence and the State*. London: Routledge, 2010.

Tindal, Matthew. *An Essay Concerning the Law of Nations, and the Rights of Soveraigns*. London: Richard Baldwin, 1694.

Toaldo, Mattia. "The Reagan Administration and the Origins of the War on Terror: Lebanon and Libya as Case Studies." *New Middle Eastern Studies* 2 (2012): 1–17.

Tomlinson, Stephen. *Head Masters: Phrenology, Secular Education, and Nineteenth-Century Social Thought*. Tuscaloosa: University of Alabama Press, 2005.

Truman, Harry S. "President Harry S. Truman's Address before a Joint Session of Congress, March 12, 1947." Yale Law School. Accessed September 10, 2013. http://avalon.law.yale.edu/20th_century/trudoc.asp.

Trutkowski, Dominik. "Concepts of Totalitarianism—Representatives, Reception and Perspectives." In *Totalitarianism and Liberty: Hannah Arendt in the 21st Century*, edited by Gerhard Besier, Katarzyna Stołosa, and Andrew Wisley, 125–51. Krakow, Poland: Księgarnia Akademicka, 2008.

Tuitt, Patricia. "Law and Violence in Richard Wright's *Native Son*." *Law and Critique* 11, no. 2 (2000): 201–17.
Turley, Hans. *Rum, Sodomy and the Lash: Piracy, Sexuality, and Masculine Identity*. New York: New York University Press, 1999.
Turner, Frederick Jackson. "The Significance of the Frontier in American History." In Frederick Jackson Turner, *Frontier and Section: Selected Essays of Frederick Jackson Turner*, edited by William E. Leuchtenburg and Bernard Wishy, 37–62. Englewood Cliffs, NJ: Prentice-Hall, 1964.
United Nations. "The Universal Declaration of Human Rights." 1948. Accessed November 12, 2015. http://www.un.org/en/universal-declaration-human-rights/index.html.
Van Ittersum, Martine Julia. Introduction to Hugo Grotius, *Commentary on the Law of Prize and Booty*, edited by Martine Julia van Ittersum, xiii–xxi. Indianapolis, IN: Liberty Fund, 2006.
Varon, Jeremy. *Bringing the War Home: The Weather Underground, the Red Army Faction, and Revolutionary Violence in the Sixties and Seventies*. Berkeley: University of California Press, 2004.
Vasilache, Andreas. "Gibt es überhaupt 'Homines sacri'? Das nackte Leben zwischen Theorie und Empirie." In *Die gouvernmentale Maschine: Zur politischen Philosophie Giorgio Agambens*, edited by Janine Böckelmann and Frank Meier, 58–74. Münster, Germany: Unrast, 2007.
Vattel, Emer de. *The Law of Nations: On Principles of the Law of Nature, Applied to the Conduct and Affairs of Nations and Sovereigns*. Philadelphia, PA: T. and J. W. Johnson, 1867.
Voelz, Johannes. *Transcendental Resistance: The New Americanists and Emerson's Challenge*. Hanover, NH: Dartmouth College Press, 2010.
Vonnegut, Kurt. "Do You Know What a Humanist Is?" In *A Man without a Country*, edited by Daniel Simon, 79–93. New York: Seven Stories, 2005.
———. *Mother Night*. London: Vintage, 2000.
Waldron, Jeremy. "Terrorism and the Use of Terror." *Journal of Ethics* 8 (2003): 5–35.
———. "Torture and Positive Law: Jurisprudence for the White House." *Columbia Law Review* 105, no.6 (2005): 1681–750.
Washburn, Wilcomb E. *Red Man's Land/White Man's Law: The Past and Present Status of the American Indian*. Norman: University of Oklahoma Press, 1995.
Watt, Ian. *The Rise of the Novel: Studies in Defoe, Richardson and Fielding*. London: Pimlico, 2000.
Weeks, William E. *Building the Continental Empire: American Expansion from the Revolution to the Civil War*. Chicago: Ivan R. Dee, 1996.
Weibust, Knut. *Deep Sea Sailors: A Study in Maritime Ethnology*. Stockholm: Nordiska Museet, 1969.
Wheelan, Joseph. *Jefferson's War: America's First War on Terror 1801–1805*. New York: Carroll and Graf, 2003.
Wiemer, Hans-Ulrich. *Alexander der Große*. Munich: C.H. Beck, 2005.
Wills, David C. *The First War on Terrorism: Counter-Terrorism Policy during the Reagan Administration*. Lanham, MD: Rowman and Littlefield, 2003.

Wormuth, Francis D., and Edwin B. Firmage. *To Chain the Dog of War: The War Power of Congress in History and Law*. 2nd ed. Urbana: University of Illinois Press, 1989.

Wright, Richard. "Blueprint for Negro Writing." In *The New Negro: Readings on Race, Representation, and African American Culture, 1892–1938*, edited by Henry Louis Gates Jr. and Gene Andrew Jarrett, 268–74. Princeton, NJ: Princeton University Press, 2007.

———. "How 'Bigger' Was Born." In Richard Wright, *Native Son*,1–31. London: Vintage, 2000.

———. *Native Son*. London: Vintage, 2000.

Yoo, John C. "Memorandum for William J. Haynes II, General Counsel of the Department of Defense: Re: Military Interrogation of Alien Unlawful Combatants Held Outside the United States." Washington: Department of Justice, Office of Legal Counsel, 2003.Accessed May 1, 2013. https://www.aclu.org/sites/default/files/pdfs/safefree/yoo_army_torture_memo.pdf.

Zalman, Amy. "What's So New about the 'New Terrorism'?" *About.com*, 2008 (updated October 30, 2014). Accessed March 5, 2016. terrorism.about .com/b/2008/03/01/whats-so-new-about-the-new-terrorism.htm.

Zanker, Paul. *Augustus und die Macht der Bilder*. Munich: C.H. Beck, 2009.

Žižek, Slavoj. "The Depraved Heroes of 24 Are the Himmlers of Hollywood." *Guardian*, January 10, 2006. Accessed August 28, 2013. http://www.the guardian.com/media/2006/jan/10/usnews.comment.

INDEX